Individual Development From 3 to 12

This book describes the findings of a long-term, comprehensive longitudinal study conducted at the Max Planck Institute for Psychological Research in Munich from 1984 to 1993. The major goal of the study was to analyze developmental changes in the cognitive, social, and personality domain and to explore possible interrelationships in developmental changes across domains. A sample of about 200 children was first tested in 1984 when they were almost 4 years old and first entering German kindergarten. Children's cognitive, social, and personality development was followed up on a regular basis (2–3 times a year) for about 9 years (until 1993). Data analyses focused on both the issue of continuity versus discontinuity of the developmental function in the various domains and on the issue of stability or variability in interindividual differences in developmental change. The study is unique in that developmental changes in several important domains were assessed simultaneously over a period of almost 10 years.

Franz E. Weinert is Director of the Center for Behavioral and Cognitive Development at the Max Planck Institute for Psychological Research. He has previously been Professor of Psychology at Heidelberg University and he has served as President of the German Psychological Association.

Wolfgang Schneider is Professor of Psychology and Dean of the Faculty of Philosophy, Education, and Social Sciences at the University of Würzburg. He has published widely on issues of cognitive development and educational psychology.

Individual Development From 3 to 12

Findings From the Munich Longitudinal Study

Edited by

FRANZ E. WEINERT

WOLFGANG SCHNEIDER

CAMBRIDGE
UNIVERSITY PRESS

PUBLISHED BY THE PRESS SYNDICATE OF THE UNIVERSITY OF CAMBRIDGE
The Pitt Building, Trumpington Street, Cambridge CB2 1RP, United Kingdom

CAMBRIDGE UNIVERSITY PRESS
The Edinburgh Building, Cambridge CB2 2RU, UK   http://www.cup.cam.ac.uk
40 West 20th Street, New York, NY 10011-4211, USA   http://www.cup.org
10 Stamford Road, Oakleigh, Melbourne 3166, Australia

First published 1999

Printed in the United States of America

Typeset in Times Roman 10/12.5 pt. and New Century Schoolbook in LaTeX 2_ε [TB]

A catalog record for this book is available from the British Library

Library of Congress Cataloging-in-Publication Data

Individual development from 3 to 12 : findings from the Munich
   longitudinal study / edited by Franz E. Weinert, Wolfgang Schneider.
       p.   cm.
   Includes bibliographical references and indexes.
   ISBN 0-521-58042-0
   1. Child development – Germany – Munich – Longitudinal studies.
   I. Weinert, Franz E., 1930–   . II. Schneider, Wolfgang.
   HQ792.G3I53   1999
   305.231 – dc21   98-42346
                                                            CIP

0 521 58042 0 hardback

Contents

Contributors

Jens B. Asendorpf, Humboldt University of Berlin, Germany

David F. Bjorklund, Florida Atlantic University, Boca Raton, Florida, USA

Augusto Blasi, University of Massachusetts at Boston, USA

Jack Block, University of California, Berkeley, USA

Peter Bryant, University of Oxford, England

Merry Bullock, Estonian Academy of Sciences, Tallinn, Estonia

Susan R. Goldman, Vanderbilt University, Nashville, Tennessee, USA

Andreas Helmke, University of Koblenz-Landau, Landau, Germany

Walter Kintsch, University of Colorado, Boulder, USA

David Klahr, Carnegie Mellon University, Pittsburgh, Pennsylvania, USA

Monika Knopf, Max Planck Institute for Psychological Research, Munich, Germany, and J. W. Goethe University of Frankfurt/Main, Germany

Jan Carol Näslund, University of New Mexico, Albuquerque, USA

Gertrud Nunner-Winkler, Max Planck Institute for Psychological Research, Munich, Germany

Peter A. Ornstein, University of North Carolina at Chapel Hill, USA

James W. Pellegrino, Vanderbilt University, Nashville, Tennessee, USA

Josef Perner, University of Salzburg, Austria

Kenneth H. Rubin, University of Waterloo, Ontario, Canada

Beate Sodian, University of Würzburg, Germany

Wolfgang Schneider, University of Würzburg, Germany

Jan Stefanek, Max Planck Institute for Psychological Research, Munich, Germany

Elsbeth Stern, Max Planck Institute for Human Development, Berlin, Germany

Richard E. Snow, Stanford University, California, USA

Deborah Stipek, University of California, Los Angeles, USA

Gerhard Strube, University of Freiburg, Germany

Marcel A. G. van Aken, University of Nijmegen, the Netherlands

Angelika Weber, University of Applied Sciences of Würzburg, Germany

Franz E. Weinert, Max Planck Institute for Psychological Research, Munich, Germany

Albert Ziegler, University of Munich, Germany

1 LOGIC: Introduction and Overview

Franz E. Weinert, Wolfgang Schneider, Jan Stefanek, and Angelika Weber

We would probably all agree that the main task of developmental psychology is to describe, predict, and explain change in human behavior and to uncover its determinants across the life span. Indeed, a look at the literature shows that it is full of empirical findings about age-related changes in behavioral, physical, cognitive, social, and personality variables. Thus, it would appear that the scientific study of human development is meeting its goal. However, this is only true at first glance.

A closer look at the literature provides the surprising information that more than 90% of psychological statements about developmental change are based on data that include no direct measures of change. For many developmental psychologists it is self-evident and unquestionable that one can infer laws of developmental change from observations of developmental differences between different age groups. Therefore, cross-sectional designs have become the rule, and longitudinal studies the exception.

From a theoretical point of view, taking mean age differences as indicators of individual change is a reasonable and valid research strategy, if – but only if – the developmental phenomena are universal; that is, if the laws that govern these phenomena are valid for all normal members of the human species. To be sure, for many aspects of human development, such a strong assumption may not pose any problems.

However, there is one risk and there are several disadvantages associated with this dominant mainstream position. The risk is that the one dominant methodological orientation and the one dominant theoretical perspective legitimize each other, which serves to immunize the theory against data that would support other possible perspectives. In addition to this fundamental problem, there are several obvious disadvantages to the exclusive use of cross-sectional methodology. These include its relative inability to describe individual growth functions; to identify individual patterns of change; and to describe, predict, or explain interindividual differences in intraindividual change.

In the following chapters of this volume, we concentrate on only one issue – that of interindividual differences in human development. A cross-sectional orientation

1

typically reduces interindividual differences (both in how they are defined and how they are analyzed) to variations in the speed with which universal, age-related sequences develop.

Since the time of Albert Binet at the beginning of the twentieth century, it has been popular to predict subsequent development from early differences in developmental rate. These predictions are very often based on the implicit assumptions (a) that interindividual differences in the rate of development are, at least in some cognitive domains, stable over time and (b) that there is substantial correlation between the rate of development in a particular competence and the asymptotic level of that competence that can be attained. This is the primary theoretical and empirical basis of much prognosis within the psychometric approach to development. In the last 80 years or so there have been hundreds, maybe thousands of papers supporting or criticizing this view. However, continuing the discussion on the pros and cons of this approach is not our purpose in this volume.

Rather, we simply want to make the point that it seems both desirable and necessary to study interindividual differences in intraindividual change within a broader framework of reference and with more adequate methodologies. Longitudinal research designs of course meet some of the criteria for studying individual differences.

In spite of the many pragmatic, theoretical, methodological, and statistical problems with longitudinal studies, there is agreement that only this type of research design offers an opportunity to describe and analyze individual differences and to identify patterns of causes for their genesis and for the stability or variability of such differences.

The term *longitudinal design* refers, of course, to an omnibus concept that includes a large variety of empirical designs that show just one common feature (repeated measures of the same entity) and that differs in many ways, for example, in sample size (from single case studies to broadband panel designs including thousands of participants), in time-span (short-term and long-term studies), in the density of measurement points (many observations a day to a few observations over a 30- to-40-year span), in the number of variables (from one variable to hundreds of variables), and in the rigidity or openness of the particular design (in goals, instruments, time intervals, and so on).

Because there is no standard methodological instruction for longitudinal designs, planning a longitudinal study requires many explicit decisions, and the design that is developed depends, among other things, on the preferred theoretical framework, the aims of the investigation, and the opportunities and constraints afforded by the empirical data collection.

Basic Assumptions, Constraints, and General Aims of LOGIC

When the staff members of the developmental unit at the newly founded Max Planck Institute for Psychological Research started to think about a longitudinal project on child development in 1982, our first task was to consider those decisions necessary for designing a longitudinal study (LOGIC).[1]

Although the fields of research experience varied among the individual scientists in our group (e.g., cognitive development, memory, motivation, personality, social development, and moral judgment), we all shared an interest in knowing more about the genesis and course of individual differences in cognitive and personality development. This focus, rather unpopular and widely ignored in mainstream developmental psychology, arose from a sense of discomfort with the current state of theoretical thinking in the field. The value of the universal approach is that it offers an opportunity to describe behavioral development as a sequence of changes from the immature state of the infant to the species-specific level of the mature adult. To quote John Flavell's (1970) strong definition of development, "It is the underlying presence of a biological growth process that lends to childhood changes their inevitability, magnitude, directionality, within-species uniformity, and irreversibility" (Flavell, p. 248).

However, this perspective is only one side of the coin. To avoid misunderstandings, let us be clear that we agree that this side is necessary – one side of a coin cannot exist without the other. A look at the other side of the coin, however, reveals not the homogeneity of adult behavior but the obvious, huge, and overwhelming differences among adults. How do these differences emerge? What are early indicators of such differences? How stable are individual differences in various domains over time? What are the prospects for long-term prediction of individual differences in cognitive and personality development?

In our early discussions, we reached a decision to study several aspects of development, with a strong focus on the genesis of individual differences. In addition, we also agreed on the following points, derived not from a unified theoretical position, but more as the pragmatic result of combining several specific research orientations in various developmental domains:

1. We chose early and middle childhood as the age group to study. We decided to start with 3- to 4-year-old children just after they had entered preschool. From the very beginning of the study, we planned to observe the individual children at regular time intervals for at least 9 years, or until the average beginning of puberty. Indeed, this is what we did.
2. To study interindividual differences in intraindividual development across a variety of cognitive and personality domains, we followed the research interests of the scientific members in our team. Following this rule, we concentrated our efforts in cognitive development on
   • memory development (M. Knopf, W. Schneider, B. Sodian, G. Strube, and A. Weber) and
   • development of thinking (M. Bullock, H. Wimmer, J. Perner, B. Sodian, and A. Ziegler).
   Because some members of the research group were very much interested in

---

[1] LOGIC = Longitudinal Study on the Genesis of Individual Competencies (Longitudinalstudie zur Genese individueller Kompetenzen).

connecting developmental and educational issues we also focused on some domain-specific skills from the elementary school curriculum:
- development and acquisition of arithmetic skills and mathematical understanding (E. Stern);
- acquisition of reading and spelling skills (W. Schneider, J. Näslund); and
- development of analytical reasoning in the science domain (M. Bullock).

Regarding the areas of personality and social development we focused on
- learning and achievement related behavior, motives, attitudes, and self concepts (A. Helmke);
- development of social competencies and inhibition (J. Asendorpf and M. van Aken);
- development of moral judgment, motivation, and behavior (G. Nunner-Winkler); and
- individual differences in selected personality characteristics (J. Asendorpf and M. van Aken).

To study such a variety of developmental domains we did not focus on a common, general theoretical orientation, but rather we explored domain-specific models, guiding questions, and research strategies – each with the common focus on individual differences.

To be able to provide a normative description of the sample, to make comparisons between the LOGIC data and other longitudinal data sets, and to have a common standardized set of reference variables within the LOGIC project available, we administered several selected standardized and widely used instruments at regular time intervals or at critical points of development. These instruments included
- measures of intelligence
- measures of social cognition
- assessments using Piagetian type tasks
- measures of school readiness in the preschool years
- measures of attention
- measures of motor skills

From this brief overview of the guiding principles and concrete decisions about the goals and topics of the project it should be clear that LOGIC was and is not a rigid fixed study with a set of invariant instruments but is more a variable and flexible longitudinal investigation that allowed some decisional options during the course of the study – all in all a procedure with some advantages and, of course, some disadvantages.

3. LOGIC is more or less – in our belief more than less – a descriptive study. The main goal was to describe the genesis and the stability and variability of individual differences in development and not to identify or even to analyze the causes of such developmental differences. In addition, there was neither a strong nor a systematic effort to gather data describing the social environment of the children, the living situation of their parents and siblings, or the educational atmosphere at home. We came to these decisions for two reasons: First, it seemed impossible to separate genetic and environmental factors in family effects on child development (without the frame of twin and adoption studies). Second, we assumed that descriptive models for individual differences are a necessary precondition for analyzing the causes of such differences. The lack of such models has perhaps been one main reason for the failure to integrate developmental and socialization research in the past. Thus, we decided not to attempt to take the attractive second step of looking at social–environmental causes before completing the necessary first step of describing individual differences in developmental sequences.

4. Nevertheless, looking for causal explanations is too strong a scientific temptation to ignore this second step completely. We used the fact that parents of elementary school

children in Germany do not have the opportunity to freely choose their child's classroom or teacher. As a consequence, the variation in school environments (teacher personality and quality of instruction) is not confounded with genetic and environmental conditions in the family. Thus, to look at effects of school environment, we decided to supplement the individual-centered LOGIC study with a classroom-centered school project, the so-called SCHOLASTIC study.[2]

It was possible to observe more than half of the LOGIC sample together with their classmates in 54 classrooms (a total of more than 1,200 participants) during the 4 years of elementary school. We were able to observe, test, and interview these students five to nine times a year under regular classroom conditions. This design gave us the opportunity (a) to analyze the SCHOLASTIC data for the entire SCHOLASTIC sample and (b) to combine the data sets from the SCHOLASTIC and LOGIC projects for the overlapping sample to study the impact of classroom differences on individual development and on the genesis of interindividual differences.

LOGIC Sample

The sample size of a longitudinal study is always a compromise between scientific needs and pragmatic restrictions. After discussing the goals and strategies of the project and calculating the manpower necessary for a long time period, we came to the conclusion that 180 participants would be the minimal size of the sample – not only in the first but also in the expected last wave of the study. We were able to meet this criterion. Table 1 shows the original sample and changes over the time of the study.

Four points are of special interest from Table 1. First, finding enough participants for the LOGIC study was not an easy task. We decided that the sample should consist of children between the ages of 3 and 4, with German as their first language. Another decision was that the participant pool should consist only of children who enrolled in one of 20 carefully selected preschools in the fall of 1984. These preschools were in central Munich and in a suburban area; had a representative distribution of people with high, moderate, and low socioeconomic status (SES); had approval to participate in the study from the relevant authorities; and met our criterion of convenience for doing the empirical work. It was finally possible to recruit the initial sample of 205 children with full permission of their parents to participate in the study.

After having 13 children drop out in Wave 1, we included 25 additional children in the sample in Wave 2 to ensure that the longitudinal sample would not be reduced below our criterion level over the long run. There were no age differences between the new subsample and the original sample (but of course the 25 participants were tested in the second wave for the first time).

The ages of the original sample ranged from 3.4 to 4.7 years, with a mean of 4.0 years. Table 2 shows the distribution of SES of the parents – defined by father's occupational status. This distribution of SES seems representative and, in contrast

---

[2] SCHOLASTIC = School Learning and Socialization of Talents, Interests, and Individual Competencies (Schulorganisierte Lernangebote und Sozialisation von Talenten, Interessen und Kompetenzen).

Table 1. *Original LOGIC Study Sample and Changes in the Sample Over Time*

	Wave								
	1	2	3	4	5	6	7	8	9
Sample	84/85	85/86	86/87	87/88	88/89	89/90	90/91	91/92	92/93
n	205	217	213	204	200	195	194	189	186
Increase	0	25	0	0	0	0	0	0	0
Decrease	0	13	4	9	4	5	1	5	3
Boys	105	113	111	105	104	101	101	100	99
Girls	100	104	102	99	96	94	93	89	87

Table 2. *Distribution of Socioeconomic Status (SES) of the Participants in the LOGIC Study*

SES	n	%
Low	$n = 57$	28
Average	$n = 127$	63
High	$n = 19$	9

to many other longitudinal studies, provides no indication that the sample is biased with more participants from higher SES families.

The second point to note in Table 1 is that the dropout rate from Wave 2 to 9 was very low (31 participants altogether, from a sample of $N = 217$). Considerable efforts were made to keep the children and parents motivated to participate in the three testing sessions each year. These efforts included steady contact with the parents in the form of letters and evening presentations to discuss the study (without any information about individual children). Dropout was caused primarily by the families' moving away from the area, although in a few cases the child or the parents refused to participate further in the study. The credit for this low dropout rate goes especially to the research assistants.

To check for continued representativeness we compared the dropout sample and the remaining sample for sex, SES, and intelligence. No significant differences could be found.

Third, because of the large number of observations (27 across the 9 years) and the huge number of variables measured, the number of children with complete data sets is relatively small. As a consequence, statistical analyses are based on different numbers of participants. Because the principle of listwise deletion would have reduced the sample size too much, the principle of pairwise deletion was used in most cases to allow us to retain as much information as possible.

Table 3. *Intelligence Scores for Girls and Boys*

Wave	IQ verbal boys	IQ verbal girls	IQ nonverbal boys	IQ nonverbal girls	Total IQ boys	Total IQ girls
Wave 1[a]	106.33	106.91				
Wave 2[a]	107.98	105.96	104.00	106.56	105.99	106.26
Wave 4[b]	102.21	98.72				
Wave 6[b]	109.06	105.22	98.74	96.43	104.45	100.51
Wave 9[b]	112.76	104.66				

[a]Indicates the Wechsler Preschool and Primary Scale of Intelligence was used to measure intelligence.
[b]Indicates the Wechsler Intelligence Scale for Children was used to measure intelligence.

Fourth, over the course of some longitudinal studies, the sample seems to become a unique population, perhaps as a result of repeated testing with its resulting opportunities for coaching, training, or feedback effects. To check for such effects, we compared the verbal IQ, the nonverbal IQ, and the overall IQ for boys, girls, and the whole sample across different waves. Table 3 shows this information. Analyses of variance with these data sets did reveal a significant main effect of time and a significant interaction between time and sex. However, despite these rather small changes in intelligence measures, we can state with some confidence that our sample did not develop into a nonrepresentative population over the course of the LOGIC study.

LOGIC Design

Figure 1 shows the sample and the course of the LOGIC study, as well as an overview of the sample and the course of the SCHOLASTIC study.

As Figure 1 illustrates, the LOGIC study lasted for more than 9 years with three measurement points per year (October–December, January–March, and April–June). Each measurement point provided the opportunity to observe, test, and interview each individual child for more than 2 hours. The children were tested individually, except in some cases in which groups of two or more children were observed to assess indicators of social behavior.

In September 1987, most children in the sample entered the first grade of elementary school. As mentioned earlier, from this point in time a subsample of 108 children from the LOGIC group together with more than 1,000 classmates in 54 classrooms participated in the SCHOLASTIC project.

In this project, testing took place during regular school hours and included five to nine measurement sessions per year. The measurements comprised tests of fluid intelligence, the solution of mathematic word problems and math tasks requiring arithmetic skills, reading comprehension, spelling, and analytic reasoning in the science domain. School grades for each of these topics were also available. In addition,

8

WEINERT ET AL.WEINERT ET AL.

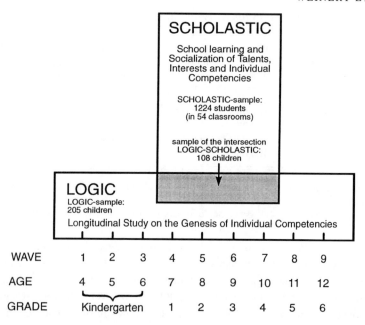

Figure 1. Samples and time course of the longitudinal LOGIC and SCHOLASTIC studies.

information concerning various aspects of the motivation to learn, achievement motivation, and the academic self-concept was gathered by questionnaires; children's attentive behavior in the classroom during instruction was measured with a low-inference, time-sampling observation instrument. These data were complemented by regular ratings by observers in the classroom concerning teaching and teacher behavior, allowing the construction of a large number of high-inference scales addressing different aspects of teaching and management quality.

In the following chapters we report on selected results from the main topics of the LOGIC study; in one chapter we use data from the SCHOLASTIC study. However, the findings represent only a small part of the results from the LOGIC study. A longitudinal investigation is like a machine for generating a huge amount of data and provides the opportunity not only for one comprehensive presentation but for many special presentations and publications. It will take us years to exploit the whole data set. In taking a bottom-up perspective, we are trying to go beyond the domain-specific type of analyses and are looking for more general developmental regularities.

Reference

Flavell, J. (1970). Cognitive change in adulthood. In R. Goulet & P. B. Baltes (Eds.), *Life-span developmental psychology: Research and theory* (pp. 248–253). New York: Academic Press.Flavell, J. (1970). Cognitive change in adulthood. In R. Goulet & P. B. Baltes (Eds.), *Life-span developmental psychology: Research and theory* (pp. 248–253). New York: Academic Press.

2   Development of Intelligence and Thinking

Wolfgang Schneider, Josef Perner, Merry Bullock,
Jan Stefanek, and Albert Ziegler

This chapter is concerned with developmental changes in aspects of intelligence and thinking assessed in the Munich Longitudinal Study on the Genesis of Individual Competencies (LOGIC). Although the majority of measures used in the study stemmed from a psychometric approach, several experimental procedures assessed constructs typical of a cognitive developmental approach. One purpose of the present analysis is to relate cognitive developmental tasks assessing general developmental milestones with psychometric intelligence at different time points to explore the interrelationships among these variables for different ages. Because of time constraints, the design used to investigate this issue was not as systematic as that of many longitudinal studies focusing solely on intellectual development (e.g., Schaie 1994). Before we present the measures and the results in more detail, we provide a short overview of the existing literature on developmental changes in intelligence and thinking.

The Starting Point: Psychometric Perspectives on the Development of Intellectual Ability

The study of the development of mental abilities has a long tradition in the field of psychology. Since the 1880s, numerous tests of psychometric intelligence have been used worldwide to explore children's cognitive abilities and to characterize the structure of these abilities. From the very beginning, the definition of the term *intelligence* aroused much controversy, because there were diverse views of the structure and organization of intelligence. This divergence was first illustrated in 1921 when the editors of *Journal of Educational Psychology* collected definitions of intelligence from several experts in the field and was replicated again in later, similar attempts where the diversity among experts' views was striking (Sternberg and Detterman 1986; cf. Berg 1992). However, despite problems in agreeing on a narrow definition of intelligence, most researchers dedicated to the psychometric approach agree that the nature of intelligence and intellectual development can be fruitfully studied by examining individual differences in performance on tests of mental abilities (cf. Kail and Pellegrino 1985; Siegler and Richards 1982; Sternberg and Powell 1983). From

9

this perspective, the primary developmental interest has been in assessing the stability of individual differences over time.

It is, however, important to note that the study of individual differences is only one aspect of the overall picture of the development of psychometric intellectual ability (cf. Gardner and Clark 1992). Focusing exclusively on individual differences and their stability overlooks the fact that change or stability in individual differences (indicated by correlations across various intelligence tests) is logically independent of growth in the average level of mental ability (cf. McCall 1981; Schneider 1989). Ignoring this difference can yield misleading conclusions. One famous example concerns Bloom's (1964) claim that 50% of an individual's adult intelligence is already developed by the age of 4. This claim was based on the finding from previous studies that the correlations among IQs assessed at age 4 and at age 18 average around .7, which means that they share about 50% variance. The reason that this conclusion is misleading is that Bloom's claim is based solely on the stability of individual differences and not on the absolute level of mental abilities. Undoubtedly, a 4-year-old's performance level is far less than 50% of the 18-year-old's.

Both individual differences and overall growth were assessed in several famous longitudinal studies conducted during the first half of this century at different places in the United States (for overviews, see Bayley 1970; Gardner and Clark 1992; Goodenough 1946). Although most of these studies focused on individual difference questions such as stability over time, some studies also explored the question of developmental changes in mental growth rates. Typically, participants in these studies were recruited at an early age (during infancy or the preschool years) and followed until adolescence or adulthood.

Findings regarding the stability issue can be summarized as follows:

1. Infant tests of intelligence do not predict later intelligence levels (cf. Bayley 1949, 1970; McCall, Hogarty and Hurlburt 1972). McCall et al. pointed out that the lack of a correlation is not due to poor infant test reliability. Rather, they give the plausible explanation that the competencies measured in infancy are different from those measured in the preschool years and later.
2. Later intelligence levels can be predicted with sufficient accuracy from age 3 on (cf. Bayley 1949; Honzik, MacFarlane, and Allen 1948; Sontag, Baker, and Nelson 1958). For example, stable patterns were found in an 11-year follow-up study by Yule, Gold, and Busch (1982), who tested a sample of 85 children on the Wechsler Preschool and Primary Scale of Intelligence (WPPSI, Eggert 1978) at about 5 years and then on the Wechsler Intelligence Scale for Children (WISC, Tewes 1983) at about 16 years. Long-term predictive validity of the WPPSI was found to be high: The intercorrelation between the full-scale IQs on the two tests was .86. Generally, correlations between IQ scores across different ages show the familiar simplex pattern, with values increasing as the intervals between tests decrease. For instance, Hindley and Owen (1978) reported a test–retest correlation of .53 for IQ scores assessed at the ages of 3 and 17 years, compared with .74 for scores assessed at ages 8 and 17 and .87 for scores assessed at ages 14 and 17.

Although most longitudinal studies on intellectual development showed high temporal stability between the preschool period and adolescence, they did not support the notion of a "constant IQ." Most longitudinal researchers noted considerable intraindividual change in the level of IQ (e.g., Bayley 1955; Honzik et al. 1948; Sontag et al. 1958). For instance, IQ changes of 20 points and more between the ages of 6 and 18 occurred in about 35% of the participants in the Honzik et al. (1948) study. The patterns of intraindividual change observed in most studies were typically quite idiosyncratic, including periods of loss in IQ followed by a gain, periods of gain followed by little change, and yet still differing patterns of change. Sontag et al. (1958) reported larger increments of change during the preschool years than during the school years.

This finding was also confirmed by Bayley (1949), who used "intelligence lability scores" for the Berkeley Growth Study children. Whereas the use of IQs or standard scores seems suited for assessing a child's shifts in status relative to the norm, a child's progress in relation to his or her own past is better represented by lability scores indicating the degree of variation from his or her own central tendency over time. More precisely, a lability score represented a child's standard deviation from his or her own mean standard score averaged across all testing points. Bayley (1949) found that lability scores decreased consistently as a function of testing age: Lability scores were highest for infancy, lower for the preschool period, and lowest for the school-age period. Accordingly, it appears that children are more likely to maintain their own relative status as they grow older. However, Bayley also emphasized the considerable individual differences in lability at all ages. Overall, these and a variety of other findings demonstrate that patterns of mental growth differ widely across individual children.

Results from a recent longitudinal study (Moffitt, Caspi, Harkness, and Silva 1993) based on an analysis of profiles of IQ changes basically support this view. Moffitt et al. studied the reliability, magnitude, and meaning of IQ change using scores on the Revised WISC (WISC–R) obtained from a representative sample of about 800 children at ages 7, 9, 11, and 13. The authors interpreted their findings to show that changes in intellectual performance during the period from childhood to adolescence may reflect several distinct phenomena. Whereas IQ change was either negligible in amount, unreliable, or both in the majority of children, it was quite marked and reliable in a nontrivial minority (about 14%) of their participants. One of the most intriguing aspects of their data was that there did not seem to be any differences in intellectual ability between stable and labile children. The question regarding "who changes" could not be answered in this study because no reliable correlates of IQ change were found.

Taken together, the findings from psychometric studies of intelligence indicate that intellectual development is highly stable between the preschool years and adolescence. Although interindividual differences in intraindividual change decrease with age, patterns of mental growth differ more widely across individual children than has been assumed in the classic literature.

Cognitive–Developmental and Domain-Specific Perspectives on Intellectual Development

It is well-known that Piaget's perspective on intellectual development was formed during his early psychological studies in Binet's psychometric laboratory (Piaget 1952).

Piaget was particularly critical of the scoring procedure (pass vs. fail) used in all psychometric instruments. This dissatisfaction led him to develop the "clinical method," which explores the reasoning behind a child's answer. The tasks and methods that Piaget subsequently used and his basic theory of intelligence differed considerably from theoretical approaches and test procedures used within the psychometric tradition. The central questions that guided Piaget's perspective on intellectual development were the description and explanation of universal changes in mental functioning that take place from infancy to adolescence. Piaget viewed the child as similar to a young scientist, constructing theories of the world, and he defined *intelligence* as an interactive instrument that achieved an equilibrium between a child's internal cognitive structures and the environment. Piaget identified four broad stages of intellectual development, characterized by the types of cognitive structures used to interact with the environment: (a) sensorimotor stage, (b) preoperational stage, (c) concrete operational stage, and (d) formal operational stage. Unlike the psychometric approach, which characterized intellectual development as continuous change, the Piagetian approach characterized intellectual development as a sequence of qualitatively different stages and emphasized the similarity in cognitive structures among children at a given developmental period or stage. As noted by Bidell and Fischer (1992), the Piagetian focus on similarities among children of a given age has drawn attention away from the extensive literature illustrating variability in cognitive development.

New perspectives on cognitive development ("neo-Piagetian" perspectives with an information-processing component as well as other perspectives that focus on concept structure and content) evolved during the 1970s, as an increasing number of concerns were raised about Piaget's theory. For example, Piaget's theory was formulated in a way that was difficult to test in any straightforward empirical fashion (cf. Brainerd 1978), and when it was tested it revealed data that were not easily reconciled with its underlying theoretical claims. Although many of the post-Piagetian perspectives on cognitive development preserve central ideas of Piaget's perspective on intellectual development (e.g., the concept of cognitive structures), several underlying claims have been modified. In particular, current cognitive developmental theorists seem to be interested in (a) exploring the basic mechanisms of developmental change, (b) understanding individual differences, (c) investigating cognitive structures more locally within a given domain and not universally across domains, and (d) investigating the role of specifiable biological factors that regulate cognitive development and determine the possible upper limits to be achieved (cf. Case 1985, 1992; Demetriou 1988; Fischer 1987; Fischer and Rose 1994).

The Contribution of the LOGIC Study to the Understanding of Intellectual Development

Before describing the goals and contributions of the LOGIC study to the description and explanation of interindividual differences in intraindividual change in cognitive development, we first want to mention a few constraints in the study that limit the scope of our analyses. First, the development of children's intellectual competencies was not a core issue of the LOGIC project. This does not mean that the available database is scarce. Psychometric tests of mental ability were regularly given throughout the study, and tasks assessing various areas of conceptual-growth were applied both in early and later phases of the study (cf. Table 1 in the next section). Thus, we do possess longitudinal data that can be used for the assessment of developmental changes in intellectual competencies.

However, unlike other domains such as social inhibition, memory, or mathematical thinking, intelligence measures were included primarily for pragmatic rather than theory-based considerations. There were two main reasons for including psychometric tests of intelligence in the LOGIC study. First, they provided information on the representativeness of the sample. Most longitudinal studies investigating intellectual development have not been representative because the IQ levels of their participants were high, that is, 120 and above (cf. Bayley 1949, 1970; Hilden 1949; Sontag et al. 1958). Needless to say, such lack of representativeness can seriously bias the conclusions concerning important developmental issues such as the general growth of intelligence or the stability of individual differences over time.

The second reason was to assess practice effects. Although classic longitudinal studies (e.g., Sontag et al. 1958) reported only minimal effects of repeated testing on IQ, we wanted to be certain we could generalize this finding to the LOGIC study. Compared to most longitudinal studies on intellectual development, the amount of testing time per child in the LOGIC study was immense, and we could not exclude the possibility of significant practice effects for our sample. Thus, tests of verbal and nonverbal intelligence were administered at least once a year to control for changes in overall IQ level.

Although this pragmatic orientation restricts the range of meaningful data analyses, it still allows us to investigate topics not sufficiently covered in the available literature. In the analyses to be discussed here, we focus on four major questions. The first two questions concern replications and extensions of traditional research on psychometric intelligence, and the second two issues explore possible links between psychometric and cognitive perspectives.

Specifically, we addressed the following issues:

1. Are there changes in the intercorrelations of verbal and nonverbal intelligence over development? Other longitudinal studies have focused on general intelligence (e.g., as assessed by the Stanford–Binet test) but have not addressed verbal (cf. Burt's verbal: educational) and nonverbal (kinesthetic: mechanical) components separately.
2. Is IQ test performance assessed in preschool related to IQ performance in the later school years? If so, does the quality of prediction differ for verbal and nonverbal IQ components? Although plenty of evidence from American longitudinal studies indicates that mental ability assessed in the preschool years predicts later IQ scores rather well (see above), most of this evidence dates back to the first half of this century and may be methodologically biased in that several measurement points per year were aggregated into a single score (cf. Bayley 1949).

Table 1. *Overview of Intelligence Assessments in the LOGIC Study*

	Chronological age								
Test	4	5	6	7	8	9	10	11	12
Verbal IQ									
HAWIVA (WPPSI)	x	x							
HAWIK (WISC)			x		x				x
Nonverbal IQ									
CMMS	x		x		x				
CFT							x		x
Piagetian tasks									
False belief	x	x							
Number conservation	x		x						
Arlin test								x	x
Logical reasoning								x	
Scientific reasoning									x

3. Are there any significant relationships between measures of psychometric intelligence and indicators of cognitive performance as assessed by Piagetian and other cognitive tasks, and do these relationships change with age? The issue of interrelationships between psychometric intelligence and other cognitive variables was explored to some extent in the 1970s and early 1980s (e.g., Hunt 1980). However, most of this research was conducted with adults and did not consider longitudinal evidence.

4. Does the growth of mental ability between ages 7 and 12 show linear increases, or are first signs of the eventual leveling off at asymptote already discernible at this early age? Whereas the first three research questions listed above focus on interindividual differences in cognitive ability, the last issue deals with intraindividual changes over time and explores the topic of cognitive variability, which has been ignored in most models of cognitive development (cf. Siegler 1994).

Descriptions of Tasks and Results

Indicators of Psychometric Intelligence

An overview of the psychometric tests used in the LOGIC study is given in Table 1. As is seen, different psychometric tests were administered during the preschool and kindergarten years. The Hannover–Wechsler–Intelligence Scale for Preschool Children (HAWIVA; Eggert 1978) was administered twice. This test is roughly comparable to the WPPSI used in English-speaking countries. Because of time constraints, only the verbal part of the test was administered during the first year of the study. This part consists of three subtests: General Knowledge, Vocabulary, and General Comprehension. One year later, both the verbal and nonverbal ("performance") parts of the HAWIVA were administered. Because the nonverbal component of the HAWIVA is not considered in our analyses, we report only the means and standard deviations of the verbal component of the HAWIVA test obtained at Waves 1 and 2.

From Wave 4 on, the Hamburg–Wechsler–Intelligence Scale for School Children (HAWIK) replaced the HAWIVA, which was no longer applicable because the oldest children in the normative sample were younger than the LOGIC children (who averaged 7 years of age in Wave 4 and had just entered elementary school). The HAWIK test (equivalent to the WISC) can be used for children between 6 and 16 years of age. Only performance on the verbal part of the test is considered in the present analyses. This part consisted of the following subtests: General Knowledge, Vocabulary, General Comprehension, Commonalities, Numerical Thinking, and Digit Span.

The Columbia Mental Maturity Scale (CMMS; Burgemeister, Blum, and Lorge 1972) was chosen to assess children's nonverbal intellectual skills. The test is designed to tap general reasoning abilities of children aged 3 years 6 months to 9 years. Test items consisted of picking out the odd item in a group (i.e., selecting the picture that is different from or unrelated to all the others in a series of three to five drawings). The number of correct answers gives the sum raw score, which is then used to calculate a standardized score. Depending on children's age level, an increasing number of items were administered. Because the raw scores for children of different ages are derived from different numbers of items, the standardized age deviation scores, comparable to IQ scores, were used. The results obtained in Waves 1, 3, and 5 were used for the present analyses.

As noted earlier, the CMMS covered the age range between 3.6 and 9 years. This test was no longer appropriate after children had entered Grade 4. Thus, we used the German version of the Culture Fair Intelligence Test (CFT) first developed by Cattell and Horn (Weiss 1976) as a measure of nonverbal intelligence from Grade 4 on. According to the test authors, the CFT assesses children's fluid intelligence. The test consists of two parallel forms (A and B), each containing four different subtests: The first (Series) requires the identification and completion of series of geometric figures the second (Classification) requires the classification and differentiation of geometric figures, the third (Matrices) requires children to complete matrix figures, and the fourth (Topologies) requires the identification of proportions and relations of geometric areas. The speed version of the test was used on both occasions (i.e., in Waves 7 and 9).

The means and standard deviations for each of the psychometric tests administered are listed in Table 2. These data provide valuable information on the representativeness of our LOGIC sample and the impact of practice effects. First of all, the mean of most IQ scores ranged between 106 and 110 points, regardless of the measurement point or the test. Thus, although the IQ scores of the LOGIC participants were slightly above average (which could be due to a cohort effect), they were not as high as those reported for the various American and British longitudinal studies. Thus, our sample seems to be more representative than most samples used to look at the development of psychometric intelligence.

Table 2. *Mean IQs, Standard Deviations, and Ranges for the Various Psychometric Intelligence Tests Used in the LOGIC Study*

Variable	M	SD	Minimum	Maximum
HAWIVA (Wave 1)	106.62	13.14	70	137
HAWIVA (Wave 2)	107.00	11.06	78	130
HAWIK (Wave 4)	100.52	10.47	78	130
HAWIK (Wave 6)	107.22	8.89	77	131
HAWIK (Wave 9)	108.97	12.90	77	148
CMMS (Wave 1)	108.82	11.94	74	139
CMMS (Wave 3)	107.92	12.55	79	150
CMMS (Wave 5)	107.96	12.94	70	144
CFT (Wave 7)	109.63	14.60	71	152
CFT (Wave 9)	114.34	13.97	78	149

The homogeneity of IQ scores across tests at different points in time indicates that practice effects were negligible. The only exception is an increase in IQ observed for the CFT between Waves 7 and 9. Overall, this pattern of results agrees with others reported in the literature (e.g., Sontag et al. 1958 and others) who found no substantial practice effects in longitudinal studies on the development of intelligence.

Intercorrelations among the various verbal and nonverbal intelligence components are depicted in Table 3. Most intercorrelations were of moderate size and considerably lower than those reported in the literature. Although this might occur because we occasionally related subsets of psychometric tests (i.e., verbal components of the HAWIVA and HAWIK tests) with full scales (CMMS and CFT), the intercorrelations among full scales were of about the same moderate size. A more likely explanation for this discrepancy is that several of the longitudinal studies with young children (e.g., Bayley 1949) used several measurement points per year and then aggregated these IQ scores across annual measurement points. This procedure not only increases reliability scores but also leads to overestimations of true long-term stability.

The developmental pattern of correlations shows some evidence for the simplex pattern reported in most previous studies, particularly when developmental changes were considered from early starting points. The pattern also supports the claim that higher correlations occur over the school years, as compared to the preschool period.

Table 3. *Intercorrelations Among Verbal and Nonverbal Intelligence Components*

Variable	1	2	3	4	5	6	7	8	9	10
1. HAWIVA1	—	.52	.47	.46	.42	**.45**	.31	.20	.30	.27
2. HAWIVA2		—	.51	.47	.49	.27	.37	.27	.35	.25
3. HAWIK4			—	.81	.69	.40	.49	.43	.44	.35
4. HAWIK6				—	.80	.39	.43	.43	.47	.45
5. HAWIK9					—	.34	.43	.40	.54	**.43**
6. CMMS1						—	.55	.41	.36	.38
7. CMMS3							—	.53	.51	.52
8. CMMS5								—	.53	.46
9. CFT7									—	.65
10. CFT9										—

Note: Synchronous correlations are given in boldfaced type.

Although intercorrelations between verbal and nonverbal IQ tests tended to be lower than those obtained for verbal tests alone or for nonverbal tests alone, this difference was not substantial until the school years. From Grade 1 on, the stability of individual differences was rather high.

All in all, the correlational analyses yielded developmental trends similar to those found in classic longitudinal studies. The patterns found for test of verbal and non-verbal intelligence were roughly comparable, and IQ test performance assessed in preschool was significantly related to IQ performance in the later school years, regardless of the type of test (i.e., verbal vs. nonverbal). In contrast to previous studies, however, the average size of intercorrelations was generally lower for the LOGIC data.

Nonpsychometric Tests of Thinking and Reasoning

Theory of Mind. In the first (Wave 1) and second year (Wave 2) of investigation, children were tested for their understanding of false belief, a critical aspect of our commonsense psychology (belief–desire psychology). This assessment consisted of three tasks. Two were variations of the standard "unexpected transfer" test used by Wimmer and Perner (1983). In this task, a story protagonist puts an object in an original location. Then, unbeknownst to the protagonist, the object is transferred to a new location. The critical test in this task is to ask children where the protagonist will look for the object. The correct answer is that he will look in the original, now empty location. In addition to these two "unexpected transfer" tasks, children were also given one task using the "deceptive container" paradigm (Hogrefe, Wimmer, and Perner 1986). In this task, children were shown a familiar container with well-known contents (e.g., a Smarties [M&Ms] box). After indicating what they believed it contained (e.g., Smarties), they were shown that it really contained something else (e.g., a nut). Then the (unexpected) object was put back inside the box, it was closed, and children were asked what a friend who saw this box for the first time would think was inside. The correct answer, of course, was the original belief (Smarties).

At the time of the first assessments in Wave 1, children ranged in age from 3 years 9 months to 4 years 10 months. For purposes of correlating performance on these tasks with other measures, children were scored as passing 0 to 3 tasks at each point of assessment (Waves 1 and 2), abbreviated as FB1 (False Belief 1) and FB2 (false Belief 2).

The number of children passing each of the two unexpected transfer tasks was rather high even at the first time of assessment around age 4. Of the 175 children tested on both tasks, 70% passed one task, 73% the other task, and the correlation between tasks was PHI = .654. A year later 90% (N = 208) passed one task and 87% the other and the correlation was PHI = .472.

In contrast, fewer children in Wave 1 gave correct answers in the deceptive container task than on the transfer tasks: Although 43 children answered both transfer tasks correctly but gave a wrong answer on the container task, only 17 children showed the reverse pattern and answered the container task correctly but failed one of the transfer tasks; McNemar's $\chi^2(1, N = 60) = 11.27, p < .001$. This difference vanished at the second time of assessment in Wave 2 when children were about 5 years old. Here, 12 children passed both transfer tasks and failed the container task, and 21 showed the reverse pattern, McNemar's $\chi^2(1, N = 33) = 2.45, p > .10$. Indeed, at this age performance was high on all tasks: 77% answered all three tasks correctly. The difference in difficulty between the transfer tasks and the deceptive container task has also been reported by Holmes, Roldan, and Miller (1994) and by Doherty (1994), although Jenkins and Astington (1993) found no difference between the two task types.

There was a clear improvement with age. Of the 152 children who participated in all three tasks across both years, 67 children failed one or more tasks at 4 years and then passed all tasks at age 5. In contrast, only 7 children who answered all three tasks correctly at 4 years failed to do so at 5 years, McNemar's $\chi^2(1, N = 74) = 48.6, p < .001$.

Number Conservation. Number development in the LOGIC children was explored in Waves 1 and 3 with a "number invariance" test that consisted of 12 problems that assessed number invariance as defined by Piaget. Children were required to judge whether the number of items in item sets changed when they were transformed (i.e., either stretched out or compressed). The total number of items correctly answered was used as the dependent measure for the present analyses.

The mean number of number invariance problems solved correctly in Wave 1 was 3.22 (SD = 2.21; max = 12). Although this finding does not indicate a strong floor effect, it shows that the task was rather difficult for 4-year-olds. Two years later, the average number of tests passed was 7.01(SD = 4.47; max = 14), showing significant improvement, $t(186) = 9.31, p < .01$. The test–retest correlation was rather low (r = .12), indicating large interindividual differences in the degree of progress in numerical abilities from age 4 to age 6. A closer inspection of individual changes showed relatively few stagnations and even fewer regressions. Those 10 children scoring very high on the first measurement point (at least 75% correct) all maintained their level 2 years later.

Thinking and Reasoning. During the last 2 years of the LOGIC study, children's analytic thinking skills were tested with various instruments. A German version of the Arlin Test of Formal Reasoning (ATFR; Arlin 1984) was first used in Wave 8 when children were about 11 years old and was repeated 1 year later. This standardized paper-and-pencil test of operational reasoning skills focuses on the transition between concrete and formal operations. According to Arlin (1984), validation studies have shown that his test is a reliable alternative to the much more time-consuming clinical interview. The original test consists of 32 questions, arranged into eight subtests with four multiple choice questions. The questions pertaining to two formal schemes (forms of conservation beyond direct verification and mechanical equilibrium) were omitted from the German version because they were judged to be especially difficult. Thus, the resulting test contained 24 items arranged into the following six subtests:

- multiplicative compensations (conservation of water displacement with changes in size/shape)
- correlations (between variables in two dimensions)
- probability (of different outcomes in games of chance)
- combinatory reasoning (the ability to produce exhaustive combinations of 5 items)
- proportional reasoning (balance beam and amount of paper to cover different proportionally sized objects)
- coordination of two or more frames of reference (relative position of objects moving in different directions).

The score used from this test was the total number of questions correct and a qualitative classification into operational level (i.e., concrete, high concrete, transitional, low formal, and formal operational).

A *logical reasoning* task was presented in Wave 8. This task assessed two dimensions of logical reasoning skills: the ability to draw conclusions according to logical schemata regardless of contents (e.g., to draw factually false but logically valid conclusions) and the ability to differentiate logically intact from logically defective forms. The task consisted of syllogisms and sets of conditional sentences, and the subject was asked to determine whether a conclusion one might draw from the information was valid or invalid or whether one could not tell. For example, an item tapping the counterfactual version of the logical syllogism was

> "All panthers are strong.
> No strong things are black.
> What can you conclude? Are panthers black?"

Sixteen syllogisms were presented to the participant. A sum score representing the total number of correctly solved problems overall was used in the present analysis. Split-half reliability of the logical reasoning scale was .76.

Finally, a scale tapping *scientific reasoning* assessed in Wave 9 was also included in the present analysis. This scale consisted of scores assessing different components of scientific reasoning: (a) the production of controlled experiments, (b) the discrimination of controlled from uncontrolled experiments, (c) the generation of essential features of an empirical test, and (d) the detection of flaws in experiments described to the participants. The overall reliability of the scientific reasoning scale was .84.

As noted above, repeated measurements were only available for the ATFR, which was given in Waves 8 and 9. The percentage of correct answers obtained for the first measurement point was .40 ($SD = .14$), and it only slightly increased in Wave 9 (.45; $SD = .13$). Thus, the test proved to be rather difficult for 11- to 12-year-olds.

Stability over the time of about a year was found to be of moderate size, with a test–retest correlation of .57. A closer inspection of changes across the five operational levels described above showed that instability was highest for those children initially judged to be "transitional." From the 34 children initially classified as "low formal" or "formal," 24 maintained their position, whereas 7 moved down to the "transitional" stage.

Interrelations Among Cognitive and Psychometric Tasks: Developmental Patterns

Intercorrelations among measures of psychometric intelligence and cognitive developmental tasks were computed separately for preschool and school periods (n.b., German children attend preschool – which is called *kindergarten* – between the ages of 4 and 6 and then directly enter the first grade). The data obtained for the preschool period are depicted in Table 4.

As can be seen from this table, most intercorrelations were of low-to-moderate size, ranging between 0 (verbal intelligence and number conservation) and .35 (verbal intelligence and false belief) measured at the age of 4. Overall, the correlations are considerable lower than those obtained among various psychometric tests in the preschool period. With the exception of the correlation between false belief assessed in Wave 1 and number conservation measured in Wave 3 ($r = .40$), the interrelations among measures of children's theory of mind (i.e., false belief) and number invariance were also negligible.

The pattern or relations found for psychometric variables and indicators of formal reasoning assessed during the school years looks completely different, as shown in Table 5. Most of the correlations ranged between .45 and .60, indicating interrelations of moderate to high size. It is interesting that diachronous and synchronous correlations did not differ much. For example, the interrelation between the HAWIK measured in Wave 4 (first grade) and the Scientific Reasoning Scale administered in Wave 9 (Grade 6) exactly corresponds to the synchronous correlation between both variables obtained in Wave 9 ($r = .46$). Overall, the intercorrelations found among measures of formal and scientific reasoning also ranged between .45 and .60 and thus

Table 4. *Intercorrelations Among Measures of Psychometric Intelligence and Cognitive Developmental Tasks Observed in the Preschool Years*

	False belief		Number conservation	
Scale	FB1	FB2	NC1	NC3
HAWIVA1	.35	.22	−.03	.17
HAWIVA2	.28	.25	.10	.24
CMMS1	.22	.18	.09	.03
CMMS3	.29	.21	.12	.24

Note: Number immediately following variable indicates wave number.

Table 5. *Intercorrelations Among Measures of Psychometric Intelligence and Piagetian Tasks Observed for Grades 1–6*

	Formal operation		Logical reasoning	Scientific reasoning
Scale	TFR8	ATFR9	LR8	SR9
HAWIK4	.48	.43	.56	.46
HAWIK6	.45	.52	.59	.49
HAWIK9	.48	.59	.61	.46
CMMS5	.37	.40	.41	.44
CFT7	.52	.47	.51	.48

Note: Number immediately following variable indicates wave number.

are comparable to those found between measures of verbal and nonverbal intelligence obtained for the same age range (cf. Table 3). This finding indicates that the type of assessment of intellectual skills did not seem to make a big difference after children entered school. Overall, interrelations among psychometric measures of intelligence and experimental assessments of logical thinking were substantial and reliable over the school years.

Intraindividual Changes in Psychometric Intelligence Over Time: The Impact of Individual Difference Variables

As noted above, developmental changes on the basis of raw scores of psychometric measures could not be assessed for the whole range of 9 years because different instruments had to be used for different age periods. Raw scores for the HAWIVA (Waves 1 and 2) and for the HAWIK (Waves 4, 6, and 9) could be used for longitudinal

Table 6. *Means and Standard Deviations of Raw
Scores Used for the Various MANOVAs*

	HAWIVA		HAWIK		CFT	
Wave	M	SD	M	SD	M	SD
1	34.40	9.42				
2	46.26	8.38				
4			28.51	12.13		
6			51.10	12.90		
7					29.44	5.66
9			79.39	16.05	33.98	4.90

analyses of developmental change in verbal IQ. This was not possible for some of the measures of nonverbal IQ. For instance, the CMMS could not be chosen for assessing developmental change because different item sets were used for different ages. Thus, only the CFT raw scores obtained in Waves 7 and 9 were suited for our purposes.

One of the major goals was to assess the type of developmental trend (linear vs. nonlinear). This could only be done for the HAWIK data because at least three measurement points are required. Hierarchical linear modeling (Bryk and Raudenbush 1992) was used for this analysis. Another major goal was to assess the impact of various individual difference variables such as sex, socioeconomic status (SES), family size, and initial intelligence level (high vs. low) on the change in raw scores over time. Both ratings of the social prestige of fathers' occupation (high, medium, or low) and of mothers' educational level were included as indicators of SES. Three repeated measurement multivariate analyses of variance (MANOVAs) were carried out using the individual difference variables as independent factors and the HAWIVA, HAWIK, and CFT raw scores as dependent variables. In addition, chronological age was included as a covariate given the large age range within the sample. The means and standard deviations obtained for the HAWIVA, HAWIK, and CFT raw scores are given in Table 6.

The MANOVA conducted for the HAWIVA scores yielded a main effect of social prestige, $F(2, 148) = 5.71$, $p < .01$. Subsequent univariate analyses revealed that children from families of the highest social prestige level scored higher than children from the two lower levels on both occasions. In addition, the effect of the age covariate was significant, $F(1, 148) = 30.62$, $p < .01$. Overall, older children performed better than younger children. There were no other main effects and no significant interactions. It should be noted that the effect of testing time was just short of being significant ($p < .09$). That is, although most children improved their performance from ages 4 to 5, this change was not statistically significant.

The MANOVA based on the HAWIK data revealed significant main effects of sex, social prestige, initial IQ level, and measurement point. Boys performed better than girls, and the children from families with high social prestige levels outperformed the rest of the sample. Furthermore, children with initially high IQ scores remained superior throughout the testing period, and all children improved their performance from Grade 1 to Grade 6. The main effect of measurement point was qualified by interactions with sex and initial IQ level. Subsequent analyses showed that boys improved more than girls across time, and children with initially high IQ level gained more than those with initially low IQ levels. Again, the effect of the covariate (chronological age) was significant, indicating that younger children performed worse than older ones, regardless of measurement point.

Finally, the MANOVA carried out on the CFT raw scores yielded a significant main effect of initial IQ level, $F(1, 148) = 139.78$, $p < .01$, qualified by a significant interaction with measurement point, $F(2, 161) = 28.76$, $p < .01$. Again, children with initially high IQ levels gained more than those with initially low IQ levels. The effect of measurement point was not significant, $F(1, 148) = 3.71$, $p < .06$: Although most children improved their performance over the 2-year period, the gain was not substantial. With the exception of a significant effect of the age covariate, no other effects or interactions were found.

To utilize fully the longitudinal information in the HAWIK data, we used hierarchical linear modeling (HLM; Bryk and Raudenbush 1992). The HLM consists of two models: (a) an individual growth model that represents changes in each child's verbal ability over time and (b) a between-child model that represents the differences among children in these growth trajectories. The HLM allows one to estimate the function of the mean growth curve (linear vs. nonlinear) and provides the possibility of explaining observed variability in individual growth trajectories by individual differences in background variables (e.g., sex, SES). The impact of these background variables on both the entry level (i.e., the first measurement point) and the slope of the growth function can be easily assessed.

Although the mean HAWIK scores obtained for Waves 4, 6, and 9 suggest an almost linear increase over time (cf. Table 6), this should be interpreted with caution because the time intervals between measurement points were not equidistant (16 months for the interval between T1 and T2 and 36 months for the interval between T2 and T3). To correct for this difference in time intervals, we used a transformation procedure to obtain estimates of the HAWIK raw scores assessed in Wave 9.[1] These corrected raw scores were then included in the HLM analyses.

In a first step, a linear model of growth was estimated using the individual difference variables listed above as predictors of interindividual differences in intraindividual growth trajectories. Although the reliability score obtained for the entry level was

---

[1] The following procedure was used to correct for the impact of different time intervals between T1, T2, and T3: The mean change score per month for the interval between T2 and T3 (36 months) was calculated for each child, and the resulting change score per month was multiplied by 16 (the number of months between T1 and T2). This score was then added to each child's raw score obtained at T2.

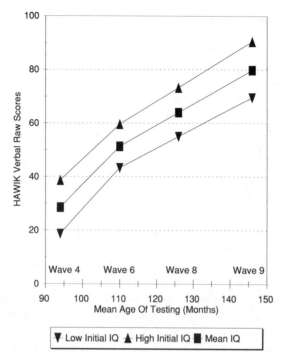

Figure 1. Changes in HAWIK (Hamburg–Wechsler–Intelligence Scale for Children) verbal raw scores between Waves 4 and 9, as a function of initial IQ level.

sufficient (.61), the reliability estimate for the growth function was low (.07). Given this low reliability score, it appears that modeling the growth parameters as a function of background variables is not warranted.

In a second step, a nonlinear model of growth was estimated. As the (corrected) HAWIK scores suggested a negatively accelerated growth curve, a root function growth model was specified. The reliability estimates for both the entry level and the growth function were found to be sufficiently high (.68 and .64, respectively), indicating a substantial signal in these data in terms of individual differences in both initial status and growth rates. The correlation between entry level and growth rate was .27, indicating that children with initially higher scores tended to gain at a somewhat faster rate. Figure 1 shows the developmental pattern of raw scores as a function of initial IQ level (high vs. low). It should be noted that the Wave 8 data represent estimated raw scores based on the transformation procedure described above. Figure 1 indicates that both IQ subsamples showed a slight slowing down in the increases in their raw scores over the age period between 9 and 12 years.

As can be seen from Table 7 sex, social prestige, and initial level of IQ were significantly related to both entry level and individual growth rates. Whereas the

Table 7. *Hierarchical Linear Modeling Results Describing the Impact of Individual Difference Variables on the HAWIK Entry Level and Nonlinear Trend*

Variable	t	p
Entry level		
Sex	−2.12	<.04
Social prestige	2.48	<.02
Family size	−1.31	<.20
Initial IQ level	18.27	<.01
Nonlinear trend		
Sex	−2.06	<.04
Social prestige	0.40	.68
Family size	0.96	.34
Initial IQ level	−2.17	<.03

impact of initial IQ level on entry level is trivial, its contribution to the growth curve confirms the correlation between entry level and growth rate already mentioned above. The root function growth model did fit the data rather well. Sex, social prestige, and initial IQ level accounted for about 77% of the parameter variance in the initial status and 43% of the parameter variance in growth rates on IQ raw scores.

Conclusions

Individual Differences in IQ and Changes in Correlational Patterns Over Time

Our findings indicate that there were moderate relationships between verbal and nonverbal IQ components from preschool age on, which did not increase substantially over the school years. It is interesting that test–retest correlations found for repeated assessments based on the same instruments were not significantly higher than correlations between measures of verbal and nonverbal intelligence for the preschool period. This pattern changed later in childhood, that is, from Grade 1 on. For the later testing period, test–retest correlations obtained for the verbal (HAWIK) IQ component were considerably higher than those found between verbal and nonverbal IQ scores. Although the results were not similarly clear for the nonverbal IQ component, our findings are compatible with the view that intraindividual changes in verbal and nonverbal components of intelligence follow different patterns. Whereas stability of individual differences within each component (verbal vs. nonverbal) increases as a function of time, cross-domain comparisons do not indicate any increase in intercorrelations over time.

*The Relation of Early Performance on Mental Ability Tests
and Later IQ Assessments*

Our findings deviate from those obtained in the classic American longitudinal studies. Compared to these studies, we found more instability in young children's performance during the preschool years, regardless of whether psychometric or Piagetian-type tasks were considered. Although early performance on psychometric IQ tests predicted later performance to some extent, our preschool measures did not explain as much variance in IQ assessments during school as reported for most classic longitudinal studies. As noted above, we suspect that the test aggregation procedure used in these studies led to an overestimation of the stability of early IQ. Our data agree with those from the classic studies in that substantial long-term stabilities in IQ were found for the school years.

*Relations Between Cognitive Developmental and Psychometric Measures
of Children's Intellectual Competencies*

Assessments for the preschool and school periods led to different results. Although there were almost no reliable interrelations between psychometric measures of intelligence and false belief or number conservation tasks, psychometric IQ and measures of formal, logical, and analytical reasoning assessed during the first 6 years of school correlated substantially. In fact, the level of these correlations corresponded with those found for verbal and nonverbal IQ indicators for the same time period. Given the high overlap in correlations, it seems unlikely that cognitive developmental measures and psychometric IQ measures used with 7- to 12-year-old children tap different intellectual abilities (cf. also Anderson 1992; Carroll, Kohlberg, and DeVries 1984).

Patterns of Interindividual Differences in Intraindividual Change

Our analyses yielded two major findings:

1. Although our database was not ideal with regard to the question of linear versus nonlinear change patterns, the HLM analyses suggest that developmental changes in verbal ability (as assessed during the school years) may be best described by nonlinear growth models. The data suggest a nonlinear slowing down of raw score gains between ages 9 and 12. Although we are tempted to interpret this as a first sign of the eventual leveling off at asymptote, further research including older adolescents and young adults is necessary to validate this claim.
2. The impact of individual differences variables (e.g., sex, SES, initial level of IQ) throughout the course of the LOGIC study was substantial, indicated by both the MANOVA and HLM analyses. Taken together, our findings agree with the view that different children show different developmental patterns as a function of both environmental and organismic factors (Fischer and Silvern 1985; Weinert 1994). Nonpredictive, unstable developmental differences seem to be particularly frequent during the preschool and kindergarten years. The cognitive system is consequently distinguished by increasing invariability and stability in individual differences over time.

References

Anderson, M. (1992). *Intelligence and development – A cognitive theory*. Oxford, England: Blackwell.

Arlin, P. K. (1984). *Arlin Test of Formal Reasoning (ATFR). Test manual for middle school, high school, and adult levels*. New York: Slossen Publications.

Bayley, N. (1949). Consistency and variability in the growth of intelligence from birth to eighteen years. *The Journal of Genetic Psychology, 75*, 165–196.

Bayley, N. (1955). On the growth of intelligence. *American Psychologist, 10*, 805–818.

Bayley, N. (1970). Development of mental abilities. In P. H. Mussen (Ed.), *Carmichael's manual of child psychology* (3rd ed., pp. 1163–1209). New York: Wiley.

Berg, C. A. (1992). Perspectives for viewing intellectual development throughout the life course. In R. J. Sternberg & C. A. Berg (Eds.), *Intellectual development* (pp. 1–15). Cambridge, England: Cambridge University Press.

Bidell, T. R., & Fischer, K. W. (1992). Beyond the stage debate: Action, structure, and variability in Piagetian theory and research. In R. J. Sternberg & C. A. Berg (Eds.), *Intellectual development* (pp. 37–52). Cambridge, England: Cambridge University Press.

Bloom, B. S. (1964). *Stability and change in human characteristics*. New York: Wiely.

Brainerd, C. J. (1978). The stage question in cognitive–developmental theory. *Behavioral and Brain Sciences, 1*, 173–182.

Bryk, A., & Raudenbush, S. (1992). *Hierarchical linear models for social and behavioral research: Applications and data analysis methods*. Newbury Park, CA: Sage.

Burgemeister, B., Blum, L., & Lorge, J. (1972). *Columbia Mental Maturity Scale*. New York: Harcourt Brace Jovanovich.

Carroll, J. B., Kohlberg, L., & DeVries, R. (1984). Psychometric and Piagetian intelligences: Toward resolution of controversy. *Intelligence, 8*, 67–91.

Case, R. (1985). *Intellectual development: Birth to adulthood*. Orlando, FL: Academic Press.

Case, R. (1992). Neo-Piagetian theories of child development. In R. J. Sternberg & C. A. Berg (Eds.), *Intellectual development* (pp. 161–196). Cambridge, England: Cambridge University Press.

Demetriou, A. (1988). *The neo-Piagetian theories of intelligence: Toward an integration*. Amsterdam: North Holland.

Doherty, M. (1994). *Metalinguistic understanding and theory of mind*. Unpublished doctoral dissertation, Laboratory of Experimental Psychology, University of Sussex, Sussex, England.

Eggert, D. (1978). *Hannover–Wechsler–Intelligenztest für das Vorschulalter* [German version of the Wechsler Preschool and Primary Scale of Intelligence]. Bern, Switzerland: Huber.

Fischer, K. W. (1987). Relations between brain and cognitive development. *Child Development, 57*, 623–632.

Fischer, K. W., & Rose, S. P. (1994). Dynamic development of coordination of components in brain and behavior. In G. Dawson & K. W. Fischer (Eds.), *Human behavior and the developing brain* (pp. 3–66). New York: Guilford Press.

Fischer, K. W., & Silvern, L. (1985). Stages and individual differences in cognitive development. *Annual Review of Psychology, 36*, 613–648.

Gardner, M. K., & Clark, E. (1992). The psychometric perspective on intellectual development in childhood and adolescence. In R. J. Sternberg & C. A. Berg (Eds.), *Intellectual development* (pp. 16–43). Cambridge, England: Cambridge University Press.

Goodenough, F. L. (1946). The measurement of mental growth in childhood. In L. Carmichael (Ed.), *Manual of child psychology* (pp. 450–475). New York: Wiley.

Hilden, A. J. (1949). A longitudinal study of intellectual development. *Journal of Psychology, 28*, 187–214.

Hindley, C. B., & Owen, C. F. (1978). The extent of individual changes in I.Q. for ages between 6 months and 17 years in a British longitudinal sample. *Journal of Child Psychology and Psychiatry, 19*, 329–350.

Hogrefe, G. J., Wimmer, H., & Perner, J. (1986). Ignorance versus false belief: A developmental lag in attribution of epistemic states. *Child Development, 57*, 567–582.

Holmes, H. A., Roldan, C., & Miller, S. A. (1994, April). *A cross-task comparison of false belief understanding in a Head Start population.* Paper presented at the Conference on Human Development, Pittsburgh.

Honzik, M. P., MacFarlane, J. W., & Allen, L. (1948). The stability of mental test performance between two and eighteen years. *Journal of Experimental Education, 17,* 309–324.

Hunt, E. (1980). Intelligence as an information-processing concept. *British Journal of Psychology, 71,* 449–474.

Jenkins, J. M., & Astington, J. W. (1993, April). *Cognitive, linguistic, and social factors associated with theory of mind development in young children.* Paper presented at the 60th anniversary meeting of the Society for Research in Child Development, New Orleans, LA.

Kail, R., & Pellegrino, J. W. (1985). *Human intelligence: Perspectives and prospects.* New York: Freeman.

McCall, R. B. (1981). Nature–nurture and the two realms of development: A proposed integration with respect to mental development. *Child Development, 54,* 408–415.

McCall, R. B., Hogarty, P. S., & Hurlburt, N. (1972). Transitions in infant sensimotor development and the prediction of childhood IQ. *American Psychologist, 27,* 728–748.

Moffitt, T. E., Caspi, A., Harkness, A., & Silva, P. A. (1993). The natural history of change in intellectual performance: Who changes? How much? Is it meaningful? *Journal of Child Psychology and Psychiatry, 34,* 455–506.

Piaget, J. (1952). Autobiography. In Boring. E. G. (Ed.), *A history of psychology in autobiography* (Vol. 4, pp. 237–256). Worcester, MA: Clark University Press.

Schaie, K. W. (1994). The course of adult intellectual development. *American Psychologist, 49,* 304–313.

Schneider, W. (1989). Problems of longitudinal studies with young children: Conceptual and methodological issues. In M. Brambring, F. Lösel, & H. Skowronek (Eds.), *Children at risk: Assessment and longitudinal research* (pp. 313–335). New York: DeGruyter.

Siegler, R. S. (1994). Cognitive variability: A key to understanding cognitive development. *Current Directions in Psychological Science, 3,* 1–5.

Siegler, R. S., & Richards, D. D. (1982). The development of intelligence. In R. J. Sternberg (Ed.) *Handbook of human intelligence* (pp. 897–971). Cambridge, England: Cambridge University Press.

Sontag, L. W., Baker, C. T., & Nelson, V. L. (1958). Mental growth and personality development: A longitudinal study. *Monographs of the Society for Research in Child Development, 23*(Serial No. 68).

Sternberg, R. J., & Detterman, D. K. (Eds.). (1986). *What is intelligence? Contemporary viewpoints on its nature and definition.* Norwood, NJ: Ablex.

Sternberg, R. J., & Powell, J. S. (1983). The development of intelligence. In J. H. Flavell & E. M. Markman (Vol. Eds.), *Handbook of child psychology: Vol. 3. Cognitive development* (4th ed., pp. 341–419). New York: Wiley.

Tewes, U. (Ed.). (1983). *Hamburg–Wechsler–Intelligenztest für Kinder, Revision (HAWIK–R)* [German version of the revised WISC]. Bern, Switzerland: Huber.

Weinert, F. E. (1994). Cognitive development: Individual differences. In T. Husen & T. N. Postlethwaite (Eds.), *International encyclopedia of education* (2nd ed., pp. 842–847). Oxford, England: Pergamon Press.

Weiss, R. (1976). *Grundintelligenztest CFT20* [Basic intelligence test CFT20]. Braunschweig: Westermann.

Wimmer, H., & Perner, J. (1983). Beliefs about beliefs: Representation and constraining function of wrong beliefs in young children's understanding of deception. *Cognition, 13,* 103–128.

Yule, W., Gold, R. D., & Busch, C. (1982). Long-term predictive validity of the WPPSI: An 11-year follow-up study. *Personality and Individual Differences, 3,* 65–71.

2a Comment: What Individual Differences Can Teach Us About Developmental Function, and Vice Versa

David F. Bjorklund

People interested in cognitive development have always been of two types (at least): those who study developmental function, changes in the form that cognition takes over time; and those who study individual differences, particularly the stability of individual differences. Researchers in the former group have typically looked at changes in cognitive processes or structures, whereas researchers in the latter group have typically looked at the stability of intelligence-test performance. Despite what would appear to a naive observer to be interest in highly similar phenomena, there has been traditionally little communication between the two groups (e.g., Cronbach 1957). The situation has changed some in recent years, with researchers acknowledging the importance of both inter- and intraindividual variability for studying developmental function (e.g., Siegler 1995) and the importance of understanding changes in developmental function for studying the stability of individual differences (e.g., Fagan 1992; McCall, Eichorn, and Hogarty 1977). To integrate properly the study of developmental function and individual differences requires not only longitudinal data but also the conceptual disposition to look for relations between these two realms of developmental psychology, something that is found in the Munich Longitudinal Study on the Genesis of Individual Competencies (LOGIC).

The chapter by Schneider, Perner, Bullock, Stefanek, and Ziegler looks at the developmental relation between changes in psychometric performance and Piagetian-type cognitive measures. As other researchers have done, they assess both the relation between and the stability of psychometric intelligence and Piagetian-type reasoning. What is unique about the LOGIC study, however, is that it examines the relations between these two sets of tasks over time; moreover, the relations between psychometric and Piagetian-type tasks are examined both synchronously, as has been done previously (e.g., Humphreys, Rich, and Davey 1985; Kingma 1984; Kuhn 1976), and diachronously, with tests administered in kindergarten correlated with tests given in later childhood. This provides a unique opportunity to examine the developmental relations between these two types of cognition not typically available (or not typically analyzed) in other longitudinal studies.

29

Schneider et al. used the LOGIC data to investigate four questions:

1. Are there changes in the intercorrelations between verbal and nonverbal intelligence over time?
2. Do verbal and nonverbal IQ tests given in the preschool years predict later IQ, and do the predictions differ for verbal and nonverbal IQ performance?
3. Are there any significant relations between psychometric and Piagetian-type tasks, and do these relations change with age?
4. Does cognitive growth between ages 7 and 12 years develop linearly or nonlinearly?

I discuss the first two issues, the relations between verbal and nonverbal intelligence and their respective predictive validity, in the first section below, then look at the relation between the psychometric and Piagetian-like tasks, and finally discuss the issue of intellectual change over childhood.

The Relation Between Verbal and Nonverbal Intelligence From 4 to 12 Years

Looking only at the psychometric results, the findings of Schneider and his colleagues both confirm and contradict some of the classic patterns reported in the literature. First, there was moderate stability of IQ scores over age, with cross-age correlations within each test type (i.e., verbal and nonverbal) increasing for measures administered during later childhood (7 years and on), especially for verbal IQ. The median of seven correlations between verbal scores when the first test was administered during the preschool years was .47; this is contrasted with a median of three correlations between verbal tests of .80 when the first test was administered at age 7 or later. This difference could not be attributed to the number of years intervening between testings. When the number of years between testings was equal (2, 3, and 5 years), the correlations obtained when the first verbal test was given during the preschool years were all lower (.51, .46, and .46, for 2, 3, and 5 years' separation, respectively) than comparable correlations when the first verbal test was administered at age 7 or later (.81, .80, and .69, for 2, 3, and 5 years' separation, respectively). A similar, though less drastic change was noted for the nonverbal tests, with median cross-age correlations being .40 for the tests first administered at age 4, .52 when the first test was given at age 6, and .53 for tests first administered in later childhood (ages 8 and 10 years). This pattern of results is consistent with past literature and indicates that psychometric intelligence becomes increasingly stable with age, with a greater move toward stability for verbal than for nonverbal intelligence.

Verbal and nonverbal IQ scores were moderately correlated at all ages, with no systematic pattern of changes in the magnitude of this relation with age. It is interesting that the median magnitude of the diachronous cross-task correlations ($n = 23$, $Mdn = .40$) was comparable to that of the two synchronous correlations (.43 and .45 at ages 4 and 12, respectively). Cross-age correlations between the verbal and nonverbal tests varied some as a function of the number of years between the tests (median of the 13 correlations between tests of 1-, 2-, and 3-year intervals = .43; median of the 7 correlations between tests of 4-, 5-, and 6-year intervals = .35; median of the 3 correlations between tests of 7- and 8-year intervals = .27). The absence of increases in the correlations between the verbal and nonverbal measures over time, as was found within each domain, and the lower correlations between the two types of tests with increasing years between testings, which was less apparent within the verbal and nonverbal tests, suggests some differences in the developmental course of verbal and nonverbal intelligence. Both skills increase with age, and the significant correlations between the two sets of tests suggest that a common factor underlies both types of intelligence; however, there are also differences, indicating different developmental patterns for these two types of intelligence.

Most of these are not new findings but essentially replicate patterns that have been reported in the literature. However, what is different is the magnitude of the cross-age correlations reported here compared to previous investigations. These correlations are somewhat lower than those reported in other studies. The authors attribute this difference to the aggregation of IQ scores in previous research (e.g., Bayley 1949), resulting in an overestimation of long-term stability.

The Relation Between Psychometric and Piagetian-Type Tests Over Childhood

Children were also given sets of Piagetian-type tests, with theory-of-mind and number-conservation tests being given at ages 4 and 5 and a series of formal-operational reasoning tasks being given at ages 11 and 12. Performances on these tasks were correlated with one another and with psychometric tests.

Looking first at the preschool data, performance on the two false-belief tasks and the number-conservation tasks are consistent with previous findings. It should be noted that the false-belief tasks are not traditional Piagetian tests; theory-of-mind theory was developed only after Piaget's death. However, I think Piaget would have approved of theory-of-mind research. Children's ability to solve the false-belief tasks, which are the central data of theory-of-mind research, reflects a form of egocentricity that Piaget would have found familiar. Moreover, although major theorists disagree with exactly what type of theory of mind younger versus older preschoolers have (e.g., Perner 1991; Wellman 1990), changes in theory of mind are described as occurring in a stagelike manner, similar to the way Piaget described development. Thus, I think Schneider and his colleagues are justified in including the false-beliefs tasks as Piagetian in nature and evaluating performance on them along with the more traditional number-conservation tasks.

The authors reported that performance on the Piagetian-type tasks during the preschool years did not correlate strongly with psychometric IQ (median correlation between IQ and false-belief tasks = .235; median correlation between IQ and number-conservation tasks = .11). This pattern suggests that different cognitive abilities underlie the "intelligences" assessed by psychometric and Piagetian-type reasoning tests during the preschool years. That is, intelligence is not best represented by a single factor, but rather the type of intelligence that is reflected by IQ tests is different from the type of intelligence that is reflected by the Piagetian-type tests. However, it should be noted that the relations among the false-belief and conservation tasks were also low, suggesting that these two Piagetian-type tasks are domain-specific in nature and do not reflect a single underlying cognitive structure, as would be predicted from Piagetian theory.

Perhaps the Piagetian-type tests used in the LOGIC study were not an adequate test of operational (or preoperational thought), and a more complete battery of tests would have yielded higher correlations. For example, Kuhn (1976) reported a correlation of .69 between a battery of Piagetian tasks (class inclusion, seriation, conservation of amount, multiple classification, and multiple seriation) and mental age for a group of 5- and 6-year-old children. Kuhn's tasks represented a more advanced form of cognition than the false-belief and number-conservation tasks used in the Munich study. Whereas the tasks used by Kuhn reflect transition from pre- to concrete operations, the false-belief tasks are typically mastered by a majority of children by age 4 (as was found in the present sample), and number invariance is one of the earliest forms of conservation that children acquire, being mastered by most children by age 6 or 7, as was found in the present sample. Thus, whereas tests that assess the transition in thinking that typically occurs during the early school years (e.g., conservation of amount, class inclusion) are highly correlated with psychometric IQ (e.g., Kuhn 1976) and presumably tap some of the same underlying cognitive abilities as assessed by IQ tests, tasks that assess the transition from early preschool thought (e.g., desire theory of mind) to later preschool thought (e.g., belief-desire theory of mind) are generally unrelated to IQ measures. This pattern may reflect the fact that the preschool child must make some basic cognitive accomplishments that are independent of the type of cognition assessed by psychometric tests. Greater overlap in the underlying cognitive abilities is assessed by Piagetian-type and psychometric tests during the early school years, however.

Overlap between psychometric intelligence and formal operational abilities is also substantial, with the cross-age correlations between these two sets of tasks being nearly as high as the cross-age correlations for the psychometric tests. This finding is contradictory to those of Kuhn (1976), who reported a nonsignificant correlation (.22) between mental age derived from the Wechsler Intelligence Scale for Children (Wechsler, 1949) and a battery of formal operational tasks, but it is consistent with the findings of other researchers (e.g., Humphreys 1980; Humphreys and Parson 1979; Humphreys et al. 1985; Keating 1975). Although Humphreys and his colleagues did not report correlations broken down by ages, they found correlations in excess of .80 between a battery of Piagetian and psychometric tests of intelligence in samples of children ranging in age from 6 to 18 years. The correlations reported in the LOGIC study are somewhat lower, but what is impressive about the LOGIC findings is the high correlations between psychometric tests administered at ages 7 and 9 and tests of formal reasoning administered at ages 11 and 12 years.

On the basis of these findings, Schneider and his colleagues reached what seems to be an inescapable conclusion. They wrote, "it seems unlikely that cognitive developmental measures and psychometric IQ measures used with 7- to 12-year-old children tap different intellectual abilities" (p. x). Despite the high correlations, I recommend a bit more caution before concluding that Piagetian and psychometric tests are isomorphic in the types of intelligence they assess. For example, Humphreys et al. (1985) reported significant relations between Piagetian tests, verbal and nonverbal IQ, and academic achievement, and they claimed that each was a valid measure of general intelligence. However, although IQ and Piagetian tasks correlated significantly, each also accounted for some unique variance, suggesting that, despite the significant overlap, the two tests were not measuring exactly the same cognitive abilities.

I have been intrigued and somewhat perplexed by previous research and by the findings of the current study, of high correlations between psychometric and Piagetian tasks. As typically construed, both psychometric and Piagetian theory postulate a domain-general mechanism underlying development. In psychometric theory, that domain-general mechanism is g, a general factor of intelligence that influences all aspects of cognition. In Piagetian theory, the general mechanism is the underlying cognitive structures that, at any point in time, are highly integrated and produce homogeneity of cognitive functioning. Although both are domain-general theories, there is a major difference between the two approaches. In psychometric theory, g, is usually thought of as varying continuously over time, so that individual differences in g at one age should predict individual differences of g at another age. That is, there is continuity of developmental function, and it yields stability of individual differences. Piaget, of course, was the classic stage theorist, who postulated discontinuity of developmental function. A child's cognitive structures become reorganized between stages. As such, there is no reason to predict that individual differences remain stable over time. The suggestion here is that there is an inherent relation between developmental function and individual differences: When developmental function is continuous, individual differences over time are stable; when developmental function is discontinuous, individual differences are apt to be unstable.

Continuity and stability, or discontinuity and instability, are not inevitable outcomes. Developmental function and stability of individual differences are conceptually and statistically independent, just as means (that reflect developmental function) are independent of correlations (that reflect cross-age stability). Research findings, however, have suggested a systematic relation between the two concepts. Perhaps the clearest example of this is the study by McCall et al. (1977), who evaluated changes in cognitive function over infancy, using the data from the Berkeley Growth Study (Bayley 1949). Infants were tested monthly on a precursor of the Bayley Infant Scale (Bayley 1969), and, on the basis of careful item analyses using principal component analysis, McCall et al. described developmental function across infancy and also assessed the stability of individual differences by evaluating the cross-age correlations of the principal components. They reported stagelike transitions over infancy, similar to those proposed by Piaget. When examining individual differences, they reported that the cross-age correlations were generally high when calculated between two points both within the same cognitive stage. Correlations were lower, however, when they were calculated between points within different stages. That is, cross-age correlations within a stage were high (continuity with stability), whereas cross-age correlations between stages were low (discontinuity with instability). Similar conclusions have been reached when interpreting the high correlations between measures of infant habituation or preference for novelty and later childhood IQ (e.g., Fagan 1992): The cognitive abilities that underlie the infant measures also underlie childhood IQ, presumably varying continuously over this time period. In contrast, scores on infant intelligence measures, such as the Bayley or Gesell Scales (Gesell & Amatrude 1954), do not correlate highly with childhood IQ, suggesting different underlying cognitive mechanisms reflecting a discontinuous developmental function (e.g., Fagan and Singer 1983).

How are we then to explain the high correlations between Piagetian and psychometric measures of intelligence? How can a continuously varying factor (g) correlate significantly with a discontinuously varying factor (cognitive structures)? First of all, as demonstrated in the LOGIC study, these measures do not correlate significantly before the school years. Piaget proposed that the advent of concrete operations yielded greater structural integration ("structures d'ensemble"), and perhaps this factor accounts for the significant correlations between Piagetian and psychometric tasks during the school years, but not before. Nonetheless, Piaget proposed cognitive change between the ages of 7 and 12, yet the correlations between IQ and formal-reasoning measures are high at all ages (and stay high into early adulthood, when considering the Humphreys et al. data).

Perhaps most significant are the findings from the present database of significant cross-age correlations between psychometric IQ and formal-reasoning tests. The correlations between verbal IQ at age 7 and tests of formal operations at age 11 were .48 and .56, and at age 12, .43 and .46. For nonverbal IQ administered at age 8, the correlations with formal reasoning at 11 years of age were .37 and .41, and at age 12, .40 and .44. As noted earlier, these correlations are only slightly lower in magnitude than those for the psychometric tests administered at different ages.

These data suggest to me that Piaget's proposal of discontinuous, stagelike progression across middle childhood to adolescence must be seriously questioned (as, of course, it has been by others; see Brainerd 1978). Psychometric and Piagetian tests not only correlate significantly with each other when administered simultaneously, but psychometric tests administered in early childhood predicted formal reasoning ability 5 years later. If psychometric and Piagetian tests are measuring much the same underlying general intelligence, that intelligence cannot be conceptualized as varying both continuously and discontinuously at the same time.

It is possible, of course, that the psychometric theory is wrong – that g does not vary continuously over time. However, given the careful and long history of IQ-test construction and evaluation, and the high cross-age correlations typically found for IQ, my guess is that it is Piaget's theory that is wrong. The data of the Munich study provide convincing evidence, I believe, that the changes that Piaget described between the ages of about 7 and 12 are not discontinuous in nature but can better be described as continuous. The current data do not suggest that Piaget's notion of stage must be totally abandoned or that there may not be other aspects of intelligence not tapped by either the psychometric or Piagetian tests. In fact, the preschool data are consistent with a stage-theory approach, and McCall et al.'s (1977) evaluation of cognitive changes over infancy indicate that at least some aspects of intelligence vary discontinuously over time. However, the ability of psychometric tests to predict later formal reasoning suggests that a single form of continuously varying intelligence underlies both sets of tasks. I realize the need to heed my own caution, stated earlier, that it is unlikely that psychometric and Piagetian tasks overlap perfectly in the type of intelligence they tap. Nevertheless, I agree with the authors that there is substantial commonality and that it appears to be for a type of intelligence that varies continuously over time.

Developmental and Individual Differences in the Nature of Cognitive Growth Over Childhood

Schneider and his colleagues looked at a number of predictor variables and examined the pattern of developmental changes for the psychometric data. First of all, a signif-icant nonlinear trend was found for changes in verbal intelligence scores between 7 and 12 years of age, with the rate of gain slowing down between the ages of 9 and 12 years. Second, several factors predicted level of IQ scores, including social prestige and sex, with children from more prestigious homes having higher IQs than children from less prestigious homes, and boys performing better than girls. The social pres-tige socioeconomic status effect is a robust finding in the developmental literature and needs no explanation, and the authors provided no interpretation for the less robust, but presumably unexpected, sex effect, and I, too, make no attempt to interpret it here.

The most intriguing effect in these analyses, however, was that of initial level of IQ on subsequent performance. In both the multivariate analyses of variance and in the hierarchical linear modeling of the verbal IQ data, children who had higher initial IQ scores demonstrated greater subsequent gains than children with lower initial IQ scores. This finding is an example of the "Matthew Effect" (Stanovich 1986; Walberg and Tsai 1983), in which more educationally advantaged children experience greater gain from educational experience than less educationally advantaged children. Just as the "rich get richer and the poor get poorer," children who are academically accomplished (e.g., good readers) in the early grades improve their cognitive skills at a faster rate than less accomplished children. This results in an increased discrepancy between the "haves" and "have nots" over time. Apparently, this same pattern holds for psychometric intelligence and may be influenced by the same feedback effects postulated for the Matthew Effect in educational contents (see Stanovich 1986).

This is another demonstration of the interaction between developmental func-tion and individual differences: High-IQ children show more rapid acquisition (i.e., steeper developmental functions) of certain cognitive contents than low-IQ children. Both groups displayed similar nonlinear patterns of gains in verbal intelligence over the 7- to 12-year age range (see Schneider et al.'s Figure 1), suggesting that these two groups were following similar developmental paths and that the difference is primarily one of rate. However, these finding make it clear that there is not a single developmental function that all children show, regardless of level. Rather, patterns vary in often subtle but important ways as a function of a number in endogenous and exogenous factors.

Some Final Comments

The findings of Schneider, Perner, Bullock, Stefanek, and Ziegler provide some insight into the relation between individual differences and developmental function. Their findings add to the psychometric literature that has long demonstrated stability of individual differences and suggest some possible reinterpretations of "classic" results. The longitudinal data of the LOGIC study permitted the authors to evaluate the relation between psychometric and Piagetian-type intelligence in a way not previously possible and provided, I believe, some interesting and important insights, not only about the relation between these two types of intelligence but about the developmental nature of each as well.

One must be cautious in interpreting the findings, of course. The conclusion that one might draw from much of this research is that a single, domain-general mechanism underlies much of cognitive development, at least from the age of 7 onward. As the authors realize, this is too simplistic, and this is reflected by other findings in the Munich study (e.g., Sodian and Schneider's analysis of memory strategy development, this volume). Moreover, different patterns of change were found for verbal and nonverbal intelligence, the relations between the psychometric and Piagetian-type tasks varied with age, and cross-task correlations were only of moderate magnitude, all suggesting that, even for the sample of tests administered here, a single, domain-general mechanism cannot adequately capture the development of intelligence across childhood. Had a greater variety of cognitive tasks been given and related to both the psychometric and Piagetian-type data, I am confident that different patterns of cross-task and cross-age correlations would have been found, providing a more complicated but more complete picture of intellectual growth. That, however, would be asking too much of the authors, whose goal in this chapter was to address several frequently asked questions about the relations between and stability of two much-studied types of intelligence. To that extent, Schneider et al. did their job well, with their results indicating that developmental function and individual differences can be fruitfully studied together, providing a clearer picture of each.

In fact, data such as these make it difficult for cognitive developmentalists ever to consider one realm of cognitive development without also considering the other. Individual differences can best be understood by knowing something about the developmental nature of the ability under question; individual differences are not just noise in developmental data but rather have important consequences for understanding ontogeny. The findings from the Munich longitudinal study, and the results provided by Schneider and his colleagues in their chapter, make these points clear.

References

Bayley, N. (1949). Consistency and variability in the growth of intelligence from birth to eighteen years. *Journal of Genetic Psychology, 75*, 165–196.

Bayley, N. (1969). *The Bayley Scales of infant development*. New York: Psychological Corporation.

Brainerd, C. J. (1978). *Piaget's theory of intelligence*. Englewood Cliffs, NJ: Prentice Hall.

Cronbach, L. J. (1957). The two disciplines of scientific psychology. *American Psychologist, 12*, 671–684.

Fagan, J. F., III. (1992). Intelligence: A theoretical viewpoint. *Current Directions in Psychological Science, 1*, 82–86.

Fagan, J. F., III, & Singer, J. T. (1983). Infant recognition memory as a measure of intelligence. In L. P. Lipsitt & C. K. Rovee-Collier (Eds.), *Advances in infancy research* (Vol. 2, pp. 31–78). Norwood, NJ: Ablex.

Gesell, A., & Amatrude, C. (1954). *Developmental diagnosis*. New York: Paul B. Holber.

Humphreys, L. G. (1980). Me thinks they do protest too much. *Intelligence, 4*, 179–183.

Humphreys, L. G., & Parsons, C. K. (1979). Piagetian tasks measure intelligence and intelligence tests assess cognitive development. *Intelligence, 3*, 369–382.

Humphreys, L. G., Rich, S. A., & Davey, T. C. (1985). A Piagetian test of general intelligence. *Developmental Psychology, 21*, 872–877.

Keating, D. P. (1975). Precocious cognitive development at the level of formal operations. *Child Development, 46*, 276–280.

Kingma, J. (1984). Traditional intelligence, Piagetian tasks, and initial arithmetic in kindergarten and primary school grade one. *Journal of Genetic Psychology, 145*, 49–60.

Kuhn, D. (1976). Relation of two Piagetian stage transitions to IQ. *Developmental Psychology, 12*, 157–161.

McCall, R. B., Eichorn, D. H., & Hogarty, P. S. (1977). Transitions in early mental development. *Monographs of the Society for Research in Child Development, 42*(Serial No. 171).

Perner, J. (1991). *Understanding the representational mind*. Cambridge, MA: MIT Press.

Siegler, R. S. (1995). Children's thinking: How does change occur. In W. Schneider & F. E. Weinert (Eds.), *Research on memory development: State of the art and future directions* (pp. 405–430). Hillsdale, NJ: Erlbaum.

Stanovich, K. E. (1986). Matthew's effects in reading: Some consequences of individual differences in the acquisition of literacy. *Reading Research Quarterly, 21*, 360–407.

Walberg, H. J., & Tsai, S. (1983). Matthew's effects in education. *American Educational Research Journal, 20*, 359–373.

Wechsler, D. (1949). *Manual for the Wechsler Intelligence Scale for Children*. New York: The Psychological Corporation.

Wellman, H. M. (1990). *The child's theory of mind*. Cambridge, MA: MIT Press.

3   Scientific Reasoning: Developmental and Individual Differences

Merry Bullock and Albert Ziegler

The focus of this chapter is on selected aspects of children's scientific reasoning over the period from 8 to 12 years of age. To put this work in context, we first delineate what we mean by *scientific reasoning*, explain which aspects of scientific reasoning we studied, and present our specific focus within this topic.

Research on Scientific Reasoning: Two Lines

The development of scientific reasoning has been addressed in two largely unrelated lines of research. In one, the focus is on thinking and reasoning about the contents of science, that is, about the concepts, definitions, and principles that characterize particular scientific disciplines (cf. Carey 1985; Clement 1993; Kaiser, Profitt, and McCloskey 1985; Smith, Carey, and Wiser 1985). Here, developmental research is concerned with describing initial, intuitive ideas about scientific concepts (e.g., biological categories, mechanical functions, laws of physics, or the nature of matter) and with assessing how these ideas change over the course of development or instruction. In the other line of research, the focus is on the processes involved in scientific activities rather than the content of what is reasoned about, that is, how information is collected, how experiments are designed and implemented, how empirical results are interpreted, and how hypotheses or theories are developed and revised. Developmental research in this line is concerned with describing when and how children engage in these processes of scientific inquiry, for example, when they can produce valid experimental tests or evaluate evidence in systematic and unbiased ways (e.g., Demetriou, Efklides, Papadaki, and Papantoniou 1993; Dunbar and Klahr 1989; Kuhn, Amsel, and O'Loughlin 1988; Schauble 1990).

Our work on scientific reasoning broadly followed the second of the two lines of research and was concerned with how children engage in and understand the processes of doing science. This focus by no means implies that we assumed that mastery of the processes of scientific reasoning is independent of domain or content. We were, however, primarily interested in addressing general questions of children's understanding of scientific inquiry for everyday contents that did not assume specialized domain knowledge. Across nearly 4 years of the longitudinal study (we began the study of scientific reasoning first in Wave 6, when children were about 8 years old), we addressed several different aspects of scientific inquiry. These included tasks measuring experimentation (including hypothesis formation, information gathering, and hypothesis testing), the use of empirical information (including the evaluation and interpretation of evidence and inferences with uncertain or incomplete information), and "meta" information about scientific inquiry (including understanding the distinction between theory and data and explicit verbal knowledge about setting up an experiment). A full account of these tasks and results is provided elsewhere (Bullock, Ziegler, and Martin 1993, and Bullock and Ziegler 1993, 1994). Because of space contraints, in this chapter we concentrate on an account of one core aspect of scientific inquiry, children's experimentation skills, that is their understanding and use of the logic of experimentation, or the "scientific method."

Children's Scientific Reasoning Skills: Differing Views

A review of the literature on the development of experimentation skills provides a fairly consistent opinion that grade school children do not understand the basics of experimentation (Karmiloff-Smith and Inhelder 1974; Klahr, Fay, and Dunbar 1993; Kuhn 1989). Indeed, even adults are characterized as biased and uncritical in scientific reasoning tasks (e.g., Evans 1989; Mynatt, Doherty, and Tweney 1977; Wason 1960, 1968). Despite a robust ability to experiment with events and to detect causal relations, evident even in preschoolers (Bullock, Gelman, and Baillargeon 1982; Bullock and Gelman 1979), preadolescent children are generally characterized as incapable of applying these abilities in a systematic and analytic way to test causal relations in experiments or to understand evidence produced by such experiments. Indeed, there is general agreement that scientific reasoning is not engaged in before adolescence and even then not by everyone at all times. In particular, grade school children are characterized as having several sorts of difficulties with experimentation:

1. They are said to be unable to separate questions that ask whether something affects an outcome, that is, hypothesis-based questions, from questions that ask how to make an outcome occur, that is, pragmatic concerns (Kuhn and Phelps 1982; Tschirgi 1980).
2. This leads them to prefer simply to confirm that a potential cause is effective (e.g., to demonstrate a causal relation), rather than to test effects of the presence and absence of a potential cause under controlled conditions. This is because they are really attempting to produce outcomes, not test hypotheses (Tschirgi 1980).
3. Even when they do manage to perform an empirical test, children are said to lack an ability to interpret or use empirical information properly or to understand that information from an uncontrolled test is not conclusive (cf. Klahr and Dunbar 1988; Kuhn et al. 1988; Schauble 1990; Schauble and Glaser 1990).

There is certainly evidence for these claims. When children are given complex, multivariable tasks and are asked to test the possible causal role of one variable, they do tend to construct unsystematic, uncontrolled experiments, and apparently they do not realize that the results from such experiments are uninformative. Even worse, when they themselves have a prior hypothesis about the role of a variable, they tend to arrange situations that can at best confirm their hypotheses, not test whether these hypotheses are valid. All this supports the contention that grade school children do not understand the logic of experimentation (e.g., Kuhn et al. 1988).

The reasons given for why children do not understand the logic of experimentation are varied and include (a) such conceptual problems as an inability to take a hypothetical perspective (Inhelder and Piaget 1958; Piaget 1987); an inability to differentiate determinate from indeterminate situations (e.g., Acredolo and O'Connor 1991; Byrnes and Beilin 1991); a lack of differentiation between beliefs, hypotheses and data; or a failure to understand the goal of experimentation (e.g., Kuhn et al.1988); (b) procedural problems deriving from a lack of prerequisite cognitive skills such as logical inference (e.g., Byrnes and Overton 1986; Mynatt et al. 1977) or from an inability to represent the problem-solving situation appropriately and explicitly (e.g., Klahr and Dunbar 1988); and (c) structural problems that limit reasoning schemes, such as a lack of formal operations (e.g., Karmiloff-Smith and Inhelder 1974).

When one looks more closely at the literature, however, a few recent studies have presented more simplified tasks and have asked about single components of scientific thinking. Some of these studies do suggest that children may understand some of the basics of experimentation. For example, Beate Sodian and her colleagues (Sodian, Zaitchik, and Carey 1991) have shown that children can propose informative tests of simple hypotheses involving single variables (e.g., they understand that if one wants to know whether a mouse in the house is large or small and can leave cheese in one of two boxes with a large door or a small door, a conclusive answer can be obtained only if one leaves cheese in the box with the small door); Barbara Koslowski (e.g., Koslowski, Susman, and Sterling 1991) has shown that children prefer tests that involve a control group comparison over those that do not; and Ruffman, Perner, Olson, and Doherty (1993) have argued that even 6- to 7-year-olds can distinguish evidence and hypotheses under simplified conditions. However, it is important to note that children in these studies are not asked to produce their own experiments but rather to evaluate experiments.

Thus, two seemingly discrepant characterizations of scientific reasoning suggest both early competence and later incompetence. Those tasks on which younger children seem to do well tend to be tasks where their understanding of experimental tests is assessed; in contrast, those tasks where even older children have difficulties tend to be tasks in which they are actively asked to produce experiments and interpret their own productions.

Our approach to the different characterizations of scientific reasoning and accounts of the development of experimentation skills was to take these two seemingly discrepant sets of findings as complementary rather than contradictory. Specifically, it may be that children first acquire an understanding of experiments and only then acquire the skill to use this understanding systematically to produce adequate experiments. There are, to our knowledge, no systematic studies that have compared understanding and production components of scientific reasoning, and no theoretical models that predict different performance in this domain depending on response type. Because of this, and because there are no clear models that specify what other skills are necessary for the acquisition of the ability to produce (not just understand) scientific tests, our approach when beginning this work was to be pragmatic and to use the unique possibilities offered by a longitudinal study such as LOGIC to take a componential approach in which we focused on tracing different aspects of how children understand and produce experiments, what skills might underlie these abilities, and how these abilities change over the course of development as children do, in fact, become more competent scientific thinkers.

The goals of the research we describe here included three things: (a) to provide a description of general developmental changes in understanding the logic of experimentation and to use this knowledge to produce controlled tests, (b) to ask how we might account for developmental changes and individual differences in these skills, and (c) to test the role of possible underlying skills by asking whether it is possible to provide selected training to improve performance.

Overview of the Sample, Tasks, and Measures

The data we used to meet these goals came from LOGIC children across four waves of the longitudinal study, from the third through the sixth grades. In each year we presented a battery of scientific reasoning tasks (including tasks on interpretation of evidence, hypothesis generation, and so on, that are not discussed here.) Our core information that we focus on here came from one type of story task included each year that addressed the logic of experimentation. Additional information was gathered in the last 2 years in Waves 8 and 9 on children's explicit knowledge about experimentation (understanding the distinction between theory and data, detection, and explanation of a range of errors in experimental design). We also used a selection of other tasks to assess some of the potentially important underlying skills contributing to developmental and individual differences in scientific reasoning. Table 1 provides an overview of some of the measures that are discussed in this chapter.

Test Understanding and Test Production: The Core Task

An illustration of the core task on the logic of experimentation that was presented in each measurement year provides a sense of what we asked children to do. This task was a story problem that always followed an identical format, although the content changed across adjacent years. In the stories, a protagonist wanted to make some product and wanted to test whether a particular dimension was important for producing successful outcomes. As an example, in one story children were told about Mr. Miller, an airplane engineer, who was given the task of making airplanes that were fuel efficient. Children were told that Mr. Miller thought about how to make the airplanes and considered three sorts of things, that is, three variable dimensions

Table 1. *Overview of Measures Used in Waves 6–9*

Measure	Wave 6	Wave 7	Wave 8	Wave 9
Scientific reasoning				
Logic of experimentation	×	× × ×	×	× ×
Explicit verbal knowledge			×	×
General skills				
IQ	×	×	×	×
Memory span		×		×
Specific related skills				
Logical reasoning	×	×	×	
Combinations	×	×		
Operational level	×	×	×	×

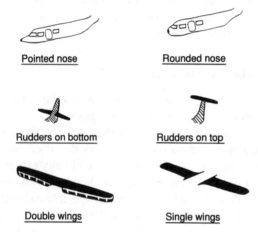

Figure 1. Variable dimensions used in the core tasks.

that might make a difference. These variable dimensions were named and pictures of each variable, grouped by dimension, were shown, as in Figure 1.

Children were then told that Mr. Miller wanted first to test whether one of the dimensions, which we called the *focal dimension* (e.g., rudder position), made a difference on the plane's fuel efficiency. There were two measures for children's understanding of the logic of experimentation. One measure was children's responses when they were asked to produce a test that would allow one to see whether the focal dimension (in the airplane example, rudder position) made a difference, and our question was whether children would produce a controlled test. A controlled test consisted of varying the focal dimension (rudder position) and keeping the other dimensions (wing placement, nose shape) constant. After children's first response, the question was repeated if they had not suggested at least a test in which the focal dimension was varied. The second measure was children's performance when they

Table 2. *Story Task, Coding Examples*

Variable	Coding Category	Example
Experiment production	Controlled test focal dimension varied; other dimensions held constant	"Then he should make two exactly just the same, only one with the rudder on top and one with the rudder lower"
Experiment choice	Contrastive test only focal dimension varied	"One with the rudder above, and one with the rudder below"
	Noncontrastive test or no test	"Two airplanes, one with a sharp nose and the other with double wings." "Just make one with the rudder on top"

were asked to choose an appropriate test. To do this, they were shown small cards with pictures of all the eight possible objects (e.g., the different airplanes) that could be constructed from combining the two values on each of the three dimensions (in this case, 2 nose shapes × 2 wing positions × 2 rudder positions). Children were asked to pick those cards that would make a good test of whether the focal dimension made a difference, first with no constraints on how many cards they picked, and then with the instruction to pick just two cards. Coding for both of the measures, as illustrated in Table 2, took into account whether children suggested varying the focal dimension (rudder position) and whether they held the other dimensions (wing placement, nose shape) constant, that is, whether they produced a controlled test. For both measures there was a first, more or less spontaneous answer and a second more probed answer, which were combined to yield scores for the first response and best responses. This basic task was repeated in Waves 6, 7, 8, and 9 (children were in Grades 3 to 6) and was given twice in Wave 8 with a training condition between the two presentations. The contents of the stories included building kites, making egg warmers, constructing cars, making lanterns, and, as in the example above, constructing airplanes.

The Development of Scientific Reasoning: Results From the Core Tasks

Figures 2 and 3 show the best production and choice answers for Waves 6 through 9, with performance from a sample of adults for comparison purposes.

The distribution of childrens' test production responses in Figure 2 shows that most children, even those in Waves 6 and 7 (third and fourth graders), suggested a contrastive test, showing at least that they could vary the focal dimension. A very small number of younger children did produce controlled tests, holding one or both of the other dimensions constant. This performance improved relatively steadily in the fifth and sixth grades. Indeed, performance of the sixth graders was generally equivalent to that of the adult comparison subjects. Thus, in contrast to the literature on hypothesis testing that suggests that preadolescent children are limited to attempting

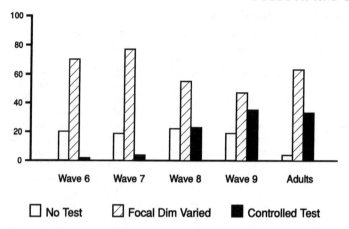

Figure 2. Percentage of best test production answers for Waves 6–9 and a sample of adults.

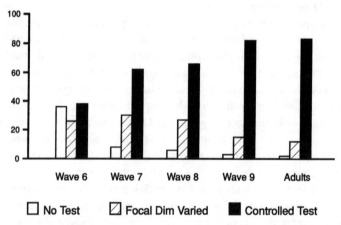

Figure 3. Percentage of best test choice answers for Waves 6–9 and a sample of adults.

only to produce successful outcomes, that is, not producing tests at all, these results suggest that certainly by the third grade, children can produce a test in which a focal dimension is varied. However, in agreement with the literature on the use of a controlling variables scheme, neither children (nor many adults) were likely to produce controlled tests.

The distribution of choice task responses, coded into the same categories, shows the same general improvement with age as in the production task, but the performance level, at least for the older children and adults, was much higher: More than a third of the third graders, about 60% of the fourth and fifth graders, close to 80% of the sixth graders, and almost all the adults could choose or recognize a controlled test, even when they did not produce one. That is, although only a few children produced controlled tests (e.g., said that the protagonist should hold everything except the focal dimension constant), many more chose cards that did just that.

To summarize from these results, when children are asked to produce experimental tests, their performance suggests that they do not understand the logic of experimental control. In contrast, when children are asked to choose a controlled test, their performance at least by the fourth grade suggests that they do understand the logic of experimental control. Furthermore, and this is important, of those who chose controlled tests, more than 50% of the fourth graders, about 80% of the fifth graders, and almost all of the sixth graders also justified this choice in terms of controlling variables, suggesting that their understanding is also somewhat explicit.

This discrepancy between production and choice performance was stable. First, it was stable within individuals: If one collapses across all waves, of those children who produced a controlled test ($n = 217$), nearly all (92%) also chose a controlled test. However, choosing a controlled test ($n = 594$) provided no guarantee that a child would produce a controlled test (34% of the time). The production–choice discrepancy was also stable across tasks: In one wave we included other tasks that also had production and choice measures but with very different contexts (see Bullock and Ziegler 1993, pp. 59ff). One of these was a hands-on task in which children were to experiment and discover what made springs stretch differently when weights were hung on them. In another task, which was designed to be a more complex and rich version of the basic story-task design, children were asked to take the role of forest researchers and make tests to find out which chemicals in the air and water were responsible for deforestation. Although the absolute levels of performance differed, the pattern of results was similar across these other tasks, too, suggesting that the discrepancy found across each wave in the story task is generalizable across specific task type.

How then should children's understanding of experimentation be characterized, and how should we characterize the difference between those children who showed they understood the logic of experimental control in their choice responses and those children who used this understanding to produce controlled tests? This is essentially a question of how to characterize both developmental changes and individual differences. Because our longitudinal data fairly well cover the range of performance variance from very poor performance (at least in test production) at earlier ages to relatively good performance in test choice behavior and at least adultlike performance in test production behavior, they were well suited for such a question. We adopted four different strategies to address individual differences and developmental change: (a) To gather a broad picture of the predictors of individual differences, we looked at intercorrelations over time between scientific reasoning and a range of skills in other areas such as logical or analytical ability, processing speed, and metacognitive knowledge about scientific inquiry; (b) to ask whether we could account for differential developmental changes, we performed a hierarchical structural modeling of performance changes in scientific reasoning; (c) to ask whether we could predict those skills that differentiated children who understood the logic of experimentation from those who both understood it and produced controlled tests, we performed a discriminant analysis; and (d) to test hypotheses about the nature of the choice–production discrepancy, we provided selective training to see whether it would improve performance.

What Predicts Individual Differences in Performance?
Results of the Correlational Analyses

One view in the literature is that scientific reasoning skills form a domain that has specific prerequisites, for example, an understanding of the logic of necessity and possibility, or formal operations, and that adequate performance rests on the acquisition of these skills. Another view is that scientific reasoning is a complex of skills that do not necessarily cohere together and that there are no necessary and sufficient prerequisite cognitive skills. To provide a very rough picture of what might contribute to individual differences and whether some skills are indeed prerequisites, we constructed a table showing the average correlations between experiment production/experiment choice performances and earlier scientific reasoning performance (scales summarizing performance in the earlier measurement waves), "metaknowledge" about scientific theories and experimentation from interview tasks, selected specific component skills (e.g., logical reasoning, combinatory skills, understanding of indeterminacy, logical search skills), and general cognitive ability (IQ, memory span, and operational level). Table 3 shows a greatly condensed overview of the correlations among the different measures across each wave for production and choice performance. This table is meant to provide simply a general flavor of the "lay of the land," that is, where the sources of individual differences might lie.

The rough overview in Table 3 shows that early performance (which, because of floor effects in Waves 6 and 7, refers primarily to test choice performance) was only predicted consistently by intelligence and memory span. It is especially noteworthy that early performance (e.g.,Wave 7) is predicted by general cognitive skills, not domain-specific scientific reasoning performance. Stronger intertask correlations appeared first in Wave 8, for both choice and production performance. Here, performance was predicted by earlier task-specific variables (scientific reasoning), explicit verbal knowledge about theories and experiments, and general cognitive variables. In Wave 9, in contrast, choice behavior was predicted only by earlier scientific reasoning, whereas production performance was predicted from each of the other variables.

Across the waves, there was a consistent pattern in how the correlations change – component skills first predict choice performance, then both choice and production performance, and finally only production performance. This pattern can be understood in various ways. From a statistical standpoint, the pattern of early prediction of choice performance and later prediction of production performance might appear because of floor effects in production in Wave 6 and ceiling effects in choice performance in Wave 9. A more interesting possibility is that correlations between scientific

Table 3. *Intertask Correlations Between Choice and Production Measures and Other Variables in the Same and Earlier Waves*

Measure	Wave 6		Wave 7		Wave 8		Wave 8,t		Wave 9	
	C	P	C	P	C	P	C	P	C	P
Earlier scientific reasoning	—	—	*ns*	*ns*	x	x	x	x	x	x
Explicit scientific knowledge					x	x	x	x	*ns*	x
Operational level combinations	*ns*	*ns*	x	*ns*	x	x	x	x	*ns*	x
Logical reasoning	x	*ns*	*ns*	*ns*	x	x	x	x	*ns*	x
IQ	x	*ns*	x	*ns*	x	x	x	x	*ns*	x
Memory span	x	*ns*	x	*ns*	x	*ns*	*ns*	x	*ns*	x

Notes: The measures listed in Table 3 were based on the following: IQ was measured in Waves 6, 7, and 9 with standardized tests; memory span was assessed by number, word and sentence span procedures; the scientific reasoning measure was an overall scale calculated from responses to all scientific reasoning tasks in each specific wave; science metaconceptual knowledge was measured with interview tasks assessing the understanding of theories, evidence, and selected factors in experimental design; logical reasoning was assessed by the evaluation of conditional sentences and syllogisms; the understanding of indeterminacy was measured by an avoiding premature closure task, which assesses the understanding that sometimes answers are indeterminate; combinatory reasoning consisted of generating exhaustive combinations of four variables; deductive search skills were measured with a variant of the game "Mastermind"; and operational level was measured with a standardized test designed to track the transition from concrete to formal operations. Wave 8, t = performance after training; C = Choice task; P = Production task; *ns* = nonsignificant correlation; x = significant correlation.

reasoning and other variables appear only in later waves because both sets of skills are themselves developing and are either not sufficiently stable or are not sufficiently developed to make a difference in scientific reasoning. In any case, the pattern does show that knowledge of what makes a good experiment (choice) is best predicted by general cognitive abilities. In contrast, acquiring the ability to also produce a good experiment is predicted by both domain-specific and general cognitive skills. That is, to produce an experiment requires not only knowledge of experimentation but also general cognitive skills to put this knowledge into action.

Differential Developmental Changes: Results of the HLM Analyses

To address differential developmental sequences in scientific reasoning, we used a hierarchical linear modeling (HLM) procedure (Bryk and Raudenbush 1992). We used this procedure to investigate differential growth from Wave 6 through Wave 9 and to test whether other variables predict these growth curves. To do this, we constructed scales from the story task for performance in each wave. Children received 1 point for the production or choice of a controlled test in their first and best responses, resulting in a score that could range from 0 to 4 points. Table 4 lists the relevant data for the scales for each measurement wave.

Table 4. *Mean, Standard Deviation, Minimum, Maximum, and Number of Valid Observations for Scores in Each Wave*

Wave	Score	*SD*	Minimum	Maximum	Valid observations
6	0.68	0.90	0	3	190
7	1.08	0.98	0	4	193
8	1.53	1.31	0	4	187
9	2.13	1.39	0	4	183

The HLM analysis confirmed that developmental changes were described by a significant linear growth curve and a significant positively accelerated growth curve. Furthermore, the growth parameters were related to entry level. The linear growth curve correlated .28 with the entry level. Because HLM controls for statistical regression effects, this suggests that those children whose scientific reasoning was better in Wave 6 also improved at a faster rate than those who were less skilled (or to put it colloquially, those who were already blessed received more). The quadratic growth curve was negatively correlated (−.67) with the entry level. It is interesting that the linear and quadratic trends showed a negative correlation (−.33), suggesting that individual developmental curves could be characterized as linear or as quadratic but not as both. That is, those children who were worse in scientific reasoning at the beginning had an accelerated growth curve later on, although generally they did not catch up to the same level as those who began at a higher level.

The advantage of the HLM model is that it also allows these interindividually different developmental growth curves to be explained. That is, it provides information about the degree to which these growth curve differences can be clarified by other individual differences. We tested the effects of a variety of predictors assessed at earlier points, most in Wave 6. These included intelligence test scores, logical reasoning, memory measures, logical search, concrete-formal operational level (taken from a later wave because this was not measured in Wave 6), socioeconomic status, age, sex, and school class (part of the sample was one grade behind). Table 5 shows the beta weights, *t* values, and probability estimates for those predictors that showed the strongest effects.

The results depicted in Table 5 show that the variables that contributed most significantly (and positively) to explaining the interindividual differences in the score from the first measurement point (in Wave 6) were age and intelligence, although the absolute value of the explained variance, 21%, is low. This low explained variance arises in part because performance in general was low at the first measurement point, and most of the score variance came from responses to the test choice tasks, tasks that may be easier for older children or children with a generally higher cognitive ability level to answer.

Table 5. *Results for the Most Robust Group Factors for Entry Level, Linear Trend, and Quadratic Trend*

Factor	Beta weight	t	p	Explained variance (%)
Entry level				
Age	.012	4.41	<.0001	16.34
Intelligence	.082	5.94	<.0001	21.20
Linear trend				
Knowledge test	.021	3.96	<.0001	29.14
Logical reasoning	.003	3.23	<.0001	41.77
Quadratic trend				
Numerical intelligence	.0009	5.29	<.0001	34.44
Logical search	.0146	3.93	<.0001	37.00

About 42% of the linear growth was explained by two variables, logical reasoning and general knowledge (from the general knowledge subtest from the Wechsler Intelligence Scale for Children, Tewes 1983). This suggests that, in addition to the ability to draw inferences, which is plausibly seen as an important component of scientific reasoning, general world knowledge, that is, an experiential component, helps to account for interindividual differences in the rate of development of scientific reasoning. This result is consistent with the many findings over the last years showing an important knowledge component in cognitive development.

To summarize from these results, the entry level for understanding the logic of experimentation is best explained by relatively nonspecific measures: age and IQ. This makes sense when scientific reasoning is seen as a complex skill that consists of many subcomponents that older and more intelligent children may have begun to master to a greater degree. Individual differences in the linear developmental trend were best explained by both a knowledge component and a logical reasoning component reflecting systematic inference skills. Individual differences (about 37% of the variance) in the quadratic trend were best explained by numerical IQ (subtest from the Wechsler scales that requires inductive reasoning) and analytic search (measured in a task adapted from the game "Mastermind" in which children had to compare feedback for a series of patterns of markers and infer a hidden pattern). Both of these predictors are from tasks in which success requires generating a rich problem space and systematically reasoning within this problem space, suggesting that a poorer beginning in scientific reasoning may be compensated for when knowledge, inference, and representation skills improve.

Equally interesting to the identification of those variables that were significantly related to individual differences is the identification of those that were not related: Operational level was unrelated to entry level or developmental growth curves, which suggests that attaining formal operations is not necessary for improvement in scientific reasoning in these types of tasks. Also, contrary to our expectations, metacognitive measures were unrelated to individual differences. This may be, however, because the measures available were measures of metamemory and not metaconceptual measures specifically related to scientific reasoning.

Differential Prediction of End-State Performance:
Results of the Discriminant Analysis

The HLM analyses modeled the entire developmental course from Waves 6 through 9. Our second set of analyses was concerned with looking not at individual differences in entry level characteristics and developmental changes, but rather at those variables that could predict performance in the last measurement point, in Wave 9, when children were about 12 years old. By Wave 9, the large majority of children chose controlled tests over uncontrolled tests, and we wanted to explain why many children were not able to activate their already demonstrated knowledge of the logic of experimentation to produce controlled tests actively.

To do this, we performed a discrimination analysis on only two groups of children: those who chose controlled tests but did not produce them and those who both chose and produced controlled tests. The variables we tested included logical reasoning and operational level, because these cognitive skills are among those assumed to be necessary for mature scientific thinking; explicit verbal knowledge about theories and experimentation, because we reasoned that these represent second-order knowledge that can assume a control function in activating knowledge about the logic of experimentation to produce controlled tests; and word span as an index of the capacity to generate a rich problem space, a capacity that we hypothesized as important for being able to actively use knowledge about experimental control.

The analysis with six predictors showed that over 76% of the children could be correctly classified. Considering the small number of predictor variables, this is a satisfactory result. The eigenvalues showed that the best predictor differentiating the two groups were those tapping explicit verbal knowledge about experimental control from an interview in Wave 8, planning an experiment from an interview in Wave 9, and memory span (74% correct classification), with logical reasoning and operational level not improving the classificatory power of the discrimination function to a notable degree, although these components were strong predictors of performance in Wave 9. Before discussing the implications of these results, we first describe the results of our fourth strategy, a training study.

Can Test Performance Be Improved? Results of a Training Intervention

Our last analysis actually took place during Wave 8 but is theoretically a culmination of the results from our attempts to predict developmental growth and to account for the differences between those children who only chose and those children who both chose and produced controlled tests. To produce a controlled test clearly involves a knowledge component that the discriminant analysis suggested might be explicit knowledge about scientific tests. However, other component skills also predicted performance, including logical reasoning, analytic search, memory span, and operational level. When one considers what these tasks have in common, they all seem to involve mental operations within a specific problem space: For example, logical reasoning entails applying logical inference rules to specific problem contents, or combinations involve the mental generation of specific object groupings. Furthermore, children who are better in these tasks are more likely to produce controlled tests. One question one might ask, then, is whether it was necessary to improve each of the component reasoning skills (i.e., logical inference, compensation rules, analytic search, combination rules, and so on) to improve test performance, or whether the common feature of needing to generate a rich problem representation is the important feature. Our hypothesis is that demonstrating an understanding of experimentation is related to better active representation of the problem space, a characterization compatible with Klahr and Dunbar's (1988) approach in which scientific thinking is conceptualized as search in a dual problem space.

We reasoned that increasing the saliency of what is to be varied and what is to be held constant might help children's active representation of the problem and thus facilitate the production of controlled experiments. To test this idea, we provided children with a short training intervention (in the context of a separate task on "attention") that would induce them to generate actively (and thus represent) all the variable dimensions and combinations of variables used in the story task. The results of this intervention were quite clear: Such simple training that fostered representation of the entire problem space made a dramatic difference in performance – children's production of controlled tests jumped from 23% before training to 56% afterward (see Bullock and Ziegler 1994 for details).

Summary and Conclusions

Scientific reasoning is an omnibus term for a set of complex cognitive skills. In our contribution to the overall LOGIC project we included tasks that addressed a wide variety of these skills. In this chapter, we have focused on the "heart" of scientific reasoning, understanding of the logic of experimentation. Even in this clearly circumscribed area, there is not complete agreement in the literature on when this skill develops or on what it is that develops. As noted in the introduction, some studies suggest that even adults and trained scientists are not experts in the logic of experimentation; others suggest that even younger children show considerable competence.

In planning our research in this area, we proceeded from the assumption that these seemingly contradictory results are a result of experimental procedures: Studies that require that individuals understand experimentation tend to show competence even in younger children; in contrast, studies that require that individuals produce experiments tend to show poor performance, even in adults. We thus decided to separate the development of understanding experiments and the development of producing experiments both conceptually and empirically. In doing so, our first goal was to provide a description of developmental changes that would move us beyond a simple description of preadolescents' inadequacies.

Our distinction between understanding experiments and using understanding to produce experiments proved fruitful: Most children acquired the knowledge of what constitutes a good experiment by the end of elementary school. This is an important finding and different from the general view in the literature (e.g., Demetriou et al. 1993; Inhelder and Piaget 1958; Kuhn et al. 1988). This distinction also pinpoints production as the more difficult and crucial milestone: When left to their own devices, only a minority of children could apply their understanding to actually produce an adequate, controlled experiment. To our mind, acquiring the ability to put knowledge about experimentation into practice is the most important general developmental change.

Our second goal was to investigate differential developmental changes in scientific reasoning skills and the role of underlying component skills. The results of the correlation analysis showed that understanding the logic of experimentation and *producing* controlled experimental tests were predicted by cognitive variables in somewhat different ways. There were strong relations with general cognitive measures such as IQ or word span at younger ages for the earlier developing understanding of experiments, and these relations decreased over time. In contrast, performance for the later developing production of experiments was predicted by domain-specific measures and general cognitive measures, a set of findings that is compatible with approaches that postulate both domain specific and general components to scientific reasoning (e.g., Klahr et al. 1993).

The impression of two types of influence dependent on the age of the children was supported by the results of the HLM analysis: Although the entry level of scientific reasoning was best explained by general measures such as age and IQ, interindividual differences in development were best explained by more inferential skills and a knowledge component.

These findings were supported by the results of the discrimination analysis, which we conducted to ask if there were good predictors for the end-state performance and if we could provide a more precise specification on the knowledge component suggested by the HLM analysis. The statistical analysis showed that the best predictors for differentiating end-state performance were explicit verbal knowledge about experimental control and memory span, that is domain-specific knowledge and a capacity measure. Consistent with the SDDS approach discussed by Klahr and Dunbar (1988), this suggests that the capacity to produce a good experiment is dependent on (a) conceptual knowledge about the production of experiments and (b) a component that facilitates representation and that allows the child to use his or her knowledge in a problem space. If this conclusion is correct, it should be possible to compensate for representational difficulties in those children who already understand the components of a good experiment, to improve their performance in experiment production tasks. Our training intervention showed that this was indeed the case: A brief procedure that facilitated problem representation improved performance selectively for those children who already showed understanding of experimental control.

Summarizing from these results provides the following characterization of the development of scientific reasoning: The early development of scientific reasoning, which is substantial by the end of elementary school, consists of the acquisition of an understanding of what constitutes a good experiment. Individual differences are best predicted on the basis of nonspecific factors such as age or IQ. A later developmental change consists of translating this domain specific knowledge about experimentation into action, to produce an experiment. This ability is related to skills that facilitate the generation and operation of an adequate problem space.

What can we conclude about the development of scientific reasoning, and what can we conclude about the origins of individual differences? Our patterns of results suggest that an approach that posits strict structural constraints (e.g., formal operation) is less appropriate for explaining scientific-reasoning performance and development than an approach that posits knowledge-based and procedural constraints. The results of our studies suggest that the acquisition of scientific-reasoning skills consists mainly of two components: the specific and verbalizable knowledge about what constitutes a controlled experiment as well as the ability to generate and operate in a rich, full representation of the problem space. Such a perspective should allow a better integration of the available information on the development of scientific reasoning, for example, by considering research findings on the acquisition of explicit experiment production strategies (e.g., Kuhn et al. 1988; Kuhn, Schauble and Garcia-Mila 1992) together with research findings on abilities to operate within a problem space (e.g., Klahr and Dunbar 1992).

We hope that our distinction between understanding and producing experimental tests, our description of the early stages in the acquisition of the skills, and our suggestions about how these skills might change over development and individuals provide an interesting stimulus to further specification of the development of scientific reasoning across the age span.

References

Acredolo, C., & O'Connor, J. (1991). On the difficulty of detecting cognitive uncertainty. *Human Development, 32*, 204–223.

Bryk, A. S., & Raudenbush, S.W. (1992). *Hierarchical linear models: Applications and data analysis methods*. Newbury Park, CA: Sage.

Bullock, M., & Gelman, R. (1979). The young child's understanding of causality: Temporal ordering. *Child Development, 50*, 89–96.

Bullock, M., Gelman, R., & Baillargeon, R. (1982). The development of causal reasoning. In W. Friedman (Ed.), *The developmental psychology of time* (pp. 209–254). New York: Academic Press.

Bullock, M., & Ziegler, A. (1993). Scientific thinking. In F. E. Weinert & W. Schneider (Eds.), *The Munich Longitudinal Study on the Genesis of Individual Competencies (LOGIC): Report No. 10* (pp. 59–89). Munich: Max Planck Institute for Psychological Research.

Bullock, M., & Ziegler, A. (1994). Scientific thinking. In F. E. Weinert & W. Schneider (Eds.), *The Munich Longitudinal Study on the Genesis of Individual Competencies (LOGIC): Report No. 11* (pp. 56–76). Munich: Max Planck Institute for Psychological Research.

Bullock, M., Ziegler, A., & Martin, S. (1993). Scientific thinking. In F. E. Weinert & W. Schneider (Eds.), *The Munich Longitudinal Study on the Genesis of Individual Competencies (LOGIC): Report No. 9* (pp. 66–110). Munich: Max Planck Institute for Psychological Research.

54   BULLOCK AND ZIEGLER

Byrnes, J. P., & Beilin, H. (1991). The cognitive basis of uncertainty. *Human Development, 34*, 189–203.
Byrnes, J. P., & Overton, W. F. (1986), Reasoning about certainty and unvertainty in concrete, causal, and propositional contexts. *Developmental Psychology, 22*, 793–799.
Carey, S. (1985). *Conceptual change in childhood*. Cambridge, MA: MIT Press.
Clement, J. (1993). Using bridging analogies and anchoring intuitions to deal with students' preconceptions in physics. *Journal of Research in Science Teaching, 30*, 1241–1257.
Demetriou, A., Efklides, A. Papadaki, M. Papantoniou, G. (1993). Structure and development of casual experimental thought. From early adolescence to youth. *Developmental Psychology, 29*, 480–497.
Dunbar, K., & Klahr, D. (1989). Developmental differences in scientific discovery processes. In D. Klahr & K. Kotovsky (Eds.), *Complex information processing: The impact of Herbert A. Simon* (pp. 109–143). Hillsdale, NJ: Erlbaum.
Evans, J. S. B. T. (1989). *Bias in human reasoning: Causes and consequences*. Brighton, UK: Erlbaum.
Inhelder, B., & Piaget, J. (1958). *The growth of logical thinking from childhood to adolescence*. New York: Basic Books.
Kaiser, M. K., Profitt, D. R., & McCloskey, M. (1985). The development of beliefs about falling objects. *Perception and Psychophysics, 38*, 533–539.
Karmiloff-Smith, A., & Inhelder, B. (1974). If you want to get ahead, get a theory. *Cognition, 3*, 195–212.
Klahr, D., & Dunbar, K. (1988). Dual search space during scientific reasoning. *Cognitive Science, 12*, 1–155.
Klahr, D., Fay, A. L., & Dunbar, K. (1993). Heuristics for scientific experimentation: A developmental study. *Cognitive Psychology, 25*, 111–146.
Koslowski, B., Susman, A., & Serling, J. (1991, April). *Conceptual vs. technical understanding of evidence in scientific reasoning*. Paper presented in the symposium "Evidence evaluation, conceptual change and the development of scientific reasoning" of the Society for Research in Child Development, Seattle, WA.
Kuhn, D. (1989). Children and adults as intuitive scientists. *Psychological Review, 96*, 674–689.
Kuhn, D., Amsel, E., & O'Loughlin, M. (1988). *The development of scientific thinking skills*. New York: Academic Press.
Kuhn, D., & Phelps, E. (1982). The development of problem-solving strategies. In H. Reese (Ed.), *Advances in child development and behavior* (Vol. 17, pp. 1–44). New York: Academic Press.
Kuhn, D., Schauble, L., & Garcia-Mila, M. (1992). Cross-domain development of scientific reasoning. *Cognition and Instruction, 9*, 285–327.
Mynatt, C. R., Doherty, M. E., & Tweney, R. D. (1977). Confirmation bias in a simulated research environment. *Quarterly Journal of Experimental Psychology, 30*, 395–406.
Piaget, J. (1987). *Possibility and necessity: The role of necessity in cognitive development* (Vol. 2). Minneapolis: University of Minnesota Press.
Ruffman, T., Perner, J., Olson, D. R., & Doherty, M. (1993). Reflecting on scientific reasoning: Children's understanding of the hypothesis–evidence relation. *Child Development, 64*, 1617–1637.
Schauble, L. (1990). Belief revision in children: The role of prior knowledge and strategies for generating evidence. *Journal of Experimental Child Psychology, 49*, 31–57.
Schauble, L., & Glaser, R. (1990). Scientific thinking in children and adults. *Contributions to Human Development, 21*, 9–27.
Smith, C., Carey, S., & Wiser, M. (1985). On differentiation: A case study of the development of the concepts of size, weight, and density. *Cognition, 21*, 177–237.
Sodian, B., Zaitchik, D., & Carey, S. (1991). Young children's differentiation of hypothetical belief from evidence. *Child Development, 62*, 753–766.
Tschirgi, J. (1980). Sensible reasoning: A hypothesis about hypotheses. *Child Development, 51*, 1–10.
Tewes, U. (Ed.) (1983). *Hamburg–Wechsler–Intelligenztest für Kinder, Revision (HAWIK-R)* [German version of the revised WISC]. Bern: Switzerland: Huber.
Wason, P. C. (1960). On the failure to eliminate hypotheses in a conceptual task. *Quarterly Journal of Experimental Psychology, 12*, 129–140.
Wason, P. C. (1968). Reasoning about a rule. *Quarterly Journal of Experimental Psychology, 20*, 273–281.

3a   Comment: "Scientific Reasoning"

David Klahr

The general paradigm used by psychologists who are interested in scientific reasoning is to present people with situations crafted to isolate one or more essential aspects of "real-world" science and to observe carefully their problem-solving processes. Other ways to study scientific thinking include historical analyses, retrospective reports, and "in vivo" studies of ongoing scientific work (Dunbar 1995). However, the laboratory approach – used here by Bullock and Ziegler – has several important merits, including (a) the selection of specific subject populations, (b) control over their prior knowledge and over the nature of the thing-to-be-discovered, and (c) repeated observations over either short durations (as in microgenetic studies (Kuhn, Garcia-Mila, Zohar, and Andersen 1995; Schauble, Glaser, Raghavan, and Reiner, 1991) or many years, as in the LOGIC project.

The challenge facing those who investigate the psychology of scientific discovery "on-line" is to find a way to evoke the cognitive processes inherent in scientific discovery while maintaining the experimental rigor that supports sound inferences about human cognition. In the context of a multifaceted, longitudinal study such as the LOGIC project, this challenge is exacerbated by the competing needs for "bench time" with the subject population. This constraint meant that Bullock and Ziegler had to devise some very straightforward assessments that would not only be relatively brief, but also would be suitable for children over a 4-year age span. Bullock and Ziegler are to be commended for satisfying all of these constraints. Before commenting specifically on their chapter, I place their work in the context of other efforts to study various aspects of the psychology of scientific discovery.

Laboratory Investigations of the Cognitive Psychology of Science

Laboratory investigations of scientific reasoning can be classified along two dimensions: one representing the specificity of the knowledge being investigated, and the other representing the type of processes involved. Table 1 depicts this characterization of the field.

55

Table 1. *Types of Foci in Psychological Studies of Scientific-Reasoning Processes (Adapted From Klahr and Carver 1995)*

Type of knowledge and method	Hypothesis space search	Experiment space search	Evidence evaluation
Domain-specific knowledge and strong methods	Carey 1985 McCloskey 1983	Tschirgi 1980	Ruffman, Perner, Olson, & Doherty 1993
			Shaklee & Paszek 1985
	Vosniadou & Brewer 1992		Vosniadou & Brewer 1992
		Bullock & Ziegler	
Domain-general knowledge and weak methods	Bruner, Goodnow, & Austin 1956	Bruner, Goodnow, & Austin 1956	Bruner, Goodnow, & Austin 1956
		Case 1974; Siegler & Liebert 1975	Ruffman, Perner, Olson, & Doherty 1993
			Shaklee & Paszek 1985
	Wason 1960	Wason 1960	Wason 1960
		Bullock & Ziegler	

The two rows in the table correspond to the oft-cited distinction in developmental psychology between domain-general knowledge and domain-specific knowledge. Psychologists' attempts to disentangle the relative influence of general versus specific knowledge have produced two distinct literatures: one on domain-specific knowledge and "strong methods" and the other on domain-general reasoning processes and "weak methods."

The three columns in Table 1 correspond to the major components of the overall discovery process: searching a space of hypotheses, searching a space of experiments, and evaluating evidence. This reflects a view of scientific discovery as a type of problem-solving process involving search in a problem space (Newell and Simon 1972). In the case of scientific discovery, there are two primary spaces to be searched: a space of hypotheses and a space of experiments. These spaces are sufficiently different that they require different representations, different operators for moving about in the space, and different criteria for what constitutes progress in the space.

Without getting into detail here (cf. Klahr and Dunbar 1988), I can convey the importance of the distinction between searching the hypothesis space and searching the experiment space by noting that in most of the natural sciences the difference between experimental work and theoretical work is so great as to have individuals who claim to be experts in one, but not the other, aspects of their discipline. It is clear that the problems to be solved in each space are different, even though they have obvious and necessary mutual influences. Thus, in characterizing research on scientific discovery, we emphasize three major interdependent processes: hypothesis space search, experiment space search, and evidence evaluation. In searching the hypothesis space, the initial state consists of some knowledge about a domain, and the goal state is a hypothesis that can account for some or all of that knowledge. When one or more hypotheses are active, it is not immediately obvious what constitutes a "good" experiment. In constructing experiments, participants are faced with a problem-solving task paralleling their search for hypotheses. That is, they must search in the experiment space for an informative experiment. The third process – evidence evaluation – involves a comparison of the predictions derived from the current hypothesis with the results obtained from experimentation.

During the course of scientific discovery, the various cells in Table 1 are traversed repeatedly. However, it is very difficult to study thinking processes that involve all of them simultaneously. Consequently, much of the research in the field focuses on only one or two cells, although some investigators have used complex contexts involving multiple cells. I have attempted to demonstrate what I mean by these distinctions by listing a few examples of investigations that involve various cells from Table 1. Space limitations preclude even a concise description of each of these studies, but I assume that the readers of this volume are familiar with most of them. (For a more detailed characterization of each of these studies with respect to this taxonomy, see Klahr 1994 or Klahr and Carver 1995.)

Although many investigations focus on one or two of the cells depicted in Table 1, a few studies attempt to traverse the entire matrix (e.g., Dunbar 1993; Klahr and Dunbar 1988; Klahr, Fay, and Dunbar 1993; Kuhn 1989; Kuhn, Amsel, and O'Loughlin 1988; Kuhn et al. 1995; Kuhn, Schauble, and Garcia-Mila 1992; Schauble 1990; Schauble et al. 1991).[1]

In the present study, Bullock and Ziegler focus on search in the experiment space. In their view it is "the 'heart' of scientific reasoning (p. 51)." Although I do not consider any one of the three components listed in Table 1 as more fundamental than any other, I would agree that experiment space search is worthy of investigation, and I would situate the Bullock and Ziegler study in both of the cells outlined in Table 1. Note that their subjects did not have to search for hypotheses (they were provided by the experimenter), nor did they have to evaluate evidence. That is, they did not have to decide, on the basis of some experimental outcomes, whether a hypothesis was correct. However, even though Bullock and Ziegler's intent was to use everyday contents that did not assume specialized domain knowledge I believe that their problems were likely to have activated domain knowledge that might have influenced children's choice of

---

[1] These integrative studies are not listed in Table 1. By definition, they would have an entry in each cell.

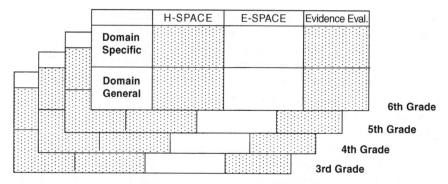

Figure 1. Longitudinal study of scientific reasoning (adapted from Klahr and Carver 1995).

experiments. For example, children are likely to have a stronger belief about the role of a pointed nose versus a rounded nose in determining airplane speed than about the effects of the location of the "rudder."[2] This is an important consideration in evaluating the validity of participant's experimental choices, because if participants have very strong biases about the irrelevance of certain factors, then they might design what, to an omniscient observer, will appear as a confounded experiment. Thus, I have categorized their study in both the domain-specific and the domain-general cells under experiment space search.

Perhaps the most valuable aspect of the present study – and the most unusual with respect to the literature on scientific reasoning – is its longitudinal design. One can depict the Bullock and Ziegler study as a series of layers of 2 × 3 tables, as shown in Figure 1. Each layer represents one of the waves in which the experiment space is searched, and the series of layers represent the time course of annual assessments. (Not shown are all the additional measures that Bullock and Ziegler use to determine the cognitive correlates of the development of skills in searching the experiment space.) Although a few microgenetic studies explore scientific reasoning with repeated trials spread over a relatively short interval (i.e., a few months), a longitudinal study of experiment space search is, I believe, unprecedented.

The results of this study reveal both the kind of improvement with age that one would expect, as well as evidence that – at all ages – the ability to select a discriminating experiment from among a set of options precedes the ability to design one. However, it is possible that these results both overstate and understate children's true abilities. The overstatement may come from not correcting for guessing. Even if children choose cards at random, once a card is chosen, there are four chances out of seven that the next card will vary the focal dimension.

The understatement may result from sources. First, if participants have strong biases that some dimensions are irrelevant, then they may choose experiments that

---

[2] In fact, it is not the rudder, but the elevator (or stabilizer) that is varied in Bullock and Ziegler's Figures 1 and 2.

appear to us to be confounded, even though they may understand the logic of a valid inference. Second, the developmental trend that is reported here may be as much a result of performance factors (such as systematically scanning all the eight options) as of an understanding of the logic of controlled tests. Perhaps we would have seen much better performance (corrected for chance responding) if there were only two dimensions (and four options) in the stimulus materials.

The final factor that may lead to an underestimate of children's understanding of the logic of experimentation is its isolation from the rest of the cycle of scientific reasoning. As I noted earlier, scientific reasoning involves a complex interaction among the processes of hypotheses formulation, experiment design, and evidence evaluation. Although the decontextualization engendered by studying only experiment choice and/or production facilitates an efficient use of subject's limited time in the full battery of LOGIC assessments, it may have produced a distorted picture of children's true understanding of the logic of experimentation. The reason is that, in the format used by Bullock and Ziegler, children never had an opportunity to see the consequences of their uncontrolled or noncontrastive tests. Even a few occasions for such feedback might have been sufficient for them to exhibit substantial improvement in their next set of experimental choices.

Bullock and Ziegler also describe various cognitive correlates that predict children's developing ability to select and design valid experiments. These results are tantalizing, and I would hope that they could be followed up with a more detailed assessment of the development of individual patterns of the emergence of effective experimental strategies using the kind of procedures that Kuhn and her colleagues have found so effective in microgenetic studies.

For example, Bullock and Ziegler do not present data on how individual children's patterns of correct productions and choices at each wave predict their pattern at the subsequent waves. Thus, it is impossible to know whether the regressions to weaker strategies discovered in microgenetic studies (e.g., Kuhn et al. 1995; Siegler and Shipley 1995) also occur over the much longer intervals studied here.

In conclusion, this is a valuable and unique study of the development of an important scientific-reasoning skill. I hope that future investigators continue to press for the convergence of short duration, but fine-grained microgenetic studies (Siegler and Crowley 1991) and long duration, but coarse-grained studies such as the one presented here.

References

Bruner, J. S., Goodnow, J. J., & Austin, G. A. (1956). *A study of thinking*. New York: NY Science Editions.

Carey, S. (1985). *Conceptual change in childhood*. Cambridge, MA: MIT Press/Bradford Books.

Case, R. (1974). Structures and strictures: Some functional limitations on the course of cognitive growth. *Cognitive Psychology, 6*, 544–573.

Dunbar, K. (1993). Concept discovery in a scientific domain. *Cognitive Science, 17*, 397–434.

Dunbar, K. (1995). How scientists really reason: Scientific reasoning in real-world laboratories. In R. J. Sternberg & J. E. Davidson (Eds.), *The nature of insight* (pp. 365–395). Cambridge, MA: MIT Press.

Klahr, D. (1994). Searching for cognition in cognitive models of science. *Psycoloquy* 5(94). ftp://ftp. princeton. edu/pub/Psycoloquy/1994. volume.5/ psyc. 94. 5. 69. scientific-cognition.12. Klahr.

Klahr, D., & Carver, S. M. (1995). Scientific thinking about scientific thinking. *Monographs of the Society for Research in Child Development, 60* (4, Serial No. 245), 137–151.

Klahr, D., & Dunbar, K. (1988). Dual space search during scientific reasoning. *Cognitive Science, 12*(1), 1–55.

Klahr, D., Fay, A. L., & Dunbar, K. (1993). Heuristics for scientific experimentation: A developmental study. *Cognitive Psychology, 25*(1), 111–146.

Kuhn, D. (1989). Children and adults as intuitive scientists. *Psychological Review, 96*, 674–689.

Kuhn, D., Amsel, E., & O'Loughlin, M. (1988). *The development of scientific reasoning skills*. Orlando, FL: Academic Press.

Kuhn, D., Garcia-Mila, M., Zohar, A., & Anderson, C. (1995). Strategies of knowledge acquisition. *Monographs of the Society for Research in Child Development, 60* (4, Serial No. 245).

Kuhn, D., Schauble, L., & Garcia-Mila, M. (1992). Cross-domain development of scientific reasoning. *Cognition and Instruction, 9*, 285–327.

McCloskey, M. (1983). Naive theories of motion. In D. Gentner & A. L. Stevens (Eds.), *Mental models* (pp. 299–324). Hillsdale, NJ: Erlbaum.

Newell, A., & Simon, H. A. (1972). *Human problem solving*. Englewood Cliffs, NJ: Prentice Hall.

Ruffman, T., Perner, J., Olson, D. R., & Doherty, M. (1993). Reflecting on scientific thinking: Children's understanding of the hypothesis–evidence relation. *Child Development, 64*, 1617–1636.

Schauble, L. (1990). Belief revision in children: The role of prior knowledge and strategies for generating evidence. *Journal of Experimental Child Psychology, 49*, 31–57.

Schauble, L., Glaser, R., Raghavan, K., & Reiner, M. (1991). Causal models and experimentation strategies in scientific reasoning. *The Journal of the Learning Sciences, 1*, 201–238.

Shaklee, H., & Paszek, D. (1985). Covariation judgment: Systematic rule use in middle childhood. *Child Development, 56*, 1229–1240.

Siegler, R. S., & Crowley, K. (1991). The microgenetic method: A direct means for studying cognitive development. *American Psychologist, 46*, 606–620.

Siegler, R. S., & Liebert, R. M. (1975). Acquisition of formal scientific reasoning by 10- and 13-year-olds: Designing a factorial experiment. *Developmental Psychology, 10*, 401–402.

Siegler, R. S., & Shipley, C. (1995). Variation, selection, and cognitive change. In G. Halford & T. Simon (Eds.), *Developing cognitive competence: New approaches to process modeling* (pp. 31–76). Hillsdale, NJ: Erlbaum.

Tschirgi, J. E. (1980). Sensible reasoning: A hypothesis about hypotheses. *Child Development, 51*, 1–10.

Vosniadou, S., & Brewer, W. F. (1992). Mental models of the earth: A study of conceptual change in childhood. *Cognitive Psychology, 24*, 535–585.

Wason, P. C. (1960). On the failure to eliminate hypotheses in a conceptual task. *Quarterly Journal of Experimental Psychology, 12*, 129–140.

4   Memory Strategy Development – Gradual Increase, Sudden Insight, or Roller Coaster?

Beate Sodian and Wolfgang Schneider

Developmental psychologists have traditionally been divided on the issue of continuities and discontinuities in development. Is development in childhood best conceptualized as a gradual, continuous process of enrichment or as a discontinuous sequence of qualitatively different steps or stages? Researchers in the field of memory development tend to be among the advocates of the former view, emphasizing continuities rather than discontinuities in development. This view is supported by a rich database from cross-sectional investigations of the development of various memory skills. The general result of these studies is that memory performance (e.g., free recall) improves gradually with age and that much of this improvement appears to be due to increasing efficiency in the use of memory strategies: Older children behave more strategically in memory tasks (e.g., show a higher level of conceptual clustering at encoding and recall in sort–recall tasks), and strategy use is more strongly correlated with recall performance in older than in younger children (Bjorklund 1987; Hasselhorn 1992; Schneider and Pressley 1989).

One of the goals of our longitudinal study was to explore whether the generalizations about the developmental course of the acquisition of organizational strategies drawn from cross-sectional studies are valid on the individual level. This is not trivially true: The improvements on the group level could be due to some children making enormous progress, whereas others remain the same or even decline. Individual developmental curves in strategy use and recall performance could be much less continuous than the cross-sectional data suggest. In fact, there are theoretical reasons to expect more discontinuity in strategy acquisition than the group data would suggest: Strategies are deliberate attempts to remember; therefore, strategic behaviors are driven by an understanding of learning and remembering. There is ample evidence from the metamemory and the theory of mind literatures indicating that children's concepts of learning and remembering change in middle childhood. Whereas preschoolers appear to understand that simple strategies such as perceptual inspection or verbalization help remembering, older children begin to understand more sophisticated strategies such as semantic organization or elaboration that depend on inferential processes. If there is conceptual change in children's understanding of the nature and purpose of

61

memory strategies (i.e., in their metamemory), then we should expect reorganization rather than continuity on the behavioral level. That is, we should be surprised to see a gradual steady increase of strategy use and corresponding memory performance over the preschool and elementary school years. Rather, we would expect periods of steep increase in strategy use once children understand the rationale for a strategy, followed by plateaus. Thus, longitudinal data on the development of strategy use can help us evaluate claims about universal changes in memory behavior.

A second goal of our longitudinal study was to explore the individual development of strategy *effectiveness*. Previous research indicates a utilization deficiency in younger children. Younger children's memory strategy use tends to be less effective than older children's; that is, even when levels of strategy use are comparable between younger and older children, younger children tend to recall less than older ones. However, this general developmental trend is qualified by considerable individual differences (Bjorklund and Coyle 1995; Miller and Seier 1994). At any given age, individual children differ in their strategy effectiveness, and these differences appear to be related to a number of cognitive and motivational factors (Miller 1994). Longitudinal data can contribute to exploring the relationship between general developmental trends and individual differences in strategy effectiveness. For example, individual differences in the effectiveness of strategy use at a given age may in part be dependent on the individual developmental course of strategy acquisition. Children who discover a given strategy (e.g., conceptual organization) for the first time at a given measurement point (e.g., at age 8) may use it less efficiently than children who discovered it earlier and who have gained some practice in using it. Such individual differences in the age of onset (and effectiveness) of strategy use may in turn be predictable from metamemory development, memory capacity, or IQ.

In the present chapter, we therefore explore the acquisition of an organizational strategy and its relation to recall performance longitudinally over a wide age range. We focus on one memory task, a sort–recall task, that was administered five times in the course of the study, at the ages of 4, 6, 8, 10, and 12. We first ask whether we can replicate the results from cross-sectional studies on the group level. In a second step we inspect the development of strategy use and recall performance on the individual level to see whether most children follow the developmental course that we expect from analyses on the group level. Finally, we investigate the relationship between performance gains in strategy use and in recall performance over the age range under study.

The Task

The item lists consisted of 16 toys (four of each of the animals, furniture, vehicles, and household items categories) for the 4- and 6-year-olds and 24 picture cards (six of each of the tools, animals, fruit, and vehicles categories) for 8-, 10-, and 12-year-olds. We instructed the children to try to remember as many items as possible and to do whatever they thought was useful for remembering them. After 2 minutes, a photograph was taken showing the final arrangement of the items, which were then hidden, and the children were asked to "tell the names of all the toys (the pictures) they had seen."

The sort–recall task was followed by a short metamemory interview in which the children were presented with photographs that showed three different arrangements of the items used in the sort–recall task, a random order, an ordering by conceptual category, and an ordering by color (by alphabet). The children were asked to rank these arrangements in terms of their usefulness for remembering; that is, to identify the arrangement that was "best for remembering" and to identify the arrangement that was "worst for remembering" (see Schneider and Sodian 1991 for a detailed description of the task).

In addition to this task-specific metamemory interview, we assessed preschoolers' metamemory with an interview modeled after a task by Wellman (1977), and we used an interview procedure modeled after Kreutzer, Leonard, and Flavell (1975) for preschool and school aged children.

Replication of Cross-Sectional Findings

On the whole, inspection of the group means for sorting during study, clustering during recall, and recall performance conveys the impression of a gradual increase in strategy use and recall performance over the age range under study. Figure 1 shows the mean RR (ratio of repetition) scores for sorting during study and clustering during recall for each age group. Although the RR scores for sorting during study suggest an almost perfectly linear increase from chance level at age 4 to complete conceptual categorization at age 12, the clustering scores at retrieval show a slight dip at age 8,

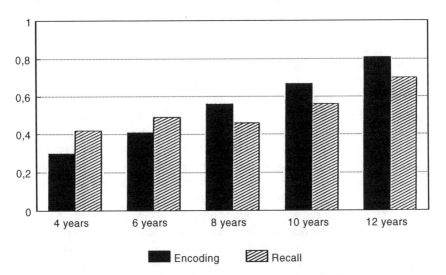

Figure 1. Conceptual organization at encoding and recall (RR scores).

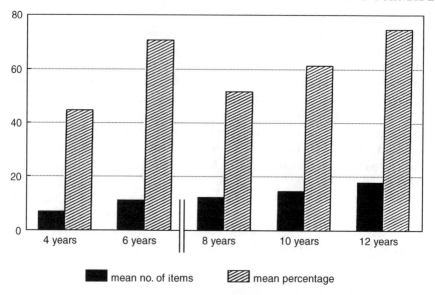

Figure 2. The development of recall performance.

indicating that clustering levels dropped when the longer item list was first introduced. On the whole, this picture is consistent with what was known from previous cross-sectional studies, except that progress in our data seems more gradual than in previous studies (usually, levels of conceptual clustering rise more steeply between the ages of 8 and 10 than in our study). Inspection of individual data will show whether the impression of gradual increase of levels of clustering is confirmed at the individual level.

Figure 2 shows the development of recall performance. The mean number of items recalled increased from about 7 at age 4 to about 18 at age 12. As a group, the children made considerable progress between the ages of 4 and 6 (mean gain of four items) and between 10 and 12 (mean gain of three items), whereas progress was slower between the ages of 6 and 10. If we take into account that list length was increased between the ages of 6 and 8, and if we consider percentage of items recalled correctly (rather than absolute numbers), we find a drop from about 70% at age 6 to little over 50% at age 8. Thus, we replicate the age trends in recall performance that were known from cross-sectional studies of preschoolers and of grade school children. In addition, we find that recall performance in young children is considerably affected by task variations (i.e., list length and presentation mode).

Previous research has shown that children not only become more strategic in sort–recall tasks as they grow older but also that the correlations between conceptual organization strategies and recall performance increase with age (cf. Hasselhorn 1990; Kee and Bell 1981; Schneider 1986). This is well replicated in our sample. Table 1 shows the intercorrelations among sorting at encoding, clustering at recall,

Table 1. *Intercorrelations Among Sorting During Study, Clustering During Recall, and Free Recall in the Sort–Recall Task, Separately for Each Age Group*

	Age				
Correlations	4	6	8	10	12
Sorting/recall	.22	.34	.58	.60	.48
Clustering/recall	.28	.42	.55	.70	.66
Sorting/clustering	.22	.45	.63	.73	.68

and recall performance for each age level. Correlations increase from about .25 at age 4 to about .70 at age 10 (with a slight drop at age 12 that was due to ceiling effects in strategy use). Thus, strategy use appears to become increasingly effective with age.

In summary, the analyses on the group level indicate that our findings are comparable to what was known about memory development from previous studies in the sort–recall paradigm.

Stability of Individual Differences

If the majority of individual children roughly followed the developmental paths that the group data suggest, then we would expect high group stabilities over time (retest correlations). The rank orders of participants should then remain relatively constant (highly strategic children at age 4 are still the top strategists at age 10, and poor strategy users remain poor strategy users over time relative to their peer group). Table 2 shows that the data are not consistent with this assumption. Although test–retest correlations for free recall are moderate (around $r = .30$), the stabilities of sorting at encoding and clustering at recall are extremely low. With the exception of the stability of clustering in recall between the ages of 10 and 12 years ($r = .29$), none of the 2-, 4-, or 6-year stability coefficients reaches an interpretable level. These findings cannot be attributed to measurement error because short-term stabilities (assessed by test–retest correlations within an interval of 2 or 3 weeks) were high even for preschoolers ($r > .60$; see Table 2). Thus, individual children seem to change considerably their relative positions in the group between measurement points. The model of gradual improvement that fits the group data well does not seem to hold for strategy acquisition in individual children.

Two alternatives to gradual improvement appear to be consistent with the data. (a) The acquisition of a conceptual clustering strategy is not a process of gradual increase (becoming more and more strategic) but is an all-or-none, insightful discovery process: Children go from chance level to perfection between successive

Table 2. *Stability Over Time for the Strategy and Recall Measures*

(a) Two-year-stability

	Age range				
Variable	4–6	6–8	8–10	10–12	Short term
Recall	.36	.29	.39	.38	.68
Sorting	.17	.12	.07	.16	.85
Clustering	.12	.16	.12	.29	.64

(b) Four-and-more-year stability	Age range			
	4–8	8–12	6–12	4–12
Recall	.30	.36	.30	.16
Sorting	.08	.16	−.09	.06
Clustering	.08	.17	.004	.22

measurement points, and individual children vary greatly in the age at which they first discover the strategy. (b) Strategy development is not a undirectional process of improvement. Children may show high levels of conceptual clustering at one measurement point, low levels at the next one, and high levels again at the third one. Such U-shaped developmental curves would be consistent with the assumption that young children sometimes behave apparently strategically without understanding the rationale for strategy use (i.e., merely reacting to item associativity, Bjorklund 1987; Lange 1978). In the following section, we explore whether either one (or both) of these possibilities can account for the remarkably low stabilities in measures of conceptual organization. In this chapter, we focus only on strategic behavior at encoding (i.e., sorting during study).

Individual Patterns of Strategy Acquisition

Inspection of the children's conceptual organization scores at encoding quickly showed that individual children tended to go from chance levels of conceptual organization to perfection or near perfection – and sometimes back to chance level at subsequent measurement points – but that a pattern of gradual, steady increase was rarely found. Eighty-one percent of the children "jumped" from chance level (RR scores < .30) to near perfection (at least 80% of the items sorted into conceptual categories) between subsequent measurement points. The remaining children fell into three groups: Three percent never discovered the strategy, 8% were nearly perfect from the start, and 8% showed a pattern of gradual increase as suggested by the group data. Figure 3 shows that there was considerable variation in the age at which children first used the strategy: As many as 40% of the children showed nearly perfect levels of conceptual organization on one of the two first measurement points; 24% discovered it at age 8,

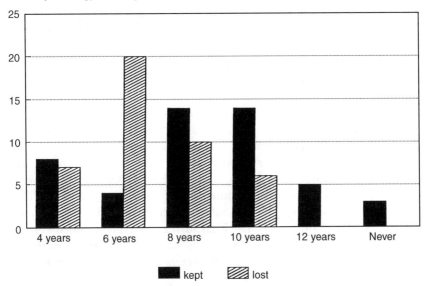

Figure 3. Age of onset and maintenance of sorting strategy.

21% at age 10, and 5% as late as age 12. Thus, some of the instability in strategic behaviors over time can be explained by individual variation in the time of strategy "discovery": Children go from chance levels of conceptual organization to perfection, but they do so at different points in time.

However, this is not the whole story. As Figure 3 shows, not everyone who once discovered the sorting strategy used it again at subsequent measurement points. On the contrary, the majority of those children who used it early (70% of those who first used it at ages 4 and 6) lost it subsequently and "rediscovered" it at some later point. Of those children who discovered the strategy late (at ages 8 or 10), 65% kept it up consistently, 21% followed a U-shaped curve (strategy use at age 8, nonstrategy use at age 10, and strategy use at age 12), and 14% lost it and did not rediscover it by age 12.

In summary, the individual patterns of strategy acquisition can be grouped as follows:

1. *Early discovery–Keep strategy.* Thirteen percent of the children discovered the strategy at the age of 4 or 6 and kept it up throughout the study.
2. *Early discovery–Lose strategy.* Twenty-eight percent of the children discovered the strategy at age 4 or 6, lost it subsequently, and rediscovered it at age 10 or 12.
3. *Late discovery–Keep strategy.* Fourteen percent discovered the strategy at age 8 and kept it subsequently, and 19% did so at the age of 10 or 12.
4. *Late discovery–Lose strategy.* Nineteen percent discovered it at age 8 or 10, and lost it subsequently (all but 6% reused it at the last measurement point).
5. *Gradual increase.* Eight percent rose from chance level to nearly perfect sorting gradually (increasing their RR indices by about 20% between subsequent measurement points).

Thus, our analyses of individual patterns show that the large majority of individual children deviate massively from the developmental pattern suggested by the group data: Children show "leaps" and U-shaped curves, and they do so at different points in time. It is therefore not surprising that it is impossible to predict the relative position of individual children at any measurement point from their ranking at a previous measurement point.

Analyses of individual developmental patterns thus helped us solve the puzzle of low individual stabilities in highly regular group data. However, so far we have merely *identified* individual developmental curves. We would like to be able to *interpret* these individual differences with respect to theoretical explanations of memory development. In the following, we focus on two questions: (a) Do children who keep a strategy once they have discovered it differ from children who give it up in their metaconceptual understanding of the usefulness of the strategy (i.e., in their task-related metamemory)? (b) How is individual strategy acquisition related to recall development? Do "strategy keepers" start with higher base levels, rise more steeply than "strategy losers", or both? Are "late discoverers" poorer in recall performance growth than "early discoverers"?

Metamemory and Strategy Acquisition

As Figure 3 shows, the proportion of children who showed almost perfect organizational behavior at one measurement point, and no such behavior at the next point, was high in the early years of the study. It has been argued that young children may show seemingly strategic behaviors in memory tasks without being strategic in the sense that they use these behaviors deliberately with the aim to remember (e.g., Bjorklund and Jacobs 1985; Hasselhorn 1992; Rabinowitz 1984). In particular, these children could be reacting to the associative relations between items and thus put those together "that go together" without having the goal of memorizing these items in mind. If this is the case, then children should be unlikely to be stable in their use of organizational behaviors, especially if the task is slightly modified (different items, different presentation mode, etc.). One way to distinguish between children who organized items into conceptual groups in a strategic way and children who "mindlessly" used organizational behaviors is to inspect their metamemorial understanding of the strategy they were using. Children who deliberately used sorting as a memory strategy should show some metaconceptual understanding of the advantages of conceptual organization over other behaviors (e.g., sorting by color or random arrangements).

Figure 4 shows how children's judgments in the task-related metamemory interview changed with age. Although many preschoolers used conceptual organization in the memory task, only a minority judged this behavior to be "best" for memorization. Most preschoolers judged organization by color to be the best strategy, even though literally nobody used this strategy in his or her own approach to the task. Figure 4 also shows a clear age trend: From the age of 8 years onward, the large majority of

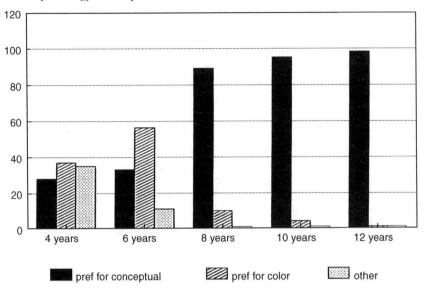

Figure 4. The development of task-related metamemory.

the children chose conceptual organization as the best strategy, and most could give memory-related reasons for their judgments.

Even though most preschoolers did not judge conceptual organization to be the best strategy, about one third of the 6-year-olds did. Similarly, about one third (32%) of those children who showed high levels of conceptual clustering at encoding at the age of 4 or 6 kept this strategy up at age 8 (and later measurement points). We hypothesized that children who understood the rationale for an organizational strategy should be more likely to keep this strategy at subsequent measurement points than children who did not possess such understanding. Therefore, we tested whether strategy users at age 6 who had adequate metamemory (preferred conceptual clustering over other arrangements) were more likely to reuse the strategy at age 8 than strategy users without metamemory. Unfortunately, this was not the case. Of 21 strategy users with metamemory at age 6, only 3 (14%) reused the strategy at age 8, and of 53 strategy users without metamemorial understanding, 18 (34%) reused the strategy at age 8 (this difference was not significant). Thus, metamemory does not appear to be related to stability versus instability in strategy use in this age range.

It is possible that the requirement that children understand the advantage of conceptual organization over color organization is too specific and does not tap the knowledge base that underlies early strategy use. In the early stages of metamemory development, children may understand that organizational behaviors in general are useful for remembering, without understanding why *conceptual* organization should be of specific value. When asked whether sorting by color might be a good idea, they accept this suggestion because it is consistent with their general understanding that organizational behaviors help you remember. In the metamemory interview that we modeled after a task by Wellman (1977), we merely asked children whether an organizational strategy was better than "just looking" and why this was so. In addition to assessing children's judgments of organizational behavior, this interview tested a number of other aspects of young children's metamemory (e.g., their awareness of the relevance of study time, list length, and a person's age). We found a marginally significant difference between children who scored high versus low in this interview in their stability of strategy use. Of those children who were highly strategic at age 6, about half (49%) reached a score of at least 4 (maximum = 6) on this interview. About 58% of those 6-year-old strategy users who reached such a high score reused the strategy at age 8, whereas only 33% of those strategy users who scored low (lower than 4) did so, and this difference approached significance ($\chi(1, N = 74) = 3.24, p < .10$). Thus, children with high general metamemory at age 6 tended to be more likely to reuse an organizational strategy under the changed task conditions at age 8 than children with low metamemory.

In summary, there is evidence from our data that preschoolers who behave in an apparently strategic way differ greatly in their metaconceptual understanding of strategy use, and there is some (although not very strong) evidence in favor of the assumption that such differences in metamemory are related to *stability* in strategy use in the sense that early metamemory is associated with high stability in strategy use. This impression is confirmed by a correlational analysis: Performance in the "Wellman interview" did not correlate with strategy use (conceptual clustering) at the ages of 4 and 6 years ($r < .10$), but there was a significant (though moderate) correlation between performance in the Wellman interview at age 4 and conceptual organization at age 8 ($r = .22$). Thus, early metamemory may have some influence on later strategy use such that an early advanced conceptual understanding of the domain of learning and remembering becomes useful once the task requirements demand "truly" strategic behavior (as was the case when the list length was increased).

Strategy Development and Recall Performance

In our analyses of individual patterns of strategy acquisition, we found that few children followed the developmental course indicated by the group data. Does this also hold for the development of recall performance? For each child, we computed regression equations on percentages of items recalled as a function of time. As a main result, only 10% of the children could be fitted to a model of linear increase (indicated by an R^2 value of .75 and above). Thus, the large majority seems to show dips and leaps. However, this is also suggested by the group data (see Figure 2): Percentage of items recalled at age 8 (when the new list was introduced) was about 20% lower than at age 6. When we inspected individual regression equations for recall development between the ages of 8 and 12, we found that two thirds of the children showed patterns that conformed to a model of linear increase. Of the remaining children, 50% showed U-shaped curves (dip at age 10), whereas 25% showed inverted U shapes, and 25%

declined from age 8 to age 12. Inspection of the raw data revealed that those children whose patterns (for the last 3 measurement points) were consistent with a model of linear increase differed greatly in the rates of improvement between successive measurement points. About half of the sample roughly followed the path suggested by the group means (15–20% increase between successive measurement points), whereas the other half showed "spurts" followed by a plateau, when a spurt was defined as a gain in recall performance between successive measurement points that was at least three times as high as the group means: Roughly 40% of the total sample showed such spurts. Spurts were about equally distributed between measurement points (half showed a spurt between the ages of 8 and 10, and half between the ages of 10 and 12). This finding helps us explain the moderate stabilities of recall performance over time (see Table 2): Although about 40% of the children remained relatively constant in their position relative to the group, another 40% massively changed their positions by gaining disproportionately at one of the time intervals while remaining constant during the other interval.

Are individual patterns of recall development related to individual patterns of strategy acquisition? We address this question in three steps: First, we explore whether the considerable improvement in recall performance that most children showed between the ages of 4 and 6 is related to the acquisition of organizational behaviors during that time period. Second, we ask whether the magnitude of the "drop" that occurred from age 6 to age 8 is related to the age of onset and the stability of strategy use, and third we explore the relation between patterns of strategy acquisition in school age (ages 8–12) and the development of recall performance.

Recall Performance and Strategy Acquisition in Preschool Age

Figure 5 shows the mean percentage of items recalled by each of the five strategy acquisition groups: Early discoverers who keep the strategy, early discoverers who (temporarily) lose it, late discoverers who keep it, late discoverers who (temporarily) lose it, and children following a pattern of gradual increase in the use of organizational behaviors. It is obvious from Figure 5 that all of these groups showed remarkable gains of comparable magnitude in free recall between the ages of 4 and 6. This can be illustrated by an inspection of the mean gains for some subgroups: Children who used organizational behaviors at both ages 4 and 6 ($N = 15$) started with a mean percentage of items recalled of 42% and rose to 77%, children who "discovered" the strategy between age 4 and age 6 ($n = 8$) rose from a mean of 47% to 73%, children who discovered the strategy only at age 8 ($n = 26$) rose from 46% to 67%, and those who discovered it only at age 10 ($n = 26$) rose from 39% to 62%. As indicated by the low correlations between strategy use and recall performance in preschool age (see Table 1), organizational behaviors do not seem to have a major influence on recall performance in this age range. As the subgroup analyses show, this was not due to low performance gains in those who used the strategy early but was due to the fact that those children who did not use it early had equally high performance gains as those who did.

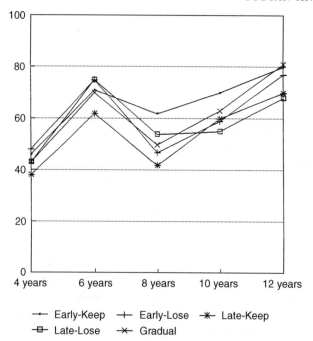

Figure 5. The development of recall, as a function of age of onset and maintenance of strategy use.

If recall performance in preschool age is not driven by strategy use, is it related to basic capacities and general intellectual functioning? Table 3 shows that the intercorrelations among memory capacity measures (word span and digit span) and recall at the ages of 4 and 6 were literally zero. The correlation between verbal IQ and recall performance at age 4 reached significance but was not any higher than the correlations between strategy use and recall performance. Similarly, some metamemory measures (based on the Kreutzer et al. 1975 interview) correlated significantly, but not substantially, with free recall in preschool age. The magnitude of intercorrelations did not change much when the coefficient gamma, a more appropriate measure of interitem association, was chosen instead (cf. Nelson 1984).

A multiple linear regression analysis with the recall performance gains between the ages of 4 and 6 as the dependent variable and including IQ (Columbia Mental Maturity Scale, Burgemeister, Blum, and Lorge 1972), strategy use, free recall at age 4, metamemory, and serial word span as the predictors, yielded significant effects of free recall at age 4 and IQ ($p < .05$). However, the correlation between recall at age 4 and recall performance gains between ages 4 and 6 was highly negative ($r = -.68$), indicating that the higher the entry level, the lower the performance gains during preschool age. Overall, 45% of the variance of the dependent variable was explained by this set of predictors. Thus, it appears that except for some predictive effect of

Table 3. *Intercorrelations Between Metamemory, Memory Capacity and IQ Measures, and Sorting During Study, Clustering at Recall, and Recall Performance, Separately for Each Measurement Point*

Variable	S1	C1	R1	S3	C3	R3	S5	C5	R5	S7	C7	R7	S9	C9	R9
MM1															
MM3											.20	.18			.21
MM5															
MM7										.22					
MM9													.34	.25	
Beal W4									.18						.27
Beal W6				.31	.24	.21			.22		.22	.25	.20	.21	.35
Wellman 1						.22			.26	.23	.23				
Wellman 3															
Kreutzer 1	.25	.20	.19	.18					.23						
Kreutzer 3									.23						
Kreutzer 7													.19		
Word span 1															
Word span 3													.19	.31	.20
Word span 8									.20						.20
Digit span 6									.20		.19	.27			.23
Digit span 4									.19			.23			
Total IQ									.29			.32		.21	.34
W1 Verbal IQ		.19		.24							.22	.21	.20		.28
W6 IQ									.25	.18	.23	.42		.31	.43

Notes: Numbers indicate measurement points. Only significant correlations are reported, $p <$ .05. S = sorting at encoding; C = clustering at recall; R = free recall; MM = task-related metamemory; Beal = retrieval cue interview (metamemory); Kreutzer = sum score general metamemory (Kreutzer, Leonard, and Flavell, 1975); Wellman = sum score general metamemory (Wellman 1977).

general intelligence, we have little success in predicting recall performance gains in preschool age from any of our measures.

Predicting the Magnitude of the Drop

Figure 5 shows that as a group, those children who discovered the strategy early and kept it up consistently showed a slighter drop in recall performance when the longer list was introduced than the other groups. This was confirmed by an analysis of variance with the magnitude of the drop as the dependent variable and strategy development pattern (groups defined as in Figure 5) as the independent variable,

$F(4, 179) = 6.91$, $p < .001$. Post hoc Newman–Keuls tests showed that the only significant difference was between the "early-keep" group and all other groups ($p < .05$). This could either be due to the fact that these children were early strategy discoverers or to the fact that they were strategy users at the time when the new list was introduced. Additional analyses suggest that the latter was the case: There was a significant correlation between sorting during study at age 6 and the size of the drop ($r = .20$), indicating that those who showed higher organization at preschool age lost more. Similarly, and more impressively, recall at age 6 was highly correlated with the size of the drop ($r = .53$), indicating that those who had more to lose lost more. An analysis of extreme groups showed that children who had high levels of recall at age 6 and showed almost perfect organizational behaviors did not differ in the magnitude of the drop from those who had comparable levels of recall without showing an organizational strategy: The mean magnitude of the drop was exactly the same for the two groups. Thus, the early use of a sorting strategy does not appear to be functional in consistently reaching high levels of recall at later measurement points.

In contrast, sorting during study at age 8 was highly negatively correlated to the magnitude of the drop ($r = -.41$), indicating that the use of a sorting strategy became functional at this age. No other correlations (i.e., between IQ measures, metamemory measures, capacity measures, and the magnitude of the drop) reached meaningful levels (i.e., higher than $r = .20$). Thus, the magnitude of the drop appears to be primarily predictable from the level of recall at age 6 (those who had most to lose lost most), with some moderating influence of sorting during study at age 8. A multiple regression analysis with the magnitude of the drop as the dependent variable confirmed this impression: Whereas recall at age 6, sorting during study at age 8, and verbal intelligence (Wechsler Intelligence Scale for Children; German version; Tewes 1983) turned out to be significant predictors ($p < .01$), metamemory and sorting at age 6 did not reach significance. Overall, 55% of the variance was explained by this set of predictors.

Strategy Use and Recall Performance at Elementary School Age

Correlational analyses (see Table 2) showed moderate to high correlations between strategy use and recall performance at the ages of 8, 10, and 12. This indicates that strategy use is functional for recall performance at elementary school age. However, cross-sectional analyses do not allow us to determine how strategy development is related to the development of recall performance. To utilize fully the longitudinal information on the strategy and recall development data, we analyzed these data with a hierarchical linear model (Bryk and Raudenbush 1992). In this analysis, we included only those children who showed performance gains in strategy use in the critical age range; therefore, 28 children who were already at ceiling in strategy use (conceptual organization) at age 8 were not included. As can be seen from Table 4, strategy use at age 8 and verbal IQ related significantly to the entry level of recall, and

Table 4. *Hierarchical Linear Modeling
Results Describing the Impact of Memory
and IQ Variables on the Entry Level and
Growth Rates in Free Recall*

Variable	t	p
Entry level		
Entry level of strategy use	6.283	$<.001$
Verbal IQ	6.197	$<.001$
Growth rates		
Entry level of recall	3.085	$<.002$
Growth rate of strategy use	5.844	$<.001$
Metamemory	-1.531	$>.10$
Serial word span	-1.104	$>.20$

the entry level of recall and the growth rate of sorting during study were significantly related to the individual growth rates in recall performance. In contrast, there was no significant relation of metamemory, memory capacity, and IQ to the growth rates in recall performance. This model explained 72% of the variance in entry level and 48% of the variance in growth rates. Thus, at elementary school age, performance gains in recall seem to be best predicted by gains in strategy use.

Discussion

In this chapter, we studied the individual developmental course of the acquisition and effectiveness of an organizational strategy over a wide age range. Our main finding is that the group data on strategy acquisition that have been reported in cross-sectional studies massively obscure the individual developmental paths. In most children, we do not find a pattern of gradual improvement in "strategicness" but a discontinuous pattern of leaps and drops in organizational behaviors. Different children begin to use organizational strategies at different ages. Many children do not maintain a strategy once they have discovered it but drop it and rediscover it at a later age. These findings explain the low-to-moderate stabilities over time in strategy use.

These findings are consistent with the view that conceptually driven reorganization processes occur between preschool and late elementary school age. However, we gain only indirect support for this assumption from the metamemory data. At preschool age, only some children who show an organizational behavior appear to have some understanding of its function. These children tend to be somewhat more likely to reuse the strategy at a later measurement point than those who use it mindlessly. We have little evidence on the conceptual understanding of learning and remembering in those children who did not show an understanding of the benefits of an organizational strategy. Further research is needed to explore children's conceptual understanding of memorization more fully and to relate this understanding to behaviors that children show on memory tasks.

Our findings on strategy effectiveness are consistent with previous research in indicating a utilization deficiency in younger children as compared with older ones. Correlations between strategy use and recall performance increase dramatically over the age range under study, and performance gains in recall can be predicted from performance gains in strategy use at elementary but not at preschool age. We explored whether individual differences in the developmental paths of strategy acquisition were related to developmental progress in strategy effectiveness. Our main finding is that strategy acquisition appears to be unrelated to recall performance gains in younger children (preschool and early elementary school age), but highly related in older children. In preschool age, children who showed no strategic behaviors were just as likely to show substantial recall performance gains between subsequent measurement points as children who were highly strategic from the start or children who discovered a strategy between subsequent measurement points. This is not surprising if the majority of children who used organizational behaviors in this age range did so without an understanding of its function for memorization. Thus, to investigate the individual development of strategy effectiveness, researchers need to use a variety of tasks in further research that taps different memory strategies, some of which should be more likely to be deliberately used by younger children.

Consistent with previous research we found a high level of strategy effectiveness in children above the age of about 8. The use of organizational behaviors was not only highly predictive of recall performance at any given measurement point, but performance gains in strategy use were an excellent predictor of performance gains in recall. This pattern of results indicates that individual differences in strategy effectiveness are fairly stable over the age range from 8 to 12.

The age range between about 6 and 8 appears to be a transitional period with regard to the acquisition and effective use of organizational strategies. Our findings indicate that organizational behaviors at age 6 were not a good predictor of recall performance at age 8. Because of a change in our sorting task, most children showed a drop in recall performance between the ages of 6 and 8. High levels of sorting at the age of 6 did not have a moderating effect on this drop, whereas organizational behaviors at the age of 8 were substantially correlated with recall performance at this measurement point. This pattern of results suggests that organizational behaviors start to become effectively used around the age of 8. To gain further insight into transitional processes in this age range, researchers should study strategy acquisition and recall performance in short-term longitudinal studies in shorter time intervals.

In summary, the main result of this preliminary analysis of the longitudinal data from one memory task is that individual developmental paths of strategy acquisition deviate substantially from what was expected from cross-sectional studies. In the present chapter, we described these individual differences. We have only made a first step toward interpreting them.

References

Bjorklund, D. F. (1987). How age changes in knowledge base contribute to the development of children's memory: An interpretive review. *Developmental Review, 7,* 93–130.

Bjorklund, D. F., & Coyle, T. R. (1995). Utilization deficiencies in the development of memory strategies. In F. E. Weinert & W. Schneider (Eds.), *Memory performance and competencies: Issues of growth and development* (pp. 161–180). Hillsdale, NJ: Erlbaum.

Bjorklund, D. F., & Jacobs, J. W. (1985). Associative and categorical processes in children's memory: The role of automaticity in the development of organization in free recall. *Journal of Experimental Child Psychology, 39,* 599–617.

Bryk, A., & Raudenbush, S. (1992). *Hierarchical linear models for social and behavioral research: Applications and data analysis methods.* Newbury Park, CA: Sage.

Burgemeister, B., Blum, L., & Lorge, J. (1972). *Columbia Mental Maturity Scale.* New York: Harcourt Brace Jovanovich.

Hasselhorn, M. (1990). The emergence of strategic knowledge activation in categorical clustering during retrieval. *Journal of Experimental Child Psychology, 50,* 59–80.

Hasselhorn, M. (1992). Task dependency and the role of category typicality and metamemory in the development of an organizational strategy. *Child Development, 63,* 202–214.

Kee, D. W., & Bell, T. S. (1981). The development of organizational strategies in the storage and retrieval of categorical items in free-recall learning. *Child Development, 52,* 1163–1171.

Kreutzer, M. A., Leonard, C., & Flavell, J. H. (1975). An interview study of children's knowledge about memory. *Monographs of the Society for Research in Child Development, 40*(Serial No. 159).

Lange, G. (1978). Organization-related processes in children's recall. In P. A. Ornstein (Ed.), *Memory development in children* (pp. 101–128). Hillsdale, NJ: Erlbaum.

Miller, P. H. (1994). Individual differences in children's strategic behavior: Utilization deficiencies. *Learning and Individual Differences, 6,* 285–307.

Miller, P. H., & Seier, W. L. (1994). Strategy utilization deficiencies in children: When, where, and why. In H. W. Reese (Ed.), *Advances in child development and behavior* (Vol. 25, pp. 107–156). New York: Academic Press.

Nelson, T. O. (1984). A comparison of current measures of the accuracy of feeling-of-knowing predictions. *Psychological Bulletin, 95,* 109–133.

Rabinowitz, M. (1984). The use of categorical organization: Not an all-or-none situation. *Journal of Experimental Child Psychology, 38,* 338–351.

Schneider, W. (1986). The role of conceptual knowledge and metamemory in the development of organizational processes in memory. *Journal of Experimental Child Psychology, 42,* 218–236.

Schneider, W., & Pressley, M. (1989). *Memory development between 2 and 20.* New York: Springer-Verlag.

Schneider, W., & Sodian, B. (1991). A longitudinal study of young children's memory behavior and performance in a sort–recall task. *Journal of Experimental Child Psychology, 51,* 14–29.

Tewes, U. (Ed.). (1983). *Hamburg–Wechsler–Intelligenztest für Kinder, Revision (HAWIK–R)* [German version of the revised WISC]. Bern, Switzerland: Huber.

Wellman, H. M. (1977). Preschooler's understanding of memory-relevant variables. *Child Development, 48,* 1720–1723.

5 Memory for Events Experienced and Events Observed

Angelika Weber and Gerhard Strube

The definition of autobiographical memory has changed over the last two decades. In the 1970s autobiographical memory was considered to be a special type of memory that differed from other memory functions not only in content but also in its mechanisms (e.g., nonstandard forgetting functions; cf. Baddeley, Lewis, and Nimmo-Smith 1978). Work in the 1980s changed this characterization of autobiographical memory and showed that it is embedded within more general memory functions, although it is somewhat special because of its content. Seminal descriptive studies such as those by Linton (1978) and Neisser (1981) gave rise to more experimental work, for instance, Wagenaar (1986), Barclay and Wellman (1986), or Strube and Neubauer (1988). The results from these and more recent studies converge on the conclusion that autobiographical memory is subject to the same constraints that hold for memory in the laboratory. Thus, the stage was set for autobiographical memory to become firmly integrated into the range of memory phenomena considered by cognitive psychology (cf. textbooks by Conway 1990 or Neisser and Winograd 1988).

Apart from case studies, autobiographical memory has only rarely been studied longitudinally. Perhaps it seemed too "personal" or uncontrolled or idiosyncratic to be studied in cognitive psychology; indeed, it is very difficult to conduct controlled experiments in this area. Well-known authors such as Rubin (1986) have argued that research in autobiographical memory should not be concerned with veridicality; that is, assessing the relationship of participants memories to what actually happened in their lives.

Research on autobiographical memory has rarely been conducted with young children or from a developmental perspective. Indeed, the topic has only begun to be treated systematically in cognitive developmental research in recent years (Fivush 1994; Fivush and Hudson 1990; Howe and Brainerd 1989), typically by interviewing children of different ages about their recent experiences. Surprisingly, a well-developed area of applied research, eyewitness research with young participants (e.g., Brainerd and Ornstein 1991; Ceci and Bruck 1993; Ornstein, Gordon, and Baker-Ward 1992; Ornstein, Larus, and Clubb 1991), is usually not cited in the context of

78

autobiographical memory and has only recently been integrated into the developmental literature. Thus, although there are a number of promising approaches, research on autobiographical memory from a developmental perspective is still in a descriptive stage. In this tradition, LOGIC offers the first study of autobiographical memory (and event memory in general) that spans children's development from age 4 to about age 12 and provides a rich context of information about intellectual and personality development. Because the literature still lacks a widely shared definition of autobiographical memory, we first explain how we have used the term.

The Construct of Autobiographical Memory

We have considered autobiographical memory to include memory for personally experienced events (autobiographical memory in the narrow sense) as well as memory for personally observed or witnessed events (autobiographical memory in the broad sense, including events experienced vicariously through such media as film).

We placed autobiographical memory into a taxonomy defined by three dimensions: *episodic–semantic, eventlike versus elementary*, and *self-relevance*. The first dimension, episodic–semantic, refers to the now classical distinction between semantic memory (Quillian 1968; the term refers to conceptual memory, or knowledge) and episodic memory (introduced by Tulving 1972 as an enormously successful "working hypothesis," and later reinterpreted as two virtually separate memory systems, Tulving 1983). In our work, we maintain the distinction between episodic and semantic memories as a functional, pragmatic difference. In this context, autobiographical memory is clearly episodic.

The second dimension, eventlike versus elementary, refers to the nature of what is represented. When Tulving (1972) introduced the term *episodic memory*, he referred, first of all, to memory for entities, such as the words presented to a participant during an experiment. Thus, the term *episodic*, while it is ostensibly event related (e.g., related to the experiment), does not at all imply that the memory contents are themselves represented as structured events. We should note that Tulving (1983, p. 28) said that he would rather have used the term *autobiographical memory*, if that term had not already acquired a different connotation. Just as "episodic" does not imply "eventlike," merely bearing the qualities of an event does not make something episodic. For example, schematic event-related knowledge such as scripts (Schank and Abelson 1977) are nonepisodic memory contents that have, or indeed define, the structure of events (Strube and Janetzko 1990).

The third dimension, self-relevance, refers to the degree of personal relevance an event or fact has for a person.

Thus, we take three dimensions as relevant for characterizing autobiographical memory: episodic quality, complexity (event quality; cf. Strube and Janetzko 1990), and self-relevance (Weber 1993). In this framework, typical autobiographical memories are for contents that have high episodic character, are highly eventlike (complex), and (usually) high in self-relevance.

Table 1. *The Taxonomy of Contents of Memory Within LOGIC*

Contents of memory	Episodic	Semantic
Complex, eventlike	(Typical) autobiographical events; Observed events	Scripts, event schemata (including generalized and decontextualized events)
Elementary, not eventlike	Items in an experiment (e.g., words from a list)	Concepts and facts known (including autobiographical facts)

Note: Contents shown here without third dimension of self-relevance.

This taxonomy (partly shown in Table 1) does not imply that any of these dimensions are dichotomous. Rather, all three dimensions together define a space, for example, from a vivid memory of a singular experience to a general representation of a number of similar experiences (e.g., "repisodic" memory; Neisser 1981) to wholly decontextualized autobiographical knowledge. In LOGIC, however, we focus on complex episodic events, both experienced and observed.

Events Experienced and Events Observed

If events form the basic category of what is stored in autobiographical memory, what is the functional difference between autobiographical memory in the narrow sense and more general memory for events? This is one of the questions that we addressed in LOGIC, with results that supported the hypothesis that they are essentially the same. Our studies complement the (nondevelopmental) experiments reported by Larsen and Plunkett (1987) and Larsen (1988), who demonstrated that event memory for reported and experienced events was compatible. This does not preclude, of course, differences in such parameters as the strength of memory traces. Ornstein et al. (1991) cited studies indicating that participation in an event (as opposed to observation) may give rise to stronger memory traces. This would be variation within the same kind of memory system, however: Autobiographical memory (i.e., memory for events experienced) may exhibit different effects due to content and circumstances, but its phenomena still follow the laws of memory that have been found in the laboratory (N.B., we agree here with the points made by Banaji and Crowder (1989), who misinterpreted Strube and Neubauer's (1988) position when citing this study in their critique of the "everyday memory" approach).

Memory for Events Experienced and Observed: Results From 4 to 12 Years of Age

The autobiographical memory issues that we addressed in LOGIC were rather basic ones because there was a lack of information about children's ability to remember autobiographical events (Ornstein et al. 1992). Our first objective was to gather base-line information about how children of different ages remember details from a complex event that was experienced or observed without the intention to remember, after a realistically long interval of several weeks, months, or even years. In doing this, we measured recall as well as recognition because each type of memory differs in its mnemonic strategies (N.B., we agree that recognition is not free of strategic factors).

We report on effects of long retention intervals, on the comparability of memory for events observed, and truly autobiographical memory, as well as, of course, baseline data for recall and recognition of events from age 4 to 12. Our main focus is a concern with longitudinal performance in these memory tasks: How stable is it over the years? How is memory for events related to memory for stories and other memory tasks, metamemory, (verbal) intelligence, and personality factors?

Procedure

Event memory was tested in each wave with tasks that tested either autobiographical memory in the narrow sense (e.g., remembering what had happened during a previous visit to the Max Planck Institute) or autobiographical memory in the broad sense (e.g., remembering the contents of an event observed, such as a movie or a puppet show). In each case, care was taken to document what actually had happened to be able to assess the veridicality of what the children remembered.

Being able to assess the veridicality of children's responses is certainly an important step toward better experimental control in realistic studies of event memory. Still, many effects escaped our control, although we tried hard to minimize them: Rehearsal by means of discussing an event with parents, peers, or other persons was never encouraged, but could of course not be suppressed; interference between the original event and later, similar experiences (e.g., the various visits to the Institute) could not be ruled out, although the events were staged to be quite distinctive; events used in the early waves might not have been sufficiently salient to the children to be well remembered after long intervals; and so on. In addition, the memory tests were not always ideally comprehensive because they had to be tailored to fit into the always tight time schedule for the assessments.

Materials and Tasks

The following is an overview of the autobiographical memory tasks used in the LOGIC study. In each wave, there were several measurement points. For each wave, the events, mean retention interval (months), kind of sample, and the procedure used are shown in Table 2. *Kernel sample* (K) refers to the subgroup of children who also participated in the assessments of the social domain (see Asendorpf, this volume).

Table 2. *Overview of Events, Mean Retention Intervals (Months), Kind of Sample, and the Procedures Used*

Wave	Event	Retention interval	Sample	Measure
1	A	2.9	K	Cued recall
	B_1	3.2	K	Cued recall
	C	2.4	K	Cued recall
2	D_1	1.1	Whole	Cued recall, recognition
	B_2	10.9	K	Cued recall
3	D_2	9.6	Whole	Cued recall, recognition
	E	7.6	K	Cued recall
4	E	3.4	K	Free recall, recognition
5	F_1	3.9	K	Free recall, recognition
6	E	12	K	Free recall, recognition
7	F_2	21.6	K	Free recall, recognition
8	G_1	15	Whole	Free recall, Cued recall
9	G_2	4.8	Whole	Free recall, Cued recall

Notes: K = Kernel sample; A = Santa Claus visits kindergarten; B_1, B_2 = first visit to Institute; C = puppet show in kindergarten; D_1, D_2 = policeman and street drill; E = recent visit to Institute; F_1, F_2 = Movie 1; G_1, G_2 = Movie 2. In contrast to the other Waves, the retention interval in Wave 8 was only 15 minutes.

Results

Effects of the Retention Interval. Variations of the retention interval within measurement points (average retention intervals for each measurement) are shown in Table 2. Because of the logistics of planning testing sessions, the retention interval within each measurement point sometimes varied considerably across participants. However, the average retention intervals were well beyond those minutes, hours, and few days in which most of forgetting occurs. We did not expect variations in the retention interval within each measurement point to have a strong impact on remembering, and our data indeed show only very minor effects, with the single exception of a correlation ($p < .05$) of $r = -.19$ between retention interval and free recall in Wave 9. Even there the effect explains less than 4% of the variance, and on average, less than 1% of the variance was due to the size of the retention interval. Consequently in the following, we report results based on the original data instead of residuals.

As also seen in Table 2, the average retention intervals across measurement points and tasks also varied considerably, ranging from about 1 month to almost 2 years, with typical values of 3 to 4 months for most assessments, and 10 to 12 months for repeated assessments. Thus, age and retention interval are confounded. However, as stated earlier, effects due to the length of the retention interval are spurious at best. Still, there might be some "compensation" for forgetting during very long intervals because the tests presented at the longest retention intervals were invariably repetitions of earlier assessments.

Table 3. *Number of Participants Tested, Mean Memory Performance (Percentage or Discrimination Index), and Standard Deviations for Autobiographical Memory Measures Used in LOGIC*

Wave	Event	n	M	SD	Measure
1	A	69	33.70	15.88	Percent recalled
	B_1	75	26.96	12.44	Percent recalled
	C	134	31.77	15.50	Percent recalled
2	D_1	194	37.16	13.52	Percent recalled
	D_1	187	0.58	0.18	Discrimination A'
	B_2	85	22.46	11.77	Percent recalled
3	E	82	31.35	14.53	Percent recalled
	D_2	176	26.90	13.92	Percent recalled
	D_2	155	0.51	0.24	Discrimination A'
4	E	128	33.78	16.93	Percent recalled
	E	115	0.83	0.12	Discrimination A'
5	F_1	113	24.00	12.20	Percent recalled
	F_1	104	0.81	0.10	Discrimination A'
6	E	113	4.16	6.10	Percent recalled
	E	112	0.50	0.18	Discrimination A'
7	F_2	91	19.73	10.14	Percent recalled
	F_2	91	0.77	0.10	Discrimination A'
8	G_1	174	29.54	7.18	Percent recalled
9	G_2	178	14.43	9.13	Percent recalled

Notes: A = Santa Claus visits kindergarten; B_1, B_2 = first visit to Instititute; C = puppet show in kindergarten; D_1, D_2 = policeman and street drill; E = recent visit to Institute; F_1, F_2 = Movie 1; G_1, G_2 = Movie 2.

Performance in Recall and Recognition. Performance in recall (percent recalled) and recognition (discrimination index A', according to Grier 1971) tasks is shown in Table 3. Average recall measures ranged between 20 and 37% remembered, with the exception of memory for an episode from a visit to the Institute a year before measured in Wave 6. The lower retention on this measure may have occurred because of the extremely long retention interval (369 days average) or because of the particular content (only one episode from a visit to the Institute, which was possibly not very salient or relevant to the children).

Recognition measures for Waves 1 to 3 show near-floor performance, which may indicate wild guessing ($A' = 0.50$ is the baseline for guessing in a two-alternative, forced-choice recognition test). For Waves 4, 5, and 7, the discrimination index was clearly above chance level.

Stabilities (Intercorrelations Over Time). There were no significant intercorrelations between measures of accuracy or discrimination in the recognition tasks, with two exceptions: a correlation of $r = .19$ between Wave 2 and Wave 3 visits to the Institute, and $r = .52$ between the movie in Wave 5 and Wave 7, both of which were repeated measurements. Thus, there was stability across waves (higher, of course, at the higher ages, Waves 5 to 7). There was consistency in recognition tasks only within the same wave (Wave 4 recognition measures all had significant positive intercorrelations), and there was inconsistency across different recognition tasks at different ages.

In contrast, the recall measures showed a rich and stable pattern of positive intercorrelations even over several waves, with correlations between repeated measurements being higher, of course. Therefore, we chose to use recall measures to form a framework of variables to compare autobiographical and event memory to other domains of development (see below).

Effects of Sex and Age. We did not find statistically significant effects of sex, with the notable exception of discrimination measures from Wave 5 on and the spurious exception of recall of the movie shown in Wave 5, $t(111) = 2.06$, $p < .05$. The sex effects for recognition were uniform from Wave 5 to 7: Boys showed better discrimination than girls (3–9% better); these differences were all significant at the 0.1% level.

Effects of age could only be controlled within a testing point. The results were unequivocal: Older children had consistently better recall and recognition, although t tests between younger and older halves of the sample (median-split) showed significant results ($p < .05$) only for recall of the puppet show (Wave 1) and recall of the curb drill event (Wave 2).

A Framework of Tasks for Longitudinal Comparison. As we noted earlier, the recall measures showed a consistent and stable pattern of positive intercorrelations, most of them significant, and indeed, many of them significantly positive over several years. However, an important result is that those intercorrelations did not differ between truly autobiographical tasks, such as remembering details from the child's last visit to the Institute, and tasks relating to observed events, such as a puppet show at the kindergarten, or a short movie.

We have selected measures from those recall tasks that were linked through positive, significant correlations and that were about equally distributed over the LOGIC waves. The very existence of this framework of correlated tasks is evidence that memory for events, both experienced and observed, may be considered a domain of cognitive development with reasonable temporal stability. Tables 4 and 5 show our selection of central measures.

Table 4 shows intercorrelations among recall tasks in the early waves (Waves 1 to 3). The test–retest correlation (curb drill) was highest, as it should be; correlations within the same wave tend to be higher than between waves.

From Wave 3 onward, significant correlations exist over considerable time spans. Table 5 shows intercorrelations among recall tasks from the later Waves (Waves 4–9).

Table 4. *Intercorrelations Among Central Measures of Autobiographical Memory, Waves 1–3*

Wave	Wave 1 (visit)	Wave 2 (visit)	Wave 2 (policeman)	Wave 3 (policeman)	Wave 3 (visit)
Wave 1 (puppet)	.25*	.25*	.06	.07	.11
Wave 1 (visit)		.34*	−.08	−.06	.11
Wave 2 (visit)			.27*	.32*	.17
Wave 2 (policeman)				.59*	.18
Wave 3 (policeman)					.23*

*Correlations significant at the 5% level.

Table 5. *Intercorrelations Among Central Measures of Autobiographical Memory, Waves 3–9*

Wave	Wave 4 (visit)	Wave 5 (movie)	Wave 7 (movie)	Wave 8 (movie)	Wave 9 (movie)
Wave 3 (visit)	.44*	.24*	.00	.15	.18
Wave 4 (visit)		.37*	.15	.36*	.26*
Wave 5 (movie)			.61*	.35*	.36*
Wave 7 (movie)				.31*	.38*
Wave 9 (movie)					.34*

*Correlations significant at the 5% level.

Relations to Other Task Domains. Intelligence: Our assessment procedures for autobiographical and event memory were based on verbal interviews (free and cued recall and recognition), and only once did we use a nonverbal procedure (forced-choice recognition through the selection of pictures). These essentially verbal procedures together with the inevitable connection of memory to intelligence led us to expect significant correlations between autobiographical memory measures and those of intelligence, especially verbal IQ.

The tasks included in our framework all show positive correlations with all verbal IQ measures (even across waves), 75% of which were significant at the 5% level. The values are typically between $r = .20$ and $r = .40$, with higher values coming from Waves 3 and 4, as Table 6 shows.

Table 7 demonstrates that in spite of those correlations, the intercorrelations among our recall measures are only slightly affected. This result indicates that the structure of autobiographical and event memory over time is not dependent on intelligence.

Short-term memory (STM) capacity and attention: Because everything that eventually gets stored in long-term memory must be processed (e.g., rehearsed) in STM, one might expect that STM capacity is a major determinant of autobiographical and

Table 6. *Correlations Between Verbal IQ and*
Autobiographical Memory

Wave	Wave 2 IQ	Wave 4 IQ	Wave 6 IQ	Wave 9 IQ
Wave 1 (puppet)	.19*	.19*	.13	.04
Wave 2 (policeman)	.16*	.23*	.26*	.25*
Wave 3 (policeman)	.26*	.25*	.29*	.21*
Wave 3 (visit)	.09	.35*	.23*	.14
Wave 4 (visit)	.15*	.43*	.36*	.28*
Wave 5 (movie)	.09	.24*	.16*	.15
Wave 7 (movie)	.15	.18*	.10	.18*
Wave 8 (movie)	.23*	.36*	.33*	.36*
Wave 9 (movie)	.07	.26*	.25*	.20*

*Correlations significant at the 5% level (one-tailed testing).

Table 7. *Original and Partial Correlations Between Central Measures*
of Autobiographical Memory From Wave 3 to 9. Controlled for Measures
of (Verbal) Intelligence

Wave	Wave 4 (visit)	Wave 5 (movie)	Wave 7 (movie)	Wave 8 (movie)	Wave 9 (movie)
Wave 3 (visit)	.44* (.36)*	.24* (.18)	.00 (−.09)	.15 (.09)	.18 (.17)
Wave 4 (visit)		.37* (.21)	.15 (.05)	.36* (.31)*	.26* (.20)
Wave 5 (movie)			.61* (.68)*	.35* (.24)*	.36* (.22)
Wave 7 (movie)				.31* (.20)	.38* (.24)*
Wave 9 (movie)					.34 (.32)*

*Correlations significant at the 5% level.
Note: Partial corrections are shown in parentheses.

event memory in addition to its well-known importance for word lists and nonsense syllables.

We found sparse evidence for this in our data. Event recall in Waves 1 and 2 showed positive correlations with STM capacity (measured in Waves 1, 3, and 5). Most of the correlations were in the range of $r = .12$ to $r = .22$ and were significant at the 5% level (one-tailed), but they explain less than 5% of the variance. In addition, there were zero correlations (recall of visit to the Institute, Wave 3) and even some (nonsignificant) negative ones.

The d2 test of attention, or "mental concentration," was only administered in Wave 8. It showed significant positive correlations with event recall at the same time ($r = .17$) and with the retest in Wave 9 ($r = .15$). However, correlations with our measures from Waves 4 to 7 were essentially zero.

Table 8. *Correlations Between Central Measures of Autobiographical Memory and Aggregated Measures of Memory for Stories (Waves 1–9)*

Event memory	Memory for stories	r
Wave 1 (visit)	Wave 1	.36*
Wave 1 (Santa Claus)	Wave 1	.15
Wave 1 (puppet show)	Wave 1	.41*
Wave 2 (policeman)	Wave 2	.24*
Wave 2 (visit, repetition)	Wave 2	.19
Wave 3 (policeman, repetition)	Wave 3	.42*
Wave 3 (visit)	Wave 3	.37*
Wave 4 (visit)	Wave 4	.30*
Wave 5 (movie)	Wave 5	.20*
Wave 7 (movie, repetition)	Wave 7	.20
Wave 8 (movie)	Wave 9	.36*
Wave 9 (movie, repetition)	Wave 9	.19*

*Correlations significant at the 5% level.

Table 9. *Intercorrelations Between Central Measures of Autobiographical Memory From Wave 3 to 9*

Wave	Wave 4 (visit)	Wave 5 (movie)	Wave 7 (movie)	Wave 8 (movie)	Wave 9 (movie)
Wave 3 (visit)	.44* (.33)*	.24* (16)	.00 (−.09)	.15 (−.02)	.18 (.11)
Wave 4 (visit)		.37* (.30)*	.15 (.06)	.36* (.22)	.26* (.22)*
Wave 5 (movie)			.61* (.61)*	.35* (.29)*	.36* (.35)*
Wave 7 (movie)				.31* (.20)	.38* (.34)*
Wave 9 (movie)					.34* (.27)*

*Correlations significant at the 5% level.
Note: Partial correlations controlling for measures of memory for text are shown in parentheses.

Memory for stories: Stories are about events, and autobiographical recollections are usually told in the form of a narrative. Fivush, Gray, and Fromhoff (1989) found that even very young children recall experienced events in a coherent narrative form. Therefore, we expected significant correlations between our measures and story recall.

The results shown in Table 8 bear out this hypothesis. One might ask, however, whether autobiographical memory is something in its own right or is simply memory for stories (or events told). As Table 9 shows, controlling for story recall only slightly affected the intercorrelations among our measures, suggesting that autobiographical memory is not identical to memory for stories.

Metamemory: Recalling events makes use of retrieval structures built during encoding and should benefit from the application of retrieval strategies (e.g., Williams and Hollan 1981). Because the metamemory measures used in the LOGIC study[1] assessed strategic aspects of memory, it seemed reasonable to expect a positive correlation between metamemory and recall performance, although it has been emphasized that autobiographical memory does not seem to be organized in terms of semantic categories (Conway and Bekerian 1987). Our results did not suggest that metamemory as measured in LOGIC was helpful to autobiographical recall. There were only some spurious correlations, and the synchronous correlations between metamemory measures and autobiographical memory measures were low and not significant.

Personality: Autobiographical memory has often been discussed in the context of personality; for instance, that such memories are instrumental in the formation of a consistent personality (Greenwald 1980). Although we had no direct measures of personality consistency overall, we did have measures of shyness. In general, we found negative correlations between our recall measures and measures of shyness. The intercorrelations with shyness were on the negative side, many of them significant, although not uniform in size. The interpretation of these correlations need not assume an association between autobiographical memory and personality, however. The relation may just be a methodological artifact because both free- and cued-recall measures put the child into a kind of examination situation, and shyness may inhibit production in recall. The absence of any significant correlations of this kind with recognition measures supports this interpretation.

In one wave, Wave 5, we designed the tasks to look explicitly at memory and personality. Specifically, we looked at personality effects on memory for the movie shown in Wave 5. Our hypothesis was that overall recall would not be affected by personality but that there should be content-specific effects; that is, certain aspects of the movie that were concordant with the child's personality should be better remembered. Because aggressiveness was also one of the main personality traits studied in LOGIC (cf. Asendorpf, this volume), we chose a movie that contained scenes of (mild) violence. The content of the movie was categorized a priori in terms of aggressor-centered and victim-centered events. If memory for the events shown was mediated by self-involvement, those children rated as being aggressive should remember the aggressor-centered events better than the victim-centered events, and better than the nonaggressive children. In addition, overall recall should not differ between aggressive and nonaggressive children. To test this hypothesis, extreme groups were drawn from the kernel sample according to Wave 5 measures of parental scale aggressiveness and shyness (there were 18 aggressive children, 18 shy children,

---

[1] Metamemory measures used for this analysis were (a) clustering during nonautobiographical recall (RR scores (RR = ratio-of-repetition index, see Schneider and Sodian, this volume); Waves 1, 3, 5, 7, and 9), (b) Wellman's (1977) metamemory interview (sum scores; Waves 1 and 3), (c) Beale's (1985) metamemory interview (sum scores; Waves 4 and 6), and, finally, (d) use of task-specific retrieval cues (Waves 2 and 4).

and 16 children with both shyness and aggressiveness scores below the median). Total recall did not differ among the groups, but aggressor-centered events were remembered significantly better by the group of aggressive children, $F(2, 46) = 3.37$, $p < .05$. Both results supported the hypothesis. (For further details, see Weber 1993.)

Discussion

The main outcome of the research presented here was that (very) long-term episodic memory for complex events, in which a child participated or witnessed, could be established as a relatively coherent and basically self-contained domain of cognitive functioning during development. "Self-contained" does not, of course, mean that there were no relations to other domains. Quite the contrary: Memory for events was significantly correlated with (verbal) intelligence throughout the years, and with the ostensibly related domain of memory for stories. However, the pattern of intercorrelations among measures of recall for events experienced and events observed did not markedly change when the effects of intelligence or story memory were partialled out.

In addition, the pattern of intercorrelations conformed to our expectations: Correlations between adjacent measurement waves were highest (around $r = .3$ to $r = .45$) and decreased when they spanned several waves (around $r = .20$). Repeated testings yielded higher correlations (around $r = .6$), as should be expected. Generally, intercorrelations were smaller for the early waves ($r = .2$ to $r = .3$) and higher in lateral years ($r = .3$ to $r = .4$), which may be interpreted as evidence that the ability becomes more stable, and our measurements became more reliable.

The Nature of Autobiographical Memory

An essential result was that there was no marked difference in the size of correlations between truly autobiographical memory tasks or between recall of events observed and the size of correlations between the two kinds of memories (events participated in or events observed). In addition, performance on the two types of memory tasks was similar. Incidental memory for complex events that were observed in a movie cannot be dissociated from autobiographical memory; that is, memory for events that the child experienced directly, by participation. This conclusion supports the position taken by Ornstein and his colleagues (e.g., Ornstein et al. 1991).

Recall Over Very Long Retention Intervals

Laboratory experiments typically use intervals of 15 to 45 minutes when testing long-term retention. In contrast, the measures reported here stem from retention intervals ranging from 1 month to almost 2 years. When we also take into account that encoding of the events was at least incidental, and that we asked for details (although cues were provided in the early waves), the 25–35% recalled seems to be a substantial amount, although there was considerable variation (*SD*s ranged from 8 to 16%). In addition, regression analysis showed that no more than 4% of total variation in recall could be explained by the length of the retention interval. Therefore, we conclude that after about 1 month, most of forgetting has already taken place, and an important amount of detail can still be remembered. Development does not seem to bring higher performance at higher ages. Overall performance also was not influenced by sex or personality. (Personality may give rise to content-specific effects.) Remarkably, we did not find substantial STM capacity effects. Verbal intelligence, however, was found to account for approximately 17% of the variance in recall.

Recall and Recognition

Contrary to the usual findings that recognition is superior to recall, we found good discrimination in recognition tests only from Wave 4 onward, where A' values around 80% were obtained. In contrast, discrimination in Waves 2 and 3 was essentially zero (A' around 50%, the guessing baseline). There is no clear-cut interpretation for this finding. A tentative explanation is that recall needs cue generation (plus checking of possible answers) and recognition needs only checking the alternatives, as many researchers suggest. Cue generation is usually considered to be the harder part, but it could be different for young children, who might not be able to decide reliably between possible alternatives. (This should affect recall only by way of intrusions, which we did occasionally find.)

   A further point with regard to recall is the possible effect of cues on performance. We had used cued recall in Waves 1 to 4 to boost performance and avoid floor effects, and we used a free-recall procedure later on. Cues were mainly framed as questions pertaining to actions ("What was it that your mommy had to do?" referring to one of the visits at the Institute) or to specific objects ("What was the color of the box?" or "Which toys did you play with?"). Thus, cues were rather specific and concrete and certainly were helpful (see Table 2): After we switched to free recall, performance dropped from over 30% to below 30% recalled. However, the stable intercorrelations between our recall measures suggest that cued-recall performance did not differ systematically from free-recall performance with respect to individual differences.

Why Study Autobiographical Memory at All?

One answer comes from the results themselves: Autobiographical memory, which in our definition includes memory for events observed, constitutes an "identifiable domain" of cognitive development – and we still know too little about it. The other answer comes from the nature of autobiographical memory: It has great practical relevance to everyday events, and in such special events as providing accurate recall in court. Memory is, of course, a limiting factor to accuracy because "it is certainly the case that children cannot provide accurate testimony about events that cannot be remembered" (Ornstein et al. 1992, p. 135). We must not forget, however, that other limiting factors exist as well. The possible lack of an ability to check incorrect memories, or to fall back on guessing in recognition tests (indicated earlier), points to some of these limitations; others (e.g., suggestibility) were not within the scope of our study.

Prospects for Further Study

The partial dissociation we observed between memory for events observed or experienced and memory for stories (i.e., intercorrelations about $r = .4$ that did not effect correlations within autobiographical measures) certainly warrants further study. What is it that makes real events (including those shown in a movie) different from stories about events? Could it be that text-related knowledge (story grammars, story schemata, etc.) can give hints that real events lack? The most plausible explanation is a trivial one: Story memory in LOGIC was assessed with very short retention intervals of only a few minutes. Relations between autobiographical and story memory might be different for long intervals, as in Bartlett's (1932) early studies.

A second line of research might focus on autobiographical memory and personality, which was explicitly addressed only once in our study (see especially Weber 1993). Possible explanations for memory–personality congruities range from selective attention during encoding (which suggests that personal interests and preferences might play a special role in the type of incidental memory tasks we used) to the deployment of content-specific knowledge (e.g., aggressive children might have more knowledge about aggressive events such as fights).

A third line of research could focus on what develops in autobiographical memory: Is it knowledge about events (either general or domain specific) or organization and strategies? Studies comparing children's and adults' performance (e.g., Rather, Smith, and Dion 1986) could suggest interesting developmental hypotheses. In summary, we found memory for events experienced and events observed a fascinating domain that has won a position of its own in cognitive development and that deserves to be studied in the context of other cognitive, personality, and social factors.

References

Baddeley, A. D., Lewis, V., & Nimmo-Smith, I. (1978). When did you last...? In M. M. Gruneberg, P. E. Morris, & R. N. Sykes (Eds.), *Practical aspects of memory* (pp. 77–83). London: Academic Press.

Banaji, M. R., & Crowder, R. G. (1989). The bankruptcy of everyday memory. *American Psychologist*, *44*, 1185–1193.

Barclay, C. R., & Wellman, H. M. (1986). Accuracies and inaccuracies in autobiographical memories. *Journal of Memory and Language*, *25*, 93–103.

Bartlett, F. C. (1932). *Remembering*. Cambridge, England: Cambridge University Press.

Beal, C. R. (1985). Development of knowledge about the use of cues to aid prospective retrieval. *Child Development, 56,* 631–642.

Brainerd, C., & Ornstein, P. A. (1991). Children's memory for witnessed events: The developmental backdrop. In J. Doris (Ed.), *The suggestibility of children's recollections: Implications for eyewitness testimony* (pp. 10–20). Washington, DC: American Psychological Association.

Ceci, S. J., & Bruck, M. (1993). Suggestibility of the child witness: A historical review and synthesis. *Psychological Bulletin, 113,* 403–439.

Conway, M. A. (1990). *Autobiographical memory: An introduction.* Philadelphia: Open University Press.

Conway, M. A., & Bekerian, D. A. (1987). Organization in autobiographical memory. *Memory & Cognition, 15,* 119–132.

Fivush, R. (Ed.) (1994). *Long-term retention of infant memories.* Hillsdale, NJ: Erlbaum.

Fivush, R., Gray, J. T., & Fromhoff, F. A. (1989). Talk about the past. *Cognitive Development, 2,* 393–410.

Fivush, R., & Hudson, J. A. (1990). *Knowing and remembering in young children.* Cambridge, England: Cambridge University Press.

Greenwald, A. G. (1980). The totalitarian ego: Fabrication and revision of personal history. *American Psychologist, 35,* 603–618.

Grier, J. B. (1971). Nonparametric indexes for sensitivity and bias: Computing formulas. *Psychological Bulletin, 25,* 424–429.

Howe, M. L., & Brainerd, C. J. (1989). Development of children's long-term retention. *Developmental Review, 9,* 301–340.

Larsen, S. F. (1988). Remembering reported events: Memory for news in ecological perspective. In M. M. Gruneberg, P. E. Morris, & R. N. Sykes (Eds.), *Practical aspects of memory: Current research and issues* (Vol. 1, pp. 440–445). New York: Wiley.

Larsen, S. F., & Plunkett, K. (1987). Remembering experienced and reported events. *Applied Cognitive Psychology, 1,* 15–26.

Linton, M. (1978). Real world memory after six years: An in vivo study of very long term memory. In M. M. Gruneberg, P. E. Morris, & R. N. Sykes (Eds.), *Practical aspects of memory* (pp. 69–76). London: Academic Press.

Neisser, U. (1981). John Dean's memory: A case study. *Cognition, 9,* 1–22.

Neisser, U., & Winograd, E. (1988). *Remembering reconsidered: Ecological and traditional approaches to the study of memory.* Cambridge, England: Cambridge University Press.

Ornstein, P. A., Gordon, B. N., & Baker-Ward, L. (1992). Children's memory for salient events: Implications for testimony. In M. L. Howe, C. J. Brainerd, & V. F. Reyna (Eds.), *Development of long-term retention* (pp. 135–158). New York: Springer.

Ornstein, P. A., Larus, D. M., & Clubb, P. A. (1991). Understanding children's testimony: Implications of research on the development of memory. In R. Vasta (Ed.), *Annals of Child Development, 8,* 145–176.

Quillian, M. R. (1968). Semantic memory. In M. Minsky (Ed.), *Semantic information processing* (pp. 227–270). Cambridge, MA: MIT Press.

Rather, H. H., Smith, B., & Dion, S. A. (1986). Development of memory for events. *Journal of Experimental Child Psychology, 41,* 411–428.

Rubin, D. C. (1986). *Autobiographical memory.* Cambridge, England: Cambridge University Press.

Schank, R. C., & Abelson, R. P. (1977). *Scripts, plans, goals and understanding.* Hillsdale, NJ: Erlbaum.

Strube, G., & Janetzko, D. (1990). Episodisches Wissen und fallbasiertes Schließen: Aufgaben für die Wissensdiagnostik und die Wissenspsychologie [Episodic knowledge and case-based reasoning]. *Schweizerische Zeitschrift für Psychologie, 48,* 211–221.

Strube, G., & Neubauer, S. (1988). Remember that exam? In M. M. Grunewald, P. E. Morris, & R. N. Sykes (Eds.), *Practical aspects of memory: Current research and issues: Memory in everyday life* (Vol. 1, pp. 247–252). New York: Wiley.

Tulving, E. (1972). Episodic and semantic memory. In E. Tulving & W. Donaldson (Eds.), *Organization of memory.* New York: Academic Press.

Tulving, E. (1983). *Elements of episodic memory.* New York: Oxford University Press.

Wagenaar, W. A. (1986). My memory: A study of autobiographical memory over six years. *Cognitive Psychology, 18,* 225–252.

Weber, A. (1993). *Autobiographische Erinnerung und Persönlichkeit [Autobiographical memory and personality].* Frankfurt: Lang.

Wellman, H. M. (1977). Preschooler's understanding of memory-relevant variables. *Child Development, 48,* 1702–1723.

Williams, D. M., & Hollan, J. D. (1981). The process of retrieval from very long-term memory. *Cognitive Science, 5,* 87–119.

4a and 5a   Comments: Toward an Understanding of the Development of Memory

Peter A. Ornstein

A truly developmental analysis of children's memory and cognition requires parallel progress on at least three different research "tasks": (a) the characterization of children's basic competence at different ages, (b) the depiction of the course of age-related changes in this competence, and (c) the articulation of factors thought to be responsible for the resulting developmental patterns. Within the area of memory development, considerable progress has been made in the last 15 years on the first of these tasks. Indeed, even though the problem of "cognitive diagnosis" is complicated considerably by the context specificity of many aspects of young children's mnemonic abilities (Flavell 1985; Ornstein, Baker-Ward, and Naus 1988), steady advances have been made in describing these skills. In contrast, as I see it, our field made less dramatic progress on the second and third tasks that confront developmentalists. Consider, for example, the kinds of data that are necessary to speak to the issue of developmental change. Depicting the changing nature of children's skills for remembering requires more than the "simple" description of performance at varying ages. At a minimum, efforts to understand the development of memory mandate moving from cross-sectional to longitudinal research designs in which individual children are tracked over time. Moreover, because longitudinal studies are necessary for discussions of developmental change, the largely cross-sectional literature (see Schneider and Pressley 1989 for an overview) does not provide much leverage on these critical issues.

Consider also the problems associated with understanding the mechanisms that bring about developmental change. Although there has been no shortage of factors thought to account for children's remembering (e.g., strategies and prior knowledge), by and large these presumed mediators have not been examined in the context of longitudinal designs. Moreover, there is no guarantee that the variables found to be

I would like to thank Beate Sodian and Wolfgang Schneider as well as Angelika Weber and Gerhard Strube for very useful conversations with them about their chapters. Thanks are also due to Catherine Haden for her helpful comments on this discussion. Preparation of this chapter was supported in part by Grant HD32114 from the U.S. Public Health Service.

94

important in accounting for memory performance at any particular age will be the same as those necessary for understanding developmental change. Even when the critical factors have been identified and explored, a truly critical developmental question remains: What are the forces (both endogenous and exogenous) that influence the emergence and operation of these mediators?

The LOGIC Study

Given this assessment of our current understanding of the central issues, it seems clear that we have a long way to go before we have a coherent account of the development of memory and cognition. Nonetheless, it is equally clear to me that the LOGIC project has boosted significantly our understanding of these complex issues. Indeed, while I have only talked about the importance of longitudinal studies (e.g., Ornstein et al. 1988), Franz Weinert and his coworkers have actually done it. The innovative and integrative LOGIC study has generated an exceptionally rich database that can be mined profitably for years to come. Moreover, this study can lead to (a) integrated analyses of cognitive and social development, (b) the design of more in-depth studies in which particular domains (e.g., memory) are examined thoroughly, and (c) greater focus on understanding the mechanisms of developmental change.

Of course, with the wisdom of hindsight, it is possible to identify problems with any study, even this very impressive collaborative venture. By definition, any research project must involve a series of (sometimes painful) compromises between the depth versus the breadth of the inquiry. In LOGIC, the consequences of these compromises can be seen in both what is and is not included in each assessment wave and in the frequency of the observations. Concerning the former, it is no doubt the case that within each area of the LOGIC investigation, the incorporation of additional measures might have been desirable to pinpoint the skills that are emerging. Concerning the latter, a greater density of observation would certainly have permitted a more precise analysis of the selected skills as they are changing (see Siegler and Crowley 1991).

Contributions of LOGIC to Understanding Memory

Development

This overall appraisal of the LOGIC project can be applied directly to the two chapters in this volume on the development of memory that have been prepared by Beate Sodian and Wolfgang Schneider and by Angelika Weber and Gerhard Strube. Both Sodian and Schneider's treatment of deliberate memorization and Weber and Strube's discussion of autobiographical memory break new ground and have the potential to alter our thinking about the development of memory. Because these pieces whet our appetites for truly developmental analyses of memory, both chapters leave us wishing for more: more measures, more assessments, and so on. In my discussion, I present my assessments of both the strengths and weaknesses of each of these chapters and comment, as well, on some matters of integration.

Sodian and Schneider

To begin my characterization of Sodian and Schneider's contribution, let me indicate clearly that this chapter is filled with interesting findings, interpretations, and challenges to conventional wisdom. The authors are no doubt correct in their depiction of the belief systems of most researchers in the area of memory development: There certainly is a general presumption of a gradual development of memory skill. Sodian and Schneider are also correct in indicating that this viewpoint is based on cross-sectional data that are inappropriate for making claims about developmental change. Most interestingly, the authors point out that this view may very well be wrong, and they make us examine anew our assumptions about factors that are associated with children's memory development.

Overview of Findings. Because it is always a bit disconcerting to feel that one has been sold a bill of goods, it is essential to examine Sodian and Schneider's claim very seriously. What, then, have they found? First, their group data are quite consistent with what we know from the cross-sectional literature. Thus, for example, with increases in age, there are corresponding increases in remembering, in strategy use, and in strategic effectiveness. Second, the longitudinal data are surprisingly inconsistent with expectations in that there is little stability over time in strategy use; that is, the ordinal positioning of the children in terms of strategy utilization changes dramatically across the different assessment points.

In a sense, the basic replication of the key findings of the cross-sectional literature in the LOGIC project provides a vantage point for examining the implications of the corresponding inconsistency of the longitudinal data. In this regard, Sodian and Schneider point out that strategy use may account for developmental change in children's performance during the course of the elementary school years, but not before school entry. And most interestingly, Sodian and Schneider report that there are different subgroups of participants who show quite different developmental trajectories in terms of strategy emergence, utilization, and maintenance – a finding that is of considerable importance in its own right as it parallels other demonstrations of alternative pathways in development (Bronfenbrenner 1979; Cairns, Elder, and Costello 1996; Morrison, Ornstein, and Hardway 1995; Quinton, Pickles, Maughan, and Rutter 1993).

Evaluation. How shall we assess these very interesting and potentially important findings? Are these data sufficient to overturn the generally held set of beliefs about the development of memory? Have those of us who work in the area of children's memory really bought into a naive view about the gradual nature of the development of strategic competence? I attempt to answer these questions in this section, all the while trying not to be too defensive about my own preference for the prevailing position. In doing so, however, I must point out that there are at least two distinct ways in which researchers think about the gradual development of mnemonic strategies. In this regard, I suggest that Sodian and Schneider have only addressed one of these senses of gradual development and that questions can be raised about their data.

To begin, Sodian and Schneider call our attention to the lack of consistency over time in the use of a type of clustering-at-input strategy. Thus, they report that the ranking of children's clustering at one age is not strongly predictive of their ranking at a later age. Such consistency would, of course, be predicted, given a view that gradual strategic development underlies the age-related increases in clustering that are reported. However, there is an alternate conceptualization of strategy development, one not dealt with by Sodian and Schneider. For example, my own view of strategy development (see Folds, Footo, Guttentag, and Ornstein 1990; Ornstein et al. 1988), which is based on a consideration of various "supports" for information processing, suggests that one would find evidence for children's initial strategy deployment in highly salient and supportive contexts and then observe transfer or generalization to less salient settings, and so forth. Admittedly, this conceptualization is based mostly on cross-sectional evidence, although we (Guttentag, Ornstein, and Siemens 1987) have presented short-term longitudinal data that are at least consistent with it. Nonetheless, I do not think that Sodian and Schneider's arguments are relevant to this view of gradual development.

Now, turning to the conceptualization of gradual development that is addressed by Sodian and Schneider, how strong are their data? It seems to me that a great deal of the argument hinges on their ability to make accurate diagnoses of the children's skills at different age levels (see Flavell 1985; Ornstein et al. 1988). More specifically, the key issue concerns the extent to which Sodian and Schneider are able to assess the children's tendencies to behave in a strategic manner in the service of a memory goal. With this in mind, I wish to raise (as a devil's advocate) a number of points.

Emphasis on a Single Strategy. Although I know that a number of strategies were measured in the LOGIC study, Sodian and Schneider clearly focus here on a single type of strategy in the context of a sort–recall task. Assuming that we are comfortable with their findings, we nonetheless need to ask about the extent to which the clustering technique is representative of other strategies in other situations. Moreover, even with regard to the chosen clustering-at-input strategy, Sodian and Schneider adopt a standard approach to measurement that may not be optimally sensitive to developmental changes in the component features of strategy deployment.

As I see it, Sodian and Schneider's treatment of age-related changes in strategy implementation would be enhanced if their assessment of clustering were expanded to include measures of (a) the processes involved in making the basic decision to use a strategy in the first place, (b) the criteria used to evaluate the effectiveness of a selected strategy, and (c) the procedures involved in modifying the chosen strategy as a result of this evaluative process. Even with this more complex view of strategies, it is also important to ask whether it makes sense to focus on a single strategy (largely in terms of whether it is used) when there is convincing evidence to indicate that much of strategy use involves a type of competition between different techniques (e.g., Siegler 1995).

"Constancy" in Strategic Deployment. Although Sodian and Schneider raise questions about stability in the rank ordering of children's strategic efforts over time, they do not pose a rather basic question about developmental changes in clustering: Is a given "strategy" the same thing at one age as it is at another? Clustering at input is being measured here by using objects with younger children and pictures with older children. In and of itself, this discontinuity raises some interpretive difficulties; for example, objects and pictures may differ in the extent to which they elicit strategy-like behavior, even without the intent to remember. However, even with identical materials, a given clustering score can arise from a variety of information-processing operations, some of which are decidedly nonstrategic (Bjorklund 1985; Lange 1978).

Sodian and Schneider are clearly aware of this interpretive dilemma, and they address it to some extent in their analyses of subgroups on the basis of contrasting metamemory scores and in terms of their discussion of "knowledge." Nonetheless, because statements about the stability (or lack thereof) of strategy usage across age require the assumption that strategy scores are measuring the same thing at different ages, the issue must be dealt with more systematically here. Thus, when Sodian and Schneider present data about the acquisition and loss of a clustering strategy among both younger and older children, can we (or they) be sure that they are talking about the same thing?

Context Specificity. Continuing with this underlying theme of diagnosis, one can ask if Sodian and Schneider (or anyone else, for that matter) can accurately diagnose a child's level of sophistication with regard to strategy use on the basis of one trial of a sort–recall task? On the basis of what is known about variability in strategic deployment across different contexts, I suggest that this cannot be done in an adequate fashion. Indeed, a great deal of evidence suggests that the context of assessments (including props or supports) exerts a strong influence on children's performance and hence the diagnostic conclusions that we can reach. Thus, two children who are alike in one context may be quite different in others, and the same child may appear to be more or less sophisticated, and so forth, depending on the setting in which an evaluation is conducted. Many contrasting perspectives, ranging from the Vygotskyian to that of information processing, focus on these issues of context specificity (see Cox, Ornstein, and Valsiner 1991; Folds et al. 1990; Ornstein et al. 1988).

To illustrate, consider Guttentag et al.'s (1987) investigation of contextual variation in young children's rehearsal. Consistent with the bulk of the literature (e.g., Ornstein and Naus 1978; Schneider and Pressley 1989), Guttentag and colleagues found that when to-be-remembered items were presented in a traditional manner, removing each word as it was presented, third-grade children tended to rehearse "passively" by repeating a single word over and over again. However, when a more supportive assessment context was established by keeping each word visible after its initial presentation, the third graders differed considerably in their rehearsal styles. Although some children continued to rehearse in a passive manner, others tended to rehearse more "actively" by including several different words in their rehearsal when they had sustained visual access to the materials. Interestingly, consistent with a zone-of-proximal-development analysis, the children's performance under the supportive assessment condition, and not their rehearsal under the traditional mode of presentation, predicted their strategic performance the next year (i.e., when they were fourth graders) under the standard conditions of presentation. Thus, an orderly developmental progression in strategy use was observed by Guttentag and colleagues, in contrast to what would be expected on the basis of Sodian and Schneider's discussion of their data.

Design Issue: Implications for Follow-Up Work. As indicated earlier, with the wisdom of hindsight it is possible to suggest design changes that would have given Sodian and Schneider greater leverage on the issues under investigation. Such wisdom, particularly when based in part on demonstrations of context specificity, leads me to the view that it would have been useful to have assessed the children under conditions that varied in terms of their information-processing supports. With such a diagnostic strategy, Sodian and Schneider might have assigned their participants more precisely to contrasting subgroups that differed in terms of strategy usage. These groups, moreover, might show different, systematic developmental trajectories.

As also indicated earlier, it seems clear that more frequent observation and assessment of the children would have been highly desirable. Although assessments every 2 years provide an overview of developmental change, a finer grained schedule of observation is necessary if there is to be a real look at the emergence and consolidation of cognitive skill. Such assessments between the ages of 4 and 6 years would be particularly important, as the period of transition to formal schooling is one in which memory skills undergo rapid change. For example, Baker-Ward, Ornstein, and Holden (1984) have shown that strategies that are ineffective at age 4 may facilitate recall at age 6, and Morrison, Smith, and Dow-Ehrensberger (1995) have found that experience in first grade (but not kindergarten) classrooms may be associated with the emergence of mnemonic skills. Thus, more detailed observation during this transition period would certainly be important, but this is not to suggest that a comparable analysis of older children's performance would not also be important to undertake. Indeed, the middle elementary school years are clearly very important ones in terms of the consolidation and extension of children's deliberate skills for remembering (see, for example, Ornstein et al. 1988; Schneider and Pressley 1989). Moreover, Sodian and Schneider's own data suggest that memory performance after 8 years of age may be increasingly driven by the use of mnemonic techniques.

In addition, I hope that follow-up studies would focus more on the forces that drive development. Of course, Sodian and Schneider do emphasize factors that they feel may underlie the children's performance, as, for example, in their discussion of the linkage between metamemory and strategy usage. This position, however was not overwhelmingly supported by the data, particular within the preschool years. However, even if it had been supported, we can ask about the forces that influence the development of strategies and metamnemonic understanding. In this regard, school observations would be rather useful, as the classroom context seems likely to play an extensive role in the development of skilled remembering, and there may very well be classroom data available on the children in the LOGIC sample that could contribute to an understanding of memory development.

Weber and Strube

In contrast to Sodian and Schneider's exploration of memory strategies, Weber and Strube focus on a longitudinal analysis of children's autobiographical memory for both personally experienced and witnessed events, all under conditions in which the "stimulus" experiences can be specified in detail. As Weber and Strube present evidence concerning children's skills in remembering complex experiences that were initially encoded without a deliberate attempt to remember, their chapter complements that of Sodian and Schneider very nicely. Moreover, the longitudinal data set that underlies Weber and Strube's report is of clear relevance for discussions of the development of long-term retention, as well as for analyses of children's abilities to provide accurate testimony in legal settings.

Overview of Findings. In many ways, Weber and Strube break new ground by providing us with a longitudinal analysis of autobiographical memory for different types of integrated events, along with a quite useful taxonomy for organizing our thinking about various forms of memory. As I see it, the contrast between events in which children are participants and those in which they are observers is very important in both theoretical and applied terms, as is Weber and Strube's demonstration that autobiographical memory for these two types of experiences seems to be comparable and consistent with basic principles of memory.

Weber and Strube also seek to relate autobiographical memory to other indices of cognitive functioning, and they report correlations that would be expected between their recall measures and the children's intelligence and memory for stories. It is particularly interesting, moreover, that the nature of the correlations among the various autobiographical measures remains essentially unchanged when the contributions of intelligence and story memory are controlled statistically. In addition, Weber and Strube present us with the beginnings of a serious examination of interaction between aspects of children's personality and their ability recall (or at least to report) their experiences. In this regard, the demonstration that aggressive children may remember the aggressive-centered experiences better than shy children is particularly promising. Finally, Weber and Strube's report of minimal (or no) age differences in recall of the events that they have programmed is interesting, but it is also unexpected and possibly problematic, as is discussed later.

Evaluation. A number of issues arise from a consideration of Weber and Strube's interesting findings, some of which involve questions about the level of analysis that has been applied to the data. These questions cannot be resolved, however, without a greater understanding of the specifics of the events that were being remembered and the interview protocols that were utilized. Accordingly, I first raise the procedural matters and then turn to the analytic questions, as well as some issues concerning the assessment of developmental change in autobiographical memory. Then I discuss a few more general issues.

The Basic Procedures. For researchers to appreciate fully the contribution of the LOGIC data to our understanding of the development of autobiographical memory, it is essential to be provided with additional procedural information. Although Weber and Strube constructed a set of interesting stimulus experiences for the children, we really know very little about the content, complexity, and organization of these to-be-remembered events. Unfortunately, without this information, I feel that it is not only difficult to understand completely the data that they present but that it is also impossible to relate the findings to others that are appearing in the rapidly developing literature on children's autobiographical memory. Thus, additional information concerning the events and their component features would be very helpful, as would some information concerning the children's understanding of these various experiences.

A parallel set of issues arises when we consider the interview protocols that were used in the recognition and recall tasks. It is important that Weber and Strube specify more precisely their procedures for interviewing the children and to provide some justification for using a cued-recall paradigm in the early waves and a free-recall procedure when the children were older. Not only do the differences between the procedures need to be specified precisely, but we need to be convinced that variations across the protocols do not interfere with our ability to make informed comparisons about developmental changes (or lack thereof) in remembering. Moreover, given that young children, in general, provide relatively little information in response to open-ended questions, most researchers construct interview protocols that involve some mixture of general and more specific probes. Assuming that Weber and Strube did so as well, it is essential to be provided with the details of the movement between the general and specific questions and, in fact, of the selection of the probes, as well as the lures that were used in the recognition tasks. Concerning the probes, we can ask if the specific questions chosen reflect Weber and Strube's analysis of the specific features or components of the to-be-remembered events.

A related issue concerns the errors that are often made in response to specific types of questions. Indeed, because of young children's reliance on yes-no forms of questioning (with the probability of a correct response being .5), it becomes essential to include in any interview protocol a number of questions about activities that had not been included in the to-be-remembered events. Only by knowing how well children are able to say no to questions about things that did not happen are we able to calibrate our understanding of their yes responses to things that did take place.

Assessing Developmental Change. A number of issues arise as we consider Weber and Strube's report of essentially no age differences in the children's reports of their experiences. Because remembering typically increases with age, it is especially important to examine situations in which this pattern is not obtained. In this regard, I wish to raise several questions that relate to diagnosis of children's mnemonic competence.

1. *How did the children respond to various types of questions?* As suggested earlier, young children typically provide relatively little information in response to open-ended questions, and interviewers have to rely considerably on specific (e.g., yes-no) types of questions. Assuming that Weber and Strube posed both types of questions in their memory assessments, it becomes very important to break the data down in terms of the children's responses to these different types of probes. As is the case in our exploration of memory for various types of medical experiences (e.g., Baker-Ward, Gordon, Ornstein, Larus, and Clubb 1993; Ornstein 1995), it may turn out that age differences are rather substantial when responses to open-ended questions are tallied but are minimized when overall recall is considered, reflecting younger children's effective use of specific probes. However, as implied earlier, performance with yes-no types of questions needs to be evaluated carefully in the context of children's responses to parallel questions about activities that were not included in the to-be-remembered events. Here, too, Weber and Strube may find that there are age differences in the children's abilities to reject (i.e., say no to) what are basically lure items. Indeed, something like this is seen in their own recognition data, with chancelike performance being observed in the earlier waves.

2. *When was the children's memory assessed?* As Weber and Strube indicate, the delay intervals prior to their memory assessments varied considerably across both events and waves of the LOGIC study, but in no case was memory evaluated within a month of the experience that was being remembered. As they point out, by assessing memory at these delays, the children's performance is captured after the initial period of rapid forgetting has taken place. However, by following this schedule, Weber and Strube may be missing out on another opportunity to obtain age differences in remembering. Indeed, this is likely to have been the case because in addition to their dependence on specific forms of questions, young children typically show more rapid forgetting than older children (Ornstein, Larus, and Clubb 1991).

3. *What are the consequences of selecting different events at the different waves?* Another difficulty that we confront in attempting to interpret the data presented by Weber and Strube stems from the differences in the events that were being remembered across the waves of the study. In a sense, we are presented with an Age × Materials type of confounding that puts us in the position of having to compare, for example, the children's memory for a visit of Santa Claus to the kindergarten when they were quite young (i.e., at Wave 1) with their recall of the details of movies when they were older (i.e., at Waves 5, 7, and 8). Without convincing evidence that the events were of comparable structure, meaningfulness, and salience for the children as they were being experienced, problems arise in the interpretation of age differences in performance (or their absence, as in the present study). Consider, for example, the children's understanding of the events. Because memory is affected seriously by comprehension of the to-be-remembered experiences (Ornstein, Shapiro, Clubb, Follmer, and Baker-Ward 1997), failure to obtain an age-related improvement in remembering might reflect the children's better understanding of the events used in the early, as opposed to the later, waves.

4. *What can the intercorrelations among the various recall measures tell us?* Even with the interpretive problems discussed earlier, it seems possible that closer attention to

the intercorrelations among the measures of the children's performance on the various tasks at the different waves should facilitate our understanding of developmental change. Indeed, additional discussion of the pattern of intercorrelations presented in Weber and Strube's Tables 4 and 5 may give us greater insight into what is and is not changing with age. How, for example, should we think about the fact that recall of the first visit to the Max Planck Institute at Wave 1 was not correlated with memory for the details of the crossing-the-street drill with a policeman at wave 2, when recall of the visit at Wave 2 was correlated with recall of the street drill at both Waves 2 and 3? Would more detailed analyses of these correlations (and others that were not shown in Tables 4 and 5) lead to additional understanding of the nature of autobiographical memory and its development?

The Role of Individual-Difference Variables. In addition to studying memory for the details of a variety of events, Weber and Strube also explore the potential impact of several individual-difference variables (e.g., intelligence, short-term memory capacity, and personality) on the children's autobiographical memory. As I see it, this research strategy is quite promising, and not just because my colleagues and I have tried it in our efforts to relate aspects of children's temperament to their memory performance (see, for example, Merritt, Ornstein, and Spicker 1994). Rather, the approach seems to me to make sense because of its potential for letting us learn something fundamental about the storage and retrieval of information. Thus, for example, the interesting difference that Weber and Strube report in the recall patterns of aggressive and nonaggressive children may pave the way for an understanding of those aspects of the self that affect attentional deployment and encoding, on the one hand, and retrieval (or at least reporting), on the other hand.

Analyses of this sort, in turn, may facilitate the development of serious models of children's changing cognitive skills that can speak to the processes that underlie the establishment and subsequent use of event representations. For me, the key questions for these models are those concerning how factors such as personality and prior knowledge work together to affect expectation and attentional deployment at input, as well as subsequent retrieval and reporting. That is, how do these factors combine to influence individual children's unique construals of seemingly standardized events? How do they affect both the retrieval and the reporting of information in the interview context? By selecting individual-difference variables that are thought to influence the flow of information within the memory system, Weber and Strube are bringing us one step closer to the establishment of these more precise models.

Design Issues: Implications for Follow-Up Work. Where do we go from here? Many of the concerns that I have expressed here can be addressed readily without additional data collection. Indeed, Weber and Strube can easily (a) provide greater detail about their autobiographical memory assessments and (b) carry out additional analyses on the underlying data sets (e.g., recall as a function of specificity of the recall probe). In addition, it would be highly desirable to work toward an integration of Weber and Strube's data sets with those of Sodian and Schneider, so as to present a composite picture of the children's changing deliberate and autobiographical memory skills.

As was the case with the Sodian and Schneider study, however, many of the issues raised here can only be addressed through follow-up research. Indeed, on the basis of the findings of numerous studies that have been reported since the LOGIC project was launched, the wisdom of hindsight indicates clearly that more focused longitudinal studies of autobiographical memory need to be undertaken. In particular, I would like to see longitudinal studies initiated in which careful consideration is applied to the selection of contrasting types of to-be-remembered experiences, combined with detailed probing of the children's memory, both immediately after event presentation and at various delays. Moreover, consistent with my comments on Sodian and Schneider's work, a greater density of longitudinal observation would be highly desirable, as it would enable increased precision in the description of children's autobiographical memory.

General Comments

The chapters by Sodian and Schneider and by Weber and Strube raise many questions, some of which can be addressed either through the provision of procedural information or by means of additional analyses of the extant data sets. Other questions, in contrast, require follow-up studies and additional efforts at data collection. The issues raised here, however, should not in any way diminish the accomplishments of this creative group of researchers. As indicated at the outset, the projects grouped together under the banner of the LOGIC study are unique and of immense importance to the developmental literature. Because of the significance of the present findings and the potential for follow-up studies that will inform our understanding of memory and cognitive development, as well as the unparalleled across-domain integration that can result from systematic analyses of the LOGIC databases, I have no doubt that the impact of this work will be felt for many years to come.

References

Baker-Ward, L., Gordon, B. N., Ornstein, P. A., Larus, D. M., & Clubb, P. A. (1993). Young children's long-term retention of a pediatric examination. *Child Development, 64*, 1519–1533.
Baker-Ward, L., Ornstein, P. A., & Holden, D. J. (1984). The expression of memorization in early childhood. *Journal of Experimental Child Psychology, 37*, 555–575.
Bjorklund, D. F. (1985). The role of conceptual knowledge in the development of organization in children's memory. In C. J. Brainerd & M. Pressley (Eds.), *Basic Processes in memory development: Progress in cognitive development research* (pp. 103–142). New York: Springer-Verlag.
Bronfenbrenner, U. (1979). *The ecology of human development: Experiments by nature and design.* Cambridge, MA: Harvard University Press.
Cairns, R. B., Elder, G. H., Jr., & Costello, E. J. (Eds.). (1996). *Developmental science.* New York: Cambridge University Press.
Cox, B., Ornstein, P. A., & Valsiner, J. (1991). The role of internalization in the transfer in mnemonic strategies. In L. Oppenheimer & J. Valsiner (Eds.), *The origins of action: International perspectives* (pp. 101–131). New York: Springer-Verlag.
Flavell, J. H. (1985). *Cognitive development.* Englewood Cliffs, NJ: Prentice Hall.

Folds, T. H., Footo, M., Guttentag, R. E., & Ornstein, P. A. (1990). When children mean to remember: Issues of context specificity, strategy effectiveness, and intentionality in the development of memory. In D. F. Bjorklund (Ed.), *Children's strategies* (pp. 67–91). Hillsdale, NJ: Erlbaum.

Guttentag, R. E., Ornstein, P. A., & Siemens, L. (1987). Spontaneous rehearsal: Transitions in strategy acquisition. *Cognitive Development, 2,* 307–326.

Lange, G. (1978). Organization-related processes in children's recall. In P. A. Ornstein (Ed.), *Memory development in children* (pp. 101–128). Hillsdale, NJ: Erlbaum.

Merritt, K. A., Ornstein, P. A., & Spicker, B. (1994). Children's memory of a salient medical procedure: Implications for testimony. *Pediatrics, 94,* 17–23.

Morrison, F. J., Ornstein, P. A., & Hardway, C. (1995, November). *"Potchkeying" with pathways.* Paper presented at the annual meeting of the Psychonomic Society, Los Angeles.

Morrison, F. J., Smith, L., & Dow-Ehrensberger, M. (1995). Education and cognitive development: A natural experiment. *Developmental Psychology, 31,* 789–799.

Ornstein, P. A. (1995). Children's long-term retention of salient personal experiences. *Journal of Traumatic Stress, 8,* 581–605.

Ornstein, P. A., Baker-Ward, L., & Naus, M. J. (1988). The development of mnemonic skill. In F. E. Weinert & M. Perlmutter (Eds.), *Memory development: Universal changes and individual differences* (pp. 31–50). Hillsdale, NJ: Erlbaum.

Ornstein, P. A., Larus, D. M., & Clubb, P. A. (1991). Understanding children's testimony: Implications of research on the development of memory. In R. Vasta (Ed.), *Annals of child development* (Vol. 8, pp. 145–176). London: Jessica Kingsley.

Ornstein, P. A., & Naus, M. J. (1978). Rehearsal processes in children's memory. In P. A. Ornstein (Ed.), *Memory development in children* (pp. 69–99). Hillsdale, NJ: Erlbaum.

Ornstein, P. A., Shapiro, L. R., Clubb, P. A., Follmer, A., & Baker-Ward, L. (1997). The influence of prior knowledge on children's memory for salient medical experiences. In N. Stein, P. A. Ornstein, B. Tversky, & C. J. Brainerd (Eds.), *Memory for everyday and emotional events* (pp. 83–111). Hillsdale, NJ: Erlbaum.

Quinton, D., Pickles, A., Maughan, B., & Rutter, M. (1993). Partners, peers, and pathways: Assortative pairing and continuities in conduct disorder. *Development and Psychopathology, 5,* 763–783.

Schneider, W., & Pressley, M. (1989). *Memory development between 2 and 20.* New York: Springer-Verlag.

Siegler, R. S. (1995). Children's thinking: How does change occur? In F. E. Weinert & W. Schneider (Eds.), *Memory performance and competence: Issues in growth and development.* Hillsdale, NJ: Erlbaum.

Siegler, R. S., & Crowley, K. (1991). The microgenetic method: A direct means for studying cognitive development. *American Psychologist, 46,* 606–620.

6 Development of Memory for Texts

Monika Knopf

There is no doubt that the conceptualization of children's memory has changed markedly in the last decade, mostly because of insights from the study of children's memory for everyday events with everyday memory materials (e.g., Baker-Ward, Ornstein, and Gordon 1993; Fivush and Hudson 1990). Although the available research on children's memory indicates that performance can be much better when learning and remembering are embedded in real-world settings and in ecologically valid tasks, the mechanisms that underlie the development of memory for real-world events are still unknown. How does memory develop when familiar events are given as memory materials? How large and how stable are interindividual differences in memory performance when everyday memory tasks are used? To what extent is everyday memory development linked to the development of other memory abilities? What is the role of more general cognitive abilities (e.g., intelligence) for memory development?

In this chapter, we focus on these issues by using texts as memory materials. In our view, the use of more natural memory material is especially important when young children's memory is studied, not only to demonstrate early memory competence but to maximize reliability of memory measurement. We hypothesize that reliability of memory measurement in young children will increase the more familiar the memory material and the memory task are.

Texts, specifically narratives about naturally occurring events, are considered to represent a type of memory material that is more familiar to children than the episodic memory materials typically used in current developmental psychology (i.e., sort–recall tasks, word span tasks, and sentence tasks): Text comprehension and text recall are familiar activities for kindergardeners and school-aged children. In addition, the knowledge structures such as scripts, schemata, and story grammars available to young children help in comprehending and recalling event-related stories (Bauer and Mandler 1990; Farrar and Goodman 1990; Kintsch 1990; Kintsch et al. 1993; Nelson 1986).

Method

Four narratives were constructed as memory materials. These four narratives were presented repeatedly across the different waves with subsequent memory tests to assess memory development. The number of texts presented in each wave varied between one and three texts. Each text was told to the children twice, and then the children were asked to retell each story as accurately as possible. The general memory performance level, assessed in each wave, was the relative overall number of text propositions recalled.

Three of the texts were similar to memory materials used in other studies that assessed the role of scripted knowledge for text recall in young children (Fivush and Slackman 1986; Hudson and Nelson 1983). These three stories, the "birthday party" story, the "playing in the afternoon" story, and the "removal" story, had familiar event sequences in their canonical or usual order. In addition, these three stories were similar in a number of features: The number of propositions (72–74), the number of sentences (15), and the number of events were kept constant. These three texts were originally designed to assess the role of scripted knowledge for text recall in young children. However, in this chapter we do not comment on this specific aspect of the study (Knopf and Waldmann 1991).

The fourth narrative ("Mauerburg" story) described the events that happened to a boy who walked through a fictitious town (Mauerburg), where he was shopping for his grandmother, and we replaced the first three texts when they became too easy for the school-aged children. The Mauerburg story comprised mostly familiar events but was much longer (362 propositions and 31 sentences) than the earlier three texts.

As shown in Figure 1, the texts were presented repeatedly in different combinations in Waves 1 through 9 of LOGIC to assess free-recall memory performance. The three shorter texts (the birthday party story, the playing in the afternoon story, and the removal story) were presented in Waves 1 through 5, and the Mauerburg story was presented in Waves 6, 7, and 9. Thus, except for Wave 8, free-recall memory performance for texts was assessed every year. Because different combinations of texts that varied in length and content were used in different waves, relative free-recall scores were used as memory indicators. Thus, the developmental function constructed on the basis of these scores is actually based on different narratives.

Results

The Developmental Function for Free-Recall Memory Performance

The developmental function showing age-related increase in memory performance level for the entire LOGIC sample is shown in Figures 2a and 2b.[1] As can be seen from Figure 2a, 4-year-olds recalled 18% of the propositions of the texts. With increasing

---

[1] The number of children in the longitudinal study varied between $n = 152$ (for the birthday party story at Wave 1) and $n = 212$ (for the birthday party story at Wave 2).

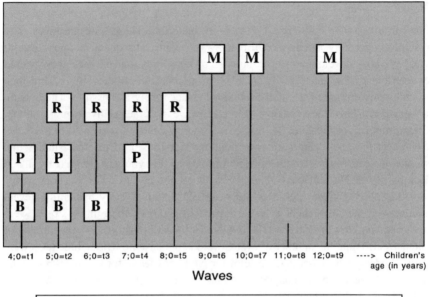

4;0=t1   5;0=t2   6;0=t3   7;0=t4   8;0=t5   9;0=t6   10;0=t7   11;0=t8   12;0=t9   ----> Children's
                                                                                               age (in years)
Waves

Note.   B = "Birthday party" story   R = "Removal" story
        P = "Playing in the afternoon" story M = "Mauerburg" story

Figure 1. Time schedule of assessments.

age, the average free-recall performance level increased steadily. In Wave 5 the average 8-year-old child recalled about 50% of the text propositions.

When the much longer Mauerburg story was given in Wave 6 for the first time, the average free-recall performance of the 9-year-old child again was 18% of the propositions of the Mauerburg text and increased steadily up to 30% (Wave 9).

Figure 2b shows the developmental function for free-recall memory performance that was constructed on the basis of these findings. Because the three easier texts and the Mauerburg story were never presented simultaneously, we had to estimate the difficulty level of the different stories by extrapolation. We estimated the mean increase in free-recall performance per year on the basis of the three easier texts. Because the empirical value of 18% remembered propositions in Wave 6 is 39% below the estimated values for the easier texts, a value of 0.39 was added to the mean empirical values of the Mauerburg story in Waves 6, 7, and 9 to equate for text difficulty.

It can be seen from these two figures that there is neither an indication of a specific increase in the rate of development nor any delay in developmental rate. Thus, at the group level, the development of free-recall memory performance was a continuous function with a steady increase in performance level. In addition, performance variation remained constant: The standard deviations were close to $SD = .10$ across the entire age range, indicating that individual differences in timing of development seem to be unimportant. All together, the continuous increase in memory performance level

Average Free Recall Performance

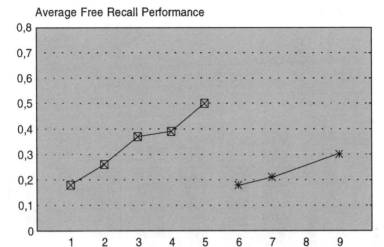

Note. In Waves 1 to 5 the "birthday party" story, the "playing in the afternoon" story, and the "removal" story were presented to assess memory development; in Waves 6 to 9 the "Mauerburg" story was presented.

Average Free Recall Performance

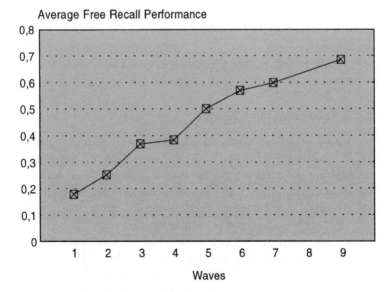

Note. In Waves 6, 7, and 9 a value of 0.39 was added to the empirical mean values; this value was computed by extrapolation.

Figure 2. (a) Development of free-recall performance. (b) The developmental function for free-recall performance.

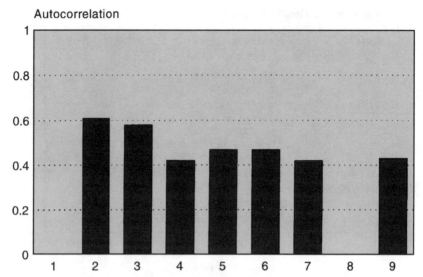

Figure 3. Autocorrelations among free-recall performance in Wave 1 and Waves 2 to 9.

and the constant individual variation level lead us to believe that age-related changes in free-recall performance are quantitative rather than qualitative in nature.

The Stability of Interindividual Differences Across Age

The second analysis focused on interindividual differences in the development of free-recall memory performance and the stability of interindividual differences across age. The mean values do not tell us whether the observed age-related memory performance level improvement is uniform across children or whether there are significant interindividual differences in developmental change across age. To answer this question, we computed autocorrelations for free-recall memory performances.

In Figure 3, autocorrelations between individual free-recall memory performance in different waves are displayed. As Figure 3 indicates, the stability of individual performance levels is statistically significant and substantial. In fact, the autocorrelation for free-recall memory performance of 4- and 5-year-olds (Waves 1 to 2) is $r = .61$. The autocorrelation for free-recall memory performance across Wave 1 and Wave 3 is still close to $r = .60$. The high stability of individual performance level seen in preschool is somewhat surprising, considering the fact that different texts were presented in the different waves.

This finding suggests that the reliability of memory testing is, in fact, high, even in 4-year-old children. This finding supports our assumption that familiarity of memory

Autocorrelation

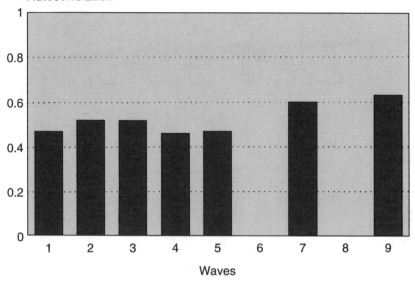

Waves

Note. p < .001 for all correlations

Figure 4. Autocorrelations among free-recall performance in Wave 6 and Waves 1 to 9.

material and memory task is a good precondition for a reliable memory assessment in young children.

As can be expected, the stability of interindividual differences decreased with time. However, the autocorrelation of free-recall scores between Wave 1 and Wave 9, which is $r = .43$, is still statistically significant and substantial.

Taken together, the data show that interindividual differences in 4-year-olds in free-recall memory performance are highly stable over time. This finding demonstrates that the normative developmental function is based on a rather stable individual change pattern. The level of stability of interindividual differences in free-recall memory performance is similar to what traditionally has been found for measures of general intelligence (McCall, 1990; for LOGIC, see Schneider and Weinert 1989) and significantly surpasses the individual stability levels found in LOGIC for other memory measures (e.g., Schneider and Sodian 1991).

There is another correspondence between these two abilities: The stability of each increases with increasing age. This is shown in the next figure. In Figure 4, autocorrelations between free-recall memory performance in Wave 6 and the other waves are depicted. As can be seen in this figure, the stability of free-recall memory performance between Wave 6 and Wave 9 is $r = .63$, whereas the stability of free-recall memory performance between Wave 1 and Wave 4 is lower at $r = .42$ (see Figure 3). The increase in the stability of interindividual differences may, of course, be partly due to the fact that the text material was identical in Waves 6 through 9, whereas it was not in earlier waves.

Table 1. *Intercorrelations of Children's Free-Recall Memory Performance in Various Narratives and Different Waves*

Wave	Birthday party, playing in the afternoon, and removal stories					Mauerburg story		
	Wave 1	Wave 2	Wave 3	Wave 4	Wave 5	Wave 6	Wave 7	Wave 9
Bartlett's fairytale (Wave 3)	.47**	.50**	.52**	.42**	.33**	.45**	.41**	.45**
Report about a soccer game (Wave 8)	.46**	.35**	.44**	.25*	.38**	.48**	.43**	.44**

$^*p < .001.$ $^{**}p < .0001.$

Text Memory as a General Faculty Versus Text Memory as a Set of Specific Abilities

Apart from the four texts described so far, two additional narratives were presented in LOGIC. One was the subtest text memory from a German standardized test assessing language development (Heidelberger Sprachentwicklungstest; Grimm and Schöler 1978, 1985). This additional text was used to assess text memory with a standardized test instrument. This text is a modified version of a fairy tale that was used by Bartlett (1932). It tells the story of a son who tries to hide from his father and is based on a specific construction principle. The successive events of this story are causally linked to each other (e.g., "The son changed into a peanut. The peanut was swallowed by a chicken. The chicken was eaten by a cat. The cat was eaten by a dog"). This narrative was presented in Wave 3, and free recall was assessed.

The second additional narrative, which was presented in Wave 8, was a report about a soccer game. This text was originally designed to explore the impact of domain-specific knowledge on the comprehension and recall of text materials. Because soccer is one of the most popular sports in Germany, it is possible to identify soccer experts even among young children. Our story was adopted from Schneider, Körkel, and Weinert (1989), and free recall of the text was used as a general verbal memory indicator.

These additional narratives differed from the other LOGIC stories with respect to text structure as well as content. This allows us to test whether text recall is a homogeneous faculty or rather a set of specific abilities by relating free-recall memory across the different texts.

In Table 1, intercorrelations among free-recall performances for the various texts at different age levels are given. As is shown, the correlations between free-recall memory performances for the four LOGIC texts and the two additional texts are highly significant and substantial, although there are clear differences among the six different narratives with respect to their content, their length, and difficulty in their structure.

Table 2. *Memory Performance Level (as a Percentage) as a Function of Age and Sex*

Age (in years)	Female	Male	t	df	p
4	19	18	−.76	135	ns
5	27	25	−.71	182	ns
6	37	36	−.46	199	ns
7	40	39	−.41	200	ns
8	50	49	−.48	195	ns
9	19	17	−1.04	188	ns
10	21	21	−.37	183	ns
12	31	29	−.85	185	ns

The size of the correlations between the different free-recall memory performances is highly similar across the total age range. This finding demonstrates that the ability to learn and recall narratives seems to be a rather global faculty and not a set of specific abilities. This holds true for the total age range tested.

Sources of Interindividual Differences in Free-Recall Memory Performance

In the next step of analysis we looked at sources of interindividual differences in free-recall memory performance. A series of hypotheses currently discussed in the literature was tested.

Interindividual Differences in Memory Development as a Function of Sex. A rather traditional hypothesis states that there are systematic sex differences in cognitive functioning, such that females typically outperform males in verbal and linguistic functions from infancy through adulthood (Anastasi 1958). Despite the fact that recent reviews are rather cautious about the effect size (Halpern 1989; Hyde and Linn 1988; Maccoby and Jacklin 1974), there are a number of recent empirical studies dealing with this topic. The main goal of these investigations was to decide where possible sex differences come from, what the timing for the appearance and disappearance of these differences is, and which types of verbal ability show the most significant sex differences (e.g., Warrick and Naglieri 1993).

We used the LOGIC data to ask if there were sex differences in text recall favoring females, and if so, at what point in development such a sex difference might appear.

In Table 2, free-recall scores for the LOGIC texts are given as a function of age and sex. As can be seen from this table, there were no significant differences in free-recall memory performance as a function of sex at any age level. Obviously, the ability to recall texts does not vary as a function of sex.

Memory Development in Different Demographic Groups. A second fairly old hypothesis states that cognitive development varies as a function of the demographic

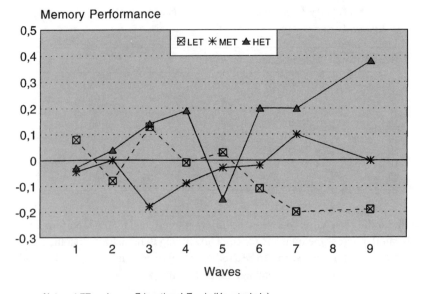

Figure 5. Children's development according to their mother's education.

background of a child. It is typically assumed that the environmental quality (e.g., availability of play and learning materials, academic stimulation, stimulation of communicative competence, variety in experience, parental involvement with child, and encouragement of maturity) is responsible for developmental differences (see for example, Bradley 1989).

To study whether the development of text recall varies as a function of the demographic status of the child, the impact of several indicators of the primary caregivers of the child was assessed (e.g., educational and professional status of the father and educational and professional status of the mother). The educational status of the mother proved to be the most significant demographic indicator for memory development of the child. We therefore concentrate on this indicator of family environment.

As is depicted in Figure 5, a three-stage scale was used to classify the LOGIC sample with respect to this variable. Our analyses were based on memory performance scores that were z standardized for each wave (z scores). Children of mothers who completed *Gymnasium* (preuniversity high school) had a higher developmental rate than all other children. Although no significant developmental differences between the three groups were found in Waves 1 to 7, children of mothers with a higher educational status outperformed the other children significantly in Wave 9 (one-way analysis of variance), $F(2, 172) = 3.76$, $p < .05$. A subsequent repeated-measures multivariate analysis of variance, comprising all waves simultaneously, additionally demonstrated that the developmental patterns of the three groups were different: approximately,

Table 3. *Intercorrelations Among Free-Recall Memory Performance and Verbal Intelligence*

Free-recall memory performance	Verbal intelligence
Wave 1[a]	.54*
Wave 2	.41
Wave 4	.36
Wave 6	.52
Wave 9	.45

[a]Only those waves are included in Table 3 in which free-recall memory performance and verbal intelligence were assessed simultaneously. *All correlations were significant ($p < .0001$).

$F(12, 232) = 1.97$, Wilks's test, $p < .05$. We conclude from these findings that the demographic status of the child is in fact a significant indicator for the development of memory ability.

Alternative explanations for this finding have to be ruled out in additional analyses. One can assume, for example, that children of well-educated mothers not only live in a more stimulating home environment but also differ with respect to school environment from children of the two other demographic groups. Our preliminary analyses show that aspects of the home environment and aspects of the school environment are important in the development of free-recall memory performance. Interindividual differences in memory performance already exist among 4-year-olds before they attend different educational tracks. Four-year-olds who will later (when they are 10 years old) be put on the higher educational track significantly outperform 4-year-olds who will later be on the lower educational track (free-recall performance: $M = 21.81$, $SD = 11.78$ for higher track; $M = 16.60$, $SD = 7.39$ for lower track), $t(98) = -2.58$, $p < .01$. These group differences in memory performance in preschool age become larger with increasing age (Wave 9–lower educational track: $M = 27.15$; $SD = 11.87$, higher educational track: $M = 33.36$, $SD = 7.81$), $t(160) = -4.45$, $p < .0001$.

The Impact of Verbal Intelligence on Memory for Texts. Learning and remembering texts not only require a good memory but also good verbal abilities. These abilities are necessary for text comprehension and for expressing the ideas kept in memory. It is thus plausible to assume that verbal intelligence is more closely linked to free-recall memory performance than nonverbal intelligence. Moreover, it is plausible to assume that the impact of both aspects of intelligence decreases with age because text difficulty also decreases.

Table 3 presents the intercorrelations of verbal intelligence and free-recall memory performance. Verbal intelligence in Waves 1 and 2 was measured with the Hannover–

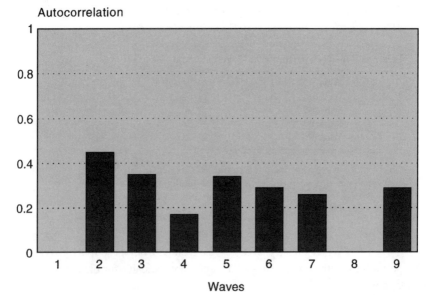

Figure 6. Partial correlation between free-recall memory performances in Wave 1 and Waves 2 to 9 controlling for verbal intelligence.

Wechsler–Intelligence Scale for Preschool Children (verbal sum score; Eggert 1978); in Waves 4, 6, and 9 it was measured with the Hamburg–Wechsler–Intelligence Scale for Children (verbal-IQ; Tewes 1983). As can be seen from Table 3, there are, in fact, strong relationships between free-recall memory performance measures and verbal intelligence measures that hold across the entire age range tested. Moreover, the correlation pattern varies as a function of text difficulty, insofar as the role of intelligence becomes less significant as the texts become easier. Although the impact of intelligence on memory performance decreased between Waves 1 and 4, the role of intelligence on memory performance increased in Wave 6 when the more difficult Mauerburg story was introduced.

Partialling out the impact of verbal intelligence resulted in a clear decrease in the autocorrelations for memory performances across different waves. This finding is depicted in Figure 6. However, the residual correlations were still statistically significant and substantial.

The intercorrelations among memory performance measures and nonverbal intelligence measures (Columbia Mental Maturity Scale, age deviation score; Burgemeister, Blum, and Lorge 1972) are shown in Table 4. These intercorrelations are, in fact, lower than those among free-recall memory performance and verbal intelligence measures. This finding supports the assumption that the role of nonverbal intelligence for free recall of texts is less important than the role of verbal intelligence. Moreover, as expected, the correlation coefficients decreased with increasing age of the children. In addition, the impact of nonverbal intelligence for free-recall memory performance varies as a function of text difficulty. Nonverbal intelligence

Table 4. *Intercorrelations Among Memory Performance Measures and Nonverbal Intelligence*

Memory performance indicator	Nonverbal intelligence		
	CMMS Wave 1	CMMS Wave 3	CMMS Wave 5
Wave 1	.26[*a]	.33**	.08
Wave 2	.30*	.25**	.13
Wave 3	.32**	.34[**a]	.20*
Wave 4	.36**	.32**	.09
Wave 5	.21*	.28**	.18[*a]
Wave 6	.24*	.26**	.19*
Wave 7	.24*	.34**	.23*
Wave 9	.31**	.31**	.25**

[a]Assessment of the two variables in the same wave. $^*p < .01$. $^{**}p < .001$.

played a role in free-recall memory performance for difficult texts even in school-aged children.

The Role of Working Memory. From an information-processing view, individual differences in free-recall memory performance are related to individual features of the information-processing system. One central aspect of the information-processing system is the amount of information encoded and retained in short-term memory and working memory (Baddeley 1986; Case 1985). Both these aspects of memory as well as their developmental change have been studied in LOGIC.

Short-term memory was assessed by using a word span test, which was adopted from Case et al. (1982). Ten different word sets that varied from three to seven items were created to assess short-term word span. Participants were asked to listen first to an entire tape-recorded set and then to recall the total set. The indicator of word span used in the following analysis was the longest set of words correctly recalled, regardless of word order.

The sentence span test was used to assess working memory capacity. In the sentence span test, adopted from Daneman and Blennerhassett (1984), children had to listen to a set of sentences read to them successively by the experimenter. At the end of a set, the children heard a tone that was a cue to recall, verbatim, each sentence in the set. The testing started with five, one-sentence sets, and if these were correct, the set size was progressively increased. Testing terminated when the child failed all five sets of a particular set size. To pass this test successfully, it is necessary to share short-term memory storage and processing capacity efficiently. This is based on a central assumption in memory theory that working memory's storage and processing functions compete for a shared limited capacity.

The sentence span task was first used in LOGIC in Wave 3. It was administered again in Waves 4, 5, and 7. The number of sentences correctly recalled across all difficulty levels was used as an indicator of working memory capacity.

Table 5. *Intercorrelations Among Two Different Memory Capacity Measures and Free-Recall Memory Performance*

Free-recall memory performance	Memory span	Working memory capacity
Wave 1	.24	
Wave 3	.27**	.33**
Wave 4		.30**
Wave 5	.23*	.27**
Wave 7		.38**

$*p < .01.$ $**p < .001.$

In Table 5, intercorrelations among free-recall memory performance scores and memory span, as well as working memory capacity measures, are given. As can be seen from this table, the findings confirm our expectation that memory capacity measures are closely linked to free-recall memory performance. In addition, these findings demonstrate that working memory capacity is more closely linked to free-recall memory performance than is short-term memory capacity. Moreover, the impact of memory capacity measures for free-recall memory performance is stable across age.

Is Verbal Memory a Homogenous Memory Ability?

As noted earlier, the close correlations between different text-related, free-recall memory performances suggest that memory for narratives is a rather homogeneous faculty. One may ask, then, whether there is a general verbal memory factor that incorporates all kinds of verbal memory skills or whether there are distinctive verbal memory subskills, and how verbal memory ability develops across age.

To address these questions, we included those five verbal memory variables in LOGIC that were assessed systematically and repeatedly across age (free recall of LOGIC texts, free recall of words in the sort–recall task, number of biographical items recalled, memory performance in the sentence span test, and memory related knowledge [metamemory]), as well as an indicator of verbal intelligence, in factor analyses. We used the data from Waves 1 to 3[2] for a first analysis, the data from Waves 4 to 6 for a second analysis, and the data from Waves 7 to 9 for a third analysis, to make sure that at least one assessment of each variable was available. The first analysis covers the preschool age, the second the beginning of elementary school (Grades 1–3), and the third the end of elementary school (Grades 4–6). Principal-component analyses showed that a single-factor model was not adequate. As Table 6 shows, two to three factors were involved in these different verbal memory performances.

The findings for the preschool children suggest three factors (eigenvalue > 1) or dimensions, explaining 67% of the variance. Factor 1 (eigenvalue = 1.71) seems to

---

[2] When more than one assessment for a variable was available, we picked assessments from the middle wave in the grouping; that is, from Waves 2, 5, and 8.

Table 6. *The Factorial Structure of Verbal Memory Across Age*

Variable	Waves 1–3 Factor			Waves 4–6 Factor		Waves 7–9 Factor		
	1	2	3	1	2	1	2	3
Free-recall texts	0.77	−0.44		0.67		0.68		
Free recall (sort–recall task)	0.51		−0.59	0.76		0.70		
Autobiographical memory (visit to the Institute event)	0.61		0.57	0.43				0.77
Sentence span		0.69		0.54	0.54	0.55		−0.54
Metamemory		0.42			0.72		0.84	
Verbal intelligence	0.52	−0.51	0.51	0.76		0.78		
Eigenvalue	1.71	1.20	1.08	2.54	1.13	2.17	1.18	0.99

Notes: Principal-components analysis was used. For each wave range, the overall explained variance is as follows: Waves–3, 67%; Waves 4–6, 61%; and Waves 7–9, 72%.

be a verbal memory factor because free recall of texts, free recall of words, and free recall of autobiographical events have the highest loadings on this factor, and verbal intelligence is closely linked to this factor. Factor 2 (eigenvalue = 1.20) seems to be a mixed factor comprising memory capacity as well as memory related knowledge. Factor 3 (eigenvalue = 1.08) is also a mixed factor that comprises memory-related knowledge and verbal intelligence.

In the second factor analysis for early school-aged children, only two factors were retained on the basis of the eigenvalue criterion (eigenvalue > 1), and 61% of the variance was explained by these two factors. This demonstrates that the different memory performances are more closely linked to each other at this age than at preschool ages. Similar to the first analysis, Factor 1 (eigenvalue = 2.54) represents a verbal memory factor because verbal memory performance scores from the different memory tasks load on this factor, and again similar to the analysis for preschool children, verbal intelligence was closely linked to this factor. Factor 2 (eigenvalue = 1.13) is a mixed factor comprising a metamemory indicator as well as a memory capacity measure.

The findings for the third factor analysis, covering the end of elementary school (Waves 7 to 9), supported three significant dimensions, explaining 72% of the variance. Similar to the two earlier analyses, Factor 1 represents a verbal memory factor (eigenvalue = 2.17). Factor 2 is a metamemory factor (eigenvalue = 1.18), and Factor 3 is an autobiographical memory factor (sightly below eigenvalue 1, eigenvalue = .99). Indeed, the three-factor solution for this third group not only explains a fair amount of performance variance of school-aged children but is also highly in accord with some recent theories of the structure of memory. Specifically, this finding supports the view that reflexive considerations about memory (metamemory), as well as autobiographical memory processes, have to be separated from episodic memory processes (free-recall memory performance in episodic memory tasks). According to this analysis, the memory performance across different episodic memory tasks, however, taps similar memory processes.

Discussion

This chapter has been concerned with the development of text recall in preschool and school-aged children by using narratives as memory material. Overall, the findings of the longitudinal study LOGIC show that free-recall performance develops steadily and continuously across the age range tested. Sudden increases or decreases in the developmental rate were not found: This large amount of continuity in memory development between preschool age and later childhood leads us to believe that the development of the ability to learn from texts is quantitative rather than qualitative in nature.

The overall result of a steady and smooth increase in free-recall memory performance is expressed in two ways: (a) steady improvement in mean performance level across the total age range, which demonstrates that the ability to learn and recall narratives improves significantly in preschool and school-aged children (thus, the present longitudinal results tracking developmental change confirm previous cross-sectional findings); (b) high level of stability in interindividual performance differences across the developmental period studied, demonstrating that the age-related increase in mean memory performance is based on stable interindividual differences. The level of stability in interindividual differences for free-recall memory performance significantly surpasses the level of interindividual stability of other memory variables tested in the LOGIC study (e.g., memory span, metamemory, and recall of clusterable objects; see Schneider and Sodian 1991).

We assume that we found high stability of early interindividual memory differences because we used more familiar memory tasks: Recent findings suggesting a lack of reliability in memory measurement in young children have been based on more unfamiliar, laboratory-based materials, which may have masked more stable performance.

Moreover, our findings suggest that the ability to recall narratives is a global faculty rather than a set of specific abilities: Interindividual performance differences in free-recall performance were relatively stable regardless of the content of the narrative, the text structure, or the length of the text. These results suggest that a more global ability develops in preschool that is used in acquiring and recalling narratives regardless of their content. How does this finding fit with recent studies that stress the role of content-specific knowledge for text comprehension and text recall? One common feature of the LOGIC texts was that the narratives were about familiar, well-known events. It is therefore quite likely that content-specific knowledge was available to all children and thus did not contribute to interindividual performance differences.

Though the ability to recall narratives appears to be rather homogeneous and global, this ability has to be differentiated from a general verbal memory ability. Our attempts to identify an even more global verbal ability that enabled children to acquire and recall verbal information successfully from the different types of verbal memory tasks used in LOGIC were not successful. Different cognitive abilities may be relevant for successfully acquiring and recalling verbal information from nontext verbal memory tasks.

On what factors, then, are interindividual differences based? In a series of analyses, we tested some hypotheses that have been proposed to explain interindividual differences in learning from texts. Correlational evidence supported the idea that interindividual differences in free-recall memory performance are closely related to verbal intelligence and working memory efficacy. The higher the verbal intelligence level and the better working memory efficacy of a child, the better the free-recall memory performance. The role of both aspects for memory performance was highly similar across the developmental period sampled.

References

Anastasi, A. (1958). *Differential psychology* (3rd ed.). New York: Macmillan.

Baddeley, A. (1986). *Working memory*. Oxford, England: Clarendon Press.

Baker-Ward, L., Ornstein, P. A., & Gordon, B. N. (1993). A tale of two settings: Young children's memory performance in the laboratory and the field. In G. M. Davies & R. H. Logie (Eds.), *Memory in everyday life* (pp. 13–41). Amsterdam: North-Holland.

Bartlett, F. C. (1932). *Remembering*. Cambridge, England: Cambridge University Press.

Bauer, P. J., & Mandler, J. M. (1990). Remembering what happened next: Very young children's recall of event sequences. In R. Fivush & J. A. Hudson (Eds.), *Knowing and remembering in young children* (pp. 9–29). Cambridge, England: Cambridge University Press.

Bradley, R. H. (1989). The use of the HOME inventory in longitudinal studies of child development. In M. H. Bornstein & N. A. Krasnegor (Eds.), *Stability and continuity in mental development* (pp. 191–215). Hillsdale, NJ: Erlbaum.

Burgemeister, B., Blum, L., & Lorge, J. (1972). *Columbia Mental Maturity Scale*, New York: Harcourt Brace Jovanovich.

Case, R. (1985). *Intellectual development: Birth to adulthood*. Orlando, FL: Academic Press.

Case, R., Kurland, D. M., & Goldberg, J. (1982). Operational efficiency and the growth of short-term memory span. *Journal of Experimental Child Psychology, 33*, 386–404.

Daneman, M., & Blennerhassett, A. (1984). How to assess the listening comprehension skills of prereaders. *Journal of Educational Psychology, 76*, 1372–1381.

Eggert, D. (1978). *Hannover–Wechsler–Intelligenztest für Kinder* [German version of the WPPSI]. Bern Switzerland: Huber.

Farrar, M. J., & Goodman, G. (1990). Developmental differences in the relation between scripts and episodic memory: Do they exist? In R. Fivush & J. A. Hudson (Eds.), *Knowing and remembering in young children* (pp. 30–64). Cambridge, England: Cambridge University Press.

Fivush, R., & Slackman, E. (1986). The acquisition and development of scripts. In K. Nelson (Ed.), *Event knowledge: Structure and function in development* (pp. 71–96). Hillsdale, NJ: Erlbaum.

Grimm, H., & Schöler, H. (1978). *Heidelberger Sprachentwicklungstest, HSET*. Göttingen: Hogrefe. [*The Heidelberg language development test.*]

Grimm, H., & Schöler, H. (1985). *Sprachentwicklungsdiagnostik. Was leistet der Heidelberger Sprachentwicklungstest?* Göttingen: Hogrefe. [*Diagnosis of language development. How efficient is the Heidelberg language development test?*]

Halpern, D. (1989). The disappearance of cognitive gender differences: What you see depends on where you live. *American Psychologist, 44*, 1156–1157.

Hudson, J., & Nelson, K. (1983). Effects of script structure on children's story recall. *Cognitive Development, 19*, 625–635.

Hyde, J. S., & Linn, M. S. (1988). Gender differences in verbal ability: A meta-analysis. *Psychological Bulletin, 104,* 53–69.

Kintsch, E. (1990). Macroprocesses and microprocesses in the development of summarization skill. *Cognition and Instruction, 7,* 161–195.

Kintsch, W., Britton, B. K., Fletcher, C. R., Kintsch, E., Mannes, S. M., & Nathan, M. J. (1993). A comprehension-based approach to learning and understanding. In D. L. Medin (Ed.), *The psychology of learning and motivation* (Vol. 30, pp. 165–214). New York: Academic Press.

Knopf, M., & Waldmann, M. (1991). Die Rolle von Ereignisschemata beim Lernen in Vorschulalter. *The role of event knowledge for memory in preschool children. Zeitschrift für Entwicklungspsychologie und Pädagogische Psychologie, 23,* 181–186.

Maccoby, E. E., & Jacklin, C. N. (1974). *The psychology of sex differences.* Stanford, CA: Stanford University Press.

McCall, R. B. (1990). Infancy research: Individual differences. In F. D. Horowitz & J. Colombo (Eds.), *Infancy research* (pp. 141–172). Detroit, MI: Wayne State University Press.

Nelson, K. (1986). *Event knowledge–Structure and function in development.* Hillsdale, NJ: Erlbaum.

Schneider, W., Körkel, J., & Weinert, F. E. (1989). Domain specific knowledge and memory performance: A comparison of high- and low-aptitude children. *Journal of Educational Psychology, 81,* 306–312.

Schneider, W., & Sodian, B. (1991). A longitudinal study of young children's memory behavior and performance in a sort–recall task. *Journal of Experimental Child Psychology, 51,* 14–29.

Schneider, W., & Weinert, F. E. (1989). *The Munich longitudinal study on the genesis of individual competencies (LOGIC)* (Report No. 6). Munich: Max Planck Institute for Psychological Research.

Tewes, U. (Ed.). (1983). *Hamburg-Wechsler Intelligenztest für Kinder, Revision (HAWIK-R)* [German version of the revised WISC]. Bern, Switzerland: Huber.

Warrick, P. D., & Naglieri, J. A. (1993). Gender differences in planning, attention, simultaneous, and successive (PASS) cognitive processes. *Journal of Educational Psychology, 85,* 693–701.

6a   Comment: Developmental Trends in Story Recall

Walter Kintsch

Three findings about memory development stand out among the wealth of material in Knopf's "The Development of Memory for Texts." First, there are the age-related trends that she has observed in memory performance. Second, there are the intriguing data she reports on individual differences. Finally, these data emphasize that memory is not something to be studied on its own, but that one must analyze memory in the context of other cognitive activities.

First, memory develops. Children get better at recalling stories as they grow older. This is not quite as trivial as it sounds. Folk wisdom is of two minds about memory development. On the one hand, there is a strong belief that, at least for certain kinds of events and materials, children's memories are exceptional: Freud's neurotics can never forget their traumatic childhood memories, even though they may not be able consciously to recall them; early experiences are equally indelible for Lorenz's ducks and Tinbergen's gulls; more trivially, it has often been claimed (though less often demonstrated to the satisfaction of memory researchers) that children are especially good at rote recall for meaningless materials. Nevertheless, careful and well-replicated research has shown that memory for standard laboratory materials improves as children become older. For instance, in a classic study published in 1932, Brunswick, Goldscheider, and Pilek reported a monotonic increase in memory performance between the ages of 6 and 18 (Figure 1.1 in Schneider and Pressley 1989). Indeed, between the ages of 6 and 13, the increase was almost linear. Others have extended these developmental functions both downward into infancy and upward into adulthood (the increase does not flatten out until about age 25). Knopf shows that memory for text is in complete agreement with these findings for other types of memory. Between the ages of 4 and 12 there is a steady, almost linear increase in text recall, as shown in her Figure 2b.

Mean recall performance thus increases with age, but the standard deviations remain relatively constant. Indeed, the relative rank ordering of the students over this 9-year period remains remarkably constant. Recall in consecutive years correlates .61, and over a 9-year span, the correlation is still as high as .43. Given the measurement unreliability of the recall task, these are very impressive correlations indeed.

123

However, what is the cause of these stable individual differences in story recall? Knopf shows convincingly that some common assumptions are wrong. First, there are no sex differences. A century ago it was argued that girls do not have as good a memory as boys and should therefore be instructed separately. Subsequently, claims were made that the girls are better on verbal tasks than the boys. We see here that neither claim is justified for story recall. Although there are big and stable individual differences, they are not linked to sex. Even more striking are Knopf's findings that these differences are not strongly linked to environmental variables either. Of the many environmental and socioeconomic variables she considered, only a single one, the educational status of the mother, had a significant (but by no means huge) effect at all. This is a surprising and important finding with very positive educational implications.

Story recall was linked to verbal ability, as one might suppose, but even when verbal ability was partialled out, significant individual differences in story recall remained. Thus, if text memory is only partially determined by verbal intelligence, and relatively independent of such global variables as sex and socioeconomic status, where do the pronounced individual differences that were observed in this study come from?

The analyses presented by Knopf do not provide an answer to this question, but they do invite some speculations. Story recall is a complex cognitive task, in which memory is usually incidental. It involves comprehension of the story, and that in itself is a complex, multifaceted process, with linguistic aspects, situational understanding and knowledge-based inferences, global organizational processes, and so on (van Dijk and Kintsch 1983). Once understood, the story must also be retrieved from memory and reconstructed for recall. Thus, story recall involves many different skills and abilities.

It remains to be seen just which of these skills and abilities are the most significant sources of individual differences in the overall recall task. Of these possibilities, Knopf has explored short-term memory and working memory differences. She reports a correlation between digit span measures and story recall. In general, digit span is unrelated to text memory in most of the studies reported in the literature, but Knopf's correlations are small (on the average, 6% of the variance in story recall is accounted for by her short-term memory measure) and therefore are within the range of other results. Her results on working memory are actually more unusual: In the present study the reading span measure predicts story recall rather poorly (between 7 and 14% of the variance), compared with other results reported in the literature. However, as I have argued elsewhere (Ericsson and Kintsch 1995), the reading span is not really a measure of memory capacity at all, but of comprehension skills, and so we still have the task of finding out which comprehension skills are responsible for Knopf's findings. Perhaps the results of Knopf's factor analysis point to some likely candidates: Factors that had to do with reflection on performance, metamemory, and autobiographical memory assumed importance in the later years of development, and it is quite possible that early individual differences in these areas might have something to do with how a person's comprehension skills develop. However, there are many other possibilities that need to be considered: skills in overall organization of a text, inferencing, retrieval processes, and reconstruction processes – to name just a few. Knopf's conclusion that memory development for text is primarily quantitative rather than qualitative is therefore not entirely convincing. To uncover qualitative differences in story comprehension one would require more than just the analysis of overall recall scores. I think this issue is still quite unresolved. Knopf has given us a beautiful and unique set of developmental data with some striking properties; researchers can now focus on the factors that might explain these results.

References

Brunswick, E., Goldscheider, L., & Pilek, E. (1932). Zur Systematik des Gedächtnisses. [Systematizing memory.] *Beihefte zur Zeitschrift für angewandte Psychologie, 64*, 1–158.

Ericsson, K. A., & Kintsch, W. (1995). Long-term working-memory. *Psychological Review, 102*, 211–245.

Schneider, W., & Pressley, M. (1989). *Memory development between 2 and 20.* New York: Springer.

van Dijk, T. A., & Kintsch, W. (1983). *Strategies of discourse comprehension.* Orlando, FL: Academic Press.

7 Impact of Early Phonological Processing Skills on Reading and Spelling in School: Evidence From the Munich Longitudinal Study

Wolfgang Schneider and Jan Carol Näslund

Longitudinal research on the preschool prediction of reading and spelling has been accumulating over the last three decades. Although results from such studies have always caught considerable attention in the scientific literature, there were at least two general problems with most of the earlier studies that mitigated their power. (a) One problem was that the choice of predictor measures was not guided by theoretical considerations concerning reading and spelling processes or their possible precursors. A vast array of mostly psychometric measures were used that, in most cases, were not proximal to reading and spelling (e.g., motor skills, general cognitive ability, and behavioral–emotional functioning; for reviews, see Horn and Packard 1985; Tramontana, Hooper, and Selzer 1988). Interestingly, many of these measures predicted later reading and spelling performance rather well, particularly when the focus was on univariate prediction. (b) A second, related problem was that the discriminant validity of predictor variables was not assessed or was found to be low. In the latter case, measures important for the prediction of reading and spelling were almost equally powerful in predicting achievement in unrelated areas such as mathematics.

Fortunately, these problems were avoided in more recent longitudinal studies that derived predictor measures from theoretical assumptions concerning possible prerequisites of reading and spelling (e.g., Bradley and Bryant 1985; Juel 1988; Lundberg, Frost, and Petersen 1988; Skowronek and Marx 1989; Stanovich, Cunningham, and Feeman 1984). In all of these studies, it was shown that phonological awareness (the ability to detect and differentiate phonemic units in speech) was a very good predictor of children's later reading and spelling performance (see also Tunmer and Nesdale 1985; Wagner and Torgesen 1987). Further, several studies demonstrated that indicators of memory capacity and information-processing speed were also related to reading ability (e.g., Daneman and Blennerhassett 1984; Ellis and Large 1987; Perfetti and Lesgold 1978; Skowronek and Marx 1989) and that the presence or absence of preschool letter knowledge or early literacy was strongly related to predicting early reading skills (cf. Bradley and Bryant 1985; Lundberg et al. 1988).

We are grateful to Merry Bullock for her valuable comments on a draft of this chapter.

126

Although these studies greatly enhanced our knowledge of the important roles of factors such as phonological awareness, memory capacity, and early literacy for the acquisition of reading and spelling, they still left us with a few open questions. For instance, one controversial question was the impact of letter knowledge on the development of phonological awareness. Whereas one group of researchers (Bradley and Bryant 1985; Lundberg et al. 1988) demonstrated phonological awareness in preschool children who did not know about phoneme–grapheme correspondence rules, another group (Morais, Cary, Alegria, and Bertelson 1979; Read, Yun-Fei, Hong-Yin, and Bao-Qing 1986) claimed that phonological awareness associated with reading and spelling cannot develop in the absence of grapheme–phoneme knowledge.

Furthermore, a problem experienced with many of the older longitudinal studies was that the range of predictor variables included in the analyses was restricted. Typically, studies focusing on the role of phonological awareness did not include indicators of working memory or early literacy, and vice versa. As a consequence, we do not know much about the relative contribution of these theoretically relevant measures to the prediction of reading and spelling when simultaneously considered in multivariate analyses. In this regard, an interesting question is whether the relative contribution of predictor measures varies as a function of the criterion measure under study (i.e., reading vs. spelling).

Another issue of current debate is whether models of reading acquisition developed in English-speaking countries transfer to other languages as well. For example, Wimmer and colleagues (e.g., Wimmer, Hartl, and Moser 1990) have demonstrated for German-speaking children that the universality of this assumption may not be valid because the English and German orthographies vary in difficulty (regularity). Accordingly, predictor variables important for the explanation of reading and spelling processes in German children may differ from those relevant for British or U.S. children.

The design of our LOGIC study seemed suited to explore these issues. The study began when children were about 4 years of age and included numerous measures of children's early cognitive abilities assessed during the first 2 years of kindergarten. Thus, we chose to carry out a prospective study of prerequisites of reading and spelling, starting with the third (and last) year of kindergarten. We assessed a variety of cognitive measures (to be described later) tapping skills that, according to the literature, seemed suited to predict reading and spelling in elementary school.

Major Goals of the Study

Our study focused on the following problems (for details, see Näslund 1990; Näslund and Schneider 1991, 1993; Schneider & Näslund 1992, 1993).

1. We were interested in exploring the interplay among IQ, phonological awareness, memory capacity, and early literacy in predicting reading ability (i.e., decoding speed and reading comprehension) and spelling. We made a distinction between phonological awareness in the broad and narrow senses (cf. Skowronek and Marx 1989).

Although the earlier refers to the ability to segment the stream of speech sounds into larger units such as syllables and rhyme words, the latter requires children to segment speech into the abstract linguistic units of phonemes. Combining indicators of phonological awareness in the broad and narrow senses in one single predictor set enabled us to judge the relative importance of each phonological awareness component for the acquisition of reading and spelling. Furthermore, memory variables and indicators of early literacy were included to provide information on the relative importance of each variable as a function of the criterion under study (i.e., reading vs. spelling) and measurement point (i.e., early vs. late elementary school period).

2. A second related focus was the relative influences of early literacy and phonological awareness in the broad and narrow senses on later reading and spelling performance. As noted earlier, this issue has generated controversy in the literature for quite awhile (cf. Bradley and Bryant 1985; Morais 1991; Morais et al. 1979, Read et al. 1986). The major issue is whether phonological awareness can be acquired without knowledge about the alphabet. In our view, one source of confusion was that Bradley and Bryant referred to phonological awareness in the broad sense, whereas Morais and colleagues focused on phonological awareness in the narrow sense. Because German kindergarten children, unlike U.S. or British children, do not learn to read before elementary school, their knowledge of the alphabet and phoneme–grapheme correspondences is usually very poor. Thus, our study seemed suited to explore whether phonological awareness does have an effect on later reading, independent of letter knowledge.

3. A third goal of the study was to explore the interrelationships among the various sets of independent variables (e.g., IQ, memory capacity, and phonological awareness) in predicting reading and spelling during school. Because traditional regression analyses are not suited to explore this issue, a latent causal modeling approach (analysis of linear structural relationships, or LISREL) was chosen. Again, one of the questions of major interest was whether different structural models would hold for reading and for spelling.

4. A final issue of interest was sex differences in reading and spelling. Most German studies on dyslexia have found that the number of dyslexic boys considerably exceeds that of dyslexic girls. However, we do not know for sure whether boys generally perform worse than girls, or whether this is true only for the lowest quartile of the distribution. Furthermore, it remains unclear from the available literature whether sex differences are observable from the very beginning of reading instruction or whether they develop later during the school career. Our longitudinal database covers the period from the second to fifth grades and thus is ideally suited to deal with this issue.

Description of Sample and Test Instruments

Participants

A total of 210 children was initially recruited for the study. Of these, 22 children stayed in kindergarten for 1 more year and did not enter elementary school with the rest of the sample. Reading and spelling data for these participants were not considered in our analyses. Complete data sets from 163 children were available for the analyses dealing with spelling performance across the first 5 school years. Because of organizational problems, not all of the children participated in the decoding and reading comprehension tests. Thus, the analyses focusing on these variables were based on only 121 participants. Additional data on classroom behavior and quality of classroom instruction were available for 120 of the children.

Our children began kindergarten at about age 4. On average, they were almost 6 years old when assessed with the phonological processing, memory capacity, and IQ tasks during the last year of kindergarten. Reading comprehension, decoding speed, and spelling skill were assessed both at the beginning and at the end of second grade. Additional spelling tests were given in the third, fourth, and fifth grades.

Predictor Tasks

The following tasks were presented during the last year of kindergarten: (a) The *Bielefeld screening test* consists of eight different tasks that tap children's phonological awareness, attention, and memory performance (cf. Jansen et al. 1986; Marx 1992; Skowronek and Marx 1989); (b) a *sound categorization task* developed by Bradley and Bryant (1985) that taps children's phonological awareness in the broad sense (rhyming); (c) verbal memory capacity assessed by a *word span task* (Case, Kurland, and Goldberg 1982) and a *listening span (sentence span) task* developed by Daneman and Blennerhassett (1984); (d) early literacy assessed by *children's letter knowledge, name writing,* and *sign knowledge*; and (e) verbal and nonverbal intelligence indicated by children's performance on the *Hannover–Wechsler–Intelligence Test for Preschool Children* (HAWIVA; Eggert 1978) and the *Columbia Mental Maturity Scale* (CMMS; Burgemeister, Blum, and Lorge 1972).

Four subtests of the Bielefeld screening instrument (Jansen et al. 1986) assessed components of phonological awareness. The *rhyming task* consisted of 10 word pairs, half of which rhymed. Children had to indicate which word pairs did rhyme and which did not. In the *syllable segmentation task*, 10 words were presented on audiotape. The task was to segment each word into its syllables, and the children were to clap their hands for each syllable. In the *sound-to-word matching task*, children were presented with a total of 10 audiotaped words. After repeating each word, children had to indicate whether a specific sound pattern (e.g., an "au") could be identified in the test word (e.g., *Auge*). Finally, the *sound-blending task* tapped children's awareness of isolated sounds. The words presented were segmented into their constituent sounds, and the children's task was to identify the words.

The remaining four subtests of the Bielefeld screening instrument tapped memory and attentional processes. The *visual word-matching task* required children to identify the "twin" (identical word) of a target word out of a number of four alternatives. The target word was always given in the upper row of a card, and three distractor items and the target word were depicted in a second row below. The number of correct solutions (maximum = 12) was the dependent variable. In the *repetition of nonsense words subtest*, children were asked to listen carefully to a series of pseudowords (*Zippelzak* and *Binne-basselbus*) and repeat them as accurately as possible. The number of pseudowords correctly repeated was the dependent variable. Finally, two different *rapid-naming tasks* were given because there is evidence in the literature that poor readers cannot access information in semantic or lexical memory as quickly as normal and good readers (cf. Blachman 1984; Denckla and Rudel 1976). The first task required rapid naming of the colors of objects from uncolored line drawings. Here, the children's task was to indicate the correct colors as quickly as possible. The second task was structurally similar and required rapid naming of the correct colors of objects with incongruent colors (e.g., a blue lemon). This task differs from the first in that the child has to cope with interference and distraction problems. In both tasks, the number of mistakes and the time needed to complete the trials were the dependent variables.

The *sound categorization task (phonological oddity measure)* developed by Bradley and Bryant (1985) consisted of three different components. Each subtest consisted of a series of four one-syllable words. In the *first-sound oddity task*, children had to identify the word with a different first sound (e.g., *Fest, Feld, Fels,* and *Helm*). In the *middle-sound oddity task*, children had to find out which of four words did not share the same middle sound (e.g., *Hahn, Sohn, Lohn,* and *Mohn*). In the *end-sound oddity task*, the same experimental structure was used. This time, the children's task was to identify the word that had a different end sound as the other three (e.g., *Speck, Dreck, Stern,* and *Fleck*). In each subtest, the number of correct solutions (maximum = 9 per test) was the dependent variable.

To assess verbal memory capacity, we used two different tasks. The *word span task* developed by Case et al. (1982) consisted of 10 sets of one-syllable words. The set sizes ranged from three to seven items. Beginning with the smallest set of three words, children were given two trials for each set size. They were instructed to listen to the entire set and then to repeat the words they heard. Children's word span was defined as the largest set size that could be repeated in the correct order.

The second verbal memory capacity measure was the *sentence span/listening span task* adapted from Daneman and Blennerhassett (1984). A maximum of 75 sentences, ranging in length from three to seven words, was read to each child. Sentences were grouped in five sets each of one, two, three, four, and five sentences. Children were asked to repeat the sentences in each set verbatim. Testing terminated when the child failed to recall all five sentences at a particular level. The total number of sentences and words recalled correctly was chosen as the dependent variable.

Three different tasks assessed early literacy and concepts about printed information in our kindergarten children. A *letter-naming task* assessed children's knowledge about phoneme–grapheme correspondences. The number of letters correctly identified was used as the dependent variable. The second task (*sign knowledge* or *Logo task*) was originally developed by Brügelmann (1986) and was later modified by the Bielefeld group (Skowronek and Marx 1989). The Logo task tapped children's knowledge of letters and words that are hidden in familiar settings. Typical examples are traffic signs (e.g., the STOP sign) and trademarks. In some trials, only the original letters were given without any graphic context. In others, only the graphic context was given, and the letters were omitted. The dependent variable in the present analysis was the number of correct responses in trials focusing on the letters. Finally, *word writing* was chosen as another variable tapping early literacy. Children were asked to write down as many words as they already knew. The number of words correctly spelled was used as the dependent variable.

Tests of verbal and nonverbal intelligence were given to assess the importance of nonspecific predictors of reading and spelling. General verbal ability was measured by the verbal section of the HAWIVA test for preschoolers. This section includes vocabulary and verbal comprehension items. The CMMS developed by Burgemeister et al. (1972) was considered an appropriate test to assess children's nonverbal intellectual ability. This test taps general reasoning ability of children aged 3 years 6 months through 9 years 11 months. Depending on the participants' age level, between 52 and 65 pictorial and figural classification items were administered. For each item, children were asked to look at the pictures on a card (varying between 3 to 5) and to select the one that was different from or unrelated to the others. The number of correct solutions was taken as the dependent variable.

Criterion Tasks Assessed in Elementary School

The task assessing word and nonword decoding speed was adapted from Rott and Zielinski (1986). The items (four-letter words and pseudowords) were presented on a computer screen. An internal timing device measured children's responses from the moment of presentation on the screen. A total of 30 words and 30 nonwords was provided. Mean decoding speed was calculated separately for both types of words. The decoding speed tasks were first given at the beginning of second grade and repeated at the end of the school year.

A 30-item test developed by the second author was used to measure reading comprehension and word knowledge within the context of single sentences and longer texts (short stories). A total of 18 multiple-choice items tapped word knowledge. They included finding synonyms and antonyms within the context of a sentence. The text comprehension part consisted of five short stories followed by two or three multiple-choice questions. This task was designed to test children's understanding of the text, deducing answers from inferences based only on information in the stories. The test was first given at the beginning and was then repeated near the end of the school year.

Finally, the first two spelling tests (word dictation) consisted of two partially overlapping versions: the first presented at the beginning of second grade, and the other shortly before the end of second grade. Each test included about 20 target words that were taken from different sources and that were designed to be particularly suited to assess spelling competence in second grade. The spelling tests provided in Grades 3, 4, and 5 were more comprehensive (60 words, 81 words, and 88 words, respectively) and were given as sentence dictations. About two thirds of the materials consisted of familiar words taken from the official vocabulary list for third and fourth graders that is distributed by the Bavarian Ministry of Education. The remaining items were less familiar and were irregular words. For all spelling measures, the number of correctly written words was the dependent variable.

Table 1. *Means, Standard Deviations, and Range for the Predictor Variables Included in the Study*

Variable	M	SD	Minimum	Maximum
Nonverbal IQ	109.51	11.70	79	137
Word span	3.48	0.97	1	6
Sentence span	14.04	6.64	2	38
Sign knowledge	0.94	1.45	0	5
Letter knowledge	6.75	7.44	0	26
Words written	2.06	1.93	0	12
First-sound oddity	4.21	2.07	1	9
Middle-sound oddity	7.03	2.22	2	9
End-sound oddity	6.62	2.31	2	9
Bielefeld screening				
Rhyming task	8.12	1.39	3	10
Syllable segmentation	8.41	1.79	3	10
Sound-to-word matching	6.83	2.20	0	10
Sound blending	6.98	1.95	0	10
Visual word matching	10.13	2.11	0	12
Repetition of nonsense words	7.21	2.04	0	11
Rapid naming (timed)	65.47	18.73	27	149

Results

Table 1 gives the means, standard deviations, and the ranges for the various predictor variables used in the present analyses. As can be seen from Table 1, children performed very well on most subtests of the Bielefeld screening test (Jansen et al. 1986). This finding is in accord with the principles of test construction used by the Bielefeld research group. That is, only those subtests were included in the final version of the screening test that particularly discriminated in the lower third of the distribution. A comparison of the Bielefeld rhyming test and Bradley and Bryant's (1985) sound categorization task showed pronounced differences in task difficulty: On average, about 80% of the children succeeded on the Bielefeld rhyming test, whereas fewer than 50% were correct on the first-sound oddity task.

Compared with the Bielefeld (Jansen et al. 1986) screening subtests, the various tasks concerning early literacy were rather difficult. In particular, most German kindergarten children did not know much about grapheme–phoneme correspondences. Almost 50% of the children knew 2, 1, or 0 letters; only a small minority (about 9%) knew between 22 and 26 letters and could thus be considered familiar with the alphabet. This finding certainly differs from those typically reported for 6-year-olds from Great Britain or the United States.

The means and standard deviations of the various criterion measures are given in Table 2. Although both word-decoding accuracy and word-decoding speed were

Table 2. *Means, Standard Deviations, and Range for the Criterion Variables Included in the Analyses*

Variable	*M*	*SD*	Minimum	Maximum
Word decoding (Grade 2/1)	1.85	0.57	.9	3.2
Word decoding (Grade 2/2)	1.68	0.62	.8	3.3
Reading comprehension (Grade 2/1)	22.17	6.45	7	28
Reading comprehension (Grade 2/2)	25.98	4.19	8	29
Spelling (Grade 2/1)	10.22	2.18	4	17
Spelling (Grade 2/2)	11.04	3.97	5	18
Spelling (Grade 3)	31.07	5.92	8	40
Spelling (Grade 4)	51.69	6.30	25	60
Spelling (Grade 5)	76.41	9.81	39	88

assessed in Grade 2, only the speed measure was used in the present analyses. It turned out that most children were already very accurate readers at the beginning of Grade 2, leaving us with a ceiling effect for the accuracy variable. On average, participants also performed well on the reading comprehension and spelling tests, although we did not observe ceiling effects for these measures.

Relative Importance of the Various Predictor Variables for Subsequent Reading and Spelling

A series of multiple stepwise regression analyses was performed to determine the relative influence of the various predictor variables on reading-related and spelling skills in elementary school. The dependent measures were word-decoding speed, reading comprehension, and spelling. We adopted the procedure used by Bradley and Bryant (1985) in that (nonverbal) IQ was always the first variable to enter the regression equation, followed by those other predictor variables that additionally explained significant proportions of the variance in the respective criterion variable. Although such a procedure probably overestimates the influence of intelligence on the reading and spelling variables, it seems appropriate for our purposes because it ensures that the impact of the remaining predictors on the criterion variables is not confounded with IQ. Contrary to expectations, the nonverbal IQ variable was generally more predictive of later reading and spelling than its verbal counterpart. Thus, only nonverbal IQ was considered in the following analyses.

The results concerning word-decoding speed are depicted in Table 3. As can be seen from Table 3, different patterns of results emerged for the two testing occasions. IQ and letter knowledge accounted for most of the variance in decoding speed measured at the beginning of second grade, whereas memory capacity (listening span), attentional features (word matching), phonological awareness in the narrow sense (phoneme–word matching), and information-processing speed (rapid naming) all

Table 3. *Results of Stepwise Regression Analysis Using Word-Decoding Speed as the Criterion Variable*

Predictor	R^2	$R^2 \Delta$
Beginning of Grade 2		
Nonverbal IQ	.07	
Letter knowledge	.15	.08
Listening span	.21	.06
Word matching	.24	.03
Sound-to-word matching	.26	.02
Rapid naming	.28	.02
End of Grade 2		
Nonverbal IQ	.03	
End-sound oddity	.15	.12
Rapid naming	.21	.06
Letter knowledge	.25	.04
Word matching	.27	.02

Table 4. *Results of the Stepwise Regression Analysis Using Reading Comprehension as the Criterion Variable*

Predictor	R^2	$R^2 \Delta$
Beginning of Grade 2		
Nonverbal IQ	.15	
First-sound oddity	.28	.13
Middle-sound oddity	.33	.05
Sound blending	.35	.02
End of Grade 2		
Nonverbal IQ	.17	
Rapid naming	.21	.04
Syllable segmentation	.24	.03
Middle-sound oddity	.27	.03

made a significant but numerically small contribution. By comparison, only phonological awareness in the broad sense (end-sound oddity task) and information-processing speed contributed substantially to the prediction of word-decoding speed assessed at the end of second grade. Regardless of measurement point, the total amount of variance explained in the criterion variable was only modest (28% vs. 27% for the first and second measurement points, respectively).

The findings for reading comprehension are given in Table 4. A closer inspection of this table shows that nonverbal IQ explained a considerable proportion of the variance in reading comprehension for both measurement points. Three indicators of phonological awareness (first-sound oddity, middle-sound oddity, and phoneme blending)

Table 5. *Results of the Stepwise Regression Analysis Using Spelling at the End of Grade 2 as the Criterion Variable*

Predictor	R^2	$R^2\Delta$
Nonverbal IQ	.11	
Rapid naming	.21	.10
Letter knowledge	.26	.05
Sound-to-word matching	.29	.03
Sound blending	.32	.03
Sign knowledge	.34	.02
Listening span	.35	.01
Word writing	.36	.01

accounted for the rest of the variance in reading comprehension assessed at the beginning of Grade 2. Although IQ explained about 15% of the variance in reading comprehension, the combined additional contribution of the phonological awareness variables was even greater (about 20% of the variance was explained by these variables).

The findings for the second measurement point differed from those for the first in that the impact of phonological awareness (middle-sound oddity and syllable segmenting) was comparably low and that IQ was by far the most influential predictor. Only 10% of the variance in reading comprehension assessed at the end of second grade was explained by the three other predictors included in the regression equation.

Because the findings for spelling assessed in second grade were very similar for both measurement points, only the results for the second point (end of second grade) are presented in Table 5. In addition to IQ, information-processing speed (rapid naming) and letter knowledge had a substantial impact, followed by two phonological awareness variables (sound-to-word matching and sound blending). The impact of the remaining predictor variables (sign knowledge, listening span, and name writing) was comparably small. Overall, about 36% of the total variance in spelling assessed at the end of second grade was explained by the various kindergarten predictors.

Interestingly enough, the predictor quality of the kindergarten variables seemed to improve over time. When spelling in Grade 3 was chosen as the dependent variable, almost 50% of the variance could be accounted for by eight predictor variables. Again, IQ and letter knowledge made the comparably strongest impact. In addition, listening span and sound categorization (middle-sound oddity and end-sound oddity) contributed significantly to the prediction of spelling skill at the end of third grade. Inspection of Table 6 shows that the four major predictor domains (IQ, letter knowledge, memory capacity, and phonological awareness) accounted for similar proportions of the variance in the criterion variable. The fact that the kindergarten measures explained more variance in Grade 3 spelling than in Grade 2 spelling may be due to the larger performance variance in the later spelling tests. Results of the regression

Table 6. *Results of Stepwise
Regression Analysis Using Spelling
in Grade 3 as the Criterion Variable*

Predictor	R^2	$R^2 \Delta$
Nonverbal IQ	.13	
Letter knowledge	.29	.16
Listening span	.36	.07
Rapid naming	.40	.04
Word writing	.42	.02
Sound-to-word matching	.44	.02
Sign knowledge	.46	.02
Nonword repetition	.47	.01

analyses performed for spelling at the end of fourth and fifth grades were similar to those reported in Table 6 and are not discussed in detail because of space restrictions.

*The Interplay of Phonological Awareness and Early Literacy in Predicting
Reading and Writing in Elementary School*

As noted earlier, there is controversy in the literature about the causal status of phonological awareness in learning to read. Some researchers argue that the emergence of phonological awareness is simply a by-product of learning to read (e.g., Morais 1991; Morais et al. 1979), whereas others propose that phonological awareness and the ability to segment the speech stream into units of phonemic size allow children to understand the alphabetical principle (cf. Bradley and Bryant 1985; Lundberg et al. 1988). A third alternative suggested by yet others is reciprocal causation; that is, a causal connection running in both directions (cf. Perfetti, Beck, Bell, and Hughes 1987).

Although our data are correlational in nature, which prevents us from making causal inferences, they do allow us to test the assumption that phonological awareness (in the broad and narrow sense) can be found among nonreaders. Those 58 children in our sample who did not identify more than two letters obviously did not understand the alphabetic principle. This subgroup, on average, scored lower than the rest of the sample on most tests of phonological awareness. However, performance was significantly above chance level, even for this subgroup. These findings nicely replicate those reported by Lundberg and Hoien (1991) for Danish and Swedish children.

A second question of interest was the status of IQ, phonological awareness, and memory capacity as predictors of reading and spelling for the subgroup of children with minimal letter knowledge. In particular, we asked the question whether phonological awareness without corresponding insight into the alphabetic principle can predict reading and spelling in elementary school.

Multiple stepwise regression analyses carried out for the subgroup of children with phonological awareness but no letter knowledge showed that it can. As seen in

Table 7. *Results of the Stepwise Regression Analysis Using Word-Decoding Speed and Reading Comprehension in Grade 2 as the Criterion Variables*

Predictor	R^2	$R^2\Delta$
Word-decoding speed		
Nonverbal IQ	.15	
First-sound oddity	.31	.16
Sound blending	.44	.13
End-sound oddity	.52	.08
Rapid naming	.58	.06
Nonword repetition	.64	.06
Reading comprehension		
Nonverbal IQ	.12	
First-sound oddity	.32	.20
Rapid naming	.43	.11
Syllable segmentation	.57	.14
End-sound oddity	.67	.10

Note: Results of the subgroup with minimal letter knowledge.

Table 7, three phonological awareness measures (first-sound oddity, end-sound oddity, and phoneme blending task) accounted for about 37% of the variance in the word-decoding speed measure. The results were similar when reading comprehension was used as the dependent variable: The ability to categorize sounds (first-sound oddity and end-sound oddity) and to segment syllables explained most of the variance in the dependent variable (about 44%). Similar results were obtained for the various spelling measures.

From these findings, we can conclude that it is possible to develop phonological awareness in the narrow sense despite a very limited knowledge of the alphabet and that phonological awareness in the broad sense that has developed without letter knowledge predicts subsequent reading and spelling. On the other hand, it is important to note that letter knowledge was positively related to phonological awareness. Those children with more letter knowledge were better than the children with low letter knowledge on most metalinguistic tasks at the end of kindergarten. Moreover, this early advantage persisted over the elementary school years: On average, children who acquired the alphabetical principle before school turned out to be the better readers and spellers in elementary school.

Findings From Causal Modeling Procedures

Although the regression analyses summarized earlier provided first important insights into the predictor quality of various kindergarten measures with regard to later reading and spelling, they must be interpreted with caution because of the methodological problems typically related to this approach. The large number of predictors and the significant interrelationship among predictors give rise to problems of multicollinearity. Consequently, parameter estimates are often biased, leading to overestimations of "true" explained criterion variance.

To cope with these problems, we also used a latent variable causal modeling approach (LISREL; cf. Jöreskog and Sörbom 1989). The major advantage of this structural equation modeling (SEM) approach is that it distinguishes between a *measurement model*, which represents the relationships among observed variables and latent, theoretical constructs, and a *structural model*, which represents the relationships among latent variables. Because causal relationships are estimated at the level of theoretical constructs and not at the level of observed variables, the number of variables considered in the structural model is comparably small. Another advantage of this causal modeling approach is that there are several so-called goodness-of-fit tests that indicate the degree of fit between the causal model and the data set to which it is applied. Causal models are said to be "confirmed" when the goodness-of-fit parameter indicates better-than-chance fit between the model and the data.

The SEM analysis on the LOGIC data provided in this chapter represents an extension of an approach reported several years ago (Schneider and Näslund 1992). In the earlier work, we estimated and tested separate causal models for the prediction of reading comprehension and spelling in Grade 2. A total of five predictor domains were used in these analyses. On the basis of a theoretical framework suggested by Wagner and Torgesen (1987), three components of phonological processing abilities were distinguished: (a) *phonological awareness*, that is, the awareness of and access to the sound structure of one's language. The sound categorization measure developed by Bradley and Bryant (1985) and three tasks used in the Bielefeld screening (Jansen et al. 1986) procedure (rhyming, syllable segmentation, and sound-to-word matching) were chosen as indicators of phonological awareness; (b) *phonological recoding in lexical access*, that is, accessing the referent of a word in a semantic lexicon by retrieving the phonological codes associated with an object from long-term memory. The two rapid-naming tasks of the Bielefeld screening procedure were suitable for representing this component; and (c) *phonetic recoding in working memory*, that is, recoding information into a sound-based representational system that enables it to be maintained in working memory during ongoing processing. The two verbal memory span tests (i.e., word span and listening span) were chosen to represent this component.

In addition to these three components of phonological information processing, two more predictor domains were included in the model: (a) *early literacy*, which was represented by letter knowledge, sign knowledge, and name writing, and (b) *intelligence*, represented by the tests of verbal and nonverbal IQ described earlier.

First analyses based on this data set were already discussed in the earlier publication (Schneider and Näslund 1992). At that time, criterion measures (i.e., reading comprehension and spelling) assessed in second grade were available for analysis. We first summarize the results of these analyses and then describe findings obtained for an extended causal model for the spelling criterion variable that included additional spelling measures assessed in Grades 3, 4, and 5.

Figure 1 shows the best fitting LISREL models for the reading comprehension and spelling criterion measures. For each model, only the causal links (i.e., structural coefficients) among the six latent variables are included for the sake of clarity. First, note that different structural models fit the data for the reading comprehension and spelling models. The two models were similar in that two of the three phonological processing components (phonological awareness and phonetic recoding in lexical access) had direct effects on the criterion variables, and working memory only indirectly influenced the two outcome variables. Although early literacy showed direct effects on both reading comprehension and spelling, these effects were rather modest. Similarly, IQ did not have much impact in either model. The total amount of variance explained in the two models was 47% and 62% for the reading comprehension and spelling models, respectively. Overall, the three phonological processing variables had a stronger impact on spelling than on reading comprehension.

The model describing and explaining spelling at the end of Grade 2 and depicted in Figure 1 was taken as a starting point for the additional analyses, including spelling measures for Grades 3, 4, and 5. Here, the major question was whether the five predictor domains assessed in kindergarten would still show direct effects on spelling assessed near the end of elementary school. The only changes in the modeling procedure were that both indicators of verbal and nonverbal intelligence were used to represent the intelligence factor and that spelling measures obtained at the end of fifth grade served as the dependent variable. The results of the LISREL runs for this model can be summarized very briefly: The model did not fit the data. There were large specification errors indicating that theoretically important variables were not included in the model.

In a second step, the model was extended by including all spelling measures assessed from Grade 2. Figure 2 shows the best fitting model resulting from this analysis. As can be seen, the five predictor variables influenced spelling assessed at Grade 2, but they had no direct impact on spelling measures assessed in subsequent years. In accord with several other longitudinal studies exploring the development of academic achievement in school (e.g., Helmke, Schneider, and Weinert 1986; Schneider and Treiber 1984), individual differences in knowledge and competence concerning a specific academic domain (i.e., spelling) assessed at an early point in time turned out to be the only relevant predictor of performance in this domain assessed at later measurement points. Overall, 68% of the variance in spelling assessed in Grade 5 was explained by the various predictors.

It should be noted that we also estimated several alternative models including socioeconomic status (SES) and sex as predictor variables. However, SES and sex were only moderately correlated with spelling outcome measures and did not show significant effects. Thus, the findings shown in Figure 2 represent the most parsimonious solution to the problem.

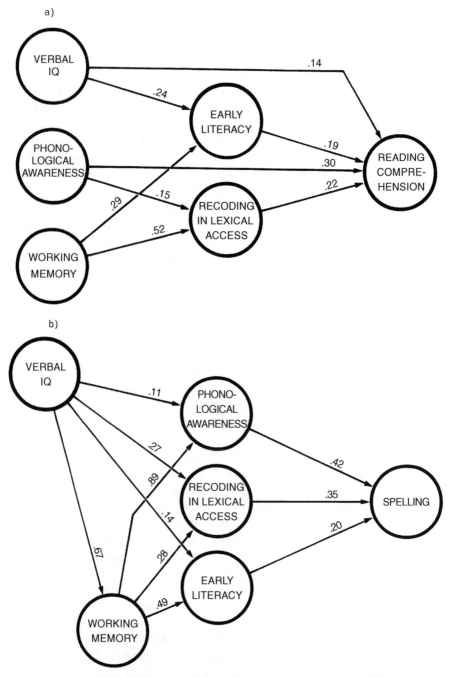

Figure 1. Best fitting structural equation models for reading comprehension (a) and spelling (b) assessed at the end of Grade 2.

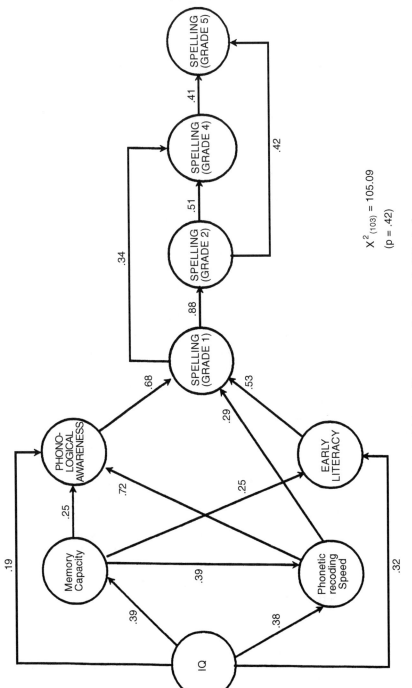

Figure 2. Best fitting structural equation model for spelling assessed at the end of Grade 5.

$X^2_{(103)} = 105.09$

$(p = .42)$

The lack of a strong impact for SES may have arisen because only a single indicator (the prestige of father's occupation) was available. However, the lack of a strong sex effect was surprising. In the following section, we present more detailed analyses exploring sex differences in the various predictor and criterion domains included in the LOGIC study.

The Role of Sex Differences

The hypothesis that girls score higher than boys on tests of metalinguistic ability was only partially confirmed for our sample. We found no sex differences on the subtests of the Bradley and Bryant (1985) sound categorization task, nor on most of the Bielefeld (Jansen et al. 1986) screening tasks. There were a few exceptions. Girls outperformed boys on the word comparison task (10.27 vs. 9.51; $p < .05$), and girls were faster than boys on the two rapid-naming tasks. As the rapid-naming measures are supposed to assess children's ability to access quickly their semantic lexicon, girls' advantage on these tasks may indicate somewhat superior language skills. However, we do not have any direct evidence for this. Although girls tended to be better on some of the Bielefeld screening subtests, the overall risk score (computed by summing up the risk points for each task) did not differ between boys and girls.

The findings concerning early literacy were also mixed. Girls and boys did not differ in their letter knowledge, nor were there sex differences in sign knowledge. However, girls were able to write down more names than boys (3.5 vs. 2.3; $p < .05$). Taken together, these findings indicate that although slight differences in favor of girls were occasionally observed, precursors of reading and spelling assessed during the last year of kindergarten did not differ much as a function of sex.

Did the situation change across the school years? We could not detect any sex differences for the word-decoding speed and reading comprehension measures administered in Grade 2. The analysis conducted for the spelling tests obtained for Grades 2 to 5 shows a somewhat different picture. Table 8 gives the means and standard deviations for these tests as a function of sex. There were no sex differences in the mean number of words spelled correctly at the two testing points in Grade 2, although girls tended to be better at the end of the school year, $t(118) = 1.77$, $p < .10$. More pronounced performance differences between girls and boys were observed for the tests in Grades 3 and 4. On each occasion, girls were significantly better: $t(118)$s $= 2.18$ and 2.17 for Grades 3 and 4, respectively, all ps $< .05$. Although these differences were reliable, they did not indicate substantial effects. Girls also outperformed boys in Grade 5. Because of ceiling effects, however, these differences did not reach statistical significance.

All in all, our findings support the view that performance differences between boys and girls increase with age and amount of schooling. They also confirm the finding reported in earlier studies (e.g., Vellutino et al. 1992) that considerably more boys than girls belong to the lowest quartile of the performance distribution from the very beginning. Stability of individual differences in spelling performance over time was

Table 8. *Number of Correct Words in the Various Spelling Tests, as a Function of Sex.*

Grade	M	SD	Minimum	Maximum
Grade 2 (beginning)				
Boys	10.31	2.16	4	16
Girls	10.06	2.26	5	17
Grade 2 (end)				
Boys	10.71	4.25	2	18
Girls	11.72	3.70	3	18
Grade 3				
Boys	27.93	8.29	7	40
Girls	30.27	6.55	13	39
Grade 4				
Boys	48.56	9.02	17	60
Girls	51.10	7.08	23	60
Grade 5				
Boys	75.92	10.60	39	88
Girls	77.51	8.10	56	88

Table 9. *Intercorrelations Among the Various Spelling Tests of the LOGIC Study as a Function of Sex*

Variable	1	2	3	4	5
1. Test Grade 2/1	—	.60	.52	.49	.46
2. Test Grade 2/2	.42	—	.84	.77	.59
3. Test Grade 3	.55	.85	—	.86	.79
4. Test Grade 4	.51	.70	.87	—	.81
5. Test Grade 5	.46	.60	.78	.86	—

Note: The coefficients for boys are depicted above the diagonal, those for girls are presented below the diagonal.

found to be high from the end of Grade 2 on, regardless of sex (cf. Table 9). Interestingly, the correlations were also very high for the time between Grades 2 and 3, despite the fact that new teachers had taken over the classrooms at the beginning of Grade 3.

Conclusions

The longitudinal analysis of the LOGIC data provided valuable information on the relative impact of phonological awareness, memory capacity, early literacy, and intelligence on the development of reading and spelling in German school children. It seems important to note that all four predictor domains assessed during the last year of kindergarten had a significant impact on the acquisition of reading and spelling skills in elementary school. This impact differed as a function of the dependent measure tested and the measurement point considered. Individual differences in word-decoding speed assessed in Grade 2 were only partially explained by the kindergarten predictor variables. The quality of prediction was better for the reading comprehension criterion measures obtained at about the same time and was best for the spelling measures in Grades 3 and 4.

The best predictors for word-decoding speed at the first assessment (the beginning of Grade 2) were children's letter knowledge and IQ, whereas phonological awareness and information-processing speed were considerably more important at the end of Grade 2. IQ was also a significant predictor of children's reading comprehension. However, indicators of phonological awareness in the broad sense (i.e., subtests of the sound categorization task) proved even more important for the prediction of individual differences in this criterion variable. As indicated by the regression analyses for the various spelling measures, the overall impact of the four predictor domains increased with time. Altogether, they accounted for almost 50% of the variance in spelling assessed at the end of Grade 3. Given that the type of stepwise regression analysis chosen generally overestimated the impact of IQ, the results indicate that indicators of early literacy (letter knowledge, name writing, and sign knowledge) had the comparably strongest impact, followed by measures of memory capacity, phonological awareness in the narrow sense, and information-processing speed.

Our findings concerning the "causal" status of phonological awareness in the process of learning to read and spell confirm those obtained in the British and Scandinavian longitudinal studies (e.g., Bradley and Bryant 1985; Lundberg et al. 1988). These findings indicate that phonological awareness in both the broad and the narrow sense predict later reading and spelling, even in those children who did not learn to break the alphabetic code before the end of kindergarten. The fact that a few children in this subgroup performed very well in the sound-blending and sound-to-word matching tasks contradicts the position that letter knowledge is a necessary condition for phonological awareness in the narrow sense (e.g., Morais 1991). However, it should be noted that phonological awareness in the subgroup with minimal letter knowledge was generally lower than that observed for the rest of the sample. Thus, letter knowledge in kindergarten clearly makes a difference with regard to phonological processing skills. Children who had already acquired letter knowledge in kindergarten performed better on most reading and spelling tests administered in elementary school. This indicates that early differences in letter knowledge seem to have long-lasting effects.

Overall, sex differences did not play a major role. We found only a few performance differences in favor of girls in the various kindergarten measures of metalinguistic abilities and memory capacity. Similarly, boys and girls did not differ on our measures of decoding speed, reading comprehension, and spelling assessed in Grade 2. The fact that girls outperformed boys in spelling tests administered later in time suggests that noncognitive factors such as attentional behavior, learning motivation, and attitude toward school may underly the sex differences in spelling frequently observed during the late school years.

Taken together, our findings show that phonological awareness, early literacy, and memory capacity do qualify as important predictors of reading and spelling. These variables proved to be specific predictors for the acquisition of literacy in that they did not relate to other subjects such as math. Our findings thus confirm the results of major Anglo-American and Scandinavian longitudinal studies, indicating that the importance of these predictor domains generalizes across several languages. These domains go beyond those obtained in most other longitudinal studies in that the relative impact of the various predictor domains was found to vary as a function of the criterion measure under study. For instance, indicators of phonological awareness in the broad sense, such as rhyming, were important for the prediction of decoding speed and reading comprehension in Grade 2. However, they were less relevant than letter knowledge or memory span in predicting spelling performance in subsequent school years. Finally, the results of this study clearly suggest that the role of IQ in predicting reading and spelling was overrated in earlier longitudinal studies. The predictive power of general cognitive abilities is greatly reduced when measures more specifically related to processes of reading and spelling are simultaneously considered.

References

Blachman, B. A. (1984). Relationship of rapid naming ability and language analysis skills to kindergarten and first-grade reading achievement. *Journal of Educational Psychology, 76*, 610–622.

Bradley, L., & Bryant, P. (1985). *Rhyme and reason in reading and spelling.* Ann Arbor: University of Michigan Press.

Brügelmann, H. (1986). *Lese- und Schreibaufgaben für Schulanfänger.* Universität Bremen: Studiengang Primarstufe.

Burgemeister, B., Blum, L., & Lorge, J. (1972). *Columbia Mental Maturity Scale.* New York: Harcourt Brace.

Case, R., Kurland, D. M., & Goldberg, J. (1982). Operational efficiency and the growth of short-term memory span. *Journal of Experimental Child Psychology, 33*, 386–404.

Daneman, M., & Blennerhassett, A. (1984). How to assess the listening comprehension skills of prereaders. *Journal of Educational Psychology, 76*, 1372–1381.

Denckla, M. B., & Rudel, R. G. (1976). Rapid "automatized" naming (R.A.N.): Dyslexia differentiated from other learning disabilities. *Neuropsychologia, 14*, 471–479.

Eggert, D. (1978). *Hannover–Wechsler–Intelligenztest für das Vorschulalter* [German version of the WPPSI]. Bern, Switzerland: Huber-Verlag.

Ellis, N., & Large, B. (1987). The development of reading: As you seek so shall you find. *British Journal of Psychology, 78*, 1–28.

Helmke, A., Schneider, W., & Weinert, F. E. (1986). Quality of instruction and classroom learning outcomes: The German contribution to the IEA Classroom Environment Study. *Teaching and Teacher Education, 2*, 1–18.

Horn, W. F., & Packard, T. (1985). Early identification of learning problems: A meta-analysis. *Journal of Educational Psychology, 77*, 597–607.

Jansen, H., Knorn, P., Mannhaupt, G., Marx, H., Beck, M., & Skowronek, H. (1986). *Bielefelder Screening zur Vorhersage von Lese- und Rechtschreibschwierigkeiten* [Bielefeld Screening test for the early identification of children at risk in reading and spelling]. University of Bielefeld, Germany.

Jöreskog, K. G., & Sörbom, D. (1989). *LISREL VII–Analysis of linear structural relationships (User's Guide)*. Mooresville, IN: Scientific Software.

Juel, C. (1988). Learning to read and write: A longitudinal study of 54 children from first through fourth grades. *Journal of Educational Psychology, 80*, 437–447.

Lundberg, I., Frost, J., & Petersen, O. P. (1988). Effects of an extensive program for stimulating phonological awareness in preschool children. *Reading Research Quarterly, 23*, 261–284.

Lundberg, I., & Hoien, T. (1991). Initial enabling knowledge and skills in reading acquisition: Print awareness and phonological segmentation. In D. J. Sawyer & B. J. Fox (Eds.), *Phonological awareness in reading–The evolution of current perspectives* (pp. 73–96). New York: Springer Verlag.

Marx, H. (1992). *Vorhersage von Rechtschreibschwierigkeiten in Theorie und Anwendung* [The prediction of reading and spelling problems in theory and practice]. Unpublished habilitation, University of Bielefeld, Germany.

Morais, J. (1991). Constraints on the development of phonemic awareness. In S. A. Brady, & D. P. Shankweiler (Eds.), *Phonological processes in literacy–A tribute to Isabelle Y. Liberman* (pp. 5–27). Hillsdale, NJ: Erlbaum.

Morais, J., Cary, L., Alegria, J., & Bertelson, P. (1979). Does awareness of speech as a sequence of phones arise spontaneously? *Cognition, 7*, 323–331.

Näslund, J. (1990). The interrelationships among preschool predictors of reading acquisition for German children. *Reading & Writing: An Interdisciplinary Journal, 2*, 327–380.

Näslund, J., & Schneider, W. (1991). Longitudinal effects of verbal ability, memory capacity, and phonological awareness on reading performance. *European Journal of Psychology of Education, 6*, 375–392.

Näslund, J., & Schneider, W. (1993). Emerging literacy from kindergarten to second grade: Evidence from the Munich Longitudinal Study on the Genesis of Individual Competencies. In H. Grimm & H. Skowronek (Eds.), *Language acquisition problems and reading disorders: Aspects of diagnosis and intervention* (pp. 295–318). New York: de Gruyter.

Perfetti, C., & Lesgold, A. (1978). Coding and comprehension in skilled reading and instruction. In L. Resnick & P. Weaver (Eds.), *Theory and practice of early reading* (Vol. 1, pp. 57–84). Hillsdale, NJ: Erlbaum.

Read, C., Yun-Fei, Z., Hong-Yin, N., & Bao-Quing, D. (1986). The ability to manipulate speech sounds depends on knowing alphabetic writing. *Cognition, 24*, 31–45.

Rott, C., & Zielinski, W. (1986). Entwicklung der Lesefertigkeit in der Grundschule [The development of reading skills in elementary school]. *Zeitschrift für Entwicklungspsychologie und Pädagogische Psychologie, 18*, 165–175.

Schneider, W., & Näslund, J. (1992). Cognitive prerequisites of reading and spelling: A longitudinal approach. In A. Demetriou, M. Shayer, & A. Efklides (Eds.), *Neo-Piagetian theories of cognitive development: Implications and applications for education* (pp. 256–274). London: Routledge.

Schneider, W., & Näslund, J. (1993). The impact of early metalinguistic competencies and memory capacity on reading and spelling in elementary school: Results of the Munich Longitudinal Study on the Genesis of Individual Competencies (LOGIC). *European Journal of Psychology of Education, 8*, 273–287.

Schneider, W., & Treiber, B. (1984). Classroom differences in the determination of achievement changes. *American Educational Research Journal, 21*, 195–211.

Skowronek, H., & Marx, H. (1989). The Bielefeld longitudinal study on early identification of risks in learning to write and read: Theoretical background and first results. In M. Brambring, F. Lösel, & H. Skowronek (Eds.), *Children at risk: Assessment, longitudinal research, and intervention* (pp. 268–294). New York: de Gruyter.

Stanovich, K., Cunningham, A. E., & Feeman, D. J. (1984). Intelligence, cognitive skills, and early reading progress. *Reading Research Quarterly, 19*, 278–303.

Tramontana, M., Hooper, S., & Selzer, S. (1988). Research on the preschool prediction of later academic achievement: A review. *Developmental Review, 8*, 89–146.

Tunmer, W. E., & Nesdale, A. R. (1985). Phonemic segmentation skill and beginning reading. *Journal of Educational Psychology, 77*, 417–427.

Vellutino, F. R., Scanlon, D. M., Clark, R., Small, S., Fanuele, D., & Pratt, A. (1992, April). *Gender differences in early reading, language and arithmetic abilities in kindergarten children*. Paper presented at the annual meeting of the American Educational Research Association, San Francisco.

Wagner, R., & Torgesen, J. (1987). The nature of phonological processing and its causal role in the acquisition of reading skills. *Psychological Bulletin, 101*, 192–212.

Wimmer, H., Hartl, M., & Moser, E. (1990). Passen "englische" Modelle des Schriftspracherwerbs auf "deutsche" Kinder? Zweifel an der Bedeutsamkeit der logographischen Stufe [Do "English" models of reading acquisition apply to German children? Doubts concerning the significance of the logographic stage]. *Zeitschrift für Entwicklungspsychologie und Pädagogische Psychologie, 22*, 136–154.

7a Comment: Sound Logic

Peter Bryant

The evidence for the importance of children's phonological sensitivities in learning to read is now so overwhelming that we have nearly reached the stage – rather rare in psychology – when we can say, "Enough research has been done, we know the answer, let's get on to something else."

The clear answer is that the link between phonology and learning to read is crucial: Dyslexic children are for the most part very bad at phonological analysis (Hulme and Snowling 1994). Children's scores in phonological tasks given to them long before school predict their progress in reading and spelling many years later, and predict it better than other measures such as their IQ (Goswami and Bryant 1990): The predictive power of these phonological measures is specific, in that they are related to the children's achievements in reading and spelling but not to their performance in other educational areas such as mathematics (Bryant, Bradley, MacLean, and Crossland 1989; Bryant, MacLean, Bradley, and Crossland 1990). Extra training in phonological analysis has the consistent effect of improving children's reading and spelling quite appreciably (Lundberg, Frost, and Petersen 1988). Each of these results has come up in several different studies in several different countries with several different languages.

So what new insight can be gained by Schneider and Näslund's new investigation into the relationship into the phonological connection? Why should this investigation have been part of the grand LOGIC design? The reply to this question is rather simple: So far, the link has been studied mainly on its own. For example, studies of dyslexic children's phonological difficulties tend to be studies of just those difficulties and little else (Hulme and Snowling 1994). The strikingly successful longitudinal predictions of reading on the basis of phonological tasks have typically concentrated only on those tasks. Training studies have looked at one form of intervention – phonological – and at one outcome measure – reading. This concentration on one variable has given the research done so far a certain power and has certainly established the importance of that variable. However, it has also left us with two worrying questions.

One is about the origins of this skill. It is quite possible that the cause–effect relationship is one way that children's phonological sensitivities simply influence

148

their reading and that is all. However, children are introduced to reading often quite early in their lives, and they are usually taught about the alphabet and letter–sound correspondences even earlier than that, so it is also possible that the experience of being taught about the alphabet and how to read an alphabetic script may considerably affect their awareness of sounds (Mann 1986; Morais, Bertelson, Cary, and Alegria 1986; Morais, Cary, Alegria, and Bertelson 1979; Read, Zhang, Nie, and Ding 1986).

The other question is about the relation of this particular ability to other abilities. Is it, so to speak, freestanding and independent of other abilities? Or are phonological measures simply a rather effective way of measuring a broad linguistic ability that is the main determinant of how well children learn to read? It is even possible that the phonological tasks that have proved to be such effective predictors of literacy owe their success to the fact that they measure some other skill as well. For example, most phonological tasks involve memory, and it has been suggested that their connection with reading can be at least partly explained by this fact (Gathercole and Baddeley 1993). There plainly has been a need for longitudinal data that include other cognitive measures, and particularly memory tasks, in addition to the phonological ones.

Schneider and Näslund's contribution to the LOGIC project is a heartening instance of a good research opportunity being recognized and seized. The comprehensive way in which the LOGIC longitudinal project was planned, the imaginative choice of questions, and the meticulous analysis of its results surely make it the most ambitious and in the end the most impressive and informative longitudinal study of intellectual development in educational settings that has ever been done. The fact that this was not just a study of reading, or of mathematics, or of scientific understanding, but of all these topics and many more, enhances the power of each part of the project immensely. Although it will take many years for us to appreciate the full richness of the data, the possibilities of finding solutions to questions about the relationship between different aspects of cognitive development and educational experience are already clear.

When Schneider and Näslund designed the part of the project that dealt with reading, they recognized the need to answer the two questions that I have mentioned already, and they saw that the LOGIC framework gave them the chance to find an answer to both. The first of the two questions, about the origins of phonological skills and the cause–effect relationships with reading, had already been the subject of a great deal of discussion, but very little of the relevant research had been longitudinal. The opening shots in this particular controversy came from the Brussels team, who argued on the basis of two comparisons of literate and illiterate people that the awareness of phonemes is largely the product of being taught to read (Morais et al. 1986; Morais et al. 1979). In the first of these experiments, Morais and colleagues compared groups of people in rural Portugal. The people in the first group had been illiterate for most of their lives, but comparatively recently they had taken part in an adult literacy program and had learned to read and write. They compared this group to another that had not taken these courses and were still illiterate. Morais and colleagues gave both groups a set of tasks that was designed to test their abilities to deal with phonemes: They had either to add a phoneme to the beginning of a word (add *p* to *urso*) or a nonword or to remove one (take *p* from *purso*).

The illiterate group was far worse at this than the literate group, and this result was repeated in the second study. In this study, an illiterate group also fared much worse than an ex-illiterate group in a phoneme task, and they also were much worse in a rhyme detection task. The Brussels team was more interested, however, in the consistent difference in the phoneme task and argued that this demonstrated that on the whole, people understand that words and syllables can be broken down into phonemes as a direct rule for learning to read. Their conclusion was borne out by subsequent cross-linguistic comparisons made by Read et al. (1986) and by Mann (1986) showing that people who are taught scripts (Chinese and Japanese) that are not alphabetic are also at a relative disadvantage when they are given the kind of phoneme task previously described.

The studies certainly showed that the experience of being taught to read an alphabetic script might well affect children's awareness of phonemes. However, other work on other aspects of children's phonological awareness made it clear that there was more to be said about cause and effect in the study of phonological awareness and learning to read. In many of the studies in which children's performance in phonological tasks successfully predicted the progress that they made in reading later on, these tasks were given to the children long before they could read (Goswami and Bryant 1990). This might seem surprising given the results, just cited, that show that people who have not been taught an alphabetic script flounder in phoneme tasks. However, there is no puzzle, for the phonological tasks given to preschool children that predict their reading successfully operate at a different phonological level. Although preschool children usually find phoneme tasks impossible, they do quite well when they have to produce rhymes or to judge whether words rhyme (Bradley and Bryant 1983). Such tasks are indubitably phonological because they involve judgments about the similarity of phonological segments, but they typically involve phonological segments that are considerably larger than the phoneme: To recognize that *string* and *thing* rhyme is to deal in a phonological segment *ing*, which is a sequence of three phonemes. In one-syllable words, it should be mentioned, the rhyming sound corresponds to the intrasyllabic unit for which the linguists' term is the *rime*.

The fact that children are amply aware of intrasyllabic units before they can read and the fact that their proficiency with these units is so strongly related to their reading later on provide us with something of a puzzle. Why should awareness of phonological segments that look considerably cruder than the phoneme be related to the way in which children learn to cope with the alphabetic code when, prima facie, it seems that the code operates at the level of the phoneme because on the whole, alphabetic letters represent phonemes?

There are two possible answers to this question. One is that though the children in question may not have been able yet to read when they were given these rhyme tests, they still may have been taught about the alphabetic code. There is considerable evidence that children's knowledge of letter–sound relationships is also a good predictor of their reading later on, and yet there has been no attempt in longitudinal studies of the phonology and reading connection to check whether this connection can be explained away in terms of children's knowledge of letter–sound relationships. It is quite possible that the young children's awareness of rhyme and alliteration in these studies was actually a product of being taught about letter–sound relationships before they had begun to read.

The second possibility is that children acquire their sensitivity to rhyme independently of their learning about the alphabet and that this sensitivity allows them to realize that groups of words that have sounds in common also have sequences of letters in common. *Sight, fight,* and *light* rhyme, and they also share a letter sequence that represents the rhyming sound. So, children's awareness of rhyme may be important to learning to read because it gives them a chance to learn about sequences of letters.

The Schneider and Näslund study provides an interesting and in some ways surprising answer to this question. They had the wisdom to include a letter–sound task as well as their various phonological measures, and they found that although the phonological scores consistently predicted reading later on, this relationship was particularly powerful with those children who had very little knowledge of letter–sound relationships when the phonological measures were taken. Here, then, is an interaction that tells us at least two things. One, the phonological connection probably does not depend on instruction in the alphabet: Quite the reverse, the children who lack this knowledge are particularly dependent on their phonological skills to learn to read. Second, early and successful instruction in the alphabet might to some extent actually remove the need for this dependence. We may be dealing with two different and alternative routes into reading, and it should be added that the latent variables analyses reported by Schneider and Näslund at the end of their chapter reinforce this possibility. The contributions of early literacy and phonological awareness to reading and spelling are independent in the successful models in these analyses.

The main answer to the second question – about other skills and their role in the phonological connection – is mainly to be found in the data in this study on memory. For some time now it has been claimed that memory, particularly working memory, is a crucial variable in learning to read (Gathercole and Baddeley 1993), and much of the argument has centered again on the phonological connection. The reason for this is that phonological tasks involve memory. The child invariably has to remember sounds and words in order to perform these tasks. Although some attempts have been made to control for the possible effects of differences in memory capacity in these tasks (Bradley and Bryant 1983), the claim has still been made that the controls were not adequate and that the memory hypothesis is still a persuasive alternative.

Before going into the actual results, it is as well to consider the various possibilities. There are two extremes. One is that memory, not phonological sensitivity, determines how well children read and therefore, the phonological connection is no more than artifact. The other is that memory plays no part: It is the phonological connection and nothing more than that. In between these two extreme hypotheses lie several rather more complex but less crude ideas: Memory plays a part but an indirect one; it contributes to the children's phonological skills, and these skills then contribute to reading.

Schneider and Näslund's structural equation models support the idea of the indirect contribution, but the direction of this contribution varies with the outcome measure. With spelling, the story is easy to grasp: The children's memory capacity contributes very strongly to phonological awareness, quite appreciably also to their early literacy (letter knowledge, etc.), and to their ability to read single words (recoding) – and all three of these variables play a considerable part in the children's success in spelling. However, when reading comprehension is the outcome measure, working memory continues to make an indirect contribution through recoding and early literacy, but this tie is not through phonological awareness. Why should this be so?

It seems to me that the most plausible reason is that letter–sound relationships may pose a greater demand on memory in spelling than in reading. The young child, after all, is a great deal more familiar with sounds than with letters, and, therefore, it might be easier for him or her to remember appropriate sounds rather than letters. It may, therefore, impose a far greater burden on children to start with a sound and have to remember the appropriate letter (which is what happens in spelling) than to start with a letter and have to remember the appropriate sound (which is what happens in reading).

Whether or not this speculation is correct, there is no doubt that the Schneider and Näslund study has provided a new and more sophisticated insight into the tripartite relation between memory, phonological awareness, and reading and spelling. At the very least it demonstrates that the introduction into the debate about the phonological connection is justified and that we still need to think deeply about the relation between phonological awareness and other skills.

Finally I want to remark on the last of the structural equation models presented by Schneider and Näslund, which demonstrates the power of having several successive measures of the same outcome measures – in this case, spelling at Grades 2, 3, 4, and 5. The successful model is extraordinarily explicit and suggests an important conclusion about the precursors of literacy. The model confirms that phonological awareness, early literacy, recoding, and memory contribute, either directly or indi-rectly, to the children's performance in spelling at Grade 1. However, it also suggests that the contribution comes, so to speak, all in one dollop. Thereafter there is no direct contribution of any of these variables to the children's spelling. Grade 2 spelling is influenced directly by Grade 1 spelling, Grade 3 spelling by Grades 1 and 2 spelling, and so on. There is no sign here of any long-term delayed effect of early experience in phonology or in learning about alphabetic letters. It influences reading and spelling at the start – and that is it. It is a valuable and sobering result.

The Schneider and Näslund study is a remarkable demonstration of the power of a well-conceived longitudinal study, and yet what we have read in this study is, it seems to me, the formidable tip of an even more formidable iceberg. For the study is part of the wider LOGIC study and thus will give us, in time, a great deal of additional information about the same children in different intellectual areas. Thus, in time, we will find out about the connections between their reading and other aspects of their intellectual development, between the phonological measures and other educational achievements, and between the memory scores and other cognitive tasks. It is, at the same time, a comforting and exciting prospect.

References

Bradley, L., & Bryant, P. E. (1983). Categorizing sounds and learning to read: A causal connection. *Nature, 30*, 419–421.

Bryant, P. E., Bradley, L., MacLean, M., & Crossland, J. (1989). Nursery rhymes, phonological skills and reading. *Journal of Child Language, 16*, 407–428.

Bryant, P. E., MacLean, M., Bradley, L. L., & Crossland, J. (1990). Rhyme, alliteration, phoneme detection and learning to read. *Developmental Psychology, 26*, 429–438.

Gathercole, S., & Baddeley, A. (1993). *Working memory and language*. Hillsdale, NJ: Erlbaum.

Goswami, U., & Bryant, P. (1990). *Phonological skills and learning to read*. Hillsdale, NJ: Erlbaum.

Hulme, C., & Snowling, M. (1994). *Reading development and dyslexia*. London: Whurr Publishers Ltd.

Lundberg, I., Frost, J., & Petersen, O. (1988). Effects of an extensive program for stimulating phonological awareness in preschool children. *Reading Research Quarterly, 23*, 263–284.

Mann, V. A. (1986). Phonological awareness: The role of reading experience. *Cognition, 24*, 65–92.

Morais, J., Bertelson, P., Cary, L., & Alegria, J. (1986). Literacy training and speech segmentation. *Cognition, 24*, 45–64.

Morais, J., Cary, L., Alegria, J., & Bertelson, P. (1979). Does awareness of speech as a sequence of phones arise spontaneously? *Cognition, 7*, 323–331.

Read, C., Zhang, Y., Nie, H., & Ding, B. (1986). The ability to manipulate speech sounds depends on knowing alphabetic spelling. *Cognition, 24*, 31–44.

8   Development of Mathematical Competencies

Elsbeth Stern

In structuralistic theories as well as in domain-specific theories of cognitive development, improvement of mathematical competencies is considered to be an important issue. Structuralistic views as developed by Piaget (1950), Case (1985), and recently by Halford (1992) use mathematical problems requiring number conservation or proportional reasoning to demonstrate progress in general information-processing efficiency or cognitive structures. Structuralistic theories of cognitive development have been challenged seriously by nativistic views that see the neonate as preprogrammed to make sense of specific information sources. There is a compelling line of evidence for an innate origin of mathematical knowledge. All aspects guiding the cardinal understanding of numbers, such as counting, seem to be guided more or less by innate principles (Gelman 1990; Wynn 1990). Therefore, the basic principles of mathematics are acquired easily by young preschool children without systematic instruction. In contrast, however, the acquisition of advanced mathematical concepts that are products of cultural evolution takes place during a long and continuous process that requires systematic instruction (Gelman 1991; Resnick 1989). Advanced mathematical understanding necessary for school-based mathematics entails radical restructuring of early cardinal number understanding. Advanced mathematical understanding is based on the mathematical symbol system that is characterized by a dual role: On one hand, symbols are used to describe and model concrete, real-world situations and events, whereas on the other hand they derive their mathematical power from the fact that their intrinsic meaning is divorced from concrete contexts. One can solve problems such as $3 + 5 =$ without referring to real situations in which elements of sets are combined. To have advanced understanding of mathematics means knowing that numbers are understood not only as counting instruments but are also used to describe the relation between sets and symbolic systems.

The importance of advanced mathematical understanding becomes clear when considering mathematical problems that go beyond the counting function of numbers. Three types of mathematical competencies fulfilling this criterion are considered in this chapter. (a) Strategy use in arithmetic: Solving complex arithmetic problems such as $16 + 8 - 8 =$ can be considerably facilitated by using principles such as commutativity and the neutral element. The use of a shortcut strategy instead of a computing strategy requires flexibility in dealing with quantitative symbols. (b) Solving arithmetic word problems: Understanding and solving word problems requires modeling real-life situations with the help of mathematical symbols. In particular, understanding statements that describe the relations between sets such as "Peter has five marbles less than John" requires understanding that the function of numbers goes beyond counting (Stern 1993a). (c) Proportional reasoning: When faced with situations that require considering at least two different units (e.g., situations dealing with speed), principles guiding the counting function of numbers must be ignored; although it is true that larger numbers refer to larger quantities for counting numbers, only the relation between the involved numbers allows inferences about the size of quantities for proportional units.

Mathematics provides an example of a domain in which huge performance differences are obtained at all age levels. Similar to the question of whether between-age differences are due to domain-specific or domain-general differences, within-age differences are considered to be explained by differences in general or in specific abilities. G-factor theories explain individual differences by referring to differences in general processing efficiency. Support for these theories comes from data showing correlations across performances in different domains (e.g., Spearman 1927). The correlation between measures of general intelligence and achievement in mathematics is higher than with most other school subjects (Gustaffson and Balke 1993). There are two main approaches toward explaining what Factor G might be. Low-level models focus on differences in basic information-processing aspects, such as speed and capacity (Jensen 1982). High-level approaches, on the other hand, focus on metacognitive competencies (Sternberg 1985). Both high-level and low-level theories can explain individual differences in mathematics because in this domain very complex facts are described with the help of a very sparse system of symbols. Understanding a sequence of mathematical symbols entails activating complex knowledge structures, which presupposes a high processing efficiency. At the same time, the complexity of most mathematical problems requires metacognitive abilities for planning the problem-solving process.

Domain-specific approaches such as those developed by Thurstone (1938) or recently by Gardner (1983) are based on empirical findings that indicate that individuals may show high competencies in some domains, although they are only average or even below average in other domains. There are good reasons for considering specific factors to explain variance in mathematical achievement: Intelligent persons with poor performance in mathematics exist, as do participants showing the opposite pattern.

Open Research Questions

Theories of general development and theories of individual differences focus on similar distinctions and processes: In both research approaches, domain-specific competencies are contrasted with general competencies. Moreover, the competencies considered in Factor G theories of intelligence, such as speed, capacity, or processing efficiency, correspond to competencies focused on some neo-Piagetian theories of development. Combining theories of cognitive development and psychometric theories means developing a theory that is able to explain coherently individual differences within and between age groups. According to the theory developed by Anderson (1992), competencies arise from domain-specific modules that are restructured with development. For example, individual differences in understanding rational numbers are caused by individual differences in the speed of restructuring conceptual primitives into more advanced and abstract knowledge structures. Innate differences in general information-processing speed are responsible for within-age level performance differences. Applied to the acquisition of mathematical competencies, this means that participants differ in the speed of restructuring cardinal numbers into more abstract numerical concepts.

It is the goal of this chapter to shed light on the impact of general and domain-specific abilities on longitudinal development of individual differences in advanced mathematical competencies between and within age levels by addressing the following issues:

1. *The impact of age-related developmental levels on mathematical competencies.* If the general cognitive competencies obtained at a particular age level have a strong impact on performance across many specific competencies as predicted by structuralistic theories, high correlations between general and specific measures within the same measurement point will be obtained. If, however, domain-specific performance is determined by successive acquisition and restructuring of specific knowledge, high correlations between similar measures presented at different measurement points are expected.

2. *The impact of preschool performance on later mathematical competencies.* If interindividual performance differences in mathematics are caused by the speed with which basic concepts are restructured into more abstract and advanced concepts, performance differences measured in preschool are expected to predict later mathematical performance because participants who began restructuring basic concepts earlier are expected to be able to develop more advanced concepts. A question of interest in this context is whether general or specific competencies have a stronger impact on later mathematical achievement.

3. *The impact of competencies in elementary school on proportional reasoning.* As mentioned before, the acquisition of proportional reasoning is considered to be an important transition in all theories of cognitive development, and therefore this issue merits further research. Individual differences in proportional reasoning in middle grades might be determined by performance differences in domain-specific knowledge in elementary school. Because advanced mathematical knowledge is developed from restructured basic competencies, the earlier such competencies are acquired, the earlier they might be restructured. According to structuralistic theories of development, however, advanced general cognitive abilities are considered to be the necessary precondition for proportional reasoning. Therefore, a substantial within-measurement point correlation between general abilities and proportional reasoning is expected.

4. *The impact of broader abilities on mathematical performance.* Differences in domain-specific knowledge cannot be expected to be the only source of within- and between-

age level differences in mathematical competencies. Low-level abilities such as speed of information processing as well as high-level abilities such as metacognitive skills and crystallized intelligence might have an impact on mathematical competencies. Moreover, besides such general competencies, former studies on mathematical litera- ture abilities have shown an impact of spatial abilities on mathematical performance. The age level at which different kinds of abilities will influence mathematical per- formance is analyzed.

Method

Participants

In every wave of the LOGIC study, measures of mathematical competencies were presented. However, for the following reasons, the full sample of children could not be considered in the analyses. As mentioned in the introduction of this volume, not all children entered school in the same year. As the time spent on attending school has clear effects on mathematical competencies, only the children who had entered school by 1987 were considered in the following analyses. As measures of word-problem solving were presented only in the SCHOLASTIC sample, analyses considering these measures were based only on 110–120 participants.

Measures of Mathematical Competencies

In the LOGIC study, we focused on the acquisition of mathematic competencies that demand numerical understanding beyond a cardinal understanding of numbers. Three problem types were considered: (a) word problems dealing with the comparison of sets, (b) numerical problems requiring the use of elaborated strategies, and (c) problems dealing with proportions.

Word Problems Dealing with the Comparison of Sets. The first time that children's numerical understanding goes beyond the cardinal understanding of numbers might be when they understand the quantitative comparison. Understanding sentences such as "John has three marbles more than Peter" requires the understanding that the difference between the sets is not a concrete, existing set of elements, but it rather describes the relation between the two sets. Quantitative comparison is generally not understood before entering school (Stern 1993b). Arithmetic word problems dealing with the comparison of sets are more difficult than problems dealing with the exchange, combination, and equalization of sets (Riley, Greeno, and Heller 1983; Stern 1993b). A well-known result first published by Hudson (1983) and replicated several times (Davis-Dorsey, Ross, and Morrison 1991; Stern 1993b) illustrates young children's difficulties: Although nearly all children solve problems such as "There are five birds and three worms. How many birds won't get a worm," fewer than 20% of the participants solve the problem if it ends with the question "How many more birds than worms are there?" An explanation for these differences might be that children have difficulties accessing the appropriate mathematical model (Stern 1993a, 1993b; Stern and Lehrndorfer 1992). Although the question "How many birds won't get a worm?" asks for a concrete, countable set, the question "How many more birds than worms are there?" asks for the relation between two sets. Understanding that numbers can be used not just for counting but also for describing the relation between sets might be the first step to an extended mathematical understanding. Stern (1993b) has found several lines of evidence indicating that understanding and solving word problems dealing with the comparison of sets is the precondition for developing advanced mathematical competencies such as understanding rational numbers.

To find out which children understand the quantitative comparison at a very early age and what consequences early understanding of the quantitative comparison might have on later mathematical understanding, we presented arithmetic word problems dealing with the comparison of sets in Waves 5, 6, and 7 (second, third, and fourth grade, respectively)[1] in a written test. In each test, there were 10 comparison problems: 2 were one-step problems, such as "John has five marbles. He has two marbles less than Peter. How many marbles does Peter have?" and 8 were multiple-step problems, such as "John has five marbles. He has two marbles less than Peter. How many marbles do John and Peter have together?" or "Susan and Mary have 14 dolls altogether. Susan has 2 dolls less than Mary. How many dolls does Mary have?"

For each wave, the number of correct problems, defined as the correct answer and the correct equation, was scored.

Strategy Use in Arithmetic. The use of simplifier strategies to solve arithmetic problems also requires an advanced understanding of mathematics. The use of simplifier strategies, such as $8 + 5 = 8 + 2 + 3$, is based purely on symbol manipulation. Detached from any concrete context, symbols can be manipulated in different ways with the only constraint being that the sum total remains constant. In all waves, two kinds of problems requiring the use of simplifier strategies were presented: inversion problems and estimation problems.

1. *Inversion problems.* Only a few children younger than 10 use shortcut strategies to solve inversion problems such as $a + b - b =$ (Bisanz and LeFevre 1990; Stern 1992), although children at this age level can be expected to have mastered the principles underlying the shortcut strategy: commutativity and the neutral element. In a computer-based procedure presented in Wave 5 (second grade), Wave 6 (third grade), and Wave 7 (fourth grade), problems requiring facilitating strategies were presented. A problem (e.g., $35 + 8 - 8$) was presented in the middle of a computer screen, and the correct answer was presented in one corner of the screen while an incorrect answer was presented in another corner. Children had to press a button corresponding to the correct answer, and if no button was pressed within 9 s, the next problem was presented. The time required to solve the problem was measured. A maximum of 9 s was given.

2. *Estimation problems.* With the same procedure, the use of the estimation strategy was investigated. Estimation problems were one-step subtraction and addition problems

---

[1] Only the LOGIC children who were also in the SCHOLASTIC study were given these tasks.

with one number being larger than 20. The wrong answer was always a number that contradicted basic mathematical principles. For example, in a subtraction problem, the incorrect answer presented might be larger than the numbers used in the equation. Participants who first checked whether one of the two possible answers contradicted basic principles of mathematics did not have to compute an answer.

The number of correctly solved problems and the mean solution times for correct answers were scored. Alpha analyses indicated that the score "number of correctly solved problems" was more reliable at all measurement points than scores based on solution times. Participants who did not use strategies failed in most cases to solve the problem within the required time and, therefore, were not given credit for a correct answer.

Proportional Reasoning. Dealing with proportions requires giving up principles that guide the understanding of counting: Larger numbers do not always refer to larger quantities than smaller numbers. Being able to reason proportionally means knowing that one has to consider at least two sources of information before drawing a conclusion. Adolescents' difficulties with understanding proportions, decimal numbers, and fractions are well documented. The most frequent mistake made is that larger numbers are considered to refer to larger values than smaller numbers; for instance, that $6/8 > 6/7$ (Hiebert 1986).

Proportional reasoning in elementary- and middle-grade children is a well-researched field: Several standardized tasks have been developed, and several studies describe five steps leading to correct proportional reasoning (Case 1978; Karplus, Pulos, and Stage 1983; Noelting 1980). Using as an example a task in which one has to determine which of two beverages made from glasses of raspberry juice and glasses of water will taste more intensive, we define the stages as follows. (a) In the stage of *isolated centration*, participants only consider whether raspberry juice was added or not. (b) In the stage of *unidimensional comparison*, participants ignore the amount of water and only consider which beverage contains an absolute greater amount of raspberry juice. (c) In the stage of *bidimensional comparison*, both dimensions are considered, but without quantification. The children only compare the quantity of water and juice in each beverage, and they pick the beverage having an excess of juice over water. When this is the case for both beverages, participants guess. (d) In the stage of *bidimensional comparison with quantification*, children compute the difference between water and juice for each beverage and choose the beverage with the larger difference. (e) Only in the stage of *ratio comparison* do participants use division strategies to find out in which beverage the proportion of juice is larger.

Summarizing from the results reported by Noelting (1980) and Karplus et al. (1983), participants begin to make bidimensional comparisons at about 7 years of age, bidimensional comparisons with quantification at about 10 years of age, and ratio comparison only after 15 years of age. In the longitudinal study, we focused on the transition from the bidimensional comparison (Stage 3) to the bidimensional comparison with quantification (Wave 5). In Waves 7 (Grade 4), 8 (Grade 5), and

9 (Grade 6), problems were presented that could be solved correctly by using the strategies typical for Stages 2–4. The problems were embedded in different context stories, such as testing the taste of mixed raspberry, estimating the weight of pieces of cheese differing in size, or collecting money for a good purpose.

Although they differ in their superficial structure, problems measuring arithmetic strategy use, understanding the quantitative comparison, and proportional reasoning are all similar in that they are based on elaborated mathematical understanding. Mathematical comprehension beyond counting is required to solve each type of problem. Therefore, close connections between these kinds of problems are expected. There are good reasons for assuming that an early use of elaborated strategies and early competencies in solving quantitative comparison problems might be good predictors of early competencies in proportional reasoning. Moreover, it may even be that mathematical performance in preschool is a good predictor of later performance in mathematics: Children who acquire basic mathematical competencies earlier than others may use this knowledge for developing more elaborated knowledge structures at an earlier time than other children.

Measures of Mathematical Competencies in Preschool

Counting Abilities. Long before entering formal school, children spontaneously acquire counting abilities at about age 4 (Wynn 1990). Differences in counting abilities in early childhood might predict differences in mathematical performance in elementary school. The earlier children learn to count, the earlier they might understand that counting is not the only function of numbers, and therefore they extend their mathematical understanding. In Wave 1 of the longitudinal study, counting abilities were observed: The children were asked to count sets of sizes varying between one and five.

Number Conservation. In Piaget's (1950) theory, the number-conservation test was considered to measure the transition from the preoperational stage to the concrete operational stage. Longitudinal studies by Stevenson and Newman (1986), however, indicated performance in number conservation to be a good predictor of mathematical performance in elementary school. Mastering the number-conservation task means understanding that verbal expressions such as "more than" and "less than" refer to the given number of elements in a set rather than to the spatial expansion of the elements. Thus, the number-conservation task might be an indicator of early quantitative reasoning ability rather than of the general cognitive level. In Wave 1 and Wave 3, children were presented with number-conservation problems.

Estimation of Quantities. Another measure of early quantitative abilities was quantity estimating, which is part of a German school-readiness test developed by Kern (1971). Children were presented with a set of three to nine small cubes and had to determine the number without counting them. Although this test was developed long before sophisticated theories of knowledge representation existed, a post hoc theoretical basis of this test is that it measures the efficiency with which visual information is transformed into mathematical symbols.

Numerical Abilities Measured with the Hannover–Wechsler–Intelligence Scale for Preschool Children (HAWIVA). In Wave 2 and in Wave 4, the Numerical Abilities subtest in the HAWIVA (Eggert 1978) was regarded as a measure of numerical abilities. In this subtest, participants had to solve addition and subtraction word problems.

Measures of General Cognitive Abilities

In each wave, measures of general cognitive abilities were presented. Three types of general measures were considered.

Nonverbal Intelligence. The Columbia Mental Maturity Scale (CMMS, Burgemeister, Blum, and Lorge 1972) was presented in Waves 1, 3, and 5. In Waves 7 and 9, a German version of the Raven test (Weiss and Osterland 1979) was presented.

Measures of Basic Information Processing. Measures of capacity and speed were presented as follows. (a) Capacity, the number span was measured in Waves 4 and 6 with a subtest of the Hamburg–Wechsler–Intelligence Scale for School Children (HAWIK, Tewes 1983). Word span was measured in Wave 3. (b) Speed, paper-and-pencil measures of speed were presented in Waves 6 and 8. Under time pressure, participants either had to relate numbers to digits or had to mark signs with particular features.

Verbal Intelligence. The General Knowledge, Analogies, and General Understanding subtests of the HAWIK and HAWIVA were combined and considered to be a measure of verbal intelligence.

Spatial Abilities. Spatial abilities are considered to have an influence on mathematical competencies. In Wave 8, Subtests 7 (folding) and 8 (field dependance) of the German Intelligence Test PSB (Prüfsystem für Schul- und Bildungsberatung [Testing System for educational counseling]), developed by Horn and Cattell (1966), were used. The PSB test is based on Thurstone's (1938) multiple-intelligence theory.

Results

Growth of Competencies

For all mathematical tests presented at different age levels, an increase in performance level was obtained, as expected.

Percent correct

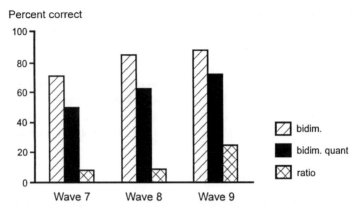

Figure 1. Percentage of correctly solved proportional reasoning problems separated by problem types: (a) Problems that could be solved correctly by qualitative bidimensional comparison, (b) problems that could be solved correctly by quantitative bidimensional comparison (difference strategy), and (c) problems that could only be solved correctly by the use of the ratio strategy.

Number Conservation. In Wave 1, only 10% of the participants passed the number-conservation task, whereas in Wave 3, 56% of the participants mastered it.

Word-Problem Solving. The mean solution rate for compare problems was .36 ($SD =$ .24) in Wave 5, .47 ($SD = .32$) in Wave 6, and .56 ($SD = .28$) in Wave 7. The correlations between the three measurement points were substantial (Waves 5–6 = .61; Waves 6–7 = .73; Waves 5–7 = .54, $p < .001$).

Strategy Use. The mean solution rate for problems requiring the use of facilitating strategies was .32 ($SD = .27$) in Wave 5, .45 ($SD = .28$) in Wave 6, and .76 ($SD = .18$) in Wave 7. The correlations between the three waves, although significant, were lower than for word-problem solving (Waves 5–6 = .43; Waves 6–7 = .50; and Waves 5–7 = .32, $p < .01$).

Proportional Reasoning. In accordance with other reported results (e.g., Noelting 1980), a transition from unidimensional comparison to bidimensional comparison took place. Figure 1 depicts the mean solution rates for problems requiring the use of different strategies. The results indicate that the bidimensional comparison strategy was used frequently in Wave 7, but the bidimensional strategy with quantification was used less frequently. In Wave 8, in contrast, the bidimensional strategy with quantification was quite common, but the ratio strategy was very uncommon. Even in Wave 9, only a few of the problems requiring the ratio strategy were solved correctly. The results depicted in Figure 1 indicate reduced variance in Waves 8 and 9. The correlations between the three waves were significant, but rather low between Waves 8 and 9, indicating that many participants were in a transition phase (Waves 7–8 = .39; Waves 8–9 = .28; and Waves 7–9 = .38, $p < .01$).

The Development of Individual Differences

The Impact of Age on Mathematical Competencies. A principal-components factor analysis with the 31 measures was conducted to find out whether different measures presented at the same age level show higher correlations than similar measures presented at different age levels. If this is the case, the analysis will produce age-level factors; that is, different measures presented at the same measurement time will load on the same factor. The analysis explained 70% of the variance and revealed the nine factors depicted in Table 1. There were no age-level factors at all, and measures presented at different age levels showed high loadings on the same factor. This result does not support models of development nor of individual differences that emphasize the impact of general abilities on mathematical competencies.

The Impact of Preschool Performance on Later Mathematical Competencies. Separate path analyses for strategy use, word-problem solving, and proportional reasoning were conducted to obtain information about the impact of general abilities and numerical competencies obtained in preschool on mathematical performance later during school. The results depicted in Figure 2 indicate that the general and specific preschool measures had a considerable impact. The results show that performance on the number-conservation task and the estimation-of-quantities task obtained in Wave 3 has a strong impact on later mathematical performance. Given that both tasks contained only a few items and were therefore less reliable than intelligence tests, their impact is especially remarkable. Knowing at an early age that verbal expressions used in number-conservation tasks such as "more than" and "less than" refer to the number of elements of sets rather than to their spatial extension seems to be helpful in understanding situations involving quantitative comparison and proportions. Participants who were good estimators of set sizes before they entered school were inclined to develop conceptually based computing strategies in the middle of elementary school.

However, although the number-conservation task and the estimation-of-quantities task both contributed to later mathematical performance, they were only moderately related to each other ($r = .32$, $p < .01$), and therefore it was not possible to combine them into a latent variable. Mathematical competencies measured in preschool seem to be quite task specific and may be restructured into broader abilities only later in development. The earlier participants acquire mathematical competencies such as number conservation and estimation of quantities, the greater the chance seems to be for developing knowledge structures that allow them to cope with more sophisticated mathematical problems.

Number estimation may measure efficiency in combining information and mathematical symbols. Participants showing good performance in this task may be able to transform visual information into symbolic information, and vice versa. This ability may help in switching between symbolic and visual representations, and representing a problem visually may help with shortcut strategies. In addition, solving problems

Table 1. *Factor Loadings of the Principal-Component Factor Analysis*

Variable	Factor 1: Verbal intelligence	Factor 2: Mathematical abilities	Factor 3: Number sense	Factor 4: Nonverbal intelligence	Factor 5: Number sense	Factor 6: Capacity	Factor 7: Nonverbal intelligence	Factor 8: Proportional reasoning	Factor 9: Number conservation
NC1	.09	.06	.13	.07	.06	.11	.03	.03	**.82**
NC3	.26	.18	.07	.09	**.47**	.08	.08	.34	-.22
EQ3	.19	-.01	**.42**	.10	**.40**	.19	.32	.26	-.15
MA2	.32	.26	.15	**.53**	.15	.19	.02	.15	-.11
MA4	.22	-.02	**.50**	.08	**.52**	.24	-.14	.07	-.00
MA6	.10	.30	.23	.10	**.63**	.10	-.08	-.01	.21
MA9	.19	**.48**	**.47**	.15	.22	.05	.01	.24	.13
WP5	.30	**.63**	**.39**	.18	.24	-.00	.02	.16	-.00
WP6	.24	**.77**	.23	.21	.10	.11	.05	.09	.02
WP7	.15	**.45**	.24	.34	**.59**	.01	.14	-.12	.07
PR7	.28	.28	.27	.20	.17	.13	-.06	**.58**	.08
PR8	.08	.18	.09	.05	-.01	.05	-.07	**.77**	.03
PR9	.20	**.60**	.05	-.21	.30	.05	.10	.22	-.14
AA5	.04	.24	**.68**	.09	.29	.20	.12	-.00	.06
AA6	.13	.12	**.77**	.02	.13	.06	.21	.05	.08
AA7	.13	.32	**.66**	.11	-.09	-.05	.03	.15	.08
CAN4	.10	.17	.08	.11	.04	**.84**	.03	.07	.11
CAN6	.06	.00	.10	.15	.15	**.84**	.09	.16	.03
CAS3	.33	**.38**	.10	.19	.02	**.55**	-.15	-.21	.01
DS6	-.00	.00	.16	.16	-.14	-.03	**.81**	-.19	-.09

Table 1. (Cont.)

Variable	Factor 1: Verbal intelligence	Factor 2: Mathematical abilities	Factor 3: Number sense	Factor 4: Nonverbal intelligence	Factor 5: Number sense	Factor 6: Capacity	Factor 7: Nonverbal intelligence	Factor 8: Proportional reasoning	Factor 9: Number conservation
NVI1	.17	.00	.16	**.75**	.01	.18	.12	-.00	.10
NVI2	.02	.31	.05	**.44**	.14	.13	**.35**	.10	-.02
NVI3	.07	.14	-.10	**.61**	**.43**	.06	.14	.18	.20
NVI5	.11	**.35**	.05	.34	.13	.17	.31	.29	.05
NVI6	.18	.33	.09	.10	.14	.03	**.74**	.04	.18
NVI7	.17	**.68**	.17	.12	.08	.20	.34	.16	.08
NVI9	.04	**.54**	.25	.27	.02	.20	.23	.23	.31
VI1	**.67**	.12	.21	**.47**	-.05	.04	.05	-.11	-.23
VI2	**.69**	.17	.12	.33	-.08	.01	.01	.12	-.16
VI4	**.84**	.08	.07	.11	.24	.16	.01	.04	.12
VI6	**.84**	.16	.12	.01	.17	.10	.16	.16	.21
VI9	**.76**	.31	.13	-.04	.19	.12	.08	.20	.14

Note: The numbers at the end of the variable names refer to the wave. Factor loadings > .35 are bold. NC = Number conservation; EQ = Estimation of quantities; MA = Mathematical abilities; WP = Word problems; PR = Proportional reasoning; AA = Arithmetic abilities; CAN = Capacity numbers; CAS = Capacity sentences; DS = Digit–Symbol Test; NVI = Nonverbal intelligence; VI = Verbal intelligence.

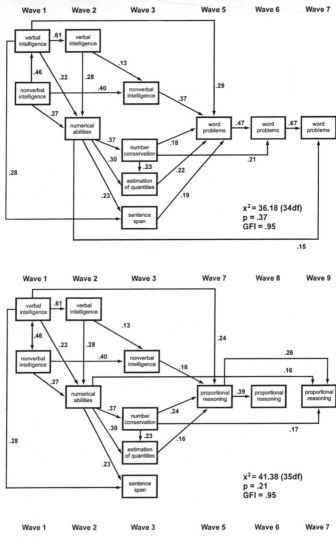

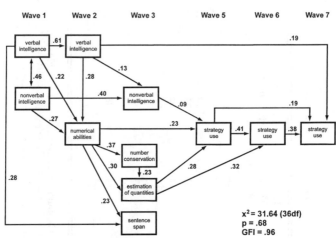

Figure 2. Results of the path analyses.

presented verbally, such as arithmetic word problems, may be facilitated if one is flexible in switching between visual and symbolic representation.

The number-conservation task may measure an ability to consider quantitative features rather than spatial extension features when verbal information about quantities is given. Participants who solved the conservation task at an early age were rather good at solving mathematical problems dealing with quantitative comparison (i.e., dealing with quantitative information).

The results indicate that the general abilities measured by verbal and nonverbal intelligence also contribute to mathematical performance. Taken together, our results show that different types of mathematical competencies correlate within and between different age levels. Early competencies acquired without systematic schooling have an effect on the acquisition of mathematical competencies in elementary school.

The Impact of Competencies in Elementary School on Proportional Reasoning. A regression analysis was conducted to find out what variables predict proportional reasoning in fifth and sixth grade because considerable individual performance differences are obtained at this age level. Although some participants already used ratio strategies, others still relied on bidimensional comparison. The results, depicted in Table 2, show that word-problem solving in Wave 7 is the best predictor of proportional reasoning in Wave 9 and that performance on intelligence tests and basic information-processing tasks assessed in Waves 8 and 9 play only a minor role. This result again shows the impact of domain-specific competencies. Good performance on word-problem solving 2 years earlier was more helpful for proportional reasoning than high general abilities at the same measurement point. The results emphasize the importance of long-term knowledge acquisition.

The Impact of Broader Abilities on Mathematical Performance. The former analyses suggested a strong impact of domain-specific competencies on individual differences in mathematical competencies within and between different age levels. However, general competencies might additionally contribute to the explanation of individual differences in mathematics. In a stepwise regression analysis, performance at the end of elementary school (Wave 7) in the three types of mathematical competencies considered in this chapter was predicted by verbal and nonverbal intelligence measures in Waves 1–7, as well as by measures of basic information processing (word capacity, Wave 3; number capacity, Waves 4 and 6; and speed, Wave 6). In addition, the measures of spatial abilities were included.

The results, depicted in Table 3, indicate that performance in verbal and nonverbal intelligence tests at all age levels had a clear impact on mathematical competencies. However, our results do not support any impact of basic information-processing efficiency, such as processing speed and capacity. Thus, the influence of general factors may be due to high-level abilities such as metacognitive strategies rather than to basic processing efficiency.

168 ELSBETH STERN

Table 2. *Results of the Stepwise
Regression Analyses*

Predictor	Proportional reasoning
Verbal intelligence	
Wave 4	—
Wave 6	—
Nonverbal intelligence	
Wave 5	1
Wave 7	1
Stragtegy use	
Wave 5	1
Wave 6	—
Wave 7	—
Proportional reasoning	
Wave 7	3
Word-problem solving	
Wave 5	2
Wave 6	—
Wave 7	25
R^2	33

Notes: Proportional reasoning in Grade 6 (Wave 9) was predicted by general and specific competencies measured during elementary school time. The percentage of explained incremental variance is depicted.

Final Conclusions

What do our longitudinal data tell us about sources of development in mathematical competencies and sources of individual differences in mathematics? Our results clearly suggest a considerable domain-specific impact on differences within and between age levels. However, there is an additional impact of high-level general abilities at all age levels. The results indicate that with growing age, the relation between mathematical performance and general abilities increases, especially for nonverbal intelligence. However, our results clearly indicate that high-level rather than low-level abilities influence mathematical performance. Reductionistic approaches to intelligence such as those suggested by Jensen (1982) or Anderson (1992) are not supported at all by our data.

Emphasizing the domain-specific impact on differences between and within different age levels does not at all mean that mathematical competencies are isolated knowledge structures that develop independently from other competencies. To the contrary, mathematical competencies are developed by using mathematical language to describe situations and events in quite different domains. Rich knowledge about the world provides opportunities to use mathematical language for modeling and

Table 3. *Results of Stepwise Regression Analyses*

Predictor	Criteria		
	Strategy use	Word-problem solving	Proportional reasoning
Verbal intelligence			
Wave 1	—	—	—
Wave 2	—	2	1
Wave 4	—	1	3
Wave 6	—	1	1
Nonverbal intelligence			
Wave1	1	—	2
Wave 3	1	1	1
Wave 5	—	—	1
Capacity sentences			
Wave 3	—	1	7
Number conservation			
Wave 3	—	1	2
Number estimation			
Wave 3	—	1	1
Strategy use			
Wave 5	2	—	1
Wave 6	26	—	27
Word-problem solving			
Wave	—	1	—
Wave 6	7	54	—
R^2	38	63	47

Note: Strategy use, word-problem solving, and proportional reasoning at the end of elementary school in Grade 4 (Wave 7) was predicted by general competencies. The percentage of explained incremental variance is depicted.

simulating real-life situations. By doing so, one might not only extend subject-matter knowledge but also acquire metastrategies that generally help one deal with complex and abstract problems.

References

Anderson, M. (1992). *Intelligence and development*. New York: Blackwell.

Bisanz, J., & LeFevre, J. (1990). Strategic and nonstrategic processing in the development of mathematical cognition. In D. Bjorklund (Ed.), *Children's strategies: Contemporary views of cognitive development* (pp. 213–244). Hillsdale, NJ: Erlbaum.

Burgemeister, B., Blum, L., & Lorge, J. (1972). *Columbia Mental Maturity Scale (CMMS)*. New York: Harcourt Brace.

Case, R. (1978). Intellectual development from birth to adulthood: A neo-Piagetian interpretation. In R. S. Siegler (Ed.), *Children's thinking: What develops?* (pp. 37–71). Hillsdale, NJ: Erlbaum.

Case, R. (1985). *Intellectual development: Birth to adulthood*. Orlando, FL: Academic Press.

Davis-Dorsey, J., Ross, S. M., & Morrison, G. R. (1991). The role of rewording and context personalization in the solving of mathematical word problems. *Journal of Educational Psychology, 83*, 61–68.

Eggert, D. (1978). *Hannover–Wechsler–Intelligenztest für Kinder* [German version of the WPPSI]. Bern, Switzerland: Huber.

Gardner, H. (1983). *Frames of mind: The theory of multiple intelligences.* New York: Basic Books.

Gelman, R. (1990). First principles organize attention to and learning about relevant data: Number and the animate–inanimate distinction as examples. *Cognitive Science, 14*, 79–106.

Gelman, R. (1991). Epigenetic foundations of knowledge structures: Initial and transcendent constructions. In S. Carey & R. Gelman (Eds.), *The epigenesis of mind: Essays on biology and cognition* (pp. 293–322). Hillsdale, NJ: Erlbaum.

Gustaffson, J. E., & Balke, G. (1993). General and specific abilities as predictors of school achievement. *Multivariate Research, 28*, 391–405.

Halford, G. S. (1992). Analogical reasoning and conceptual complexity in cognitive development. *Human Development, 35*, 193–217.

Hiebert, J. (Ed.). (1986). *Conceptual and procedural knowledge: The case of mathematics.* Hillsdale, NJ: Erlbaum.

Horn, J. L., & Cattell, R. B. (1966). Refinement and test of the theory of fluid and crystallized ability intelligences. *Journal of Educational Psychology, 57*, 253–270.

Hudson, T. (1983). Correspondences and numerical differences between disjoint sets. *Child Development, 54*, 84–90.

Jensen, A. R. (1982). Reaction time and psychometric g. In H. J. Eysenck (Ed.), *A model for intelligence* (pp. 93–132). Berlin: Springer.

Karplus, R., Pulos, S., & Stage, E. K. (1983). Proportional reasoning of early adolescents. In R. Lesh & M. Landau (Eds.), *Acquisition of mathematics concepts and processes* (pp. 45–90). New York: Academic Press.

Kern, A. (1971). *Grundleistungstest zur Ermittlung der Schulreife* (7. Aufl.) [Basic performance test on school readiness]. Munich: Ehrenwirth.

Noelting, G. (1980). The development of proportional reasoning and the ratio concept. *Educational Studies in Mathematics, 11*, 217–253.

Piaget, J. (1950). *The psychology of intelligence.* London: Routledge & Kegan Paul.

Resnick, L. B. (1989). Developing mathematical knowledge. *American Psychologist, 44*, 162–169.

Riley, M. S., Greeno, J. G., & Heller, J. H. (1983). Development of children's problem-solving ability in arithmetic. In H. P. Ginsburg (Ed.), *The development of mathematical thinking* (pp. 153–196). New York: Academic Press.

Spearman, C. (1927). *The abilities of man.* New York: Macmillan.

Stern, E. (1992). Spontaneous use of conceptual mathematical knowledge in elementary school children. *Contemporary Educational Psychology, 17*, 266–277.

Stern, E. (1993a). *Die Entwickung des mathematischen Verständnisses im Kindesalter* [The development of mathematical understanding in childhood]. Habilitationsschrift. Munich. Ludwig-Maximilians-Universität.

Stern, E. (1993b). What makes certain arithmetic word problems involving the comparison of sets so hard for children? *Journal of Educational Psychology, 85*, 7–23.

Stern, E., & Lehrndorfer, A. (1992). The role of situational context in solving word problems. *Cognitive Development, 7*, 259–268.

Sternberg, R. J. (1985). *Beyond IQ.* Cambridge, England: Cambridge University Press.

Stevenson, H. W., & Newman, R. S. (1986). Long-term prediction of achievement and attitudes in mathematics and reading. *Child Development, 57*, 646–659.

Tewes, U. (Ed.). (1983). *Hamburg–Wechsler–Intelligenztest für Kinder Revision (HAWIK-R)* [German version of the revised WISC]. Bern, Switzerland: Huber.

Thurstone, L. L. (1938). *Primary mental abilities.* Chicago: University of Chicago Press.

Weiß, R., & Osterland, J. (1979). Grundintelligenztest CFT 1 (2. Aufl.) [Basic intelligence test CFT]. Braunschweig: Westermann.

Wynn, K. (1990). Children's understanding of counting. *Cognition, 36*, 155–193.

8a   Comment: "Development of Mathematical Competencies"

Susan R. Goldman and James W. Pellegrino

The LOGIC database provides a unique opportunity to examine important questions about the acquisition of complex cognitive skills, as this volume demonstrates. In the Stern chapter, the research project pursues the developmental predictors of performance on advanced mathematics. Because of the battery of assessments administered in the various waves of the LOGIC study, it is possible for Stern to examine relationships in the preschool years among tasks and performances representing fundamental numerical competencies, measures of verbal and nonverbal intelligence, and speed and capacity to deal with number symbols, with three tasks that assess various aspects of advanced mathematical understanding – strategy use, word-problem solution, and proportional reasoning. These tasks involve mathematics and cognition "beyond counting." To varying degrees, all three complex tasks involve understanding mathematics as a system for modeling the world in symbols. They also involve the objectification, coordination, and manipulation of those symbols. These tasks stand in contrast to the preschool numerical competencies that seem to be acquired with no formal educational mechanisms.[1]

Our commentary considers two issues: relationships among the preschool and advanced mathematics tasks and the implications of these findings for assumptions about the role of formal education.

Relationships Among Earlier and Later Mathematics Competencies

Stern's basic findings are that domain-specific skills (viz., the early math competencies) predict later performance on all three complex tasks, and they make more of a contribution than general and specific capacity measures. However, early verbal and

---

[1] It is an empirical question as to whether all preschoolers enter school with the numerical competencies discussed by Stern. In the United States, for example, many students from low socioeconomic status levels enter school with qualitatively different verbal literacy skills and lower levels of numerical skills. Accordingly, it is perhaps better to indicate that preschool numerical competencies are acquired with the informal educational opportunities available to many preschoolers. This distinguishes them from those mathematical competencies that seem to depend on formal educational opportunities.

171

nonverbal indices of intelligence do predict all three complex tasks, albeit at levels lower than those of the domain-specific indices. There are also some interesting differences in how the predictor variables relate to the three beyond counting tasks. For example, verbal intelligence is quite a strong predictor of performance on word problems and proportional reasoning, although not of strategy use. As well, one of the efficiency measures (sentence span) predicts word-problem performance, although the other measures of information processing are not predictive of performance on any of the three tasks. Strategy use is the task best predicted solely by domain-specific indices: numerical abilities, number conservation, and estimation of quantities.

The variations in the results of the path analyses confirm what might be predicted from rational task analyses of the three advanced mathematics tasks. Although these tasks have in common the fact that they require mathematics skills beyond counting, they each require different cognitive skills for successful performance. For example, the word problems administered in this LOGIC study require some complex linguistic parsing skills to understand and correctly map the problem information to the solution. The common but complex wording for these comparison problems is "How many more Xs than Ys are there?" This complex linguistic expression requires the comparison of two sets and the relationship, whereas a simpler form of the question ("How many Xs won't get a Y?") suggests a counting or simpler correspondence strategy. Indeed, Stern notes data indicating that when the language of the question does not use the complex expression, children can more frequently solve these types of word problems (Stern, this volume). Another aspect of the complex expression that may make the problem difficult is the mapping of the language of the question onto the arithmetic operation that is required. Although subtraction is what is needed to solve the problem, the question uses the phrases "how many" and "more." These may cue addition. As well, the "direction" of the linguistic form (i.e., more than) may appear to conflict with the usual direction of the subtraction operation (i.e., less than or a reduction in quantity).

In other words, solving the comparison form of the word problems presented in this study requires mapping the symbol system to the conceptual system, determining the relationship, and mapping the language of the question to the appropriate arithmetic operation. There is a large symbolic (numerical and nonnumerical) processing load in these word problems. It makes sense that performance is predicted by a general linguistic variable and sentence span to a greater degree than their respective contribution to the other mathematics tasks.

In contrast to the word problems, similar rational analysis of the strategy-use task suggests that the only connection with linguistic skills is in terms of being able to treat symbols (in this case numbers) as objects to be manipulated or patterns to be completed. Solutions to the strategy-use problems do not require dealing with sets, symbols, and relations. Furthermore, knowledge of certain principles of the mathematical system make the strategy-use task totally noncomputational. Indeed, the fact that there were numbers in the problems might have been irrelevant to the children. The strategy-use problems could be solved through a pattern-matching algorithm:

As long as the patterns reflected in the numerical sequences are recognized as instances of various mathematical principles (e.g., commutativity), correct solutions can be determined. These strings could have been presented as algebraic expressions, and the shortcut strategies would have applied just the same. Stern indicates that strategy-use problems require symbol manipulation. Perhaps, but as suggested earlier, an alternative method of solution is pattern matching to mathematical laws and principles.

The proportional reasoning task, like the word problems, requires a focus on the relationship between sets of two numbers. A focus on either number or relation within a pair is insufficient to arrive at the correct answer. Thus, the proportional reasoning task involves interpreting sets of symbols and then mentally manipulating them. It makes sense that the results of the path analyses suggest greater similarity in predictors for the proportional reasoning and word problem tasks than for other paired comparisons of the tasks. To the degree that the children did engage in symbolic manipulation to solve the strategy-use task, there should be some consistency between proportional reasoning and strategy use in terms of the predictors. That there is only moderate overlap suggests that symbolic manipulation may have played only a small role in solutions for the strategy-use problems.

There are also some interesting patterns in terms of the level of predictive contribution of each task for performance on that same task in subsequent waves. For two tasks, word problems and strategy use, performance across waves is strongly predicted by performance on the previous wave in which it was tested (e.g., Wave 5 performance predicting 6 and Wave 6 predicting 7). However, for the proportional reasoning task this within-task predictability is not as strong. Wave 7 performance on proportional reasoning weakly predicts Wave 8 and Wave 9 performances. Wave 8 performance does not predict Wave 9 performance at all. It is difficult to determine if this is a function of age or the task, but it is interesting to speculate that the lack of correlation suggests that some major cognitive reorganizations in dealing with sets, relations, and symbolic manipulation may be occurring at these points in time. This is very likely a consequence of formal instruction.

Implicit in the discussion to this point is that it would be beneficial to have additional data on the advanced mathematics tasks; namely, information on the strategies that the children used to solve the problems. With this additional information it would be possible to pursue some of the data interpretations that we suggested earlier. At the same time that we note this limitation in the LOGIC study of mathematics, we recognize that collecting such data was not feasible pragmatically, given the resources available to the LOGIC project. Rather, we merely point out that solution strategy information would elucidate some of the possible explanations for the interesting patterns of prediction reflected in the path analyses. Note further that the failure of the basic information-processing measures to predict performance may be because accuracy is the performance measure being predicted. The information-processing measures may still be related to speed or efficiency of solution in the form of rate of strategy execution.

However, despite the limitations of an accuracy measure, the current results suggest interesting additional analyses of the database. For example, to augment the correlation regression approach reflected in the factor and path analyses, it would be interesting to look at performance patterns across the three advanced mathematical tasks for individuals. Such pattern analyses could allow the examination of whether there are any developmental priority relationships among the three tasks (e.g., Brainerd and Brainerd 1972; Froman and Hubert, 1980; Goldman 1982). Findings of systematic relationships could lead to identifying subsets of individuals who might differ in terms of the predictive power of the measures administered in the early waves (i.e., Waves 1, 2, and 3) of the LOGIC study. Taking this a step further, one might do similar pattern analyses across the preschool tasks, taking one advanced mathematics task at a time. These might produce important insights into the variability manifest in the sample. There might well be interesting individual differences in the role of domain-general and specific knowledge. We note, however, that the sample sizes may preclude detailed statistical comparisons and strong inferences for various subsets of children. Nonetheless, the results may be intriguing in their own right.

The Role of Schooling and Experience in Advanced Mathematical Competencies

Stern notes that one of the reasons that it is interesting to look at the prediction of performance on the advanced mathematics tasks is that they require formal education, unlike the measures that are used to predict them. This claim, and the findings we have already reviewed, raise a number of questions about the educational enterprise. Foremost, it would be nice to know what the children in the LOGIC study received in the way of formal instruction relevant to the advanced mathematics tasks and also whether individuals within each cohort experienced the same or similar instructional environments. The educational literature is replete with examples of mathematics instruction that makes little or no impact on children's understanding of mathematics (for reviews see, Cognition and Technology Group at Vanderbilt, 1990, 1992a, 1992b; 1993, 1994). Even those who score extremely well on standardized mathematics achievement tests do rather poorly when asked to engage in complex mathematical problem solving (e.g., Cognition and Technology Group at Vanderbilt, 1992a, 1994).

Furthermore, what is assumed about the role that formal instruction should play? If early measures of domain-specific competence still predict later performance, does that mean that the educational system has only succeeded in enhancing the knowledge and skill of those who come to school with basic or prerequisite knowledge relative to their peers? If that is what the school system is accomplishing, should we be asking more of it? These are complex issues, open to much debate in the United States. We are poorly enough equipped to address them in the United States' context, let alone pretend to know how to address these issues in other countries and cultures.

An educational system that preserves individual differences among students is one contextual explanation for Stern's findings. These entry-point differences are differences in the knowledge base that are exacerbated by the educational setting. However, the situation may be a bit more complex than this. Suppose, for example, that there are underlying processes that account for the fact that individuals benefit differentially from the same environment, all other things (e.g., knowledge) being equal. Perhaps children who do well on the preschool measures are better able to capitalize on what is offered in schools, just as they have been better able to capitalize on the information in their informal educational environments. If the societal goal of education is to help all individuals achieve competency on advanced mathematics tasks such as the ones considered in LOGIC, the educational system needs to consider alternative instructional models that may make it possible for a greater diversity of individuals to achieve mastery of them.

These speculations about the role of education clearly go well beyond the goals of the LOGIC project. However, the LOGIC project and analyses such as Stern's introduce these important issues into the conversation. The LOGIC project is unique in providing a database that makes it possible to identify some of the important educational issues that are considered from preschool through early adolescence. This contribution is in addition to those being made regarding developmental theory and the empirical information that has been gained regarding some complex interrelationships among knowledge, processes, and individual differences in cognition.

References

Brainerd, C. J., & Brainerd, S. (1972). Order of acquisition of number and quantity conservation. *Child Development, 41,* 1401–1406.

Cognition and Technology Group at Vanderbilt. (1990). Anchored instruction and its relationship to situated cognition. *Educational Researcher, 19* (6), 2–10.

Cognition and Technology Group at Vanderbilt. (1992a). The Jasper series: A generative approach to mathematical thinking. In K. Sheingold, L. G. Roberts, & S. M. Malcolm (Eds.), *This year in science series 1991: Technology for teaching and learning* (pp. 109–140). Washington, DC: American Association for the Advancement of Science.

Cognition and Technology Group at Vanderbilt. (1992b). The Jasper experiment: An exploration of issues in learning and instructional design. *Educational Technology Research and Development, 40,* 65–80.

Cognition and Technology Group at Vanderbilt. (1993). Integrated media: Toward a theoretical framework for utilizing their potential. *Journal of Special Education Technology, 12,* 71–85.

Cognition and Technology Group at Vanderbilt. (1994). From visual word problems to learning communities: Changing conceptions of cognitive research. In K. McGilly (Ed.), *Classroom lessons: Integrating cognitive theory and classroom practice* (pp. 157–200). Cambridge, MA: MIT Press/Bradford Books.

Froman, T., & Hubert, L. J. (1980). Application of prediction analysis to developmental priority. *Psychological Bulletin, 87,* 136–146.

Goldman, S. R. (1982). Coincidence or causality in linguistic and cognitive skills: A reply to Van Kleek. *Merrill-Palmer Quarterly, 28,* 267–274.

9 Schooling and the Development of Achievement Differences

Andreas Helmke and Franz E. Weinert

Only 20 years ago, Good, Biddle, and Brophy (1975) wrote, "Do teachers make a difference? No definite answer exists because little research has been directed to the question in a comprehensive way" (p. 3). Is this conclusion still legitimate today? It is true that research on instructional processes and schooling outcomes has yielded a good deal of empirical evidence showing that there are stable differences in the quality of instruction and classroom management across teachers. Furthermore, these differences do significantly affect academic performance and other achievement-related cognitive, affective, and motivational outcomes of classroom instruction (Helmke & Weinert 1996; Weinert and Helmke 1988, 1993, 1995a, 1995b; Weinert, Schrader, and Helmke 1989). There is also no doubt that schooling has a substantial impact on the development of intelligence: "Schooling emerges as an extremely important source of variance, notwithstanding historical and contemporary claims to the contrary" (Ceci 1991, p. 719).

However, beyond such general statements on the significance of schooling, there is little known about when, how, and to what extent differences in schooling experiences, in particular, differences in classroom environment and instructional quality, contribute to the development of interindividual differences in achievement. This is particularly true for elementary school experiences (for a recent overview of the literature, see Einsiedler 1997; Helmke and Weinert 1996).

The goal of this chapter is to help close this gap and to examine the following questions by using data collected in the SCHOLASTIC longitudinal study.

1. Which role do class differences play in determining interindividual differences in learning, cognitive, and motivational variables? To estimate this effect, we calculate how much of the variance of cognitive, affective, and conative student characteristics is accounted for by individual classroom membership with the help of simple determination coefficients.
2. How stable are features of instructional quality and classroom management during the course of elementary school? Can the reasonable assumption be confirmed that a high degree of continuity exists during third and fourth grade (same teacher) and a break follows the transition from second to third grade (a change of teachers is mandatory in Bavaria)?

176

3. How do elementary school classes differ from each other with respect to aspects relevant to instruction, such as classroom composition (e.g., proportion of girls or percentage of students whose native language is not German) and classroom size, cognitive entry characteristics, and homogeneity versus heterogeneity of learning prerequisites? And how relevant are such differences in classroom composition for gains in achievement?

4. Which are the most important characteristics of "successful" instruction – successful in the sense of maximum achievement increments in principal subjects? Does this apply to both principal subjects (German and math) to the same degree?

5. What can be learned from the instructional profiles of particularly successful teachers in reference to the necessary and sufficient conditions for successful learning, as well as possibilities and limitations of reciprocal compensatory effects of achievement-promoting instructional characteristics?

6. Finally, are relations between motivation and academic achievement universal, or are they moderated (or mediated) by aspects of classroom context?

Method

Sample

The majority of the analyses presented in this chapter are based on a sample of 54 elementary school classes (for details, see Helmke and Weinert 1997) of the elementary school project SCHOLASTIC (see Figure 1). Only a short description of the sample of third- and fourth-grade teachers and their classes is provided.

The sample consists of teachers between 28 and 53 years old ($Mdn = 42$), and it is predominantly female (45 of 51 teachers). Class size ranges from a minimum of 14 to a maximum of 29 students. The percentage of girls varies between 32% and 69% ($Mdn = 47\%$), and the percentage of students whose first language is German ranges from 63% to 100% ($Mdn = 93\%$).

Instruments

Characteristics of instructional quality were assessed by experienced classroom observers with the help of an inventory consisting of a highly inferential rating scale (5-point Likert-type scale). Total scores were obtained on the basis of evaluations of all classroom visits for each grade. Because the object of interest in this section is the development of scholastic achievement during third and fourth grade, we aggregated the scores across both grade levels in order to obtain more robust measures.

The following variables of instructional quality were used in the analyses presented later: (a) *classroom management* (intensity of time used for subject matter and efficiency of instructional organization, such as quick and smooth transitions from one phase of instruction to the next); (b) *structuredness* (clearness of teachers' mode of expression, organization of material through teachers' comments, and other helpful hints to direct attention); (c) *individual support* (individual subject-specific help, diagnosis, monitoring, intervention, and supervision, especially during group

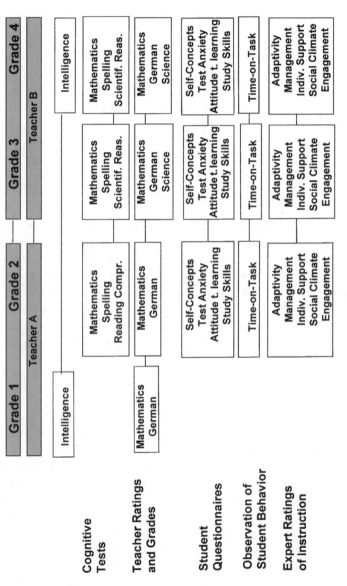

Figure 1. Design and instruments of the SCHOLASTIC study ($N = 1,200$ students from 54 elementary school classrooms). $t.$ = toward.

and silent work); (d) *orientation toward deficit compensation* (the promotion of poor students as a matter of priority and intensive efforts to bring the degree of difficulty of demands and questions into line with the learning prerequisites of these students); (e) *social climate* (acceptance of and direct reference to students' emotional feelings and importance of the teacher as a person to confide in, rather than someone who just imparts knowledge); and (f) *variability* (variety of selected forms of instruction).

From the viewpoint of the students, the perceived clarity of instruction was assessed (however, in contrast to the ratings of class instruction, these questionnaires were administered only once; namely, at the beginning of fourth grade). To measure this variable, we asked students how often they were not able to comprehend the teacher's questions, instructions, and statements. To build a clarity score, the polarity was changed.

Finally, with the help of a low-inferential observation schedule (Münchner Aufmerksamkeitsinventar [Munich Attention Inventory]; Helmke 1990; Helmke and Renkl 1992), various aspects of attentiveness were assessed. In this section we use the rate of "passive" forms of inattentive behavior ("off-task"), such as drowsing, staring out of the window, etc. After changing the polarity, this measure can be interpreted as an indicator of motivational quality of instruction on the level of the class.

Performance increments in spelling and mathematics were used as dependent variables. We computed residuals, in other words, for each participant the total score for fourth grade was calculated after having accounted for class differences in entry characteristics assessed at the beginning of third grade. In contrast to the class means in achievement tests in mathematics, which were highly correlated ($r = .59$, $.61$, and $.53$ in Grades 2, 3, and 4, respectively), a correlation of only $r = .26$ (*ns*) was found between both residuals. Therefore, it is inappropriate to build an overall score "total performance increment" across subjects, and so the following analyses were conducted separately for each criterion.

Results

The Role of Class Differences

The question concerning the importance of classroom differences for the development of scholastic achievement of students and classes can be answered in a variety of ways, as far as methods are concerned. The computation of determination coefficients is both a relatively robust and illustrative way to approach this question. These coefficients provide information concerning what percentage of interindividual differences in a certain characteristic are due to class membership.

The findings depicted in Figure 2 (motivation and attention) and Figure 3 (academic achievements) show that the role of classroom differences varies quite strongly across characteristics. Classroom differences in various aspects of students' attentiveness (observed during regular lessons) proved to be of paramount importance. As far as motivational and affective variables are concerned, we found that besides achievement

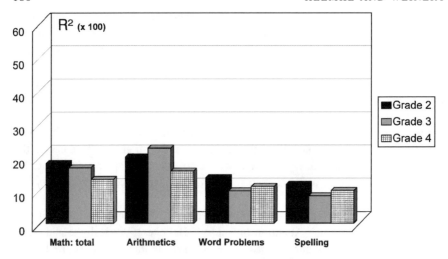

Figure 2. The role of classroom membership for differences in student motivation and attention: determination coefficients.

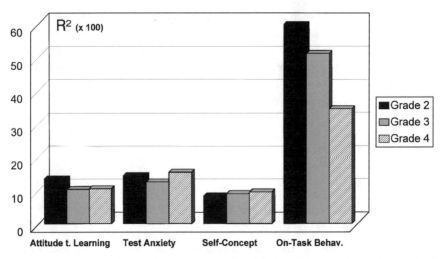

Figure 3. The role of classroom membership for differences in student academic achievements: determination coefficients. $t.$ = toward.

anxiety and different types of learning disorders, so-called *effort avoidance* – a hetero-geneous construct encompassing many facets of disturbed motivational and volitional processes (cf. Helmke and Rheinberg 1996) – also varied quite strongly from class to class. In comparison, classroom membership plays a less important role in respect to other cognitive and motivational characteristics.

With the exception of measures of learning disorders and achievement anxiety, many student variables showed a trend toward decreasing importance of class membership. How can this finding be interpreted? A number of explanations are possible. One explanation is that this leveling effect results from a general socialization effect of schooling, with highly standardized curricula and comparable learning prerequisites in the classrooms. If this assumption is correct, then the variance in the respective characteristics between classes should sink during the course of elementary school. However, this is not the case; no systematic relationship between the decreasing role of individual classroom membership for interindividual differences and differences between school classes could be detected. An alternative explanation would be that the characteristics of the individuals become increasingly stable in the course of time.

Naturally, "classroom membership" is only an omnibus variable, one that encompasses a number of different aspects: classroom composition, teacher personality, classroom climate, and instructional features. The advantage of this measure is that it provides a maximal estimation of all possible class features, thereby offering a rough frame for estimating the significance of the classroom as a context for learning and socialization. This method cannot and does not claim to provide an explanation. Therefore, we depart from the level of classroom membership and direct our attention toward specific characteristics of class context and instructional quality.

Stability of Class Differences

To obtain data concerning temporal stability, we correlated the class means of various characteristics of instruction and class. The results are presented in Table 1. As expected, the change of teachers between second and third grade is accompanied by abrupt changes in instructional quality, whereas a high degree of continuity exists between third and fourth grade. The high stability of differences between classes during the entire course of elementary school, already reported for the individual level (cf. Helmke, this volume), stands in stark contrast to this finding.

Context Variables and Quality of Instruction

Established relations between classroom context and instructional quality are presented in Table 2. The following three points summarize these findings:

1. Generally speaking, features of classroom composition play only a minor role in respect to differences in instructional quality. With the exception of class size, which is discussed below, only two of the remaining correlations reached the 5% significance level.
2. The relationship between the proportion of girls in class and positive social climate turned out as expected; the relation between the level of intelligence and the intensity of individual, subject-related support is less plausible.
3. At least at first glance, the role of class size seems to be unexpected to say the least: As class size increases, lessons become more structured, and teachers more actively supervise and monitor individual students.

Table 1. *Stability of Instructional Variables, Student Attentional Behavior, and Academic Achievements*

	Transition from grade	
Instructional variables	Grade 2 to 3 (teacher change)	Grade 3 to 4 (same teacher)
Aspects of instruction		
Management[a]	.00	.57**
Structuredness[a]	.25	.59**
Individual support[a]	.14	.51**
Orientation toward compensation[a]	−.08	.41**
Variability[a]	.04	.39**
Social climate[b]	.10	.46**
Achievement tests		
Mathematics test	.78**	.80**
Spelling test	.62**	.72**
Learning behavior		
On-task[b] (active engagement)	.30*	.65**
Off-task[b] (passive)	.23	.43**

[a]High-inferential ratings of trained observers.
[b]Low-inferential observations of student behavior during instruction.
*$p < .05$.   **$p < .01$.

Table 2. *Correlations Between Aspects of Classroom Context and Instructional Variables (n = 51)*

	Classroom context				
Variables of Instruction	Class size	Level of intelligence	Variability of intelligence	Proportion of girls	Proportion of pupils with German as first language
Management[a]	.43**	.24	−.20	.16	.13
Structuredness[a]	.40**	.25	−.17	.08	.09
Individual support[a]	.30*	.33*	−.16	.26	.12
Orientation toward compensation[a]	.00	−.20	.24	.09	−.14
Variability[a]	−.01	.05	−.21	.17	−.04
Social climate[a]	.28*	.13	−.04	.33*	.06
Clarity[b]	.01	−.10	.07	−.18	.06
Motivational quality[c]	−.23	.05	−.11	.10	.26*

[a]High-inferential ratings of trained observers.
[b]Student perceptions, assessed on individual level and aggregated on classroom level.
[c]Low-inferential observations of student behavior during instruction.
*$p < .05$.   **$p < .01$.

Table 3. *Classroom Context and Growth of Achievement in Mathematics and Spelling (n = 51 classrooms)*

	Classroom context				
Achievement gain	Class size	Level of intelligence	Variability of intelligence	Proportion of girls	Proportion of pupils with German as first language
Mathematics	.01	.22	−.08	.12	.14
Spelling	.22	.28*	−.07	.08	−.07

*p < .05.

How can this finding be interpreted? Does it indicate that classes with a greater number of students necessitate a high standard of instructional quality and, above that, efficient classroom management? But this still does not explain why, exactly, the social climate seems more positive in larger classes (*r* = .28). Another explanation could be that "large" classes are generally judged as more "difficult" ones, and so the assignment of teachers to new classes in third grade (by the school principal or educational authorities) is based on the principle that the more experienced and competent teachers receive the larger classes.

Class Context and Achievement Gains

Table 3 depicts the relations between the context variables described earlier and the two criterion variables of interest here (viz., performance increments in the spelling test and in the math test). Evidently, merely the level of intelligence (assessed at the end of first grade) plays a role, although the magnitude of this effect is not particularly large: The higher the general cognitive level of the class, the more favorable the average achievement gain. However, this applies only to achievement growth in spelling; the correlation for achievement gain in mathematics (*r* = .22) did not reach significance.

Quality of Instruction and Achievement Gains

The most important findings of this section are summarized separately in Table 4 for spelling and mathematics. Here again, this table is restricted to the gains in achievement, in other words, it does not report the correlations between features of instruction and simple test scores. In addition to correlations as a measure of the linear relationship, we also analyzed the respective relations with the help of curvilinear regression analyses (with a linear and a quadratic term), in order to identify possible curvilinear relationships. One could expect such relationships, for example, U-type relationships,

Table 4. *Correlations Between Instructional Variables and Growth of Achievement*

Instructional variables	Growth of achievement (residualized posttests)	
	Mathematics	Spelling
Management[a]	.36**	.26
Structuredness[a]	.28**	.17
Support[a]	.32**	.16
Orientation toward compensation[a]	.17	−.02
Variability[a]	.28**	−.04
Social climate[a]	.18	.02
Clarity[b]	.34**	.17
Motivational quality[c]	.35*	.27*

[a] High-inferential ratings of trained observers.
[b] Students perceptions, assessed on individual level and aggregated on classroom level.
[c] Low-inferential observations of student behavior during instruction.
$p < .05$. $**p < .01$.

under the assumption that the maximal value of an instructional variable is not identical with the optimal value. However, no such indications of curvilinear relationships were found. Certainly, this does not imply that they do not exist at all – possibly more extreme values than those found in our sample are necessary to produce curvilinear relationships.

The first main finding is that class-specific differences in instructional quality and classroom management obviously play a very different role for the two criterion variables. For the development of achievement in spelling, only one significant relation can be established with variables of instructional quality – in clear contrast to the pattern of results found for mathematics. How can this finding be explained?

The insignificance of the majority of characteristics of instructional quality for achievement gains in spelling has not yet been completely understood. This finding cannot be led back to problems with the psychometric properties of the spelling tests (cf. Chapter 7 in this volume). Does the scope of the area of competence assessed with the spelling test play a role (it is less encompassing as compared with the contents of the math tests)? How important is the curricular validity of the tests? Do didactic skills and instructional material play a greater role than the general quality of instruction and classroom management? Or is progress in spelling influenced to a much greater extent by factors outside of school (e.g., incentives given at home and learning opportunities) as compared with mathematics? Unfortunately, these questions must remain open here. Because of this pattern of findings, the following discussion is limited to the subject of mathematics.

Successful classes are characterized by a typical pattern of features. First, efficient class management is a factor of prime importance. Successful teachers (successful in the sense of a large gain in achievement; cf. Schrader, Helmke, and Dotzler in 1997, concerning the issue of competing teaching objectives) instruct in a flowing manner, transitions from one phase of instruction to the next are quick and smooth, and they occur in regular intervals; there are only short breaks between different units of instruction; and instructional material is immediately available. Furthermore, use of time is an important aspect: The time period is spent on treating subject matter; teachers keep to the point, do not deviate from the subject, and avoid unnecessary digression; procedural elements are carried out in a quick and concise manner or take place outside of regular lessons.

This type of class management is related to a high motivational quality of instruction, manifested by more active participation of students during lessons and the relatively seldom occurrence of passive forms of inattentiveness (e.g., daydreaming, dosing off, and so forth).

Another important condition for above-average gains in performance is a high degree of structuredness of the teachers' presentation. Teachers' mode of expression is direct, short, and to the point; at the same time, teachers frequently make helpful comments to direct attention ("cues") in order to facilitate comprehension of material and explicitly point out connections between different parts of the material.

The complementary construct from the viewpoint of the students is clarity. It happens much more seldomly that successful teachers' questions, suggestions, and comments hit on a void because students do not understand what they are supposed to do or what the teacher means. The intensity of individual support in the respective subject also plays an important role in the ensemble of instructional features conducive to achievement: Achievement growth is more favorable the more actively the teacher makes direct interventions (especially during phases of silent work); for example, by going from desk to desk, checking and assessing students' work, making suggestions, and intervening if necessary. The opposite of this kind of active teaching behavior is manifested by an individual who remains seated at the teacher's desk during lessons (e.g., while checking workbooks or who restricts him- or herself to general monitoring and maintenance of silence and order, without devoting him- or herself to the individual students – not meaning a few special ones – but as many as possible per time unit). Finally, successful teachers are characterized by greater variability of forms of social interaction and teaching methods.

On the other hand, for progress of the entire class, it appears to be comparatively unimportant (but not detrimental either) if teachers particularly focus on the special promotion of poor students (compensation of deficits). If this instructional characteristic – which actually reflects a general orientation toward teaching rather than a style of teaching – has a differential effect on specific subgroups (e.g., good pupils vs. poor pupils), then this presents an interesting question to be addressed by future analyses of SCHOLASTIC study data by using the aptitude–treatment interaction model. The finding that the social climate does not make any difference also fits well into the body of available empirical findings (cf. the overview given by Helmke and Weinert 1996).

Nonetheless, one cannot maneuver around the fact that the correlations between the characteristics of instructional quality and achievement growth turned out relatively low–even in mathematics – not to speak of spelling. Naturally, we cannot exclude the possibility that key variables of successful elementary school instruction have remained hidden to us or that the operationalizations were suboptimal. However, it could also mean something else; namely, that in view of the firmly fixed instructional scheme specified by the curriculum, as well as definite expectations on the side of school authorities, education authorities, and school principals, differences in teaching style, teacher–students interaction, and climate hardly play a role any longer.

Profiles of Successful Classes

In this section we turn to the question of how similar or how different the profiles or particularly successful classes are. However, in falling back on the description of single cases we are standing on shaky ground, as far as the method is concerned; above that, it is outside of mainstream research. Thus, we are leaving the level of traditional, variable-centered approaches, in which analyses are based on group statistics and relations between variables, in favor of a person-oriented approach (cf. Weinert, Helmke, and Schrader 1992). It goes without saying that such an examination of individual cases cannot lay a claim to generalizability. The only question of interest here is how homogeneous versus heterogeneous the pattern of instructional characteristics that were found to promote student achievement is across different teachers. Can we find a relatively uniform pattern in "superior" teachers, in other words, roughly the same above-average outcomes in those variables of instructional quality that were found to be important? The results of this analysis, which were transformed into z scores because of the different metrics of the variables, are illustrated in Figure 4. Only those instructional characteristics that were previously established as significant predictors of achievement growth (cf. Table 4) are reported. The resulting picture is a confusing one because above-average scores in all measures of "successful" instruction were present in only two of the six classes. The other classes display, in part, extreme negative deviations in individual features of instructional quality. If one inspects the pattern variable by variable, instead of focusing on the entire profile, then it is evident that there is only one characteristic in which all successful classes have an above-average score; namely, clarity (as perceived by students). Classroom management is the only other variable that fits half way into the picture. As far as all other characteristics are concerned, the profiles display a high degree of variation.

The figure illustrates that for the domain of instructional determinants of achievement growth, it is not possible to define the prerequisites, not even for the subject of mathematics. Evidently, many different roads can lead to success. Thus, it would be questionable to speak of key features of successful instruction or necessary conditions in any prescriptive way. These findings strongly support the assumption that

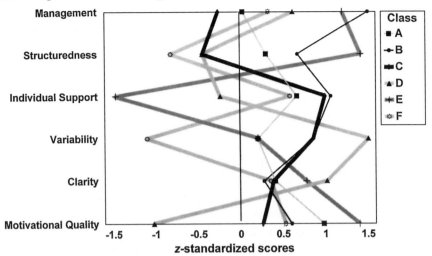

Figure 4. Instructional profiles of the six most successful classrooms (basis: achievement growth in mathematics).

the determinants of scholastic achievement are multiple and compensatory in nature (cf. Helmke and Weinert 1997).

Classroom Context as a Moderating Variable

Research on the impact of classroom instruction has traditionally focused on the level of variables. The typical process–product approach analyzes how differences in the level (frequency, intensity, etc.) of an instructional variable account for differences in outcome level. This approach often overlooks the fact that there are many other, by no means less important, ways in which classroom variables contribute to the emergence and development of achievement differences (Helmke 1988; Treiber and Weinert 1985). One approach we took was to regard classroom context as a moderating variable system that mediates the impact of student entry characteristics on schooling outcomes. We showed this moderating effect for a variety of motivational variables, such as test anxiety (Helmke 1988) and academic self-concept (Helmke 1992; Weinert & Helmke 1987). This issue has also been addressed by other research traditions – for example, ability formation theory (Blumenfeld, Pintrich, Meece, and Wessels 1982; Mac Iver 1987; Mitman and Lash 1988; Marshall and Weinstein 1984; Rosenholtz and Simpson 1984; Stipek 1984; Stipek and Daniels 1988; Stipek and Mac Iver 1989; Stipek and Tannatt 1984). See also Keeves and Larkin (1986) and the overview by Helmke (1988) for other hypotheses about classroom context as mediating variable. To illustrate this, we compare classroom differences in the correlation between test anxiety and achievement and between intelligence and mathematics achievement.

Classroom and other context differences in the covariation between motivational and cognitive variables have been (and are) analyzed surprisingly seldomly. This is because of two reasons: First, models of cognitive development are predominantly universal; that is, they claim to be valid in principle for all humans (see Weinert and Helmke 1998) and overlook individual differences. Second, instructional psychology, which does take a more differential perspective, has concentrated mainly on fundamental, noncomplex measures of effects, particularly on changes in the level of criterion variables. Few studies have investigated more complex, derived features of the classroom environment (such as correlations or variances).

In this section, we ask about classroom differences with regard to the impact of (a) test anxiety on academic achievement and (b) early intelligence (Grade 1) on math achievement in the following school years (Grades 2–4). Although the statistically more correct method would have been to use regression coefficients and to use the tool of hierarchical linear modeling (Bryk and Raudenbush 1992), we used correlation coefficients: Because the units of the variables were often arbitrary, correlation coefficients are more illustrative and easier to understand than unstandardized regression coefficients. Given this, our statements on the "significance" of classroom differences in correlations and about concomitants of these correlations should be regarded with caution.

Helmke (1988) reported classroom differences in the detrimental effect of test anxiety on math achievement (from $r = -.81$ to .38); these results were based on a longitudinal study in 39 fifth- and sixth-grade classrooms. On the basis of a domain-specific classroom context theory, he suggested two mechanisms to explain these classroom differences: a compensatory mechanism and a saliency mechanism. Independent of its level, test anxiety had a particularly impairing effect in classrooms characterized by (a) high-intensity time use and a low degree of structuring (few previews and reviews), indicating few opportunities for compensating information-processing deficits, and (b) a high incentive value of achievement in the classroom, indicating high saliency of success and failure.

The results from the present study on test anxiety and math achievement are depicted in Figure 5. The pattern of classroom differences represents an almost perfect replication of our earlier longitudinal study, the Classroom Environment Study of the International Association for the Evaluation of Educational Achievement (IEA) (see Helmke 1988).

Indeed, test anxiety appeared to have no detrimental effect at all in some classrooms, whereas it showed a negative correlation in other classrooms of almost .80. Given these results, it is difficult to maintain the widespread notion that test anxiety has a universal (i.e., independent of classroom), moderate negative impact on academic achievement. A second step of the data analysis was to identify those classroom factors that determine the anxiety and academic achievement relationship. Although the variables and assessment procedures used in the SCHOLASTIC project were not completely identical to those in the earlier project (Grades 5–6), it was nonetheless quite clear that the theoretical model developed by Helmke (1988) was not supported by the

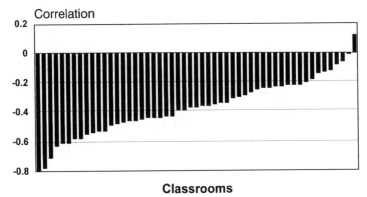

Figure 5. Correlations between test anxiety and math achievement in fourth grade elementary school classrooms.

SCHOLASTIC project data: There was no indication that classrooms with a strong correlation between anxiety and achievement – that is, with a strong achievement-impairing effect of anxiety (not to be confounded with the level of test anxiety, both variables were practically independent of each other, $r = -.01$) – were characterized by a higher incentive value of success and failure ($r = .14, ns$) or by intensive true use ($-.01$). Rather, we found that classrooms with a high negative correlation between anxiety and achievement were characterized by a particularly unfavorable social climate, low level of teacher warmth, and by little teacher engagement for the private sorrows and concerns of their pupils. It should be noted that these variables were irrelevant in the earlier longitudinal study with fifth and sixth graders. One plausible explanation is that the conditions and mechanisms of test anxiety change from elementary school to high school. For older students, the incentive value of achievement-related success and failure may be a crucial point, whereas for younger children the affective bonding and emotional attachment to the classroom teacher is a major psychosocial point. In other words, a climate of warmth and acceptance can be regarded as a social support buffer: It does not decrease the frequency of task-irrelevant worry cognitions but might compensate by decreasing threats to children's self-worth.

A second issue is the decomposition of the well-known correlation between intelligence and later achievement (Simons, Weinert, and Ahrens 1975; Weinert and Helmke 1988). This correlation is of particular interest because one criterion of good classroom instruction is a decrease in the correlation between intelligence and academic achievement: The less achievement and achievement growth are dependent on relatively stable student characteristics such as fluid intelligence, and the more they are dependent on changeable characteristics such as prior knowledge, the better the instruction. The results from the SCHOLASTIC study are depicted in Figure 6. For illustrative reasons, the correlations were rank ordered across classrooms, separately for each of the three measurement points.

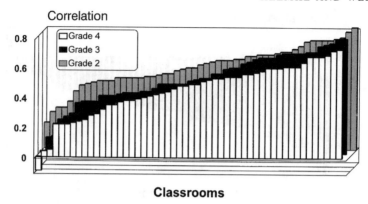

Figure 6. Classroom-specific correlations between intelligence (Grade 1) and math achievement in Grades 2, 3, and 4.

From Figure 6 it can be seen that there is some variability in the correlation coefficients between intelligence scores at Grade 1 and math achievement in Grades 2, 3, and 4 (from $r = .2$ to .8 in Grade 2 and from $r = 0$ to .6 in Grade 4). In addition, the expected decrease of the relationship between intelligence and academic achievement was surprisingly small over the 3 years as Figure 6 shows. In other words, there were classes where individual differences in intelligence determined the (development of) individual differences in math achievement, but there also were classes in which intelligence as a central predictor variable of math achievement was practically neutralized. One reason for such a finding could be that only some teachers were able to help most students in the classroom acquire a similarly rich knowledge base independent of their individual differences in intelligence. To test his hypothesis, we plan to conduct further analyses that include comparisons of the knowledge base, the level of math achievement, and the gain scores per year in classrooms that vary in the correlation coefficients between intelligence scores and mathematics achievement.

Concluding Remarks

Classroom factors, quality of instruction, and some teacher variables do have an impact on individual differences in achievement outcomes, cognitive competencies, and learning-related motives. This impact is not overwhelmingly strong, but it is certainly substantial. This is the main result and the optimistic message of the SCHOLASTIC study.

Equally important is the finding that classroom differences contribute only a minor part to achievement variance in terms of stable configurations of instructional variables. The reasons why long-term predictions are limited and why it is so difficult to explain the specific impact of schooling are because (a) interindividual differences in academic achievement are determined to a large extent by learner characteristics, specifically intellectual abilities and domain-specific knowledge, and (b) different patterns of student characteristics, instructional factors, and context variables have different effects on different types of classroom outcomes.

References

Blumenfeld, P. C., Pintrich, P. R., Meece, J., & Wessels, K. (1982). The formation and role of self perceptions of ability in elementary classrooms. *Elementary School Journal, 82,* 401–420.

Bryk, A. S., & Raudenbush, S. W. (1992). *Hierarchical linear models.* Newbury Park, CA: Sage.

Ceci, S. J. (1991). How much does schooling influence general intelligence and its cognitive components? A reassessment of the evidence. *Developmental Psychology, 27,* 703–722.

Einsiedler, W. (1997). Unterrichtsqualität und Leistungsentwicklung Literaturüberblick. [Quality of instruction and growth of achievement: A literature review]: In F. E. Weinert & A. Helmke (Eds.), *Entwicklung im Grundschulalter* (pp. 225–240). Weinheim: Psychologie Verlags Union.

Good, T. L., Biddle, B. J., & Brophy, J. E. (1975). *Teachers make a difference.* New York; Holt, Rinehart & Winston.

Helmke, A. (1988). The role of classroom context factors for the achievement-impairing effect of test anxiety. *Anxiety Research, 1,* 37–52.

Helmke, A. (1990). *Das Münchner Aufmerksamkeits-Inventar (MAI)* [The Munich Attention Inventory]. Munich: Max-Planck-Institut für psychologische Forschung.

Helmke, A. (1992). *Selbstvertrauen und schulische Leistungen* [Self-confidence and scholastic achievement]. Göttingen: Hogrefe.

Helmke, A., & Renkl, A. (1992). Dad Münchener Aufmerksamkeitsinventar (MAI): Ein Instrument zur systematischen Verhaltensbeobachtung der Schüleraufmerksamkeit im Unterricht [The Munich Attention Inventory: An instrument for the systematic observation of student attention during classroom instruction]. *Diagnostica, 38,* 130–141.

Helmke, A., & Rheinberg, F. (1996). Anstrengungsvermeidung – Morphologie eines Konstruktes [Effort avoidance – morphology of a construct]. In C. Spiel, U. Kastner-Koller & P. Deimann (Eds.), *Entwicklung und Sozialisation* (pp. 207–224). Vienna: Waxmann.

Helmke, A., & Weinert, F. E. (1996). Bedingungsfaktoren schulischer Leistungen [Determinants of scholastic achievement]. In F. E. Weinert (Ed.), *Enzyklopädie der Psychologie, Band 3 (Psychologie der Schule und des Unterrichts)* (pp. 71–176). Göttingen: Hogrefe.

Helmke, A., & Weinert, F. E. (1997). Wissenschaftliche Grundlagen, Realisierungsbedingungen und Ergebnisperspektiven des Längsschnittprojektes SCHOLASTIK [The longitudinal elementary school project SCHOLASTIK: Goals, procedure, and results]. In F. E. Weinert & A. Helmke (Eds.), *Entwicklung im Grundschulalter* (pp. 3–12). Weinheim: Psychologie Verlagsunion.

Mac Iver, D. (1987). Classroom factors and student characteristics predicting students' use of achievement standards during ability self-assessment. *Child Development, 58,* 1258–1271.

Keeves, J. P., & Larkin, A. I. (1986). The context of academic motivation. *International Journal of Educational Research, 10,* 205–213.

Marshall, H. H., & Weinstein, R. S. (1984). Classroom factors affecting students' self-evaluations: An interactional model. *Review of Educational Research, 54,* 301–325.

Mitman, A. L., & Lash, A. A. (1988). Students' perceptions of their academic standing and classroom behavior. *The Elementary School Journal, 89,* 55–68.

Rosenholtz, S. J., & Simpson, C. (1984). Classroom organization and student stratification. *The Elementary School Journal, 85,* 21–37.

Schrader, D.-W., Helmke, A., & Dotzler, H. (1997). Zielkonflikte in der Grundschule [Goal conflicts in elementary school]. In F. E. Weinert & A. Helmke (Eds.), Entwicklung im Grundschulalter. Weinheim: Psychologie Verlagsunion.

Simons, H., Weinert, F. E., & Ahrens, H. J. (1975). Untersuchungen zur differentialpsychologischen Analyse von Rechenleistungen [Individual determinants of arithmetic achievements: An empirical study]. *Zeitschrift für Entwicklungspsychologie und Pädagogische Psychologie, 7,* 153–169.

Stipek, D. J. (1984). Young children's performance expectations: Logical analysis or wishful thinking? In J. G. Nicholls (Ed.), *Advances in motivation and achievement* (Vol. 3, pp. 33–56). Greenwich, CT: Jai Press.

Stipek, D. J., & Daniels, D. H. (1988). Declining perceptions of competence: A consequence of changes in the child or in the educational environment? *Journal of Educational Psychology, 80,* 352–356.

Stipek, D. J., & Mac Iver, D. (1989). Developmental change in children's assessment of intellectual competence. *Child Development, 60,* 521–538.

Stipek, D. J., & Tannatt, L. M. (1984). Children's judgments of their own and their peers' academic competence. *Journal of Educational Psychology, 76,* 75–84.

Treiber, B., & Weinert, F. E. (1985). *Gute Schulleistungen für alle? Psychologische Studien zu einer pädagogischen Hoffnung* [High scholastic achievements for all students? Psychological studies on a pedagogic hope]. Münster: Aschendorff.

Weinert, F. E., & Helmke, A. (1987). Schulleistungen – Leistungen der Schule oder der Kinder [Scholastic achievement – institutional or individual determinants?] *Bild der Wissenschaft, 24,* 62–73.

Weinert, F. E., & Helmke, A. (1988). Individual differences in cognitive development. Does instruction make a differences? In E. M. Hetherington, R. M. Lerner, & M. Perlmutter (Eds.), *Child development in life-span perspective* (pp. 219–239). Hillsdale, NJ: Erlbaum.

Weinert, F. E., & Helmke, A. (1993). Wie bereichsspezifisch verläuft die kognitive Entwicklung [About the domain-specificity of cognitive development]? In R. Duit & W. Gräber (Eds.), *Kognitive Entwicklung und Lernen der Naturwissenschaften* (pp. 27–45). Kiel: Institut für die Pädagogik der Naturwissenschaften.

Weinert, F. E., & Helmke, A. (1995a). Interclassroom differences in instructional quality and interindividual differences in cognitive development. *Educational Psychologist, 30,* 15–20.

Weinert, F. E., & Helmke, A. (1995b). Learning from wise mother nature or big brother instructor: The wrong choice as seen from an educational perspective. *Educational Psychologist, 30,* 135–142.

Weinert, F. E., & Helmke, A. (1998). The neglected role of individual differences in theoretical models of cognitive development. *Learning and Instruction, 8.*

Weinert, F. E., Helmke, A., & Schrader, F.-W. (1992). Research on the model teacher and the teaching model: Theoretical contradiction or conglutination? In F. Oser, A. Dick, & J.-L. Patry (Eds.), *Effective and responsable teaching: The new synthesis* (pp. 249–260). New York: Jossey-Bass.

Weinert, F. E., Schrader, F. W., & Helmke, A. (1989). Quality of instruction and achievement outcomes. *International Journal of Educational Research, 13,* 895–914.

9a   Comment: "Schooling and the Development of Achievement Differences"

Richard E. Snow

Having visited the Max Planck Institute for Psychological Research just about 10 years ago, as the work on this project was beginning, it is a great pleasure to return now for this conference, to learn how it has borne such interesting and useful fruit. The project has yielded a decade of outstanding research – and it is not really at an end, as several other speakers have noted as they gave myriad suggestions for further analyses. I also have such suggestions to offer. An old rule of thumb in psychology says that you should spend as much time and resources analyzing your data as you spent collecting them. If the present project holds to this rule, then we all expect to be invited back again to this beautiful place in another 10 years time to see the really final results. That is, of course, part of the reason for our myriad suggestions! Seriously, despite the excellence of the present reports, the data are indeed rare and rich with possibilities for further analyses. So I honestly hope further resources will be invested to this end, whether or not there is ever another conference.

The Helmke and Weinert chapter concerns the SCHOLASTIC project primarily, rather than the LOGIC project. However, the two were designed to be closely interlocked, as shown by Weinert (this volume). Just as LOGIC is innovative as a longitudinal study, SCHOLASTIC is innovative as a classroom study. The interlocking design allows measures and analyses that most classroom research cannot include. Its size, with 54 classrooms, is also a rarity in work on classroom instruction. Two other points add further to its uniqueness. The design provides for combined analysis of cognitive, conative, and affective student variables. It also emphasizes person–situation interaction – the view that person characteristics and situation characteristics jointly influence learning outcome and so must be studied as mediators and moderators of one another's effects. As such, it is a good example of what I call *aptitude–treatment interaction (ATI)* research on instruction (Cronbach and Snow 1977; Snow 1989, 1992). Finally, another unique strength is the relative homogeneity of curriculum across classrooms in German schools. This allows research questions to be addressed in ways that are difficult to approximate in many other countries, especially in the United States.

193

What do the SCHOLASTIC results tell us? First come the main effect, average comparisons:

1. There are class differences that appear as average differences in student characteristics. These differences are quite large on some motivational and affective characteristics but not large on the cognitive characteristics. Furthermore, many of these variables show decreasing importance of class membership that is not due to leveling effects of increasing grade but may be due to increasing stability of individual differences.
2. Classroom instructional variables show strong stability across grades when the same teachers remain, but zero stability when teachers change. These instructional variables do not relate strongly to indicators of classroom context. However, class size does seem to moderate some aspects of instructional quality directly or indirectly, perhaps through teacher–class assignment patterns.
3. The only classroom context variable that shows notable (though small) positive relations to average achievement gain is average class intelligence level. However, several indicators of instructional quality relate positively to achievement gain in mathematics (though not in spelling). These suggest that efficient direct instruction and class management, structure and clarity in lessons, and direct interventions in support of individual students lead to more substantial average class gains. This instructional style seems to be similar to what would be called *direct, mastery,* or *high-structure instruction* in U.S. research (see, for example, Glaser and Bassok 1989; Snow 1994; Snow and Swanson 1992). The average relations of these variables to achievement over classes are not particularly strong, however.
4. Finally, an attempt to identify the combination of instructional quality indicators that identify superior teachers (i.e., those showing the highest class gains) does not produce a uniform pattern. Successful profiles vary considerably, suggesting that teacher clarity is the only candidate for a general indicator of quality. The determinants of achievement thus seem to be multiple and interacting, probably in a compensatory fashion.

Points 1–4 are simple main effects at the individual or classroom level. They are not uninteresting. However, they are rather small and without great theoretical or practical import. As Helmke and Weinert point out, what is really needed is an ATI approach, because it is usually the joint effects of student prior-aptitude variables (both cognitive and motivational) and instructional quality variables that most likely influence learning outcome. They then proceed to explore this next step by showing the correlation of anxiety and achievement, and also of intelligence and achievement, separately for each of their classrooms. These further results show striking ATI effects, as follows:

5. The anxiety–achievement relations range from $-.80$ to about $+.15$ across these elementary classrooms, replicating previous results obtained across a sample of 39 high school classrooms (Helmke 1988). This is an ATI effect. The treatment variable associated with strength of the negative anxiety–achievement relations is supposedly unfavorable social climate and low teacher warmth or empathy for students' personal concerns. In the previous, higher grade result, the treatments associated with negative effects reflected intensive use of time, low structure, and heavy emphasis on success or failure. The finding that different treatment variables influence the anxiety–achievement relation at lower grade levels is not a failure of replication. Rather it indicates higher order interaction with student and instructional variables associated with elementary versus high school classrooms.

6. The intelligence–achievement relations similarly range between about 0 and +.80 across classrooms and hold also across three grade levels. Again, this is a striking ATI. Further analysis is thus planned to determine what distinguishes teacher treatments that produce high versus low intelligence–achievement relations.

Thus, at the present state, we know that variations in student aptitudes are large and of some matter in relation to learning. We know that variations in instructional quality and context are large and that some of these also matter in relation to learning. However, we also know that what student and instructional quality variations matter differs in different classrooms. There are clear, complex ATI patterns, and the next question is how best to analyze and understand them.

Other discussants at this conference have been urging that the next step is to go beneath the correlations, to a more fine-grain or "molecular" analysis of item-by-item rules and strategies in individual student performance. I agree that such an emphasis is one important next step. However, I think it should not be taken to the exclusion of more "molar" analyses. There are at least three levels of grain-size here: item-by-item analysis; individual student, task, and treatment variable intercorrelation; and student within- versus between-classroom analysis. The problem of unraveling and making sense of the complex of variables and interrelationships operating within and between these levels brings up complicated statistical issues.

Helmke and Weinert approach this task carefully and correctly. They take first, exploratory cuts, doing detective work along the way to check both simple assumptions (e.g., linearity) and complex effects (e.g., teacher profiles). Then they can take a next cut, again with detective work to explore the complications. It is an iterative process that they know is not yet at an end. Thus, to help the process along at this stage, I offer the following observations and suggestions:

7. Intelligence and anxiety independently show markedly different relations with achievement across classrooms, as noted earlier. This is an ATI effect for each student aptitude variable. However, there is also considerable evidence that intelligence and anxiety interact with some of the same treatment variables and interact with one another in so doing (Snow 1989). For example, high-structure treatments that may be similar to the efficient, structured instruction classrooms noted here have been found effective for low ability–low anxious students but also for high ability–high anxious students, whereas these treatments have been shown not to serve high ability–low anxious or low ability–high anxious students well. It is important therefore that one further analysis take these aptitudes into account together. Across the 54 classrooms, we want to know whether classrooms that show high (or low) intelligence–achievement relations also show high (or low) anxiety–achievement relations. We also need to know the interrelation of intelligence and anxiety in each classroom. After all, the two kinds of differences are operating in the same classrooms and should not be interpreted independently.

8. An added complication here involves the pretest. Relying on residual achievement gain alone is risky; if there are joint effects of pretest with either intelligence or anxiety, or differential effects in different parts of the achievement continuum, then residual gain may mask them because this partials out not only pretest but everything that correlates with it and assumes further that gain units are equal throughout the range. What we really need is an analysis that looks at the three independent aptitude

variables jointly – prior achievement, intelligence, and anxiety can be considered coequal as aptitudes.

9. We should also look at the level of aptitude and outcome and their interrelationships together. Correlations and means analyses taken separately can be misleading; classrooms with high average outcome and low aptitude–outcome relations should be quite different from classrooms with low average outcome and the same low aptitude–outcome relation, and each should differ substantively from classrooms with intermediate average outcome and high aptitude–outcome relation. Thus, within-class raw regressions and means, not just correlations, should be examined together.

10. Following this, the next step is to move to a hierarchical analysis that allows between-class and within-class regressions to be distinguished. Each class is located in an array of classrooms along each aptitude continuum. The individuals within each class are also located on the aptitude continuum. Within-class and between-class (i.e., class average) regressions of outcome onto aptitude can differ in meaningful ways. For example, what constitutes high and low student ability in a class depends on the class average, and averages differ across classes. If teachers distribute attention among their "high" and "low" students differently as a function of class average ability, within-class regressions would be expected to change systematically as one goes up the class average ability continuum. Basic methods for between-class versus within-class analysis were given by Cronbach and Snow (1977), but nowadays there are various advanced methods for hierarchical modeling. The general point is that each classroom is located in a space defined by multivariate aptitude and achievement levels and relations. Instructional treatment variables varying across classrooms need to be understood in relation to all of the parameters of that space, not just one or two at a time.

11. The within-class versus between-class distinction also recognizes that each class is a social group. The mix of aptitudes in each group differs. What constitutes high or low prior achievement or ability, or high or low anxiety, is relative to the group norm and group process, at least in part. There is evidence that individual learning outcome depends not only on individual aptitude but also on the mix of aptitudes available in the individual's group and the social role the individual adopts in that group. The analysis needs to recognize this individual-in-group, social psychology of each classroom: These are context not just treatment interactions.

12. Finally, there is the distinction between the instructional treatment as observed or objectively described and the instructional treatment as perceived by each student. Ornstein (this volume) contrasted the nominal and the effective or functional stimulus to make the same distinction. Some evidence suggests that anxious and nonanxious students perceive the same treatment quite differently and react quite differently as a result. Other evidence shows that high- and low-ability students react differently as a function of what kind of treatment they perceive they are getting, in comparison with their classmates.

It is not suggested that Helmke and Weinert, or any other project, can attend to all of these subtleties. However, in most cases, analyses can be geared to detect some of these kinds of effects, and interpretations can at least be alert to their existence. In that regard, it should be noted that their chapter as it currently appears excludes mention of some other analyses that were conducted and presented at the conference. Hopefully, these analyses are reported elsewhere, because they add an important further message. Grade 1 intelligence was treated here as aptitude. However, Helmke and Weinert also treated their Grade 4 intelligence measures as indicants of instructional outcomes to be predicted from student and class variables measured earlier. They thus viewed education as an aptitude development program. In other words, achievement output at one stage is aptitude input at the next, and broad intellectual development, not just domain knowledge, becomes education's most important product (see, for example, Snow 1982). Intelligence is invested in learning to produce gain in domain achievement (we might call it *intelligent knowledge*), which is invested in learning to produce gain in intelligence (what we might call *knowledgeable intelligence*). Similar reciprocal relations hold between cognitive and motivational variables. In short, student intelligence, domain achievement, and motivation, as well as classroom variables, operate jointly to influence learning and also each other. Much instructional and developmental psychology does not appear to appreciate this point. As Helmke and Weinert acknowledge, we do not yet understand how these influences operate jointly, so we need to push our analyses much further to illuminate the complex interactions evident here.

If I understand correctly, also available in the SCHOLASTIC data set are measures of academic self-concept, attributional style, attitude toward learning, and study skills, taken at three grade levels. These of course are additional variables that could be included in the analysis both as aptitudes and as outcomes. It might also be profitable to consider subscores of the achievement test analyzed separately, if distinctions between computation, math concepts, and reasoning, for example, can be gotten from the tests used; such subscores represent different kinds of ability development and can operate quite differently in relation to other student and instructional treatment variables.

The work on SCHOLASTIC is ongoing, so there is no appropriate conclusion here. Suffice it to say that what has been done so far shows fascinating effects worthy of pursuit. As I said at the start, I hope the needed time and effort will be fully invested. The result could well become one of the most famous and useful multivariate classroom studies ever conducted.

References

Cronbach, L. J., & Snow, R. E. (1977). *Aptitudes and instructional methods: A handbook for research on interactions.* New York: Irvington.

Glaser, R., & Bassok, M. (1989). Learning theory and the study of instruction. *Annual Review of Psychology, 40,* 631–666.

Helmke, A. (1988). The role of classroom context factors for the achievement-impairing effect of test anxiety. *Anxiety Research, 1,* 37–52.

Snow, R. E. (1982). Education and intelligence. In R. J. Sternberg (Ed.), *Handbook of human intelligence* (pp. 493–585). Cambridge: Cambridge University Press.

Snow, R. E. (1989). Aptitude-treatment interaction as a framework of research in individual differences in learning. In P. L. Ackerman, R. J. Sternberg, & R. Glaser (Eds.), *Learning and individual differences* (pp. 11–34). New York: Freeman.

Snow, R. E. (1992). Aptitude theory: Yesterday, today, and tomorrow. *Educational Psychologist, 27,* 5–32.

Snow, R. E. (1994). Abilities in academic tasks. In R. J. Sternberg & R. K. Wagner (Eds.), *Mind in context: Interactionist perspectives on human intelligence* (pp. 3–37). New York: Cambridge University Press.

Snow, R. E., & Swanson, J. (1992). Instructional psychology: Aptitude, adaptation, and assessment. *Annual Review of Psychology, 43,* 583–626.

10   From Optimism to Realism? Development of Children's Academic Self-Concept From Kindergarten to Grade 6

Andreas Helmke

The study of developmental changes in children's achievement-related beliefs, self-concepts, motives, and attitudes has received considerable research attention in both developmental and educational psychology (Dweck and Elliott 1983; Eccles et al. 1983; Heckhausen 1984; Nicholls 1984a; Parsons, Adler, and Kaczala 1982; Ruble 1980; Stipek 1984a; Stipek and Mac Iver 1989; Stipek, Recchia, and McClintic 1992; Wigfield 1994). As the synopsis of achievement-related motivational variables in Table 1 shows, this domain also has been a focus of the LOGIC project.

The approach of the present chapter is at the same time both narrow and broad. It is narrow because I concentrate on a comparatively small segment, namely, on children's academic self-concept (see the footnoted areas in Table 1); other achievement-related motivational and affective constructs as well as self-concepts in nonacademic (e.g., social and physical) domains are disregarded. On the other hand, the approach is broad because results of a variety of different facets and perspectives of the academic self-concept development are reported: level, stability, and accuracy. Furthermore, the report of average developmental tendencies with regard to these aspects is complemented by analyses of differential effects. Here, we concentrate on differences between boys and girls and students with different school careers: those who attend high school (Gymnasium) versus continued elementary school (Hauptschule). Because the segregation of the Bavarian school system into streams begins at Grade 5, our approach can be characterized as postdictive analysis.

Method

Sample

For most of the analyses presented in this chapter, the sample consisted of those children of the LOGIC project ($N = 179$) for whom complete data for all the variables included in the analyses (for detailed descriptions of the samples, see Chapter 1) are available. As far as school data (e.g., teacher ratings and achievement tests and grades)

198

Table 1. *Repeated Measurements of the Core Achievement-Related Motivational Variables and Scholastic Achievements in the LOGIC Study*

Variable	Kindergarten: Wave 3			Grade 1: Wave 4			Grade 2: Wave 5			Grade 3: Wave 6			Grade 4: Wave 7			Grade 5: Wave 8			Grade 6: Wave 9		
	1	2	3	1	2	3	1	2	3	1	2	3	1	2	3	1	2	3	1	2	3
Motivation																					
Academic self-concept (ASC): Mathematics[a]			X	X			X			X			X			X			X		X
ASC: German[a]			X	X			X			X			X			X			X		X
ASC: First foreign language																X			X		X
Attitude toward mathematics			X	X			X			X			X			X					X
Attitude toward German			X	X			X			X			X			X					X
Attitude toward foreign language																X					X
Volitional learning problems							X			X			X			X			X		
Test anxiety							X			X			X			X					
Attribution of success and failure (open ended)			X	X										X			X			X	

199

Table 1. (*Cont.*)

Variable	Kindergarten: Wave 3			Grade 1: Wave 4			Grade 2: Wave 5			Grade 3: Wave 6			Grade 4: Wave 7			Grade 5: Wave 8			Grade 6: Wave 9		
	1	2	3	1	2	3	1	2	3	1	2	3	1	2	3	1	2	3	1	2	3
Achievement																					
Behavior rating by parents[a]	X			X						X						X					X
Teacher rating of students' competencies and grades[a]					X				X			X			X			X			X
Mathematics test[a]							X			X			X								
Spelling test[a]								X			X			X							
Science test								X			X			X							

[a]Indicates variables that were used in the study reported in this chapter.

are concerned, the underlying sample consists of the intersection of the LOGIC and the SCHOLASTIC study ($N = 102$).

Measurement Points

Table 1 also shows the location (marked by points) of the 8 measurement points underlying the following analyses. Between Grades 1 and 6, the time interval was always exactly 1 year (the administration of tests took place during the first third of every school year), whereas for the two end points of the study – before school entry and at the very end of Grade 6 – a half-year time interval was chosen.

Three characteristics of the Bavarian school system (Bavaria is one of the German states) should be noted: First, there are no marks or grades during the first year of elementary school; the first formal grades appear no earlier than in the middle of Grade 2. Second, there is an obligatory change of classroom teacher between Grades 2 and 3 in all Bavarian schools. Third, elementary school ends after Grade 4; depending on the average achievement in the core school subjects, pupils with lower achievement levels continue elementary school, and pupils with higher achievements are enrolled in high school.

Assessment of Academic Self-Concept

The items concerning self-concept of ability required the children to judge their relative standing within the reference group (which in Wave 3 was the kindergarten group and in the following waves the classroom) with regard to various domains of scholastic achievement and within the domains concerning specific subdomains and achievement-related activities (for details and methodological background, see Helmke 1991a, 1991b, 1992b). Although the global interview questions concerning one's overall relative standing in mathematics and German could remain constant over the years, self-evaluation of subdomains and specific achievement-related activities had to be changed according to changes in the curriculum. For example, at the kindergarten and first-grade level, children were asked how well they already had mastered elementary skills (such as counting, knowing numbers, reading, etc.); whereas in Grade 5, several subdomains of mathematics were covered in the interview (such as mental arithmetic, word problems, etc.; for details, see Helmke 1991b, 1992b). This procedure of measuring academic self-concept, similar to the one used by Nicholls (1978) and Stipek and Daniels (1988), was part of a comprehensive interview developed by the author that focused on various scholastic experiences and achievement-related motives, self-concepts, attitudes, and attributions of success and failure. The following example was the instruction that was given for mathematics in Grade 3 (See Figure 1):

> "Look, imagine that these figures here (*little wooden figures symbolizing persons*) are the children in your class (*N purple figures, with N = exactly the number of pupils in the respective classroom, are placed in a vertical line*). The child at the top is the best of all in math, the child at the bottom is the worst of all. And this figure (*green figure*) is you. Now show me where you belong: Are you the worst in math

Table 2. *The Scoring of Children's Self-Perceptions of Their Relative Standing Within the Classroom*

Meaning of the position	Best			Good		Medium		Not so good		Worst	
Pattern of the figures	0			000		000		000		0	
Placement of the target figure	+	+	+	+	+	+	+	+	+	+	+
Score	5	4	3	2	1	0	−1	−2	−3	−4	−5

(*interviewer places green figure underneath the bottom figure*), or are you somewhere in the middle (*interviewer gradually slides the green figure to the top*), or are you among those who are the best in math?" *To check that the task had been correctly understood by the child, two additional control questions were posed:* "Does this mean that about ... pupils are worse in math than you are?" "And does it mean that about ... pupils are better in math than you are?"

Figure 1. Instrument for measuring children's relative position within the reference group.

A simplified instruction was used for subdomains of school subjects (e.g., arithmetic, word problems, multiplication tasks, and so forth): Here, the N purple figures representing the pupils in the classroom were grouped into five units (see Table 2) consisting of (a) the "best" in the class, (b) the "good" students, (c) the "medium" students, (d) the "not-so-good" students, and (e) the "worst" in the class. The child's placement of the green figure was then scored in 1 of 11 response categories (see Table 2) that ranged from −5 (child places the figure *lower than* the bottommost figure), −4 (*next to* the bottommost figure), −3 (*between* the bottommost and the not-so-good group), −2 (*beside* the not-so-good group), and so on up to +5 (*above* the topmost figure).

Table 3. *Correlations Between Domain-Specific Self-Concepts (Mathematics and German) in Fourth Grade*

| | Academic self-concept in Grade 4 | |
Variable	Mathematics	German
Intelligence test	.21*	.18
Achievement test	.43**	.27**
Arithmetic skills	.31**	.25**
Word problems	.22*	.58**
Spelling	.22*	.58**
Grade		
Mathematics	.47**	.12
German	.31**	.45**
Sports	.12	.07
Motivational Variable		
Test anxiety	−.22*	−.07
Attitude toward mathematics	.66**	.20*
Attitude toward German	.11	.48**
Active engagement during instruction	.39**	.37**
Teacher rating of student personality		
Anxiety	−.20**	−.08
Achievement motivation	.30**	.20*
Popularity	.06	.14
Attention during instruction	.26**	.11
Learning behavior		
Observed active time-on-task	.12	.21*
Volitional learning problems	−.27**	.04

Notes: For details of the instruments see Helmke 1992b (student questionnaires and teacher ratings); Stern 1992 (math test); Schneider 1992 (spelling test); Helmke and Renkl 1992 (observed attention during instruction, time on task); and Weiß and Osterland 1979 (intelligence test).
*$p < .05$. **$p < .01$.

Assessment of Academic Achievements and Achievement-Related Judgments

At the kindergarten level, maternal and kindergarten teachers' reports concerning the mastery of specific verbal or math-related skills served as measures of achievement. After the start of elementary school, teachers' ratings (Grade 1) and later the official grades (Grades 2–6) were the achievement criteria.

Nomological Network

To give an impression of the nomological network of academic self-concept (ASC), correlations (selected from Wave 7; i.e., from Grade 4 of elementary school) between domain-specific self-concepts and selected other motivational, cognitive, and behavioral variables are reported in Table 3.

The results depicted in Table 3 underline the domain specificity of self-concepts as well as aspects of discriminant and convergent validity of the self-concept measures:

The arithmetic test correlates higher with math self-concept ($r = .43$) than with verbal self-concept ($r = .27$), and the reverse is true for the correlation of the spelling test with verbal self-concept ($r = .58$) versus math self-concept ($r = .22$). This reverse pattern is nicely complemented by the correlation of math word problems – comprising both verbal and mathematical competencies – which is about equally high for both domain-specific self-concepts. The equivalent reverse correlational pattern, underlining the discrepancy between the domains, was found for domain-specific self-concepts and grades (marks). The correlations of the self-concepts with the motivational variables are not very high but yield a consistent pattern: The lower the level of academic self-concepts, the lower are active engagement during instruction, attitude toward learning, general self-esteem, and achievement motivation, and the higher is test anxiety. Interestingly, there is no significant relation between self-concept and the (teacher-rated) popularity and social acceptance by the peers within the classroom. On the other hand, the correlations also demonstrate that there is a considerable conceptual overlap between these variables that must be taken into account for the interpretation of the results.

Development of the Level of Children's Self-Evaluations

Many studies have shown that children's perceptions of their intellectual ability and academic competence, as well as of their achievement-related expectations, tend to decline during late elementary school time (see Dweck and Elliott 1983; Eccles and Midgley 1989; Stipek and Mac Iver 1989 for reviews). Several explanations have been suggested for this trend, in particular, developmental changes in children's cognitive abilities (e.g., attending to and processing of evaluative feedback and searching and integrating social comparison information) and changes in classroom environment (changing salience of achievement, first occurrence of written marks and grades, and increasing frequency of grading activities and of within-classroom social comparisons; cf. Helmke 1992a; Rosenholtz and Rosenholtz 1981; Stipek 1984a; Stipek and Daniels 1988; Stipek and Mac Iver 1989; Stipek and Hoffman 1980). Although the majority of the studies have been cross-sectional, there appears to be evidence that children's competence beliefs decrease in a more or less linear way during the late elementary school period (Eccles et al. 1993; Marsh 1988, 1990; Valtin 1996) and that this decline continues into junior high or middle school (Eccles et al. 1983; Wigfield et al. 1989). In contrast, there is little empirical evidence for younger children (Bridgeman and Shipman 1978; Eshel and Klein 1981; Larned and Muller 1979; Marsh, Craven, and Debus 1991) concerning the course of self-concept development.

Figures 2 and 3 show the average course of self-concept development in mathematics and German from kindergarten (Wave 3) to Grade 6 (Wave 9). In this context, it should be noted (see Table 1) that Wave 9 comprises two measurements: one at the beginning and one at the end of sixth grade (in the Figures, 6 and 6-end).

The following points of the resulting pattern deserve mention. First, from a global viewpoint, there is a decreasing trend during the 6 years from the end of kindergarten

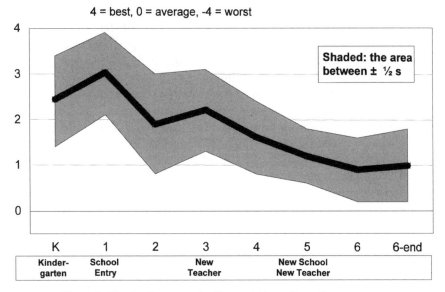

Figure 2. The development of self-concept in mathematics.

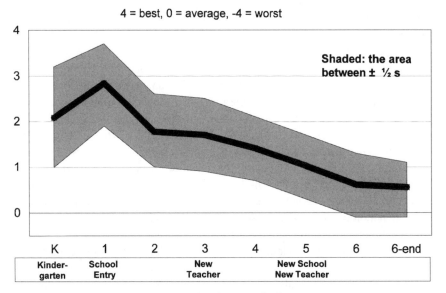

Figure 3. The development of self-concept in German.

until the end of sixth grade. This was confirmed by the repeated-measures analyses of variance (ANOVA), in combination with post hoc contrasts for self-concept of mathematics (significant time) effect: $F(7,1176) = 45.63$, $p < .01$, as well as for self-concept of German, $F(7,1176) = 32.60$, $p < .01$. So far, our results are in line with the vast majority of results reported from empirical literature.

Second, it should be noted that – on average – self-evaluation remains during the entire 6-year period in the above-average area (i.e., within the zone > 0). If students' self-evaluations were realistic, the percentage of students who judge their competence as below average should be about as high as the percentage of students judging themselves as being above the average (i.e., above- and below-average judgments should be balanced).

Third, if one regards the developmental pattern in more detail, it becomes clear that only the second half of the 7-year development – from the beginning of Grade 3 until the end of Grade 6 – can be characterized by a negative linear decrease. From kindergarten to Grade 3, the developmental trend is neither significantly decreasing nor linear. Rather, there are two "peaks," indicating that positive self-evaluation increases after kindergarten (age 5) and reaches its maximum at the beginning of Grade 1. The following decreasing trend is interrupted a second time – however, only slightly – and is not statistically significant. This more informal inspection of the data shown in Figures 2 and 3 was confirmed by analyses in which the tool of hierarchical linear modeling (Bryk and Raudenbush 1992) was used. This analysis, when applied for the first four measurement points only, revealed that the overall trend of the growth curve can best be modeled by a step trend (with down steps after Grades 1 and 3), which is superimposed by a linear trend.

The results underline that both individual personality factors and school socialization factors must be simultaneously taken into account to understand the developmental pattern of self-concept. Children improve at understanding and correctly interpreting evaluative feedback (Stipek 1984b), and they engage increasingly in social comparisons (Dweck and Elliott 1983; Nicholls 1984b). This coincides with typical changes in the school environment; namely, the increasing saliency of success and failure and the frequency and clarity of feedback given in the classroom (Blumenfeld, Pintrich, Meece, and Wessels 1982; Eccles et al. 1983; Eccles and Midgley 1989; Helmke 1991a, 1992b; Marshall and Weinstein 1984). These considerations support the notion of a steady decrease of children's academic self-concepts from a robust and strong optimism toward a more realistic self-evaluation.

However, what about the deviations of the linear decline? An obvious explanation could be that during the first grade of elementary school – at least during the first half of the year – the main goals of classroom instruction are to facilitate children's transition to school, to ensure that they become involved in school, and to establish basic social rules and norms as well as basic study skills rather than to cover content. When achievement-related feedback is given at all, it is predominantly positive, and achievement-related social comparisons within the classroom are certainly not accentuated. Under these circumstances, many children have good reasons to evaluate themselves as being "the best."

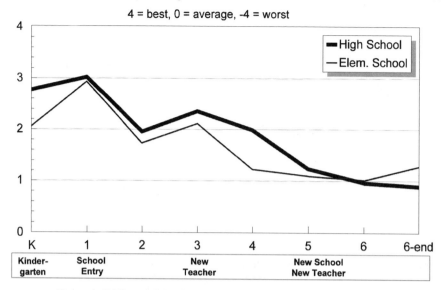

Figure 4. Differential development of self-concept in mathematics: elementary versus high school students.

The slight "re-increase" at the beginning of Grade 3 should not be overinterpreted because it failed to reach statistical significance. An explanation could be that during the first part of the school year, when new teachers are still forming images of the strengths and weaknesses of their pupils, they tend to be careful and to avoid giving negative feedback as well as unfavorable social comparisons (social reference norm). Furthermore, this could be a transition period of certainty concerning the validity of rules and standards of evaluation, leading to niches of idiosyncratic, self-serving biases in academic self-concepts (cf. Kunda 1990).

Besides the overall analysis, we analyzed differences in self-concept development of students who were (since the beginning of Grade 5) enrolled in high school (high-achievement track) versus continued elementary school (low-achievement track). A first inspection of the curves depicted in Figures 4 and 5 shows similar trends for both subjects. From the beginning of elementary school until the fourth grade, the discrepancy in the level of academic self-concept between lower and higher achievers (indicated by their different school careers after Grade 4) shows an increasing trend, whereas the opposite trend – diminishing of the discrepancy – starts after grade 5.

Although the multivariate analyses of variance main effect of school system on math self-concept did not reach the level of statistical significance, $F(1,130) = 0.86, ns$, an interaction effect was found, $F(7,124) = 2.44, p < .05$, indicating group differences in the course of self-concept development. As Figure 4 indicates, the interaction was mainly due to the adverse course of self-concept development from Grade 4 to Grade 6. This is supported by single-group contrasts showing that self-concept at the beginning of Grade 5 is still higher for the high school group ($M = 1.23$) as compared

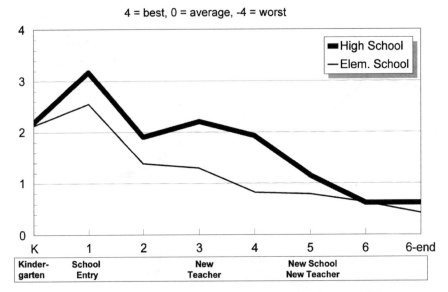

Figure 5. Differential development of self-concept in German: elementary versus high school students.

with the elementary school group ($M = 1.09$), $F(1,130) = 21.39$, $p < .01$. This superiority in self-evaluation changes at the next measurement point, however, and at the end of Grade 6, students from elementary school show a significantly higher level of self-concept than the pupils from high school.

From the standpoint of social comparison theory (Festinger 1954; Marsh 1987; Marsh and Parker 1984; Ruble 1984), this result is interpretable. Social comparison theory posits that self-concept is heavily influenced by social contexts, in particular, by social comparison processes with a reference group. In Davis' (1966) terms, it is better for one's self-concept to be a big frog in a little pond (e.g., an average or high achiever in an elementary school classroom) than a small frog in a big pond (e.g., a poor achiever in a high school class). This may explain why the discrepancy between academic self-concept in high schools versus elementary schools shows a diminishing trend. After having entered the new school type, most of the students compare themselves predominantly with their reference group (i.e., the classroom) rather than with the entire age group. This may lead to effects of relative deprivation for high school scholars and relative gratification for elementary school scholars.

Gender differences in the pattern of the average self-concept development in German and math are depicted in Figures 6 and 7. The results underline that domain-specific gender differences would have been masked if we had used overall self-concept scales, aggregated across domains: ASC in mathematics appears to be more favorable for boys, and the reverse is true for German. A two-factorial ANOVA with repeated measurements confirmed the gender difference for mathematics, $F(1,168) = 15.84$, $p < .01$, but not for German, $F(1,169) = 3.15$, ns.

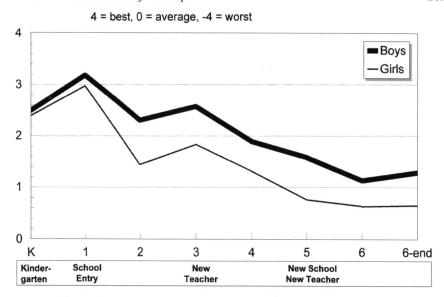

Figure 6. Development of self-concept in mathematics: gender differences.

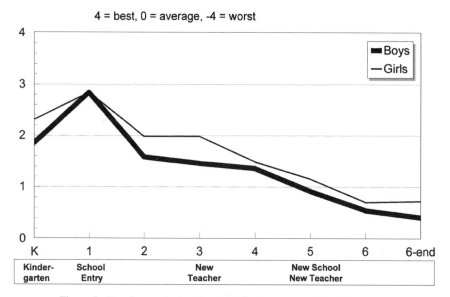

Figure 7. Development of self-concept in German: gender differences.

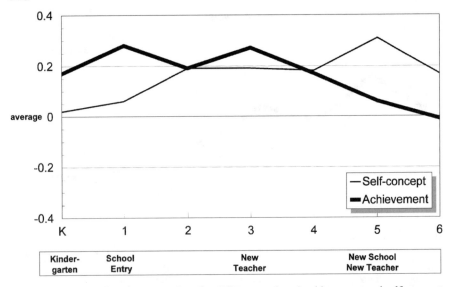

Figure 8. Development of gender differences: boys' achievement and self-concept in math (z scores). Girls' scores are exactly the mirror image below the 0-axis.

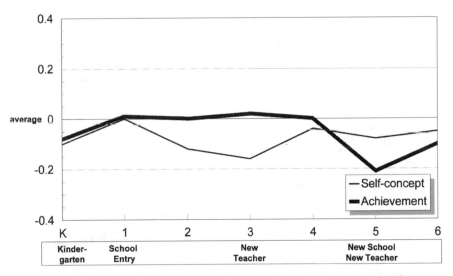

Figure 9. Development of gender differences: boys' achievement and self-concept in German (z scores). Girls' scores are exactly the mirror image below the 0-axis.

In this context, the question arises whether the domain-specific gender differences in ASC reflect actual achievement differences. To answer this question, it is necessary to establish achievement and ASC on the same metric (by means of z standardization). Figures 8 and 9 show the results for boys (girls' scores are, as a consequence of the standardization, necessarily exactly the mirror image of the boys' profile, so it would be redundant to include the data for both sexes). In mathematics, both achievement and self-concept of girls are below the average. However, there is an interesting trend: The achievement difference between girls and boys increases in favor of the boys, whereas at the same time the course of self-concept shows the opposite trend. In contrast, the results for German show no such clear pattern. The pattern found in our study is in accordance with recent meta-analyses of gender differences in achievement and achievement-related beliefs and attitudes (Hyde, Fennema, and Lamon 1990), which have shown that achievement differences between boys and girls are very small; if they occur at all, girls outperform boys in the verbal domain, whereas the contrary is true for mathematics. As far as gender differences in academic self-concept are concerned, boys are typically characterized by a (often unrealistically) high self-concept, compared with girls (see the overview of Helmke and Weinert 1996).

The Development of the Veridicality of the Self-Concept

Although the analysis of the mere average level of achievement-related self-assessments may be informative about judgment accuracy (e.g., an average overestimation can be regarded as an indicator of an optimistic bias within the sample), a more direct and straightforward approach for conceptualizing accuracy (or veridicality) of achievement-related judgments is to correlate self-evaluations with correspondent achievements. Because teachers are the major source of feedback for pupils concerning their academic abilities, we chose (from Wave 4 on) teacher ratings and official grades (marks) as criteria; in Grade 1 we used teachers' reports of children's mastery of elementary skill, and at Wave 3 (kindergarten), we used mothers' precise descriptions of their children's actual competencies. Figure 10 shows the results for the entire sample.

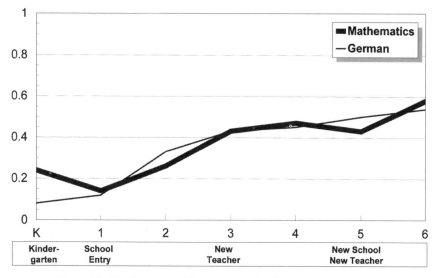

Figure 10. Development of the accuracy of self-concepts: correlation between self-concept and achievement criterion (mathematics and German).

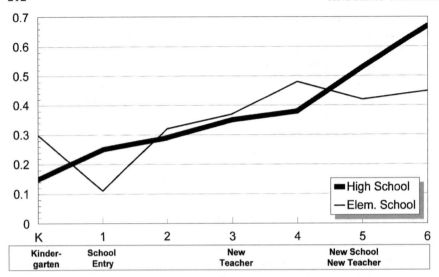

Figure 11. Differential development of the accuracy of self-concept in mathematics: elementary versus high school students.

Although in kindergarten and particularly in first grade, children's ratings of their achievements were only very weakly related to the achievement criteria, there is an increase from Grade 2 ($r = .24$) until the end of Grade 6 ($r = .78$). In contrast to earlier studies that failed to find any significant correlations between children's self-assessments of their competencies and correspondent teacher ratings (e.g., Nicholls 1978, 1979), correlations begin to reach a substantial level ($r > .40$) as early as at the beginning of third grade.

Differential developmental trends can be seen from Figures 11 and 12. First, before Grade 5 high school versus elementary school students do not differ significantly from each other in their accuracy of self-perceptions; that is, after entering the new schools (Figure 11). Although accuracy of high school scholars shows a rather linear increase, the developmental pattern of the low-achievement group is characterized by a certain delay. This effect may be caused by typical differences with regard to the saliency (associated with differences in tests, grading procedures, social comparisons, etc.) of achievement (low in elementary schools and high in high schools), which is typical for these school types.

Second, although girls' assessments of their early achievements are higher than those of boys, boys outperform girls during most of the following measurement points (Figure 12). The fact that boys – in contrast to girls, as the figure shows – reach a reasonable level of accuracy ($r = .38$) as early as at the beginning of Grade 2 deserves particular attention. Perhaps this pattern reflects one aspect of early gender-specific differential socialization, especially of school experiences. Possibly, boys receive more detailed achievement-related feedback, whether from the parents or the

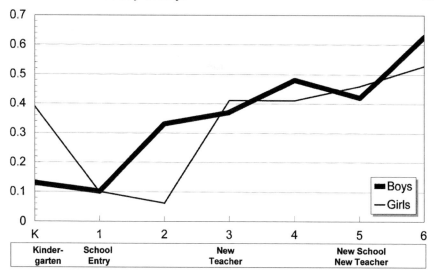

Figure 12. Differential development of the accuracy of self-concept in mathematics: gender differences.

teacher, or – and this cannot be decided on the basis of data – they are themselves more interested in achievement-related social comparison within the classroom.

Stability of Academic Self-Concept

Because of the small number of long-term longitudinal studies, little is known about the stability of academic self-concept during elementary school (Mason and Stipek 1989). From an individual developmental perspective, one would expect a steady increase in temporal stability, caused by improved cognitive abilities and by the increasing stability and validity (see previous section) of self-concept. From a social-ization perspective, the first emergence of official grades might be crucial because grades reflect the overall achievement of the pupils from the teachers' standpoint and are often publicly fed back to the students. Furthermore, one would expect that collec-tive critical life events should lead to a destabilization of self-concept. These include change of the classroom teacher (which is obligatory in the Bavarian school system between second and third grade) and the transition from elementary school to either continued elementary school or high school, including change of the reference group and the classroom teacher. To better understand the stability of achievement-related self-concepts, it appears again fruitful to contrast these results with the stabilities of the achievements. Figure 13 shows the results for the stability of achievements, and Figure 14 shows the results for the correspondent self-concepts, which are based on correlation coefficients.

As can be seen from Figure 13, achievement differences are, as early as from Grade 1 (teacher rating of students' domain-specific competencies) to Grade 2 (grades),

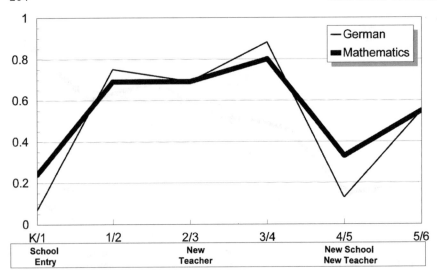

Figure 13. Stability of achievement: correlation between adjacent measurement points.

remarkably stable. Interestingly, the change of the classroom teacher (transition from Grade 2 to Grade 3), which is associated with an increase in the level of the ASC (see previous section), makes no difference for stability. In contrast, the change of the school type and change of the classroom teacher lead to a substantial destabilization of achievements – a trivial result because grades in continued elementary school and high school are not equivalent.

The decomposition of this trend of the entire sample into separate trends for students from different school systems reveals different patterns (the example is for the subject German). First, almost during the entire 6-year period, the stability of the students with poorer achievements is higher than the stability found for the high school students. Second, the high school students show a significantly stronger reaction to the teacher change between Grades 2 and 3. Thus, it would be incorrect to state that teacher change does not make any difference at all; it does, but obviously only the achievement rank order of the abler students is affected. The achievement hierarchy among the poorer students is comparatively unaffected by the change of the teacher.

The comparison of Figures 13 (stability of achievement) and 14 (stability of the correspondent self-concept) shows some similarities as well as discrepancies. On the one hand, teacher change between Grades 2 and 3 makes a difference neither for achievement nor for academic self-concept. On the other hand, although the stability of achievements decreases drastically after Grade 4, surprisingly this is not the case for self-concepts of achievement.

A comparison of the two school groups (elementary school vs. high school) in Figure 15 shows that it is the group of higher achievers that reacts much more sensibly

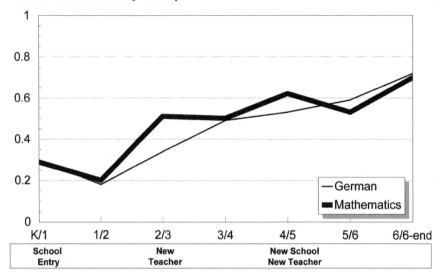

Figure 14. Stability of self-concept in mathematics and German: correlations between adjacent measurement points.

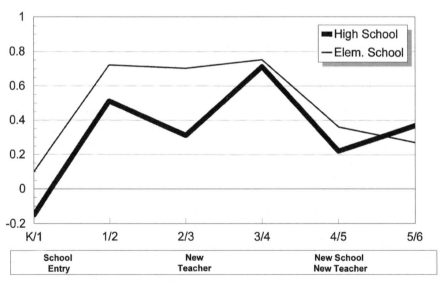

Figure 15. Stability of achievement in German: differential trends for high school and elementary school students.

Table 4. *Long-Term Stabilities of Self-Concept in Math (upper right) and German (lower left)*

Time	Ke	1b	2b	3b	4b	5b	6b	6e
Ke	—	.29	.25	.13	.23	.17	.20	.16
1b	.30	—	.20	.26	.22	.26	.11	.17
2b	.22	.18	—	.51	.35	.30	.26	.16
3b	.17	.17	.34	—	.50	.47	.43	.37
4b	.17	.17	.32	.49	—	.62	.39	.30
5b	.21	.20	.29	.37	.53	—	.53	.46
6b	.21	.20	.25	.28	.46	.59	—	.70
6e	.13	.06	.24	.26	.38	.45	.72	—

Notes: Most of the measurements took place during the first third of the school year (see Table 1 for an overview of waves and measurement points within waves); they are therefore labeled 1b, 2b, and so forth (*b* for beginning). In two cases, the measurement took place during the last third of the year, namely, during the last kindergarten year and in Grade 6 (in addition to the measurement at Time 6b); they are therefore labeled Ke and 6e, respectively (*e* for end).

to the teacher change between Grades 2 and 3. Although the stability of the elementary school group is not affected at all, classroom teacher change appears to be a much more salient life event for high-achieving pupils.

Although the figures have shown only the stabilities for adjacent measurement points, Table 4 presents a correlation matrix with all stabilities.

Differentiation of Achievements and Self-Concepts

Several developmental theorists have proposed that the development of many human traits and behaviors is characterized by a change from a global to a more differentiated state (Markus and Wurf 1987; Shavelson, Hubner, and Stanton 1976). From the standpoint of cognitive psychology, this aspect has been particularly stressed by researchers who have accentuated the issue of domain-specificity. Developmental empirical research has shown that children's competence-related beliefs and evaluations becomes increasingly distinct across the elementary school years. With regard to self-concept, several studies have shown that its structure becomes increasingly multifaceted and multidimensional (Byrne 1984; Eccles, Wigfield, Harold, and Blumenfeld 1993; Harter 1983; Marsh 1990). Harter, for example, has demonstrated that children's broad and global understandings that they are "smart" change toward an increasingly fine-grained sense of competence for specific strengths and weaknesses. Factor-analytic (both explorative and confirmatory) research has shown that children's competence beliefs form clear, distinct factors as early as in second grade (Eccles et al. 1993; Marsh et al. 1991; Wigfield et al. 1990). Even for kindergarten children it was found that competence beliefs in different domains are distinct (Eccles et al. 1993; Marsh et al. 1991).

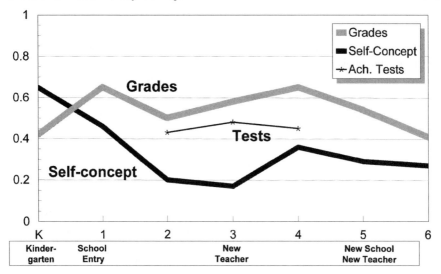

Figure 16. Differentiation: interdomain correlations (math–German) for achievement and self-concepts.

Because in this chapter the focus is on only two domains, mathematics and German, we use simple correlations between math and German self-concept (and the respective achievements). Because high correlations between teachers' grades in various school subjects may, at least to a certain degree, reflect teachers' implicit theories or may be the result of judgment biases (such as the Halo effect), we added the interdomain correlations between the tests in both school subjects. The results are depicted in Figure 16 and demonstrate very different patterns for the differentiation of achievements versus the differentiation of correspondent self-concepts.

From the standpoint of the teacher, children's achievements in both subjects covary strongly with each other as early as in the middle of the first grade. Interestingly, the change of the classroom teacher again makes no difference at all. Only after the segregation into two different school streams after the end of Grade 4 can a trend toward increasing independence of both subjects be observed. In contrast to the achievements, children's self-concepts differentiate rapidly and substantially during the first three years of elementary school. We do not yet have a satisfying explanation as to why there is an increase from Grade 3 to Grade 4. At the end of the investigated period of 6 years, the two domain-specific self-concepts no longer covary ($r = .08$).

Conclusion and Perspectives

The goal of this chapter has been to describe developmental patterns of children's achievement-related self-concepts. Previous research has mostly focused on the level component of self-evaluations, and many studies have revealed a more or less steady, often linear decline from a highly unrealistic optimism concerning one's competencies toward more realistic and adequate self-evaluation. In contrast, the present study has yielded a more complex pattern. With regard to the growth curve of self-evaluation, which is based on social comparison processes within the reference group (kindergarten group or classroom), there were remarkable deviations from a linear decrease, which are difficult to explain with the improvement of underlying cognitive abilities such as the capacity to process social comparison and teacher feedback information correctly. It appears that school socialization factors must be taken into account to understand the nonlinear shape of the self-concept decrease, in particular, first grade teachers' tendencies to protect their children from negative experiences of failure and to avoid social comparisons and, also, the transition to a new classroom teacher between Grades 2 and 3, which is, on average, associated with a destabilization of the within-class achievement and self-concept hierarchy (implying new chances and niches for self-serving evaluations) and is also associated with changed teacher expectations.

Also, the perspective of the average change of the level of children's self-concepts of ability was complemented by the description of other components, in particular, of the development of accuracy (which is conceptually not identical with the degree of the above-average effect because it is based on differences between one's subjective and objective competence) of self-descriptions, of consistency over time (temporal stability), and of differentiation (interdomain covariations). There is a rough overall trend indicating that accuracy of self-concepts and consistency increase over time, whereas the covariation of self-concepts with regard to various academic domains decreases over time. However, neither can all of the changes be described by a linear trend (e.g., increase of stability happens rather discontinuously), nor do they hold for the entire age span from 5 to 11 years (e.g., interdomain correlations decrease during the first 3 years of elementary school but then – difficult to explain – increase again). Furthermore, both individual factors (gender) and institutional characteristics (low- vs. high-achievement school track) make a difference for the course of development. Gender differences reveal the typical double asymmetry as previously found in many other studies (mostly with older children, however). On average, boys show a "too" favorable self-concept in mathematics, judged against the correspondent actual achievement (grades or tests), whereas the contrary is true for girls. In the verbal domain, however, the situation is reversed, but it is less pronounced.

Our data strongly support the notion of domain-specificity. From the beginning of elementary school, correlations between self-concepts in various school subjects are medium to low. Thus, the use of global scores, aggregating self-concepts with regard to different domains, may be legitimate from a psychometric standpoint (increase of reliability); from a theoretical standpoint, it may be misleading and may even mask differential developmental trends.

The structure of this volume and the architecture of the underlying project (the LOGIC study) are also based on separate analyses of separate domains. Thus, the focus of this chapter has primarily been the description of self-concept of ability development. This is a necessary task, but it is of course only the first step. To exhaust the richness of data from very different domains within the LOGIC study, future in-depth analyses of the LOGIC data will go beyond this restriction and combine developmental data from different domains and analyze them simultaneously. This strategy may help to solve (or at least to shed more light on) issues that had to remain unsolved in this chapter. For example, it could be fruitful to investigate whether the development of veridicality (of self-perceptions) is synchronized with the development of general cognitive capacities or with other personality characteristics such as role-taking behavior or other social competencies. Also, one could examine how strongly children's judgments of their relative achievements (as compared with the reference group) in various school domains are associated with general self-worth and aspects of the self-concept other than academic. Finally, advanced analyses of self-concept development data will increasingly take into account context factors, in particular, aspects of classroom context. Previous research on this issue (e.g., Stipek and Daniels 1988) has shown that this may be a very fruitful perspective. On the basis of the organizational and personal interlocking of the LOGIC project and the longitudinal elementary school project SCHOLASTIC (see the chapter by Helmke and Weinert, this volume), it is possible to combine individual developmental data with data of the classroom context of these individuals, such as classroom composition, social climate, instructional quality, and achievement pressure.

References

Blumenfeld, P. C., Pintrich, P. R., Meece, J., & Wessels, K. (1982). The formation and role of self perceptions of ability in elementary classrooms. *Elementary School Journal, 82*, 401–420.

Bridgeman, B., & Shipman, V. C. (1978). Preschool measures of self-esteem and achievement motivation as predictors of third-grade achievement. *Journal of Educational Psychology, 70*, 17–28.

Bryk, A. S., & Raudenbush, S. W. (1992). *Hierarchical linear models*. Newbury Park, CA: Sage.

Byrne, B. M. (1984). The general/academic self-concept nomological network: A review of construct validation research. *Review of Educational Research, 54*, 427–456.

Davis, J. A. (1966). The campus as a frog pond: An application of the theory of relative deprivation to career decisions of college men. *The American Journal of Sociology, 72*, 17–31.

Dweck, C. S., & Elliott, E. S. (1993). Achievement motivation. In P. H. Mussen (Series Ed.) & E. M. Hetherington (Vol. 4 Ed.), *Handbook of child psychology: Vol 4. Socialization, personality, and social development* (4th ed., pp. 643–691). New York: Wiley.

Eccles, J., Adler, T. F., Futterman, R., Goff, S. B., Kaczala, C. M., Meece, J. L., & Midgley, C. (1983). Expectancies, values, and academic behaviors. In J. T. Spence (Ed.), *Achievement and achievement motives* (pp. 76–146). San Francisco: Freeman.

Eccles, J., Wigfield, A., Harold, R. D., & Blumenfeld, P. (1993). Age and gender differences in children's self- and task perceptions during elementary school. *Child Development, 64*, 830–847.

Eccles, J., & Midgley, C. (1989). Stage-environment fit: Developmentally appropriate classrooms for young adolescents. In C. Ames & R. Ames (Eds.), *Research on motivation: Vol. 3. Goals and cognitions* (pp. 139–186). Orlando, FL: Academic Press.

Eshel, Y., & Klein, Z. (1981). Development of academic self-concept of lower-class and middle-class primary school children. *Journal of Educational Psychology, 73*, 287–293.

Festinger, L. (1954). A theory of social comparison processes *Human Relations, 7*, 117–140.

Harter, S. (1983). Developmental perspectives on the self-system. In P. H. Mussen (Ed.), *Handbook of child psychology: Vol. 4. Socialization, personality, and social development* (4th ed., pp. 275–385). New York: Wiley.

Heckhausen, H. (1984). Emergent achievement behavior: Some early developments. In J. G. Nicholls & M. L. Maehr (Eds.), *Advances in motivation and achievement: Vol 3. The development of achievement motivation* (pp. 1–32). Greenwich, CT: Jai Press.

Helmke, A. (1991a). Entwicklung des Fähigkeitsselbstbildes vom Kindergarten bis zur dritten Klasse [Development of academic self-concept from kindergarten through third grade]. In R. Pekrun & H. Fend (Eds.), *Schule and Persönlichkeitsentwicklung* (pp. 83–99). Ein Resumee der Längsschnittforschung. Stuttgart: Enke.

Helmke, A. (1991b). Self-concept of ability and achievement-related motives and attitudes of first graders and attributions in primary school children. In F. E. Weinert & W. Schneider (Eds.), *LOGIC Report No. 7* (pp. 68–94). Munich: Max Planck Institute for Psychological Research.

Helmke, A. (1992a). *Selbstvertrauen und schulische Leistungen* [Self-confidence and scholastic achievement]. Göttingen: Hogrefe.

Helmke, A. (1992b). Self-concept of aptitude, achievement-related motives and attitudes of second graders. In F. E. Weinert & W. Schneider (Eds.), *LOGIC Report No. 8* (pp. 82–105). Munich: Max Planck Institute for Psychological Research.

Helmke, A., & Renkl, A. (1992). Das Münchener Aufmerksamkeitsinventar (MAI): Ein Instrument zur systematischen Verhaltensbeobachtung der Schüleraufmerksam keit im Unterricht [The Munich Attention Inventory: An instrument for the systematic observation of student attention during classroom instruction]. *Diagnostica, 38,* 130–141.

Helmke, A., & Weinert. F. E. (1996). Bedingungsfaktoren schulischer Leistungen [Determinants of scholastic achievement]. In F. E. Weinert (Ed.), *Enzyklopädie der Psychologie. Serie Pädagogische Psychologie, Band 3: Psychologie des Unterrichts und der Schule* (pp. 71–176). Göttingen: Hogrefe.

Hyde, J. S., Fennema, E., & Lamon, S. J. (1990). Gender differences in mathematics performance: A meta-analysis. *Psychological Bulletin, 107,* 139–155.

Kunda, Z. (1990). The case for motivated reasoning. *Psychological Bulletin, 108,* 480–498.

Larned, D. T., & Muller, D. (1979). Development of self-concept in grades one through nine. *Journal of Psychology, 102,* 143–155.

Markus, H., & Wurf, E. (1987). The dynamic self-concept: A social psychological perspective. *Annual Review of Psychology, 38,* 299–337.

Marsh, H. W. (1987). The big-fish-little-pond effect on academic self-concept. *Journal of Educational Psychology, 79,* 280–295.

Marsh, H. W. (1988). The content specificity of math and English anxieties: The high school and beyond study. *Anxiety Research, 1,* 137–149.

Marsh, H. W. (1990). Influences of internal and external frames of reference on the formation of math and English self-concepts. *Journal of Educational Psychology, 82,* 107–116.

Marsh, H. W., Craven, R. G., & Debus, R. (1991). Self-concepts of young children 5 to 8 years of age: Measurement and multidimensional structure. *Journal of Educational Psychology, 83,* 377–392.

Marsh, H. W., & Parker, J. (1984). Determinants of student self-concept: Is it better to be a relatively large fish in a small pond even if you don't learn to swim as well? *Journal of Personality and Social Psychology, 47,* 213–231.

Marshall, H. H., & Weinstein, R. S. (1984). Classroom factors affecting students' self-evaluations: An interactional model. *Review of Educational Research, 54,* 301–325.

Mason, T. C., & Stipek, D. J. (1989). The stability of students' achievement-related thoughts and school performance from one grade to the next. *The Elementary School Journal, 90,* 57–67.

Nicholls, J. G. (1978). The development of the concepts of effort and ability, perception of academic attainment, and the understanding that difficult tasks require more ability. *Child Development, 49,* 800–814.

Nicholls, J. G. (1979). Development of perception of own attainment and causal attributions for success and failure in reading. *Journal of Educational Psychology, 71,* 94–99.

Nicholls, J. G. (1984a). Achievement motivation: Conceptions of ability, subjective experience, task choice, and performance. *Psychological Review, 91,* 328–346.

Nicholls, J. G. (1984b). Conceptions of ability and achievement motivation. In R. Ames & C. Ames (Eds.), *Research on motivation in education* (Vol. 1, pp. 39–79). Orlando, FL: Academic Press.

Parsons, J. E., Adler, T. F., & Kaczala, C. M. (1982). Socialization of achievement attitudes and beliefs: Parental influences. *Child Development, 53*, 310–321.

Rosenholtz, S. J., & Rosenholtz, S. H. (1981). Classroom organization and the perception of ability. *Sociology of Education, 54*, 132–140.

Ruble, D. N. (1980). A developmental perspective on theories of achievement motivation. In L. J. Fyans, Jr. (Ed.), *Achievement motivation* (pp. 225–244). New York: Plenum Press.

Ruble, D. N. (1984). The development of social-comparison processes and their role in achievement-related self-socialization. In J. G. Nicholls & M. L. Maehr (Eds.), *Advances in motivation and achievement: Vol. 3. The development of achievement motivation* (pp. 134–157). Greenwich, CT: Jai Press.

Schneider, W. (1992). Rechtschreibtest [Spelling test]. In Max-Planck-Institut für psychologische Forschung (Ed.), *Tätigkeitsbericht 1990–1991* (pp. 32–33). Munich: Max Planck Institute for Psychological Research.

Shavelson, R. J., Hubner, J. J., & Stanton, G. C. (1976). Self-concept: Validation of construct interpretations. *Review of Educational Research, 46*, 407–441.

Stern, E. (1992). Mathematiktest [Mathematics test]. In Max-Planck-Institut für psychologische Forschung (Ed.), *Tätigkeitsbericht 1990–1991* (pp. 31–32). Munich: Max Planck Institute for Psychological Research.

Stipek, D. J. (1984a). The development of achievement motivation. In R. Ames & C. Ames (Eds.), *Research on motivation in education. Student motivation* (Vol. 1, pp. 145–174). Orlando, FL: Academic Press.

Stipek, D. J. (1984b). Young children's performance expectations: Logical analysis or wishful thinking? In J. G. Nicholls & M. L. Maehr (Eds.), *Advances in motivation and achievement: Vol. 3. The development of achievement motivation* (pp. 33–56). Greenwich, CT: Jai Press.

Stipek, D. J., & Daniels, D. H. (1988). Declining perceptions of competence: A consequence of changes in the child or in the educational environment? *Journal of Educational Psychology, 80*, 352–356.

Stipek, D. J., & Hoffman, J. M. (1980). Development of children's performance-related judgments. *Child Development, 51*, 912–914.

Stipek, D. J., & Mac Iver, D. (1989). Developmental change in children's assessment of intellectual competence. *Child Development, 60*, 521–538.

Stipek, D., Recchia, S., & McClintic, S. (1992). Self-evaluation in young children. *Monographs of the Society for Research in Child Development, 57*(1, Serial No. 226).

Valtin, R. (1996, May). *Noten- oder Verbalzeugnisse? Zu Akzeptanz, Realisierung und Auswirkungen der verbalen Beurteilung in Ost- und Westberliner Grundschulen* [Grades versus verbal reports? Acceptance, realization and effects of verbal reports in West and East Berlin elementary schools]. Bericht zum 2. DFG- Symposium, Berlin: Humboldt-University.

Weiß, R., & Osterland, J. (1979). *Grundintelligenztest CFT 1* [Culture Fair Intelligence Test]. 3. Auflage. Braunschweig: Westermann.

Wigfield, A. (1994). Expectancy-value theory of achievement motivation: A developmental perspective. *Educational Psychology Review, 6*, 49–78.

Wigfield, A., Eccles, J., Harold-Goldsmith, R., Blumenfeld, P., Yoon, K. S., & Freedman-Doan, C. (1989). *Gender and age differences in children's achievement self-perceptions during elementary school.* Paper presented at the biennial meeting of the Society for Research in Child Development, Kansas City Missouri.

Wigfield, A., Harold, R., Eccles, J., Aberbach, A., Freedman-Doan, C., & Yoon, K. S. (1990, April). *Children's ability perceptions and values during the elementary school years.* Paper presented at the annual meeting of the American Educational Research Association, Boston.

10a   Comment: The Logic and Meaning of Declining Perceptions of Academic Competence

Deborah Stipek

Apparently children in Germany have much in common with children in the United States; they begin school with very high perceptions of their relative academic competencies, but within a year or two of school, self-evaluations begin a downward trajectory. Children in the LOGIC study had little time to enjoy their superinflated view of their competencies; the downward slide started soon after they arrived at the school door. And harbingers who would later be sorted into high school and who would continue elementary school – a placement that has long-term consequences for these students' lives – were manifest in achievement and self-concept within the first year or two of school.

Additional evidence for the importance of the first few years in school is seen in the early emergence of consistency in self-evaluations from year to year. The kindergarten-to-first-grade correlations, although modest (.30 for German and .29 for mathematics, Helmke's Table 4), are surprising, given the low correlations between self-evaluations and external indices of competencies. One wonders what these young children's somewhat stable judgments of their competencies were based on, given that their self-perceptions were not associated with the objective measures of competence used in the study.

Helmke suggests that a decline in teachers' protectiveness after first grade may explain the dip he found in children's perceptions of academic competence between the beginning of first and second grade. Although changes in teachers' treatment of children surely contribute to the decline, these changes most likely interact with changes in children. Classroom practices in second grade would have to be very different to jolt children to such a degree from their inflated views of their academic competencies. Children's increased attention to and skills in processing evaluative feedback – especially social comparison feedback – that Helmke mentions are no doubt also implicated. Making judgments about one's relative standing requires children to attend to and judge their own performance in the context of their classmates' performances – a skill that many studies suggest is not well in place until the second grade (Stipek and Mac Iver 1989). The use of the LOGIC data to examine links between changes in cognitive skills that might be required to process evaluative feed-

222

back and changes in self-evaluations during this apparently critical period might tell us something about the specific cognitive skills that underlie children's abilities to process performance feedback more realistically. My suspicion is that the increased interest in social comparison may come, in part, as a result of these increased competencies.

The pattern of the year-to-year correlations suggests that children's perceptions of their competencies become considerably less malleable at the second or third grade. The correlations jump for mathematics at second grade (to .51) and for German at third grade (to .49). The degree to which early self-evaluations predict self-evaluations at the end of the study (sixth grade) also increases substantially from second to third grade for math (from .16 to .37) and from third to fourth grade for German (.26 to .38). This "hardening" of self-perceptions of achievement, although appearing early in children's elementary careers, is delayed, in the sense that actual achievement becomes very consistent from year to year earlier – by the first grade (Helmke's Figure 13).

Teachers in the United States often complain that in third grade children begin to get discouraged about their abilities to do school work, and many show significantly less enthusiasm for learning – they suffer from what teachers often refer to as the *third-grade slump*. Helmke's data suggest that German children might begin to experience the third-grade slump by the end of the first or the beginning of the second grade. Further investigation of the developmental shifts in self-evaluation would be both theoretically and practically useful. Combining observations of classrooms with assessments of children's judgments would help researchers understand how changes in educational practice associated with children's age – in the curriculum demands, instructional approaches, ability grouping, and evaluation practices – affect changes in children's self-evaluations and thus their motivation to engage in school work.

One factor that Helmke's results suggest that is not important is the introduction of grades (marks). There is some controversy in the United States about the age at which grades should be introduced, with many educators and policymakers arguing that grades dampen young children's self-confidence and enthusiasm for learning. Ironically, the most common reaction to such concerns is to eliminate academic grades during the first year or two of school – when children appear to pay the least attention to their performance compared with others. For the children in the LOGIC study, grades were not introduced until the middle of second grade – after the biggest decline in self-evaluations. The data indicate that the introduction of grades did not have a profound effect on children's self-evaluations; at most, they assisted children on a course that they had already begun.

The gender differences in math reveal another similarity between U.S. and German children. Although not surprising, the low self-evaluations found among girls are distressing (especially for this mother of a 10-year-old girl whose self-confidence and interest in math correspond perfectly with Helmke's findings). What is truly extraordinary about these data is that gender differences in achievement decline, yet girls' evaluations of their competencies become increasingly negative compared with boys. Clearly, the gender differences are based on factors (e.g., teachers' and parents' behaviors and expectations) other than their actual performance in school.

That gender differences are less prominent in German indicates that there is something special going on with mathematics.

This and other subject-matter differences found between math and German suggest that there may be systematic differences in the nature of instruction and evaluation at the classroom level that might be systematically associated with the two subjects and with students' self-evaluations of their competencies. Children's self-perceptions stabilized in mathematics a year earlier than in German, but differences between the elementary school– and high school–bound samples were observed in German a year earlier than in math. Examining differences in instruction and evaluation in mathematics and German might help explain these subject-matter differences. Such an investigation might also provide useful information about what students attend to in the classroom and how they interpret information related to their competencies.

Rejoice or Despair?

Developmental psychologists typically lament the decline in perceptions of academic competence that this and other studies report. (Note, for example, Nicholls and Millers's title of their 1984 chapter, "Development and its Discontents"). The distress is based on considerable evidence that relatively low perceptions of competence are associated with maladaptive behavior in learning environments – avoiding difficult tasks, exerting low effort, giving up easily, and disliking academic work (Stipek, in press).

This reaction to the developmental data is nevertheless ironic, given that a decline is inevitable in the context of Western cultural definitions of competence. Although children's (and adults') apparent inclination is to put the best possible spin on their performance – most claiming to be above average (at least in the Western cultures) – as long as competence is defined in terms of relative performance, children's increased capacity to process performance information will result in declining self-ratings. By definition, only half of the class can be above average, and only a few can be the best. Children will inevitably find out where they stand relative to classmates, especially in educational contexts that provide consistent and prominent information on relative standing. Also, inasmuch as competence is defined as a relatively stable trait that is only modestly improved through practice and effort (what Dweck [1986] refers to as an *entity theory of ability*), low perceptions of competence will lead to low effort (why exert effort to change something that cannot be changed?). In brief, in cultures in which students evaluate themselves comparatively, there will always be winners and losers, and students will ultimately find out in which category they fall.

Perhaps we should not feel badly that children become increasingly realistic about how they stand. After all, is there not some practical value in knowing in which domains one excels and in which domains one is doing relatively poorly? Surely this information should help students make appropriate choices for study and lifelong pursuits.

There is some truth to this position, but many in the United States, and I suspect in Germany as well, are not prepared to celebrate children's increased awareness of their relative standing – and for good reasons. Relative standing does not tell a person anything about what he or she knows or does not know or what he or she can do with knowledge. A relatively poorly performing student in a mathematics program for gifted children may develop the perception that he or she is incompetent in math and thus eliminate math as a career option, even though the student could achieve the level of competency required for a profession requiring high-level mathematics. A student's realistic judgment that he or she is doing better compared with classmates in one domain but not in another may be equally irrelevant to any decisions the student might make about where to put his or her effort. Judgments about how much time and effort should be given to work in the respective domains must be made in the context of particular goals – such as to develop a special talent or to create an overall balanced record of performance. Only in rare cases, such as when success is defined by relative standards (e.g., making decisions about whether to enter a contest or whether to apply to medical school) is knowledge of relative competence useful.

We are left with a conundrum – Germany and the United States have a culture and an educational system that tend to focus individuals' attention on their relative performance. Eventually, children learn approximately where they stand. The increased realism, however, rarely serves any useful purpose and is often discouraging to students who come to regard themselves as incompetent. Is there a way out of this conundrum?

A Resolution

I see hope in many of the current reform movements in the United States (I am not familiar with what is going on in Germany.) In all subject areas, reform-minded researchers and educators are promoting more self- or criterion-referenced approaches to evaluation. In virtually every report and document written recently on mathematics teaching (i.e., National Council for the Teaching of Mathematics Standards, California framework), for example, teachers are urged to focus students' attention on improving their own understanding (regardless of what other students understand) and to help students work collaboratively, in ways that require every student to contribute. Teachers are encouraged to provide all students with challenge, so even those who learn quickly experience confusion and occasional "failure." I am not so naive to think that children in reform-minded classrooms will cease comparing their performance to classmates. However, evidence indicating that instructional approaches and evaluation strategies do affect students' self-perceptions (Stipek, 1996) suggests that changing educational and evaluation practices may have some positive consequences for motivation.

Another strategy is to change the meaning of relative performance so that it is not perceived as an up-or-down vote on one's value as a person. In a study I did years ago, I learned that perceptions of relative competence can have many different implications for children. In the traditional schools we studied, children easily placed themselves on the scale we used (much like the scale used by Helmke) when asked how smart they were. At UCLA's laboratory elementary school, many children responded, "that depends" and proceeded to give us a very differentiated analysis of how they stood: "For math I'm the best in class in computation speed, but about the middle on word problems; I'm close to the top in reading, but my handwriting is the worst."

The responses of the laboratory school children surprised us. The school does not give grades and has a strong ideology against social comparison (to the point that teachers occasionally refuse researchers' requests to make relative ratings of students). We expected, therefore, that students in this school would have difficulty rating their academic abilities. Contrary to our expectations, these students were unusually aware of their relative performance.

The judgments of the children in the laboratory school, however, appeared to have different meaning for them than did the judgments of students in more traditional, competitive classrooms. First, the laboratory school children described their relative competencies dispassionately, appearing to be giving information that had no bearing on their value as human beings. Although I do not have systematic data, my suspicion is that children's self-worth was less affected by relative performance in the laboratory school because teachers were unusually supportive and nurturing and did not differentiate their treatment of children as a function of their academic performance.

Another aspect of the laboratory school students' responses to our questions about their competencies is noteworthy. The children who volunteered detailed information about their competencies tended to have highly variable standing in different do mains – they believed they were very good relative to their classmates in some and not so good in others. This suggests another strategy to alleviate the negative effects of the decline in perceptions of relative competence: provide children with a broad array of valued domains in which to perform. This increases the number of students who will have some domain in which they excel and thus experience pride in school-related work.

The developmental downward trajectory in self-evaluations found by Helmke and many other researchers is inevitable as long as information about relative performance is available. Our observations at the UCLA laboratory school suggest that, at least in U.S. culture, children will make relative judgments even when information about relative performance is obscured. However, the meaning and impact of those judgments – their relevance to self-worth, immediate effort, and future plans – can be influenced by teachers' interactions with children (whether they are respectful and supportive of all children, regardless of their academic performance), the number of ways children are given an opportunity to excel, and other instructional and evaluation approaches. We cannot reverse the decline in children's perceptions of relative competence; we can affect its meaning and, thus, children's comfort and effort in educational settings.

References

Dweck, C. (1986). Motivational processes affecting learning, *American Psychologist, 41*, 1040–1048.

Nicholls, J., & Miller, A. (1984). Development and its discontents: The differentiation of the concept of ability. In J. Nicholls (Ed.), *Advances in motivation and achievement: Vol 3. The development of achievement motivation* (pp. 185–218). Greenwich, CT: JAI Press.

Stipek, D. (1996). Motivation and instruction. In D. Berliner & R. Calfee (Eds.), *Handbook of educational psychology* (pp. 85–113). New York: Macmillan.

Stipek, D., & Mac Iver, D. (1989). Developmental change in children's assessment of intellectual competence. *Child Development, 60*, 527–538.

11   Social–Personality Development

Jens B. Asendorpf

The focus of the LOGIC study in the social domain was on the longitudinal analysis of three personality constructs: shyness, social competence with peers, and aggressiveness. These constructs were investigated with multiple assessment techniques (global ratings, Q-sorts, observer ratings, self-ratings, and projective tests) across multiple settings (the preschool peer group, dyadic and triadic observation settings in the Institute, and situations watched over by parents) and, of course, over the many years of the study's duration.

The major findings for the social domain are as follows:

- Socially withdrawn children represent a heterogeneous group, within which at least three subgroups can be distinguished: unsociable, shy, and avoidant children (Asendorpf 1990a, 1993b).
- Individual differences in shyness are setting specific; both fear of strangers and social–evaluative fear contribute to shy-inhibited behavior (Asendorpf 1990b).
- High shyness with unfamiliar peers changes its behavioral appearance between 4 and 8 years of age: Younger children engage in long phases of ambivalent behavior toward the stranger, whereas older children quickly withdraw into quiet, solitary play (Asendorpf 1991).
- The longitudinal stability of children's shyness between 4 and 7 years of age is related to the stability of their extrafamilial environment: Lower environment stability is related to lower stability of shyness (Asendorpf 1992a).
- A comparison between the LOGIC children's shyness at 4 and 6 years of age and university students' shyness showed a high continuity in the behavioral expression of shyness in confrontations with strangers: Shy participants can be distinguished from participants low in shyness by a behavior pattern that is highly similar across age (Asendorpf 1992b).
- An analysis of individual developmental functions in shyness over a 6-year period from age 4 through 10 showed that high IQ and high social competence in preschool (assessed by teacher judgments) predicted a stronger decrease of shyness over the years than low IQ or social competence, both for shyness with strangers and shyness in the preschool group; it seems that more intelligent or socially competent children can learn to overcome their shyness better than less intelligent and competent children (Asendorpf 1994).
- A projective aggressiveness test similar to Lesser's (1958) showed that high scores in this test were related either to a high overt aggressiveness as judged by teachers

or to a high sensitivity to aggression as measured by a recognition test for peripheral aggression-relevant stimuli; projective tests may confound two different traits that are only loosely related: tendency toward a particular behavior and sensitivity to that behavior in others (Asendorpf, Weber, and Burkhardt 1994).

Because these findings are published or are in press, I do not wish to reiterate them in this chapter. Instead, I focus on what I consider to be the most important theoretical payoff of the LOGIC study in the social domain: The twin hypothesis that (a) individual differences in social–interactional behavior in a social setting are influenced by the emerging quality of the relationships within the setting and therefore become inconsistent with behavior in other settings and show a relatively low temporal stability during the phase of relationship formation and that (b) important social–emotional developmental outcomes such as self-esteem can be influenced more and thus be better predicted by relationship-specific individual attributes than by relationship-unspecific traits.

This hypothesis and its major empirical database are published in Asendorpf and van Aken (1994). In the present chapter, I elaborate the hypothesis in more detail within the framework of a dynamic social relations model and briefly describe a new longitudinal project aimed at testing parts of the hypothesis with a methodology that differs greatly from the methodology of the LOGIC study. The central goal of this chapter is to illustrate how a large, multifocus longitudinal study such as LOGIC that was initially not designed to test specific hypotheses on development can produce novel, testable hypotheses that stimulate further empirical research, thus testifying to its power as an important heuristic tool of developmental psychology.

The Initial Finding: Two Factors in Shyness

The assessments made in the social domain of the LOGIC study were not designed to test specific hypotheses on personality development. Instead, the underlying objective was to generate a broad database for particular constructs in order to maximize flexibility of data analysis and thereby to increase the likelihood of discovering unexpected patterns of development. This strategy proved to be most successful for the construct of shyness.

Shyness was assessed repeatedly both in naturalistic laboratory situations where we confronted the children with adult and peer strangers and in the children's preschool peer group during the regular free-play period in the morning – a setting that is ideally suited for an assessment of individual differences in social–interactional behavior because the children's activity is not constrained by tasks set up by the teachers. We observed the children's behavior directly or through videotaping and also asked knowledgeable informants to provide global judgments of the children's shyness in these two kinds of settings – parents judged shyness with strangers, and teachers judged shyness in the peer group.

I began the study with a notion of shyness that closely resembles the lay usage of this term. People call others shy when they infer from their behavior that they would like to approach others but do not dare to do so. Thus, shy behavior results from an approach–avoidance conflict: an approach motive and an avoidance motive are activated at the same time (Asendorpf 1989, 1990a). The construct of (behavioral) inhibition (Kagan 1989) also refers to such an approach–avoidance motive: an approach tendency is inhibited by some kind of fear.

This conflict view of shyness has three advantages. First, shyness is treated separately from disinterest in others (low approach motive and low avoidance motive); second, the very notion of shyness urges one to ask why shy people avoid others; and third, the avoidance motive is broad enough to include different kinds of social fears.

My research with university students had shown that shyness in adults can arise from two different kinds of fear: fear of strangers and fear of a negative or not sufficiently positive social evaluation by others. I identified these two kinds of fear in questionnaire surveys on the kinds of situations that make students shy as well as in a naturalistic laboratory study where both kinds of fear were experimentally induced independently of each other (Asendorpf 1989).

When I approached the analysis of the LOGIC data with this notion of shyness in mind, it was immediately clear to me that shyness with adult and peer strangers had to be carefully distinguished from shyness in the familiar preschool peer group and, more important, that shyness in the preschool peer group in the early stages of group socialization might be due to different fears than shyness in the later stages of group socialization. Early on in the process, the reactions of peers are largely unpredictable and are thus similar to those of strangers. Later on in the process, however, most children will have built up clear expectations of how particular peers will respond to them. If children exhibit shyness in these later stages of group socialization, they are likely to do so because of a fear of insufficiently positive or negative evaluation by peers.

This change in the nature of the fears underlying shy behavior should have consequences for individual differences in shy behavior: When the reasons for shy behavior change, the rank order of shyness within a group can be expected to change as well. This change, in turn, will produce low temporal stability for individual differences in shyness and a decreasing consistency of shyness in the laboratory-based stranger confrontations and in the preschool-based peer group observations. The correlational pattern of shyness for the first 3 years of the LOGIC study nicely confirmed this expectation (see Figure 1).

Shyness in the laboratory-based stranger confrontations showed a high temporal stability of $r = .75$ between the first assessment at 4 years of age and the third assessment at age 6. That the 1-year stabilities for shyness with strangers between ages 4 and 5, and between ages 5 and 6, were somewhat lower than the 2-year stability between ages 4 and 6 is an unusual pattern that is explained later in this chapter.

As I had expected from the two-factorial view of shyness, individual differences in shyness in the preschool class were less stable (a 2-year stability of $r = .44$, which was significantly lower than the $r = .75$ stability of shyness with strangers). This difference in stability was not due to a different reliability of the shyness assessments

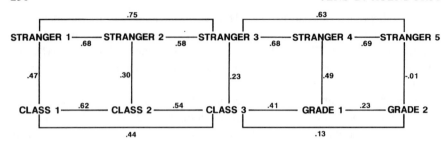

Figure 1. Consistency between shyness with strangers and shyness in the school class in the first 5 years of the LOGIC study (adapted from Asendorpf 1993a, Figure 13.6).

because the difference in stability was also found when the data were corrected for attenuation (see Asendorpf 1990b for details).

More important, the concurrent correlations between shyness with strangers and shyness in class showed a significant decrease from $r = .47$ at the beginning of group socialization to $r = .23$ (not significant) after 2 years of group socialization. Again, this pattern persisted after correcting for attenuation.

This correlational pattern was fully consistent with my two-factorial view of shyness. In the beginning of preschool socialization (assessments were made approximately 3 months after the children had entered preschool), many peers in the group were still unfamiliar to the children; therefore, shyness in the group was moderately consistent with shyness with strangers. Later, the consistency between the two kinds of shyness nearly disappeared because fear of unfamiliarity was no longer a cause of shyness; instead, other sources of fear that were based on children's differential experiences in the groups developed. The extent to which children were affected by these fears was fairly independent of their fear of strangers.

By itself, the consistency of the correlational pattern with the two-factor model of shyness alone is only a weak confirmation of this model. More direct evidence that could identify individual differences in social–evaluative fear as a cause of the correlational pattern was needed.

Fortunately, we had not only observed children's behavior during free play but had also observed their partners' responses to their contact initiation attempts. If the critical factor was indeed social–evaluative fear based on experiences of insufficient positive or negative responses by the peers, a positive correlation between peer neglect or rejection and shy behavior in the group should emerge during group socialization, particularly when shyness with strangers was partialled out.

Such a correlation between observed peer nonacceptance of contact initiation attempts and children's shyness in the group did indeed emerge (see Table 1). In the first observational period approximately 3 months after children had entered preschool, this correlation was not significant, but in the second and third year in the class it was significant, positive, and significantly higher than in the first observational period (see Asendorpf 1990b for details). Thus, shyness in the familiar classroom was linked to peer nonacceptance.

Table 1. *Relation Between Observed Peer Nonacceptance and Shyness With Peers Over 3 Years in Preschool*

Peer nonacceptance	Peer shyness		
	First year	Second year	Third year
First year	−.13	−.19	−.10
Second year	−.08	.36*	.28*
Third year	−.13	−.05	.29*

*p < .05.

Moreover, peer nonacceptance predicted shy behavior in the same and the following year of observation, whereas the reverse pattern was not found (i.e., shy behavior was not correlated with peer nonacceptance in the following year). This asymmetric correlational pattern supported a causal path running from peer nonacceptance via social–evaluative fears to shy behavior rather than vice versa (although such correlational analyses cannot prove the direction of causality, of course).

The pattern of an initial moderate consistency between shyness in the classroom and shyness with strangers that decreased over time with increasing group socialization had been expected not only for the adaptation to the preschool peer group but also for the adaptation to the (different) elementary school peer group. It was not possible to observe children directly in their classrooms in elementary school, but we were able to obtain teacher judgments of shyness with peers in Grades 1 and 2 for most of the children who made the transition to elementary school at the beginning of the fourth wave of the LOGIC study (see Asendorpf 1993a for details).

Figure 1 shows that the concurrent correlation between shyness with strangers and shyness with classmates increased to $r = .49$ in Grade 1 and then sharply decreased to zero in Grade 2. Thus, shyness in the new elementary school group was again linked to shyness with strangers (the correlation between shyness in the first year in preschool and shyness in Grade 1 was $r = .50$) but then lost the association with shyness toward strangers.

We could not test if shyness in the more familiar class in Grade 2 was again associated with peer nonacceptance because we were not able to observe peer nonacceptance in school or to perform sociometric testing in the classrooms. Thus, the elementary school data were much weaker than the preschool data. However, those data that were available confirmed the two-factorial view of shyness.

A More General Hypothesis and Heuristic Principle

Thus far, the findings on shyness have been interpreted within a theoretical framework that is specific to shyness: Shy behavior can be due to two very different kinds of fear (fear of strangers and social – evaluative fear), individual differences in shy behavior are the result of a particular admixture of these two kinds of fear in a particular social setting, and when the importance of one type of fear changes over time or across different settings, the individual differences are also unstable over time or inconsistent across situations.

We can move beyond this specific interpretation of the findings by asking about the extent to which individual differences in shyness with strangers and shyness due to social–evaluative concerns are instances of two more general classes of individual differences that, if investigated in longitudinal studies, would show a pattern of correlations similar to the one depicted in Figure 1. What might be the most general definition of such classes of individual differences? Asking such a question is a typical example of inductive reasoning in science.

My answer is this: Shyness with strangers is a special instance of a relationship-unspecific trait, and shyness due to social–evaluative concerns is a special instance of a relationship-specific individual attribute. This idea has been described and elaborated somewhat in Asendorpf and van Aken (1994). According to this view, individual differences can be ordered on a continuum of "relationship specificity" (see Stevenson-Hinde [1986] for a similar approach).

One extreme of this continuum is represented by traditional trait approaches to personality development. Traits are constructs that are used to describe individual differences in behavior that show substantial temporal stability and at least moderate transsituational consistency (see Mischel and Peake 1982). Trait approaches typically assume that traits are relationship unspecific (e.g., a shy child is shy with all sorts of people). Traditional trait taxonomies such as the Big-five model (Digman 1990) refer to relationship-unspecific traits (although this and other classifications could also be applied to relationship-specific attributes).

At the other extreme of the continuum of relationship specificity are individual attributes that are entirely relationship specific (i.e., that show no consistency across different interaction partners). Although complete relationship specificity may be difficult to find in human behavior, substantial relationship specificity has been demonstrated repeatedly in developmental research (e.g., infants' attachment to their mother versus father; see Fox, Kimmerly, and Schafer 1991).

The relationship specificity of individual differences can be described somewhat more precisely – and formally – within the framework of the social relations model by Kenny and La Voie (1984). According to this model, measures of an actor's behavior in dyadic interaction with an interaction partner can be decomposed into three main components: an actor parameter that measures the actor's disposition to show this behavior in the presence of any interaction partner, a partner parameter that measures the partner's disposition to evoke this behavior in any interaction partner, and a relationship parameter that measures the actor's disposition to deviate in the presence of the specific interaction partner from the behavior that one would expect from the actor-plus-partner parameter:

$$\text{behavior} = \text{actor} + \text{partner} + \text{relationship}.$$

This model is a special instance of the interactional approach to personality (Endler and Magnusson 1976): the actor parameter represents the Person effect, the partner parameter represents the Situation effect, and the relationship parameter represents the Person × Situation interaction.

If we add the time factor to the model, a simple and intuitively appealing solution is to assume that the actor and partner parameters represent stable dispositions, whereas the relationship parameter reflects the dynamic nature of social relationships: They can change more rapidly than broad individual dispositions, particularly in the formation phase of the relationship. Thus, in this particular dynamic social relations model, the actor and the partner parameters are constants, whereas the relationship parameter is a time-dependent variable. Formally,

$$\text{behavior } (t) = \text{actor} + \text{partner} + \text{relationship } (t).$$

When we apply this model to the LOGIC results for shyness (see Figure 1), we can describe the findings as follows: Because children do not have a social relationship with a stranger, their shy behavior in confrontations with strangers is described by the model

$$\text{behavior} = \text{actor} + \text{partner},$$

where "actor" is the disposition of children to react with shyness toward strangers in general (often considered to be a temperamental trait; see Kagan 1989), and "partner" is the disposition of the stranger to evoke shyness in children (a much less studied individual attribute).

This approach is an idealization of reality to some extent because one's reaction to strangers may be influenced by prior experiences with people who look like or behave similarly to the stranger. However, it seems clear that such "relationship" effects will be much smaller than those developing later on during the acquaintance process.

Because all children met the same stranger in the laboratory confrontations at age 4, and all children met the same stranger at age 6 (a different person than at age 4, of course), "partner" is a constant across children at both ages that does not affect the stability of individual differences in shyness between ages 4 and 6; therefore, this stability was high ($r = .75$).

The stability between ages 4 and 5, and between ages 5 and 6, was lower because different children played with different unfamiliar peers at age 5 so that the individual differences at this age reflected not only actor variance but also partner variance.

In the first months of preschool, when only few relationships had developed among the classmates, children's shyness with a particular peer in the group can be described fairly well by the above simple model without relationship parameters. To the extent that the average partner parameter is similar across different groups – which is to be expected in preschool classes where children are exposed to approximately 20 different peers – this partner parameter can be ignored for analyses of children's average shyness across partners in the group. Thus, the correlation between shyness with strangers and shyness in class depends mainly on the similarity of the actor parameters across these two different settings. Taking into account error of measurement, method variance, slightly different mean partner parameters across children, and variance due to a few early peer relationships in the classes, the consistency of $r = .49$ between shyness with strangers and shyness in class at age 4 suggests a high similarity of the actor parameters across the two settings. Thus, shyness in a peer group at the beginning of group socialization mainly reflects shyness due to the unfamiliarity of the peers.

In the second and third years of group socialization, relationship parameters must be included in the analysis because at this point many (but not necessarily all) children will have developed different kinds of relationships to different peers in the group. These relationship parameters reflect partner-specific social experiences of the children.

When the relationship parameters are averaged across the partners in the group, the average relationship parameter represents group-specific social experiences of the children (it is important to note that actor and partner parameters are treated here as general individual attributes of children that are not group specific because otherwise the relationship parameters would disappear after averaging across partners in the group). Ignoring again differences in the average partner effects across groups, and averaging children's behavior across all partners in the group, children's mean shy behavior in the familiar group can be described by the model

mean behavior = actor + mean relationship.

It is the "mean relationship" component that Asendorpf and van Aken (1994) refer to when they talk about "relationship-specific individual attributes." Please notice that "relationship specific" refers here to an "average relationship" within a particular social setting, not to one relationship at the dyadic level. When time is again added to this model, the resulting equation is

mean behavior (t) = actor + mean relationship (t).

My understanding of the correlational pattern presented in Figure 1 is that it is the emergence of this mean relationship component in shy behavior that causes the relatively low temporal stability in individual differences in shyness in class and their decreasing consistency with shyness with strangers. Different children will be differentially accepted by their classmates, not only at the level of dyadic relationships but also at the level of the average relationship in the classroom.

It is important not to confuse the mean relationship component with the mean partner component. As I use the social relations model here, the partner component is an attribute of interaction partners that is unaffected by the particular relationship between actor and partner; thus, the "mean partner" component is unaffected by children's experiences in the group. Actor and partner parameters are treated here as classic traits that may change over development, but at a much slower pace than the relationship parameters.

Having interpreted the findings for shyness within a dynamic social relations model, we can easily generalize these results: Any social behavior that is characterized by a strong relationship component is likely to produce a correlational pattern similar to that in Figure 1; that is, low temporal stability in individual differences during relationship formation phases and other phases of rapid relationship change and decreasing consistency with the same behavior in novel settings where the relationship component can be ignored. Reversing the argument, we arrive at an interesting heuristic principle: If a social behavior shows a longitudinal correlational pattern similar to that in Figure 1, it may be due to the emergence of a strong relationship component.

A Second Application

When I arrived at this more general hypothesis and heuristic principle, I looked for a different behavioral domain of the LOGIC study to which it could be applied. Aggressive behavior came to mind as a possible candidate because a strong relationship component was to be expected (as represented, for example, by specific bully–victim pairs; see Olweus 1993). We assessed aggression in the preschool group as intensively as shyness, but unfortunately our laboratory play sessions were too short to find reliable individual differences in aggressive behavior toward unfamiliar peers.

Another type of behavior looked more promising: social intelligence, or social competence. Rubin and Rose-Krasnor (1992) defined social competence as the ability to achieve personal goals in social interaction while maintaining positive relationships with interaction partners. Goal achievement in social interaction depends not only on relationship-unspecific traits such as intelligence or general social skills but also on the relationships between the actor and the partners. For example, the interaction among friends in preschool is characterized by a higher rate of successful social initiatives (Howes 1987) and a higher rate of positive conflict outcomes such as compromises or positive postconflict interaction (Hartup, Laursen, Stewart, and Eastenson 1988) than the interaction among nonfriends. Therefore, we expected that social goal achievement would be moderately consistent with test intelligence at the beginning of preschool socialization but would then become less and less consistent with intelligence because of an emerging "Mean Relationship" component.

This hypothesis was nicely confirmed by the LOGIC data (see Figure 2). Social goal achievement in the peer group was operationalized both as observed success in children's contact initiation attempts and by a teacher Q-sort index of social competence that was moderately correlated both at the beginning and at the end of preschool. The aggregate of the two variables served as a measure of peer group competence. As Figure 2 indicates, peer group competence showed a moderately positive correlation with test intelligence at age 4 ($r = .51$) that decreased later, resulting in an insignificant $r = .20$ at age 6. Furthermore, test intelligence showed a much higher stability between ages 4 and 6 ($r = .61$) than peer group competence ($r = .31$). Thus,

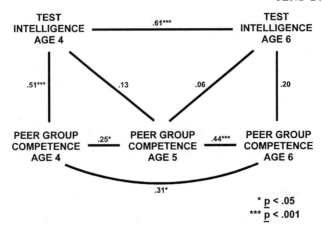

Figure 2. Consistency between test intelligence and social competence with peers in the preschool class in the first 3 years of the LOGIC study (adapted from Asendorpf and van Aken 1994, Figure 1).

the correlational pattern was very similar to the one for shyness (see Asendorpf and van Aken [1994] for more details).

Thus, we found a similar longitudinal correlation pattern for two very different kinds of individual differences (test intelligence and shyness with strangers were uncorrelated), and the similarity between the correlational patterns may be due to a similar process: relationship formation in the peer group.

A New Project

By exploratory data analysis, formalization and inductive reasoning, we had arrived at a general hypothesis about social–personality development and had found additional evidence for the hypothesis in another behavioral domain. I hasten to add that the evidence was not strong in either case because we had to rely on data that were aggregated across partners (in our behavioral observations in the preschool classroom, we did not code the name of the partner when the participant under observation reacted shyly or tried to initiate contact, and the observational data were not sufficiently aggregated for analyses of particular relationships between children; we asked the teachers to judge children, not dyadic relationships). What is required are data at the dyadic level to support the hypothesis that the emergence of relationships causes instability and inconsistency in individual differences.

Such data will be generated in a new longitudinal study at the Max Planck Institute that began in the fall of 1994. All newcomers in 14 preschool classes are directly observed during free play in the classroom over 2 years. Observers code social-interaction data at the dyadic level on a palmtop, focusing on one child for each 10-min period. Each child is observed for approximately 12 such periods within a block of 16 weeks; 2 such blocks are scheduled for 1 year.

A pilot study using videotaped behavior of a group of 10 children who knew each other for more than 1 year showed that relationship effects in interactional behavior, estimated by using the Kenny and La Voie (1984) approach, were highly stable; for example, the stability of the relationship effects for "interacts with" was $r = .84$ between two blocks of three free-play sessions. Thus, we can expect that our observational approach will generate sufficiently stable relationship effects at the dyadic level for each 12-week block when the children become familiar with their classmates.

Thus, there is a good chance that we will be able to study the emergence of relationship effects for each individual child across the 2×2 blocks of data. This first naturalistic observational study of the long-term development of dyadic peer relationships in preschool will make it possible to study the emergence of the relationship component in behavior in great detail and to test the hypothesis derived from the LOGIC study that shyness and social competence show an increasing relationship component with increasing group socialization.

At the beginning of this 2-year study, the children were also observed in a laboratory visit where they were tested for shyness with strangers, attachment to their accompanying parent, and intelligence. Together with the preschool observations, these data will enable us to study the divergence of shyness and social competence in the natural peer group from the relationship-unspecific traits assessed in the laboratory in much greater detail than in the LOGIC study.

Importance of Relationship Effects

From a more general, interactional perspective, the relationship component in social behavior is a special instance of a Person × Situation interaction. Such interaction components are sometimes regarded simply as part of the error in personality prediction based upon individual traits or as unavoidable but undesirable systematic variance that makes researchers' and diagnosticians' lives difficult. Such a statistician's view contrasts sharply with the emphasis that many developmental and personality psychologists place upon social relationships as the primary conditions for personality development.

In this view, relationships shape personality. Individual traits are considered as being outcomes of significant relationships rather than being antecedents of behavior in such relationships. For example, in attachment research, children's later social competence with peers has been related to the quality of their prior relationship with the mother (Sroufe and Fleeson 1986).

If this view is valid, the assumption that actor and partner components of social behavior are independent of the relationship component must be abandoned. Instead, it must be assumed that actor and partner parameters can (slowly) change over development because of dispositions that are first acquired in particular relationships and that are later generalized to a broader class of interaction partners.

For example, when children are strongly rejected by a parent or by a few classmates, they may acquire a generalized expectation that other adults or other peers do not accept them; in extreme cases, such expectations may even generalize from a parent to peers.

The view that the relationship component in social behavior may be an important predictor of central social–emotional developmental outcomes is supported by the finding that early peer rejection, assessed through sociometric tests, is related to later externalizing problems (Parker and Asher 1987) and that children's passive social withdrawal in kindergarten predicts later internalizing problems, including low social self-esteem, loneliness, and depressive tendencies up to age 11 (Rubin 1993; Rubin, Hymel, and Mills 1989). Rubin, LeMare, and Lollis (1990) have presented a model of possible developmental pathways to internalizing problems in late childhood and early adolescence in which experiences of peer neglect and rejection in middle childhood a major causal role.

Although it is plausible that these long-term predictive relations rest upon mean relationship components in earlier behavior, the possibility that these relations simply reflect actor components – stable relationship–unspecific traits of the children that lead to both earlier peer rejection and later poor developmental outcomes – cannot be excluded. For example, the relation between earlier sociometric peer rejection and later externalizing problems may be due simply to individual differences in aggressiveness that are both stable over time and consistent across different interaction partners.

To exclude this alternative as much as possible in our analysis of the long-term effects of high shyness and low peer competence in preschool, we contrasted two kinds of predictors for children's later self-esteem: their shyness and peer competence in the familiar peer group after more than a year of preschool socialization and then shyness with strangers and test intelligence assessed in the laboratory. Thus, we used the laboratory assessments as control conditions for the actor component in the preschool assessments.

The results of an extreme group analysis contrasting children with high or low scores with a control group of children with average scores supported the view that the mean relationship component is of particular importance for later personality development. High shyness with strangers or low test intelligence in preschool was unrelated to children's later social self-esteem in elementary school, whereas both high shyness and low peer competence in the familiar class (at ages 5–6) showed significant negative associations with later social self-esteem (see Figure 3) but were not significantly related to later cognitive self-esteem (domain-specific self-esteem was assessed in Grades 2, 3, and 4 by German adaptations of Harter's self-concept scales; Asendorpf and van Aken 1993).

Thus, it was the early mean relationship component in shy or competent behavior that was predictive of later domain-specific self-esteem, not the early actor component. It may well be, however, that a social relations analysis concurrent with the self-esteem assessments would have shown a significant concurrent correlation between the actor component and self-esteem. In this case, the early mean relationship component

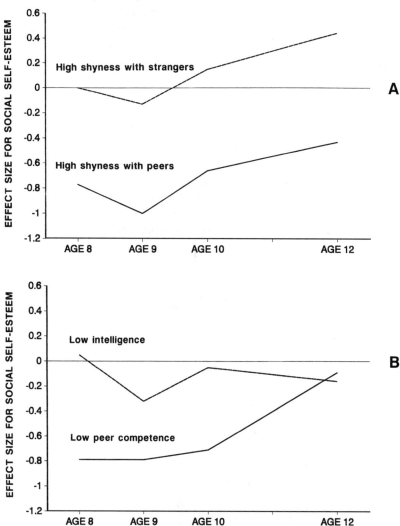

Figure 3. Relation between early shyness with strangers versus shyness with familiar peers and later social self-esteem (A) and between low intelligence versus competence with familiar peers and later social self-esteem (B) (adapted from Asendorpf and van Aken 1994, Figure 2).

would have affected the later actor component because of a process of generalizing expectations or social skills.

A longitudinal study of children's social behavior with many different members of their social network, including parents, siblings, and peers, that follows the children from the beginning of preschool through elementary school is needed to shed more light on the processes of generalization from specific relationships to mean relationship effects studied by LOGIC to late actor effects. Such a study could produce the kinds of data that are needed to confirm the oft-stated hypothesis that emotionally significant early relationships are transformed into stable individual personality dispositions later in life.

Conclusion

This chapter has not given a balanced overview of the results of the LOGIC study in the social domain. Instead, I have focused on one specific, though perhaps the most important, finding. I have tried to illustrate how a longitudinal approach that was initially not governed by specific hypotheses on development gained a sharp theoretical focus through a long interplay of exploratory data analysis, interpretation, formalization, and inductive reasoning. We began with a study on a concept as fuzzy as the lay notion of shyness and arrived at a rather complex dynamic social relations model for

Figure 4. Baron von Münchhausen's horseman.

social-personality development in general that, in turn, is already stimulating a new phase of empirical research.

According to a famous story told by Baron von Münchhausen, a horseman once got lost in a swamp. When his horse was close to perishing, the horseman rescued both his horse and himself by pulling himself out of the swamp by his hair (see Figure 4). One way natural science proceeds is similar to Baron von Münchhausen's horseman's amazing solution. Initially, we are stuck in a swamp of lay preconceptions, but by using our brains – rather than our hair – we can pull ourselves out of the swamp until we reach the sky of theory.

It is important to note that in the present case, this process was driven mainly by data, not by novel ideas. Novel ideas entered into the process at a rather late stage. To "let nature speak first" is not the only possible research strategy in psychological science, but it is the one that I personally prefer because it shields us to some extent against premature theorizing – something, that we have met too often in the history of psychology. However, there is also a danger in this strategy, of course: It needs a firm empirical database to begin with. Large longitudinal studies such as LOGIC can provide a fairly solid empirical base because of the multiplicity of assessments. In this sense, large longitudinal projects can be an important heuristic tool for developmental psychology.

References

Asendorpf, J. B. (1989). Shyness as a final common pathway for two different kinds of inhibition. *Journal of Personality and Social Psychology, 57,* 481–492.

Asendorpf, J. B. (1990a). Beyond social withdrawal: Shyness, unsociability, and peer avoidance. *Human Development, 33,* 250–259.

Asendorpf, J. B. (1990b). Development of inhibition during childhood: Evidence for situational specificity and a two-factor model. *Developmental Psychology, 26,* 721–730.

Asendorpf, J. B. (1991). Development of inhibited children's coping with unfamiliarity. *Child Development, 62,* 1460–1474.

Asendorpf, J. B. (1992a). Beyond stability: Predicting inter-individual differences in intra-individual change. *European Journal of Personality, 6,* 103–117.

Asendorpf, J. B. (1992b). A Brunswikean approach to trait continuity: Application to shynesss. *Journal of Personality, 60,* 53–77.

Asendorpf, J. B. (1993a). Beyond temperament: A two-factorial coping model of the development of inhibition during childhood. In K. H. Rubin & J. B. Asendorpf (Eds.), *Social withdrawal, inhibition and shyness in childhood* (pp. 265–289). Hillsdale, NJ: Erlbaum.

Asendorpf, J. B. (1993b). Abnormal shyness in children. *Journal of Child Psychology & Psychiatry & Allied Disciplines, 34,* 1069–1081.

Asendorpf, J. B. (1994). The malleability of behavioral inhibition: A study of individual developmental functions. *Developmental Psychology, 30,* 912–919.

Asendorpf, J. B., & van Aken, M. A. G. (1993). Deutsche Versionen der Selbstkonzeptskalen von Harter [German versions of the Harter self-concept scales]. *Zeitschrift für Entwicklungspsychologie und Pädagogische Psychologie, 25,* 64–86.

Asendorpf, J. B., & van Aken, M. A. G. (1994). Traits and relationship status: Stranger versus peer group inhibition and test intelligence versus peer group competence as early predictors of later self-esteem. *Child Development, 65,* 1786–1798.

Asendorpf, J. B., Weber, A., & Burkhardt, K. (1994). Zur Mehrdeutigkeit projektiver Testergebnisse: Motiv-Projektion oder Thema-Sensitivität? [On the multiple meaning of projective test results: Motive projection or thematic sensitivity?]. *Zeitschrift für Differentielle und Diagnostische Psychologie, 15,* 155–165.

Digman, J. M. (1990). Personality structure: Emergence of the five-factor model. In M. R. Rosenzweig & L. W. Porter (Eds.), *Annual review of psychology* (Vol. 41, pp. 417–440). Palo Alto, CA: Annual Reviews.

Endler, N. S., & Magnusson, D. (1976). *Interactional psychology and personality.* Washington, DC: Hemisphere.

Fox, N. A., Kimmerly, N. L., & Schafer, W. D. (1991). Attachment to mother/attachment to father: A meta-analysis. *Child Development, 62,* 210–225.

Hartup, W. W., Laursen, B., Stewart, M. I., & Eastenson, A. (1988). Conflict and the friendship relations of young children. *Child Development, 59,* 1590–1600.

Howes, C. (1987). Peer interaction of young children. *Monographs of the Society for Research in Child Development, 53*(1, Serial No. 217).

Kagan, J. (1989). Temperamental contributions to social behavior. *American Psychologist, 44,* 668–674.

Kenny, D. A., & La Voie, L. (1984). The social relations model. In L. Berkowitz (Ed.), *Advances in experimental social psychology* (Vol. 18, pp. 142–182). Orlando, FL: Academic Press.

Lesser, G. S. (1958). Application of Guttman's scaling method to aggressive fantasy in children. *Educational and Psychological Measurement, 18,* 543–551.

Mischel, W., & Peake, P. K. (1982). Beyond déjà-vu in the search for cross-situational consistency. *Psychological Review, 89,* 730–755.

Olweus, D. (1993). Victimization by peers: Antecedents and long-term outcomes. In K. H. Rubin & J. B. Asendorpf (Eds.), *Social withdrawal, inhibition, and shyness in childhood* (pp. 315–341). Hillsdale, NJ: Erlbaum.

Parker, J. G., & Asher, S. R. (1987). Peer relations and later personal adjustment: Are low-accepted children at risk? *Psychological Bulletin, 102,* 357–389.

Rubin, K. H. (1993). The Waterloo Longitudinal Project: Correlates and consequences of social withdrawal from childhood to adolescence. In K. H. Rubin & J. B. Asendorpf (Eds.), *Social withdrawal, inhibition, and shyness in childhood* (pp. 291–314). Hillsdale, NJ: Erlbaum.

Rubin, K. H., Hymel, S., & Mills, R. S. L. (1989). Sociability and social withdrawal in childhood: Stability and outcome. *Journal of Personality, 57,* 237–255.

Rubin, K. H., LeMare, L. J., & Lollis, S. (1990). Social withdrawal in childhood: Developmental pathways to peer rejection. In S. R. Asher & J. D. Coie (Eds.), *Peer rejection in childhood* (pp. 217–249). Cambridge, England: Cambridge University Press.

Rubin, K. H., & Rose-Krasnor, L. (1992). Interpersonal problem solving and social competence in children. In V. B. van Hasselt & M. Hersen (Eds.), *Handbook of social development: A life-span perspective* (pp. 283–323). New York: Plenum Press.

Sroufe, L. A., & Fleeson, J. (1986). Attachment and the construction of relationships. In W. W. Hartup & Z. Rubin (Eds.), *Relationships and development* (pp. 51–71). Hillsdale, NJ: Erlbaum.

Stevenson-Hinde, J. (1986). Towards a more open construct. In G. A. Kohnstamm (Ed.), *Temperament discussed* (pp. 97–106). Lisse, the Netherlands: Swets & Zeitlinger.

11a Comment: Contributions to Knowledge About Social-Personality Development: The Munich LOGIC Study

Kenneth H. Rubin

It seems like only a year or two ago that I received a letter from a young researcher who was about to begin a postdoctoral career by studying the extent to which the construct of shyness was associated with the developmental course of children's social relationships. In this letter, the young man introduced himself as someone who was schooled in personality theory and whose previous research experience involved the study of shyness in college-age adults. He wrote that he was in a remarkable position to spend full time on a funded longitudinal research project; all he had to do was formulate an acceptable research prospectus. Unfortunately, the sample for the project comprised children, not adults, and he expressed openly a lack of knowledge in developmental psychology.

This young researcher outlined several notions he had about factors contributing to the development of shyness and its putative relation with the quality of children's peer relationships. He requested that the reader of the letter provide some helpful commentary on the direction his thoughts were taking.

As one of the several recipients of the letter (apparently, the author had posted his correspondence to a multitude of researchers studying children's peer relationships), I recognized that the program of research proposed had the potential for producing a number of extraordinary contributions to the rapidly emerging field of children's social and emotional development. Not being particularly shy or reticent, I applauded the young man's proposal but then offered a number of conceptually and empirically based criticisms. My correspondence was met with almost immediate response; I was invited to spend a year, a half-year, a month, a week, or a couple of days at the Max Planck Institute (MPI) consulting with this young scholar, and his colleagues, about his piece of what was to be the LOGIC study.

Preparation of this commentary was supported by a Senior Research Fellowship from the Ontario Mental Health Foundation. Correspondence concerning this chapter should be directed Kenneth H. Rubin at the Department of Human Development, University of Maryland, 3304 Benjamin Building, College Park, MD 20742-1131.

243

Now, 11 years later, I find myself having been invited to comment on the fruits of this 10-year-long research program. During this decade, I have seen Jens Asendorpf emerge as a creative, stimulating, and productive investigator of children's social and personality development. Thus, it is with pleasure that I provide a commentary on Jens Asendorpf's contribution to the LOGIC study.

A Brief Historical Overview

After having received the invitation to visit the Max Planck Institute for Psychological Research, I decided to spend the month of June 1985 in Munich. During this visit, I was invited to give a colloquium to the members of the Institute. The title of my presentation was "Some Developmental Pathways to Competence in Childhood." Given the substance of Asendorpf's chapter herein, I believe it appropriate to provide the reader with a précis of this presentation. Needless to say, the comments offered in this chapter have been updated from those presented over 10 years ago. Nevertheless, the substance is very much the same.

In this presentation to the MPI, I described a newly developed conceptually and theoretically based model concerning the etiology of competent and incompetent, adaptive and maladaptive, and social and emotional development in childhood (see Rubin, LeMare, and Lollis 1990; Rubin and Lollis 1988; Rubin and Mills 1991 for full descriptions). Given the focus of Asendorpf's chapter, I focus on the developmental pathway to-and-from social inhibition and withdrawal.

The starting point, in this developmental scenario, is the infant dispositional characteristic generally referred to as *behavioral inhibition*. Following from the then recent work of Kagan and colleagues, (e.g., Garcia-Coll, Kagan, and Reznick 1984; Kagan, Reznick, Clarke, Snidman, and Garcia-Coll 1984), I proposed that there are some newborns who are biologically predisposed to have a low threshold for arousal when confronted with social (or nonsocial) stimulation and novelty. More recent research by Kagan (1989), Fox (Fox and Calkins 1993) and others (e.g., Davidson and Fox 1989) has shown that under conditions of novelty or uncertainty, some babies demonstrate physical and physiological changes that suggest they are "hyper-arousable" – a characteristic that may make them extremely difficult for their parents to soothe and comfort. Indeed, in my MPI presentation, I suggested that some parents might find such infantile responses of hyperarousal aversive. Consequently, under some circumstances, some parents might react to easily aroused and wary babies with insensitivity, overprotectiveness, or nonresponsivity.

I further suggested that each of these parental variables is predictive of the development of insecure parent–infant attachment relationships (Spieker and Booth 1988; Sroufe 1983). Furthermore, I noted that these parenting behaviors are associated with environmental and personal stressors such as poverty, unemployment, premature birth of the infant, marital dissatisfaction, and maternal depression (e.g., Booth, Rose-Krasnor, and Rubin 1991). Thus, I posited that an interplay of endogenous, socialization, and early relationships factors, as they coexist under an "umbrella" of negative-setting conditions, would lead to a sense of felt insecurity.

I also proposed specifically that the internal working models of insecurely attached children who are also temperamentally inhibited would lead them, as Bowlby (1973) put it, "to shrink from" their social worlds. In other words, I suggested that inhibited, insecure toddlers would be those children whom teachers and parents would describe as socially inhibited or withdrawn in preschool.

I also proposed that children who shrink anxiously away from their peers preclude themselves from the positive outcomes associated with social exploration and peer play (see Rubin and Stewart 1996 for a recent review). That is, they become socially incompetent. In turn, I suggested that social incompetence would lead to peer rejection and that the experience of being isolated and disliked by the peer group would lead the already hypersensitive, anxious child to think and feel poorly of himself or herself and withdraw further from the peer group.

At this point, let me summarize where I took this MPI audience in the summer of 1985. First, I suggested that some temperamentally hyperarousable babies may, under certain conditions, be responded to by parents with insensitivity or overcontrol. This particular admixture of infantile temperament and parental insensitivity was hypothesized to predict an insecure attachment relationship. In turn, felt insecurity was proposed to lead to an impoverished exploratory style that precludes the opportunity to experience those forms of peer exchange that promote the development of social competence. The relatively slow development of social competence, when combined with "wariness," felt insecurity, and peer rejection was proposed to result in the development of negative self-appraisals of competence, which, in turn, was posited to exacerbate withdrawal from peers. These factors, when taken all together, were hypothesized to predict difficulties of an internalizing nature, such as loneliness and depression in later childhood and adolescence.

Finally, in concluding my talk in 1985, I added a few disclaimers or provisos. First, not all infants with a fearful, wary, and inhibited temperament are "doomed" to a developmental course with an outcome of psychological maladaptation. In fact, I added that most inhibited babies receive responsive and sensitive caregiving in a relatively stress-free environment. I predicted therefore, that many, if not most, dispositionally inhibited babies develop secure relationships with their parents and do not experience the sort of parental overcontrol that I have posited to be debilitating (see Rubin, Stewart, and Chen 1995 for a full discussion).

Asendorpf's Contribution to the LOGIC Study

Having provided the reader with the conceptual rationale for research interest in inhibited and withdrawn behavior, it is appropriate to turn now to a discussion of Asendorpf's research program at the MPI. In short, in the 10 years that have passed since my visit to Munich, Asendorpf has gone quite some distance to provide substantive empirical support for the developmental model just presented.

From the outset, however, let me provide a note of clarification. In his chapter, Asendorpf used the term *shyness* to refer to reticent social behavior displayed in both unfamiliar and familiar venues. Generally, in the literature extant, shyness refers to socially reticent behavior in *unfamiliar* settings (see Rubin and Asendorpf 1993 for a discussion); *social withdrawal* is the term that is used in reference to socially avoidant or solitary behavior in *familiar* contexts.

In the longitudinal LOGIC study, Asendorpf found that social withdrawal, or the abnormally frequent display of solitary activity in the company of familiar others, was (a) relatively stable over time, (b) associated with observations of peer rebuff (Asendorpf 1993), and (c) predictive of negative self-regard vis-à-vis the child's social skills and relationships (Asendorpf and van Aken 1994). These findings are reassuring, not only because they provide support for the contentions expressed in the developmental model just presented, but also because they are completely, and in every way, in concert with those generated in our Waterloo Longitudinal Project (e.g., Rubin 1993; Rubin, Chen, McDougall, Bowker, and McKinnon 1995; Rubin, Hymel, and Mills 1989; Rubin and Mills 1988). Taken together, the results of these two longitudinal projects, drawing from data collected independently in two different countries and cultures, provide ample evidence that spending an abnormal amount of time alone, and not in the company of peers, carries with it both contemporaneous and predictive negative psychological baggage.

Furthermore, the data argue against the long-standing, but conceptually and methodologically, vacuous argument that social withdrawal is not a risk factor for maladaptive psychological "outcomes" (Ensminger, Kellam, and Rubin 1983; Kohlberg, LaCrosse, and Ricks 1972; Robins 1966). Indeed, the recent rush of studies concerning the correlates and consequences of inhibition and social withdrawal in children (e.g., Broberg, Lamb, and Hwang 1990; Hymel, Bowker, and Woody 1993; Kochanska and Radke-Yarrow 1992; LaFreniere and Dumas 1992; Parkhurst and Asher 1992; see Rubin and Stewart 1996 for a recent review) is much indebted to Asendorpf's findings in the LOGIC project.

The contributions that Asendorpf has made to the study of social, emotional, and personality development extend well beyond a focus on behavioral inhibition, shyness, and social withdrawal. For example, Asendorpf has argued rather convincingly that the expression of a given behavior may have different psychological meanings depending on (a) the situation in which it is observed and (b) the age of the child who has produced it. This is the way development should be studied; it is a realistic, and yet at the same time, creative "take" on the study of development. Specifically, Asendorpf has argued that not all forms of solitude carry with them the same psychological meanings over time and across situations. Simply put, children's expression of social reticence or shyness among adult strangers means something quite different from behavioral reticence or shyness among familiar others even though the behavioral expression of the phenomenon looks the same in the two contexts. Indeed, Asendorpf reports a nonsignificant association between the two phenomena.

A related contribution is that not all behavioral expressions of solitude carry with them identical meanings. Reticent, unoccupied, and onlooking behavior in the company of peers appears to suggest an internally based social approach–social avoidance conflict. This behavior is referred to as shyness in Asendorpf's work. Spending time alone exploring, manipulating, and creating with objects means something quite different – it conveys a lack of social interest, not shyness. As it turns out, the statistical association between reticence and solitary-constructive/exploratory behavior is nonsignificant during the preschool years. In early childhood, reticence is associated with independent markers of social anxiety, social deference, and felt insecurity (see also Coplan, Rubin, Fox, Calkins, and Stewart 1994; Rubin, Coplan, Fox, and Calkins 1995). At the same period in childhood, solitary-constructive/exploratory behavior is associated with behavioral adaptation (Rubin 1982; Rubin et al. 1995). However, over time, and with development, these different forms of solitude, as expressed in the company of familiar peers, become statistically associated, leading to the conclusion that the behavioral expression of social wariness and insecurity changes over time (Asendorpf 1993). In other words, the psychological "meanings" of particular social behaviors change from preschool to midchildhood. And that which is judged as acceptable by peers in early childhood becomes judged as unacceptable in mid-childhood.

These latter contributions are extraordinarily significant, not only to developmental psychologists but also to those who are interested in identifying children who are "at risk" for developing psychological problems associated with social withdrawal. Depending on when and how one observes and identifies "withdrawn" children, the potential candidates for the subsequent development of socioemotional problems vary. It makes a difference if one observes children in novel situations (with adults or age mates, as does Kagan 1989) or in situations with familiar others. It makes a difference if one is observing 4- versus 6- versus 10- versus 12-year-olds. It also makes a difference how one defines shyness or social withdrawal.

Recent Perspectives

In their most recent deliberations, Asendorpf and van Aken (1994) argued that children's behavior is a function of their own dispositions, the psychological inclinations of their social partners, and the relationship that exists between the dyadic mates. This suggestion derives largely from the writings of Kenny and La Voie (1984) and Hinde (1979) and is seen clearly in the elegant research concerning toddler peer relationships conducted by Hildy Ross at the University of Waterloo (e.g., Hay and Ross 1982; Ross and Lollis 1989). Ross and colleagues begin by noting that a relationship may be inferred when

> neither the characteristic behavior of Child One, nor the behavior that others typically direct to Child Two, nor the independent, additive influences of both factors taken together are sufficient to predict the behavior of Child One to Child Two. In that sense, relationships cannot be derived from the individual characteristics of the

participants; the relationship itself influences the interaction between them. (Ross, Conant, Cheyne, and Alevisos 1992, p. 1)

To this end, Ross and colleagues have demonstrated that toddlers develop reciprocal relationships, not only in terms of the mutual exchange of positive overtures but also in terms of agonistic interactions (Ross et al. 1992; Ross and Lollis 1989). Positive interactions are directed specifically to those who have directed positive initiations to the child beforehand; conflict is initiated specifically with those who have initiated conflictual interactions with the child beforehand.

With reference to Asendorpf and van Aken, it remains to be seen whether one can predict particular forms of social or unsociable behavior, given knowledge about the partners in action and knowledge about the quality of their relationship. Nevertheless, it would appear likely that Asendorpf will find support for the model.

$$\text{behavior}(t) = \text{actor} + \text{partner} + \text{relationship}(t).$$

As students of family relationships know, children bring with them to new situations *internal working models* of already established relationships. In preschool, for example, children who have "anxious-ambivalent attachment relationships" with their mothers behave in a characteristically inhibited and shy manner with strangers (e.g., Calkins and Fox 1992). A very anxious and insecure child is likely to look "shy" in most social situations involving age mates. Thus, it would be unrealistic to assume that unfamiliar peers develop interactive patterns and relationships based solely on how they behave in the given context. Clearly, the quality of already established relationships contributes to the expression of social initiatives, social confidence, and the lack thereof (e.g., Booth et al. 1991).

Similarly, the child's cognitions about the self serve to guide the demonstration of particular behaviors with unfamiliar peers. Children who believe that they are socially unskilled and that others dislike them produce fewer social initiations with unfamiliar peers than do their age mates who believe that they are socially skilled and that others like them (e.g., Lapa, Rubin, Booth, and Rose-Krasnor 1994). Furthermore, children who are negatively self-disposed produce less assertive social initiatives and are more likely to be rebuffed than are their more confident counterparts (Rubin 1985). Thus, the development of new relationships is influenced not only by characteristic behavioral displays but also by thoughts and feelings about already existing relationships and about the self.

The observations noted earlier should be taken as supportive of the Kenny and La Voie (1984) model. The critical factors in determining the predictability of the shy child's behavior in a given social situation include not only what is known about the child's disposition (or temperament), but also what is known about their working models of relationships and their feelings and thoughts about their own social competencies. I believe that this collection of variables is already on the table for Asendorpf and colleagues as they plan their new program of research.

Finally, as some small support for this new direction for Asendorpf and colleagues, I offer some findings from a study conducted quite some time ago. In this applied research program, my colleagues and I identified children who, in their preschool and second-grade classrooms, displayed a much higher than normal amount of solitary activity. These children subsequently were invited to a playroom with a normally sociable playmate; it was proposed that regular meetings with a peer (especially a younger, normal peer; Furman, Rahe, and Hartup 1979) would engender feelings of confidence and competence that would extend to their classroom behaviors. The bottom line is that the "intervention" failed. Extremely withdrawn children who participated in five extended free-play periods with one "normal" dyadic partner, and then an additional five play sessions with another normal dyadic partner, failed to increase their in-classroom social behavior or to decrease their nonsocial behavior from pre- to postintervention. However, Asendorpf's new direction concerning the significance of relationships is relevant here. Asendorpf argues that over time relationships develop between initially unfamiliar partners. These relationships interact with the individual characteristics of the play partners to produce changes in styles of interactive behavior – at least within the specific dyad being observed. In the peer-pairing study just described, each socially withdrawn child met with an initially unfamiliar partner for five play sessions; then for the 6–10 sessions, the child met with a second partner. We videotaped the 1st and last (5th) session with each partner and examined the initially shy child's behaviors as they changed over time and across partners.

When the partners were strangers, the extremely withdrawn children spent a good deal of time engaging in reticent behavior. Social initiations were relatively infrequent, and when they occurred, they were produced by the play partners. However, over time, the children began to interact more frequently, with initiations deriving as much from "actor" as from "partner." By the fifth and final session with the first dyadic partner, the initially withdrawn actor's socially initiative and interactive behaviors had increased significantly while his or her nonsocial behaviors had decreased. This suggests the importance of the developing relationship for the changing nature of the actor's behavioral profile.

Now perhaps even more important was the finding that the first meeting of the socially withdrawn child with the second partner was more like the last meeting than the first meeting with the first partner. That is, given a developing internal working model of positive peer experience and increased social confidence, the withdrawn actor looked far less "withdrawn" during the first meeting with the second partner than during the first meeting with the first partner. And by the final meeting with the second partner, our initially withdrawn children did not resemble the protype for a socially anxious and avoidant child. However, in keeping with Asendorpf's views, when the withdrawn children were observed in their classrooms, they did not appear sociable, anxiety free, and confident. Thus, behavior patterns differed across venues and across situations. Developing relationships allowed behavioral shifts; already established relationships (in the classroom) mediated against behavioral change.

Actor × Partner × Relationship is an interaction term begging for thorough investigation. However, in examining so complex an interaction term, one is required to consider the expression of human behavior as a function of still yet more variables – internal working models of relationships, thoughts and feelings about the self's competencies, and so on. Furthermore, one is required to consider factors that serve to initiate or contribute to the initial production of given patterns of social behavior. In Asendorpf's research, there has been no attempt to consider family factors such as the quality of parent–child relationships or qualitative aspects of parenting. There has been no attempt to examine the effects of stress on children's behaviors and relationships – stress leveled at the child or at his or her parents. For example, interparental conflict and marital dissolution have an impact on children's behavior. Does it contribute to the expression of social solitude and shyness in the company of unfamiliar or familiar peers? Does it influence behavior differently at different ages?

What then about child gender? Are the findings described in Asendorpf's research equally tenable for boys and girls? Recently, researchers have reported that social wariness and solitude in the company of familiar others are particularly "risky" for boys (Engfer 1993; Rubin, Chen, and Hymel 1993). Finally, what about culture? Do cultural norms, expectations, and beliefs render the findings in the literature specific to the milieus in which they were studied? We have learned today that given behaviors take on different psychological meanings, given particular situational and age constraints. However, do given behaviors mean different things in different cultures? These are questions that require some serious address – and they are questions that may provide some incentive for Asendorpf and colleagues to continue their fine work as they move to their own new venue in Berlin.

References

Asendorpf, J. B. (1993). Beyond temperament: A two-factorial coping model of the development of inhibition during childhood. In K. H. Rubin & J. B. Asendorpf (Eds.), *Social withdrawal, inhibition and shyness in childhood* (pp. 265–289). Hillsdale, NJ: Erlbaum.

Asendorpf, J. B., & van Aken, M. A. G. (1994). Traits and relationship status: Stranger versus peer group inhibition and test intelligence versus peer group confidence as early predictors of later self-esteem. *Child Development, 65*, 1786–1798.

Booth, C. L., Rose-Krasnor, L., & Rubin, K. H. (1991). Relating preschoolers' social competence and their mothers' parenting behaviors to early attachment security and high risk status. *Journal of Social and Personal Relationships, 8*, 363–382.

Bowlby, J. (1973). *Attachment and loss: Vol. 1. Attachment*. New York: Basic Books.

Broberg, A., Lamb, M. E., & Hwang, P. (1990). Inhibition: Its stability and correlates in sixteen-to-forty-month-old children. *Child Development, 61*, 1153–1163.

Calkins, S. D., & Fox, N. A. (1992). The relations among infant temperament, security of attachment and behavioral inhibition at 24 months. *Child Development, 63*, 1456–1472.

Coplan, R. J., Rubin, K. H., Fox, N. A., Calkins, S. D., & Stewart, S. L. (1994). Being alone, playing alone, and acting alone: Distinguishing among reticence, and passive- and active-solitude in young children. *Child Development, 65*, 129–137.

Davidson, R., & Fox, N. (1989). Frontal brain asymmetry predicts infants' response to maternal separation. *Journal of Abnormal Psychology, 98*, 127–131.

Engfer, A. (1993). Antecedents and consequences of shyness in boys and girls: A 6 year longitudinal study. In K. H. Rubin & J. Asendorpf (Eds.), *Social withdrawal, inhibition, and shyness in childhood* (pp. 49–80). Hillsdale, NJ: Erlbaum.

Ensminger, M. C., Kellam, S. G., & Rubin, B. R. (1983). School and family origins of delinquency: Comparisons by sex. In K. T. Van Dusen & S. A. Mednick (Eds.), *Prospective studies of crime and delinquency* (pp. 73–97). Hingham, MA: Kluwer-Nijhoff.

Fox, N., & Calkins, S. (1993). Relations between temperament, attachment, and behavioral inhibition: Two possible pathways to extroversion and social withdrawal. In K. H. Rubin & J. Asendorpf (Eds.), *Social withdrawal, inhibition, and shyness in childhood* (pp.81–100) Hillsdale, NJ: Erlbaum.

Furman, W., Rahe, D. F., & Hartup, W. W. (1979). Rehabilitation of socially withdrawn preschool children through mixed-age and same-age socialization. *Child Development, 50,* 915–922.

Garcia-Coll, C., Kagan, J., & Reznick, J. S. (1984). Behavioral inhibition in young children. *Child Development, 55,* 1005–1019.

Hay, D., & Ross, H. (1982). The social nature of early conflict. *Child Development, 53,* 105–113.

Hinde, R. A. (1979). *Towards understanding relationships.* London: Academic Press.

Hymel, S., Bowker, A., & Woody, E. (1993). Aggressive versus withdrawn unpopular children: Variations in peer and self-perceptions in multiple domains. *Child Development, 64,* 879–896.

Kagan, J. (1989). Temperamental contributions to social behavior. *American Psychologist, 44,* 668–674.

Kagan, J., Reznick, J. S., Clarke, C., Snidman, N., & Garcia-Coll, C. (1984). Behavioral inhibition to the unfamiliar. *Child Development, 55,* 2212–2225.

Kenny, D. A., & La Voie, L. (1984). The social relations model. In L. Berkowitz (Ed.), *Advances in experimental social psychology* (Vol. 18, pp.142–182). Orlando, FL: Academic Press.

Kochanska, G., & Radke-Yarrow, M. (1992). Inhibition in toddlerhood and the dynamics of the child's interaction with an unfamiliar peer at age five. *Child Development, 63,* 325–335.

Kohlberg, L., LaCrosse, J., & Ricks, D. (1972). The predictability of adult mental health from childhood behavior. In B. B. Wolman (Ed.), *Manual of child psychopathology* (pp. 1217–1284). New York: McGraw-Hill.

LaFreniere, P., & Dumas, J. E. (1992). A transactional analysis of early childhood anxiety and social withdrawal. *Development and Psychopathology, 4,* 385–402.

Lapa, L. M., Rubin, K. H., Booth, C. L., & Rose-Krasnor, L. (1994, June). *The social problem solving skills of children with low self perceptions.* Paper presented at the 13th Biennial Meetings of The International Society for the Study of Behavioral Development, Amsterdam, The Netherlands.

Parkhurst, J. T., & Asher, S. R. (1992). Peer rejection in middle school: Subgroup differences in behavior, loneliness, and interpersonal concerns. *Developmental Psychology, 28,* 231–241.

Robins, L. N. (1966). *Deviant children grown up.* Baltimore, MD: Williams & Wilkins.

Ross, H. S., Conant, C., Cheyne, J. A., & Alevisos, E. (1992). Relationships and alliances in the social interaction of kibbutz toddlers. *Social Development, 1,* 1–17.

Ross, H. S., & Lollis, S. P. (1989). A social relations analysis of toddler peer relationships. *Child Development, 60,* 1082–1091.

Rubin, K. H. (1982). Non-social play in preschoolers: Necessary evil? *Child Development, 53,* 651–657.

Rubin, K. H. (1985). Socially withdrawn children: An "at risk" population? In B. H. Schneider, K. H. Rubin, & J. E. Ledingham (Eds.), *Children's peer relations: Issues in assessment and intervention* (pp. 125–139). New York: Springer-Verlag.

Rubin, K. H. (1993). The Waterloo Longitudinal Project: Correlates and consequences of social withdrawal from childhood to adolescence. In K. H. Rubin & J. Asendorpf (Eds.), *Social withdrawal, inhibition and shyness in childhood* (pp. 291–314). Hillsdale, NJ: Erlbaum.

Rubin, K. H., & Asendorpf, J. (1993). Social withdrawal, inhibition, and shyness in childhood: Conceptual and definitional issues. In K. H. Rubin & J. Asendorpf (Eds.), *Social withdrawal, inhibition and shyness in childhood* Hillsdale, NJ: Erlbaum.

Rubin, K. H., Chen, X., & Hymel, S. (1993). The socio-emotional characteristics of extremely aggressive and extremely withdrawn children. *Merrill-Palmer Quarterly, 39,* 518–534.

Rubin, K. H., Chen, X., McDougall, P., Bowker, A., & McKinnon; J. A. (1995). The Waterloo Longitudinal Project: Predicting internalizing and externalizing problems in adolescence. *Development & Psychopathology. 7,* 751–764.

Rubin, K. H., Coplan, R. J., Fox, N. A., & Calkins, S. D. (1995). Emotionality, emotion regulation, and preschoolers' social adaptation. *Development & Psychopathology, 7,* 49–62.

Rubin, K. H., Hymel, S., & Mills, R. S. L. (1989). Sociability and social withdrawal in childhood: Stability and outcomes. *Journal of Personality, 57,* 237–255.

Rubin, K. H., LeMare, L. J., & Lollis, S. (1990). Social withdrawal in childhood: Developmental pathways to rejection. In S. R. Asher & J. D. Coie (Eds.), *Peer rejection in childhood* (pp. 217–249). New York: Cambridge University Press.

Rubin, K. H., & Lollis, S. (1988). Peer relationships, social skills, and infant attachment: A continuity model. In J. Belsky & T. Nezworski (Eds.), *Clinical implications of attachment* (pp. 167–221). New York: Guilford Press.

Rubin, K. H., & Mills, R. S. L. (1988). The many faces of social isolation in childhood. *Journal of Consulting and Clinical Psychology, 56,* 916–924.

Rubin, K. H., & Mills, R. S. L. (1991). Conceptualizing developmental pathways to internalizing disorders in childhood. *Canadian Journal of Behavioral Science, 23,* 300–317.

Rubin, K. H. & Stewart, S. L. (1996). Social withdrawal. In E. J. Mash & R. A. Barkley (Eds.), *Child psychopathology.* (pp. 277–307) New York: Guilford Press.

Rubin, K. H., Stewart, S. L., & Chen, X. (1995). Parenting factors associated with aggression and social withdrawal in childhood. In M. Bornstein (Ed.), *Handbook of parenting* (pp. 255–284). Hillsdale, NJ: Erlbaum.

Spieker, S. J., & Booth, C. L. (1988). Maternal antecedents of attachment quality. In J. Belsky & T. Nezworski (Eds.), *Clinical implications of attachment* (pp. 95–135). Hillsdale, NJ: Erlbaum.

Sroufe, L. A. (1983). Infant–caregiver attachment and patterns of adaptation in preschool: Roots of maladaptation and competence. In M. Perlmutter (Ed.), *Minnesota symposia on child psychology* (Vol. 16, pp. 41–83). Hillsdale, NJ: Erlbaum.

12 Development of Moral Understanding and Moral Motivation

Gertrud Nunner-Winkler

Theoretical Context

Underlying Kohlberg's (1976, 1981, 1984; Colby et al. 1987) theory of moral development is a supposition of cognitive–affective parallelism: At each developmental stage, the reasons people give to justify the validity of moral norms and the concerns that motivate their norm-conforming behavior are structurally equivalent. This equivalence of stage-specific reasons and concerns fits well with one of the basic tenets of stage theories: the assumption that each stage forms a "structured whole." For the preconventional level (up to about 10 or 11 years of age), both reasons and concerns are described as instrumentalistic or derived from an unconditional submission to authorities. Norms are seen as set by authorities and backed by sanctions; motives for conformity are based on cost-benefit calculations (i.e., an interest in avoiding sanctions and gaining advantages).

Although Kohlberg's (1976, 1984) description of early childhood morality is backed by a wealth of research data (cf. Blasi 1993; Damon 1977; Snarey 1985; Walker 1986), it has also been criticized on a number of grounds. Turiel (1983) has shown that even young children understand that moral rules have intrinsic universal validity and are unalterable; that is, they are binding for all people in all places and at all times, irrespective of authoritative commands or sanctions, and they cannot be changed – not even God may alter or transgress them (cf. Nucci and Lee 1993). Behaviorally, young children do not seem to be purely instrumentalistic: Observational studies on altruism have shown that children spontaneously display genuine concern over the well-being of others and help/share with and console others. Integrating these lines of evidence about children's moral understanding and behavior, Döbert (1987, on theoretical grounds) and Keller and Edelstein (1993, on empirical findings) have

I wish to thank the staff of the Institute for so carefully conducting the interviews and experiments; Tina Hascher, Yvonne Dechant, Ute Loges, and Andrea Seiderer for their assistance in the development of the coding procedures and for coding verbal responses and video tapes; and – last but not least – Merry Bullock for her editorial work. She not only corrected English grammar and style but also improved manners of presenting procedures and data and contributed conceptual clarification.

253

Table 1. *Childhood Morality: Theoretical Positions and Measurements*

Childhood morality	Kohlberg (1976, 1984)	Turiel (1983)	Research on altruism	Döbert (1987) Keller and Edelstein (1993)
Understanding:				
Validity of moral rules	Instrumental	Intrinsic	—	Intrinsic
Motives for moral conformity	Instrumental	—	Intrinsic	Intrinsic
Measurement operationalization	Justification of action decision (authorities and negative duties)	Justification of rule validity	Observation of spontaneous behavior	Justification of action decision (friendship and positive duties)

concluded that even the young child can be characterized as a morally competent actor – aware of the intrinsic validity of moral rules and motivated by truly moral concerns.

It is my contention that the apparent contradictions in theoretical interpretations and empirical findings result from differences in the conceptualization and operationalization of moral competence. Kohlberg (1984; Colby et al. 1987) questioned participants about their justifications for hypothetical *action decisions* ("What should a hypothetical protagonist do? Why?") in moral dilemmas involving authorities and negative duties. Keller and Edelstein (1993) also asked for action decisions; however, they used dilemmas involving friendship and positive duties. Turiel (1983), in contrast, questioned participants' understanding of the invariance of the *validity of moral rules* ("Is it right to do [an immoral act] if authorities allow it?"). Finally, in altruism research children's *spontaneous behavior* was observed ("Does child help/console/share with a needy peer or not?"; cf. Table 1).

These different contexts and focuses have yielded seemingly contradictory pictures of moral competence. It may well be, however, that a child understands the intrinsic validity of moral rules (moral knowledge), yet he or she does not make following these rules an important personal concern (moral motivation) and thus guides action decisions by instrumental cost-benefit calculations. It is also possible that a child acts on spontaneous altruistic impulses yet fails to take the welfare of others into account when experiencing strongly opposing (egotistic) desires and needs.

To clarify these issues and to arrive at an adequate description of early moral understanding, it is necessary to disentangle the effects of these different dimensions and to control for the possibility that they might vary independently. Thus, in the research to be presented, there were independent assessments for

- moral rule understanding (positive and negative duties)
- moral motivation

and in each assessment,

- we controlled for the concordance or discordance between spontaneous inclinations and moral commands;
- we made sure that children's understanding of authority or friendship relations and their respective psychological or moral implications (cf. Damon 1977; Selman 1980) would not interfere.

Cognitive moral rule understanding was assessed by presenting hypothetical moral conflicts and dilemmas and by using a variety of measures to explore children's knowledge and understanding of moral rules and principles, children's reasons for rule validity, and their assessments of the conditions under which exceptions from these rules might be justifiable.

Two different measures were used for strength of moral motivation: For younger children, emotion attributions to hypothetical wrongdoers were used; for older children, a global evaluation of the strength of their moral motivation based on their reactions to hypothetical moral conflicts and dilemmas was conducted (global rating). The use of emotion attributions as an index to moral motive strength was derived from a cognitivist interpretation, whereby emotions are considered to be (often) rash judgments about the personal relevance of given facts (cf. Montada 1993; Solomon 1976). By attributing an emotion to a hypothetical wrongdoer, children may indicate the relative importance they attach to moral conformity versus need satisfaction when needs conflict with norms. This operationalization is based on several assumptions that are supported by empirical results: Four- 5-year-old children are able to take intentions into account when they ascribe emotions (cf. Nunner-Winkler and Sodian 1988), they have some understanding of moral rules (cf. Turiel 1983) and morally relevant emotions (cf. Nunner-Winkler and Sodian 1988), and they tend to attribute to a hypothetical protagonist the same emotion they anticipate for themselves in a similar situation (cf. Barden, Zelko, Duncan, and Masters 1980). A different measure was used for older children because of concerns that the attribution measure might be confounded by social desirability: Rather than attributing those emotions that they would anticipate feeling in a similar situation, older children might attribute "moral" emotions to present themselves more favorably.

The justifications for negative emotions attributed to moral wrongdoers were used as indicators for type of moral motivation. One theoretical rationale for this is that children will disclose what types of concerns they assume motivate norm conformity (e.g., fear of sanctions, compassion, respect for the law, and desire for personal integrity) when they explain why they expect someone to feel bad after transgressing a moral norm.

Table 2. *Overview: Measures Used in Moral Development*

Moral development	Variable	Instruments	Waves		
Moral rule understanding	Knowledge Justification	Hypothetical conflicts (norm vs. desire/value)	2	4	6
	Exception	Hypothetical conflicts (norm vs. desire/value)	2	4	6
		Hypothetical conflicts/dilemmas (norm vs. desire/personal interest/value/norm)			8
Moral motivation	Emotion ascription to wrongdoer (strength of motivation)		2	4	(6)[a]
	Justification of emotion ascription (type of motivation)		2	4	6
	Global rating (strength of motivation)				8
Validation of measures of moral motivation	Behavior in real-life moral conflicts		3	4	8
	Q-sort ratings by kindergarten teachers		3		
	Q-sort ratings by parents				7

[a]Emotion ascription in Wave 6 no longer reliably indicates moral motivation (see section on strength and type of moral motivation).

The measurement of moral motivation was validated in several ways: Behavior in real-life moral conflicts was observed and correlated with the measures of moral motivation, and Q-sort ratings provided by kindergarten teachers and parents were compared with measures of moral motivation (cf. Table 2).

Procedure

Moral Understanding and Emotion Attributions as a Measure for Moral Motivation

Assessment. In Waves 2, 4, and 6 (ages 4–5, 6–7, and 8–9 years, respectively), children were presented the same four picture stories[1] (with minor age-appropriate adaptions in Wave 6) in which a protagonist experienced different moral conflicts and one value conflict: The stories involved a temptation to transgress a simple negative duty (Story 1: not to steal) and three positive duties (Story 2: to share one's own

[1] These stories were developed in cooperation with Beate Sodian (cf. Nunner-Winkler and Sodian 1987).

Table 3. *Moral Development Tasks (Waves 2, 4, and 6)*

Story	Transgression type	Content
Story 1: stealing	Negative duty	A child stole sweets/a toy from another child
Story 2: drink sharing	Positive duty	A child did not share a drink with a thirsty child
Story 3: prize sharing	Positive duty	A child did not share an unfairly won prize with the disadvantaged peer
Story 4: help giving	Positive duty	A child did not help another child who needed help in fulfilling a task, but rather fulfilled own achievement need; a third child did help

possession; Story 3: to share an undeserved reward with a disadvantaged peer; and Story 4: to help another child in a competitive task).

The reasons for transgressing were to fulfill hedonistic desires (Stories 1–3) or to fulfill a personal value orientation (Story 4: achievement value). All stories portrayed same-sex peers only. No adults or close friends were involved to avoid confounding children's moral understanding with their understanding of authority or friendship. In the first part of each story (the temptation situation), children were questioned about their knowledge and understanding of the moral rule in question. The protagonist was then shown to transgress the rule and satisfy his or her hedonistic desire (or his or her achievement motive in Story 4). After the transgression, children were questioned about the emotion they expected the protagonist to feel and were asked to justify their emotion attribution to the wrongdoer (for details of the measurement, see Tables 3, 4, and 5).

In Wave 8 (age 10–11), the conflicts[2] presented were systematically varied along a continuum extending from transgressions that were strictly unjustifiable to strictly called for. The conflicts involved the temptation to transgress a simple moral rule (to break a promise given to one's classmates to help clean up a mess after a party/ tents after classtrip) in order to fulfill a short-term hedonistic desire (Story 1: un-justifiable transgression); to follow up a more or less long-standing personal interest or value commitment (Stories 2 and 3: debatable justifiability of transgression); and to fulfill a (higher grade) conflicting moral norm (Story 4: justifiable and necessary transgression). To increase identification with the hypothetical moral and value con-flicts, children's own favorite candidates for hedonistic desires or personal interests were first explored and used in the hypothetical conflicts in Stories 1–3. To decrease the likelihood that children would vilify the protagonists, they were asked to attribute emotions for themselves in a similar situation rather than for a hypothetical wrongdoer (the protagonist). In addition to emotion attributions for themselves as a hypothetical

---

[2] The conflicts were developed in cooperation with Angelika Weber.

Table 4. *Measures in Moral Development Tasks (Waves 2, 4, and 6)*

Measures	Task
Control for story understanding	
"Does protagonist want to have the sweets/the toy?"	Story 1
"Was the judge fair in giving the prize to the protagonist?"	Story 3
Knowledge of moral rules	
"Is taking the sweets/the toy allowed or is it not?"	Story 1
"Must one share/help or does one not have to?"	Stories 2, 3, and 4
Justification of moral rules	
"Why is it (not) allowed to take something away?"	Story 1
"Why does one/does one not have to share/help in the given situation?"	Stories 2, 3, and 4
Emotion ascription to protagonist	
Moral wrongdoer: "How does the child who transgressed the rule (stole; did not share; did not help) feel?"	Stories 1, 2, 3, 4
Moral hero: "How does the child who conformed to the rule (helped) feel?"	Story 4
Self as wrongdoer: "How would you feel if you had (stolen/not shared/not helped)?"	Wave 6 only: Stories 1, 2, 3, 4
Justification for emotion ascription	
"Why does the protagonist feel the way s/he feels?"	Stories 1, 2, 3, 4

wrongdoer, children were asked to give and justify emotion ascriptions for themselves as a victim of or a bystander to someone else's wrongdoing (cf. Tables 6 and 7).

Coding Procedure. The following variables were defined and coded.

- "Rule validity" (indicating children's moral knowledge): all responses stating that it is wrong to steal, that one ought to share/help/keep promises.
- "Justification for rule validity" (indicating children's moral understanding): all responses to the questions: "Why is it wrong to steal?" "Why should one share/help/keep a promise?" (categories indicated in numbered list).
- "Strength of moral motivation": number of negative emotion attributions to hypothetical wrongdoers over Stories 1–4 (Waves 2 and 4).
- "Type of moral motivation": all responses to the question: "Why does protagonist feel bad?" (categories indicated in numbered list).

The same classification was used for both the reasons children forwarded in justifying the validity of moral rules as well as the concerns children referred to when explaining the protagonist's feeling bad after transgression. The following four categories were distinguished.

1. *Rule orientation.* A reference to the fact that there are binding rules (e.g., "Stealing is not allowed; one ought to share/help; one ought to keep promises") sometimes

Table 5. *Example of Moral Development Tasks (Waves 2, 4, and 6) – Story 1: Theft*

Episode 1

This is Florian and this is Thomas. They are in the cloakroom in their kindergarten/school, hanging up their coats. Thomas takes a bag with sweets out of his pocket and shows them to Florian. "Look, my aunt gave me these sweets." Florian likes this kind of sweets very much.

Episode 2 (temptation)

Later on, Florian is back in the cloakroom, where Thomas left his coat with the sweets. He is all by himself. He thinks about taking the sweets out of Thomas's coat.

Control Question: "Does Florian want to have the sweets?"

Test Question 1: Knowledge of rule: What do you think? Is Florian allowed to take the sweets? Or is he not allowed?

Test Question 2: Justification of rule: Why is he/why is he not allowed to?

Control comment (if response "no" to Test Question 1): Florian also knows that this is not allowed.

Episode 3 (transgression)

Now Florian goes to Thomas' coat, takes the bag with the sweets out of his coat, and puts it into his pocket. Then he goes back to the classroom. Nobody has seen him.

Episode 4

Soon afterwards children go out to play in the yard. Thomas puts on his coat. He notices that the sweets are no longer there. He does not know where they are. Thomas is sad.

Test Question 3: Emotion ascription to wrongdoer: How does Florian feel?

Test Question 4: Justification of emotion ascription: Why does he feel the way he feels?

Note: The girls received a version with girls as story figures.

qualified by specific context considerations, such as a reference to the relatively low costs incurred by the protagonist in fulfilling the positive duty (e.g., Story 4, helping: "S/he will still be able to fulfill part of the task.") or a reflection upon whether the recipient deserved help (e.g., Story 4, helping: "S/he was sick when instructions were given.").

2. *Moral evaluation.* Reference to the moral evaluation of the wrongdoer or the transgression (e.g., "Otherwise s/he'll be mean/a thief/will have a bad conscience; stealing/not helping/not sharing/breaking a promise is mean/unfair").

3. *Victim orientation.* Reference to the specific needs of the child affected by the rule transgression (e.g., "Victim is sad/is thirsty/would also like to have the prize/does not know how to fulfill the task/the others would have liked to go swimming, too.").

4. *Sanction orientation.* Reference to any consequences ensuring to the protagonist, such as: the workings of concrete reciprocity (e.g., "Next time the others will not return help/share either."); to impending reactions by adult authorities, spontaneously mentioned by some children despite the fact that adults had not been included in the stories presented (e.g., "The teacher will say it was nice/bad; Mother will scold/praise."); to negative institutional sanctions ("S/he will be put in jail."); or to positive or negative sanctions by peers ("The other children will/will not like him/her.").

The intercoder agreement was between 94% and 97%, and disagreements were resolved by consensus.

Table 6. *Moral Development Tasks (Wave 8)*

Story	Content of moral duty	Type of conflict	Content of conflicting issue
Story 1: Fun	Keep a promise (Cleaning up mess after party)	Moral/hedonistic	Engaging in a more pleasant activity (e.g., going swimming)
Story 2: Event	Keep a promise (Cleaning up mess after party)	Moral/ special interest	Attending a special and unique event (e.g., ballet, circus performance...)
Story 3: Course	Keep a promise (Cleaning up tents after class trip)	Moral/long-term personal interest	Registering for a summer camp course (e.g., computer course, theater group...)
Story 4: Helping	Keep a promise (Cleaning up tents after class trip)	Moral/moral	Taking home a small child that got lost
Story 5: Intervening	Intervene upon observing classmates deriding a new student who happens to stutter	Moral/fear	Fear of self becoming victimized

Moral Motivation – Global Coding Procedure

In Wave 8, a global evaluation[3] procedure was devised to assess the strength of
moral motivation. The following types of indicators were used: moral versus strategic
justification of spontaneously mentioned action decisions, attempts at repair following
a transgression, switch from moral to amoral emotion attributions to self as wrongdoer
when a transgression was seen to remain undetected, and indignation at a classmate's
transgression (Story 3: classmate broke promise because he went to register for a
summer camp course) if own transgression in the same situation is presented as
legitimate. The raters' task was to form an overall impression of the importance a child
attributed to the moral domain by paying special attention to these types of indicators,
recognizing that individual indicators were neither necessary nor sufficient for the
global impression. The question guiding raters' evaluations was, How likely is the
child to behave in a moral way in a real-life situation? Participants were classified into
one of seven categories: (a) naively amoral (moral concerns were not mentioned at all),
(b) predominantly amoral, (c) strategic moral, (d) moral strategic, (e) predominantly
moral, (f) rigidly moral (answers were "moral" but stereotyped in manner; the protocol
left the sense of low conflict intensity, indicating either that morality was already
integrated into the self, so that little temptation was experienced in moral conflicts,
or that social desirability considerations mediated the moral self-presentation), and

---

[3] I am grateful to Augusto Blasi for advising me on the development of the global evaluation procedure.

Table 7. *Measures in Moral Development Tasks (Wave 8)*

Measurement of personal desires/interests to be used in conflicts	
What would you most like do on a sunny afternoon (e.g., swimming, playing table tennis, meeting with friends . . .)?	Story 1
Which special event would you most like to attend (e.g., championship match, ballet performance, circus . . .)?	Story 2
Which course would you most like to take in a 2-week summer camp (e.g., computer course, horseback riding . . .)?	Story 3
Moral judgment	
You promised to take part in tidying up the mess/cleaning the tents – but you'd rather (fun/event/course/helping). Do you think it is right not to participate in cleaning up but rather to . . .?	Stories 1, 2, 3, and 4
How wrong do you think it was, when you decided not to keep the promise because you wanted to (fun/event/course/helping): very wrong, somewhat wrong, neither right nor wrong, somewhat right, totally right.	Stories 1, 2, 3, and 4
You observe that the new student is being made fun of. Do you think this is right or not?	Story 5
Justification of moral judgment	
Why do you think it is right/wrong to not keep the promise but to (fun/event/course/helping)	Stories 1, 2, 3, and 4
Why is it right/not right to deride the new student?	Story 5
Emotion ascription to self as wrongdoer	
You decided to (go to fun/attend the unique event/register for the course/help the child). How would you feel?	Stories 1, 2, 3, and 4
Emotion ascription to self as deceived	
You kept your promise and went to the cleaning up; there you learn that another classmate didn't come, because he went to register for a summer camp course. How would you feel ?	Story 3
Emotion ascription to self as bystander	Story 5
You did not intervene upon watching the new student being made fun of. How would you feel?	
Justification of emotion ascription to self as wrongdoer/deceived/bystander	Stories 1, 2, 3, 4, and 5
Why do you feel . . . ?	

(9) flexibly moral (moral argumentation despite high identification with conflicts, realistic and credible attempts at repair, transgression assumed as legitimate for the self is also allowed for others, and reference to universalizability of moral argumentation). After coder training, 60 protocols were coded by two independent raters. There was perfect agreement in 89% of the cases; disagreement occurred mainly for the third and fourth categories (strategic moral and moral strategic). Disagreements were resolved by consensus. For some of the analyses to be reported, the categories were further collapsed to define three groups: low moral motivation (1 and 2, naively and predominantly amoral, respectively), middle (3 and 4; mix of strategic and moral concerns); and high (4, 5, and 6, predominantly, rigidly, and flexibly moral).

Testing for the Validity of Moral Motive Measures: Moral Behavior

Assessment. Four episodes were conducted to assess children's behavior in real-life moral-temptation situations (for details see Asendorpf and Nunner-Winkler 1992; Nunner-Winkler and Asendorpf 1994).

In Episode 1 (Wave 3, age 5.11),[4] children were individually involved in a guessing game in which they could win an attractive prize. The experimenter left them alone for awhile, providing an opportunity to cheat (i.e., peek at the hidden objects) without risk of detection. Cheating behavior was recorded, and the validity of the norm not to cheat in this situation was explored in a posttask interview.

In Episode 2 (Wave 4, age 7.2), triads of children had to come to an agreement about the distribution of scarce resources; sharing behavior was recorded.

In Episode 3 (Wave 8, age 10–11), the child profited unjustifiably from an error made by an unknown experimenter; the child's reporting of this was recorded.

In Episode 4 (Wave 8, age 10–11), two children unknown to each other were to determine the order of viewing short films by operating a chance device. Unknown to the children, this device was biased to constantly favor one child – the "winner"; turn taking and adjustments were recorded. The norms holding for winners and losers were explored in a posttask interview.

Coding Procedure. The following types of behavior were coded as immoral: touching or uncovering the hidden objects in Episode 1; ruthlessly enforcing one's own interests (by pushing away other children, grabbing the desired resources, and refusing proposals for fair bargaining procedures) in Episode 2; not correcting the experimenter's error in Episode 3; and the loser's pressing hard on the winner in order to gain access to the filmbox in Episode 4.

Q-Sort Assessment

Kindergarten teachers (Wave 3) and parents (Wave 7) provided Q-sort assessments of children's typical reaction patterns and personality characteristics on a shortened version of the California Child Q-Set (CCQ; Block and Block 1980; for the German version compare Göttert and Asendorpf 1989).

Cross-Sectional Analysis: Results and Discussion

Moral Understanding

Results: Rule Validity. As can be seen from Figure 1, by age 4–5, at the first measurement almost all (96%) children held the negative duty (not to steal) to be valid, and a majority believed the positive duties to be valid (61% in Story 2: sharing drink; 65% in Story 3: sharing prize; and 82% in Story 4: helping). By age 8–9, the acceptance

---

[4] The design of this study was developed in cooperation with Beate Sodian and Angelika Weber.

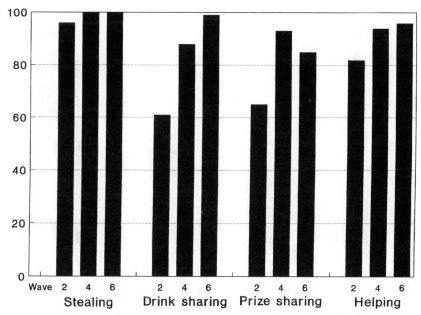

Figure 1. Percentage of children judging rule to be valid in Waves 2, 4, and 6.

of the positive duties rose to 87% in Story 2 (sharing drink), 89% in Story 3 (sharing prize), and 98% in Story 4 (helping).

Results. Justification for Rule Validity. With the exception of Story 2 (sharing a drink) the overwhelming majority of children across all waves justified the rules on deontological terms. That is, they referred to a binding obligation to follow the rule, or expressed a moral condemnation of the transgression or the wrongdoer. A small number (between 2% and 18%) mentioned consequences ensuing to the victim and a small number (between 1% and 12%) referred to positive or negative sanctions by authorities or peers. Story 2 presented a striking contrast: over two thirds of the children in Wave 2, almost half in Wave 4, and still almost a third in Wave 6 justified an obligation to share by referring to the welfare of the needy child (cf. Figure 2).

Results. Exceptions to Rules (tested only in Wave 8). Children's acceptance of a transgression of a moral obligation (breaking a promise) varied with the reason: Only 4% of the children believed one could break a promise just because another favorite pastime was available. This increased to 29% (with 11% giving amoral justifications) when the alternative was attending a very special and unique event, and to 42% (with 26% giving amoral justifications) when the alternative was to enroll for a highly desirable course. In contrast, 92% said the promise could be broken (with virtually no amoral justifications) when the reason was to take care of a small lost child (cf. Figure 3).

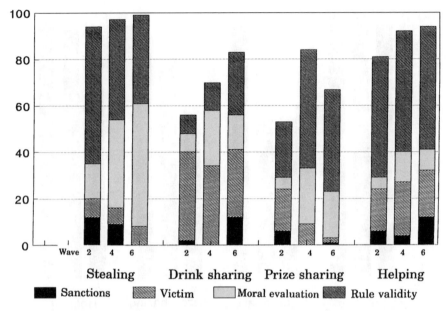

Figure 2. Percentage of children justifying rule by referring to . . . in Waves 2, 4, and 6 (children who gave no justification for their validity judgment are omitted).

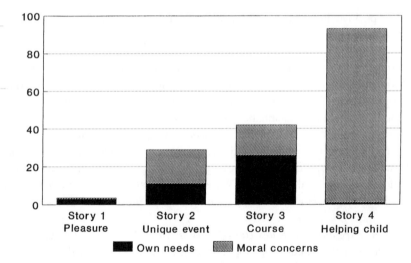

Figure 3. Percentage of children justifying an exception to the rule "promise-keeping" in different contexts in Wave 8.

Discussion. These data show that most children gave intrinsic validity to simple moral rules from very early on. That is, they saw them as binding, independent of authorities and sanctions. This is consistent with Turiel's (1983) findings. Also, most children gave *situation-specific justifications:* The needs of the victim were rarely mentioned in Story 1, yet were frequent in Story 2. This corresponds quite well to adults' prima facie moral understanding that it is always wrong to steal (one may not even take away wealth from the rich) but that the positive duty of sharing a drink only arises from the concrete needs of the thirsty. This distinction was even more clearly evident in children's justifications for the obligation to share in Stories 2 and 3. Despite the surface similarity of these two stories, children rarely referred to the needs of the victim in Story 3, but rather they argued that there was a general duty not to profit from clear-cut injustice, regardless of concrete consequences to those involved. This suggests that even young children grasped the essence of deontic moral thinking: There are individual rights (i.e., the right to enjoy one's possessions in Story 1 and the right not to be cheated in Story 3) that have a categorical obligatoriness that is not dependent on utilitarian considerations.

Nevertheless, at least by age 10–11, moral rules enjoy prima facie validity only (i.e., they are not accorded exceptionless validity). Some children morally justified breaking a promise in the face of conflicting personal interests or value commitments (Stories 2 and 3); most did so in the face of a contradictory norm (Story 4). Moral justifications were to indicate that breaking a promise could be justifiable from an impartial point of view (considering costs and benefits ensuing to all persons involved), especially if reparation was offered. Thus, contrary to Kant (1979), who maintained that strict negative duties must never be broken, children not only allowed (Stories 2 and 3) but even required breaking a promise when doing so would prevent much greater harm (Story 4). This departure from Kantian strict deontological moral thinking may reflect the historical change from an "ethics of intentions" to an "ethics of responsibility" (Weber 1956). Adequately adopting an ethics of responsibility, however, requires that morality is not seen simply as a set of ready-made rules to be strictly followed; rather it is important to understand the basic principles of morality: the command not to do harm (or avert harm) and the principle of impartiality. The fact that about 80% of the children justified breaking the promise in Story 4 by referring to the harm that would be averted from the child or his or her parents shows that they could apply moral principles in a contextualized way and that they were not limited to fixed rules.

Strength and Type of Moral Motivation – Emotion Attributions

Results: Emotion Attributions. Figure 4 shows the percentage of children attributing negative emotions to the moral wrongdoer across Waves 2, 4, 6, and 8. The percentage of children who attributed a negative emotion to the wrongdoer increased with age. Although the majority of children in Wave 2 were clearly aware of the validity of the moral rules (as shown earlier in Figures 1 and 2), they nonetheless expected the wrongdoer to feel good after transgressing (because the wrongdoer's own desires were satisfied). Only between 24% (Story 1) and 36% (Story 4) of the children expected the wrongdoer to feel bad. By Wave, 6 between 48% (Story 4) and 77% (Story 1) expected the wrongdoer to feel bad. In Wave 8, 96% expected to feel bad after having broken a promise to do something more enjoyable.

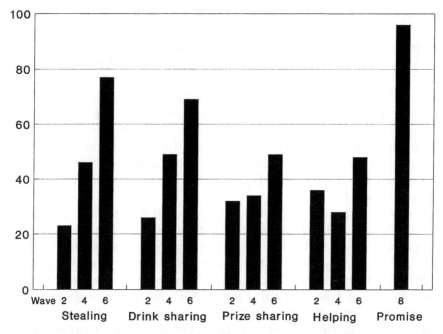

Figure 4. Percentage of children attributing a negative emotion to a hypothetical moral wrongdoer in Waves 2, 4, and 6.

Results: Type of Moral Motivation. When justifying why they expected the wrong-doer to feel bad, the majority of children referred to deontic concerns; that is, to the validity of the norm or to the intrinsic badness of the transgression or the wrongdoer (e.g., feels bad because he or she stole, he or she should have helped/shared; what he or she did was mean, and he or she was bad) (cf. Figure 5). Across all stories in Waves 2, 4, and 6, only 18% of the children referred to sanctions, and 18% referred to negative consequences ensuing to the victim.

Discussion. The high incidence of younger children's amoral emotion attributions is a surprising result: Older children and adults expect a wrongdoer to feel bad and as-sume that younger children share this same expectation (cf. Zelko, Duncan, Barden, Garber, and Masters 1986). The finding is robust, however. It results neither from a generalized positive bias (younger children expect a protagonist who resists a temp-tation [e.g., does not steal desirable sweets] to feel bad because he or she does not have the sweets), nor from a preference for tangible profits (younger children expect a wrongdoer who intentionally hurts another child for no physical benefit to feel good), nor from a failure to understand morally relevant emotions (even young children expect a protagonist who watches another child hurting him- or herself to feel em-pathy and compassion and expect an ill-intentioned protagonist who unintentionally hurts another child to feel regret and remorse; cf. Nunner-Winkler and Sodian 1988).

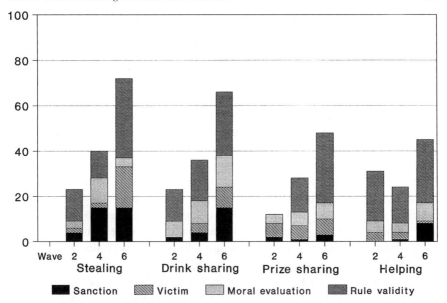

Figure 5. Percentage of children justifying a negative emotion attribution to a moral wrongdoer in Waves 2, 4, and 6 (children who did not justify a negative emotion attribution are omitted).

Neither are these amoral emotion attributions because of cognitive deficits: Most children at age 4–5 were able to integrate outcome and intentions: They expected a protagonist who successfully does what he or she wants to do (e.g., steals the sweets she wants to have) to feel good, and they expected a protagonist who does not do what he or she wants to do (e.g., resists the temptation to steal), or does what she does not want to do (e.g., unintentionally hurts another child), to feel bad. Nor are these findings because of lack of empathy: Children are quite capable of spontaneous feelings of compassion (i.e., of first-order altruistic impulses). Nevertheless, in a situation in which norms and personal desires collided (a moral conflict), most of the younger children expected a protagonist to feel good after transgressing. They seemed to give preference to the satisfaction of hedonistic desires over conformity to known moral rules (e.g., wrongdoers feel good because they do what they want to do). This indicates that most young children lack moral motivation, the willingness to do the right thing – in case this requires forgoing the satisfaction of personal desires.

The number of children who attributed a negative emotion to a hypothetical wrong-doer increased with increasing age. Older children were more likely to imply that following the norm was more important than satisfying personal interests. This occurred either because morality indeed was more important for older children (growth in moral motivation) or because older children were more aware of the fact that others might evaluate them on the basis of their responses (social desirability; cf. the following section).

The justifications for negative emotion attributions may be taken to indicate the concerns children assumed to motivate norm conformity. Instrumentalistic concerns – that is, the anticipation of external physical or social positive or negative sanctions (punishment or reward or social acceptance or rejection) – did not figure very prominently in children's justifications. Thus, for most, moral motivation was intrinsic.

When they explained why the wrongdoer felt bad, most children said a specific moral duty was obligatory in a given situation (he or she should have shared/helped), or they passed a negative judgment on the moral wrongdoer or the immoral act (he or she was mean, unfair, a thief, a miser or what he or she did was wrong, mean, unfair, etc.). Only a few children referred to the welfare of the victim of the transgression (i.e., assumed norm conformity was motivated by empathy or compassion). This was especially clear in Story 2: Although most children justified an obligation to share (rule validity) by referring to the victim's needs, they rarely mentioned the victim's welfare when explaining why the protagonist felt bad after not following the norm. Most children simply stated that he or she felt bad because it was wrong not to share, because he or she ought to have shared, or because he or she was a miser, and so forth. This suggests that moral motivation was formal for most children; that is, it was a "content-free" generalized disposition to do what is right because it is right. What it is that is the "right thing" to do must be decided in each concrete situation through a contextualized moral judgment process.

This interpretation is different from traditional conceptualizations of moral motivation: From a Freudian perspective, specific rules are internalized and generate a need for rigid adherence (e.g., punctuality as an end in itself, irrespective of contextual conditions); in Parsonian theory, motives are culturally transformed need dispositions that direct actions without conscious awareness or explicit reflection (i.e., without moral judgment). In contrast, I want to suggest that there is an analytical distinction between a moral judgment process that considers concrete contexts and moral motivation that is not tied to specific contents but that is a formal readiness to follow whatever is recognized as the right thing to do in a given situation.

Moreover, I suggest that moral motivation is best conceptualized as a second-order desire (cf. Frankfurt 1988). The attribution patterns for Story 4 in Wave 2 illustrate the difference between characterizing moral motivation as first-order altruistic inclinations and conceptualizing it as a second-order desire (i.e., as a desire that stems from a willingness to take a stance toward one's own spontaneous impulses and to act only upon those that are deemed morally justifiable). In this story, one protagonist helped a child even though it meant achieving less of a personally relevant outcome, whereas another did not help but achieved more. Responses showed that most children assumed that both protagonists, the helper and the nonhelper, would feel good because they each did what they wanted to do (i.e., fulfilled their own first-order desires and felt good thereafter). This attribution pattern does not indicate moral motivation. For, although it is good if a person acts on altruistic impulses, as is true of the helper, it is not moral. Altruistic impulses are neither necessary nor sufficient for moral behavior.

Moral motivation requires doing what is right, not only when one spontaneously feels like it but also when doing it is counter to one's first-order desires – be these altruistic or egotistic ones.

Strength of Moral Motivation – Global Coding (Wave 8)

Results. Table 8 shows the number and percentage of children classified according to the global coding procedure into each of seven categories of moral motivation strength. As can be seen, 41% displayed a purely or predominantly strategic orientation, 24% were conflicted about the relative importance of instrumental versus moral considerations, and 36% gave a clear preference to moral concerns.

Table 9 gives the percentage of children who attributed moral emotions in at least three of the four stories in Wave 8 as a function of moral motive strength category. This cross-classification shows that emotion attributions are no longer a good indicator for moral motivation: Almost half of those classified as mainly amoral and most of those at higher levels gave moral emotion attributions.

Discussion. The fact that the majority of children in Wave 8 were more self-serving than moral in their concerns lends some support to Kohlberg's (1976, 1984) global description of preconventional morality as mainly instrumental. Yet, a look at individual differences produces a more differentiated picture. By the age of 10–11 (still in the preconventional stage), over one third of the children demonstrated a strong moral motivation. Moral motive strength was independent of intelligence or rule understanding. Thus, counter to Kohlberg's assumptions, moral motivation may be analytically independent of moral knowledge and moral understanding.

The fact that some of the children rated low in moral motivation nonetheless gave moral attributions suggests that emotion attribution is no longer a reliable indicator of moral motivation. This may be because of increased attention to social desirability. By age 10, most children have become aware that others evaluate them (cf. Perner and Wimmer 1985; Selman and Byrne 1974). Even many younger children know that a person who feels bad after wrongdoing is judged to be morally better (cf. Nunner-Winkler and Sodian 1988). Children begin to make use of this knowledge in order to present themselves favorably and attribute negative emotions to self as wrongdoer only around age 8. Moral attributions, although not necessarily indicative of moral motivation, do indicate that morality is not totally irrelevant to these children – at least they want to appear moral.

Testing for the Validity of Moral Motive Measures

Moral Behavior

Results. In *Episode 1* (Wave 3; cf. Nunner-Winkler and Sodian 1989), 91 children were given an opportunity to cheat without risk of detection in a guessing game (and

Table 8. *Number and Percentage of Participants in Moral Motive Strength Categories*

	Amoral			Middle			Moral				
Measurement	Naively	Mainly	Σ	Amoral–moral	Moral–amoral	Σ	Mainly	Rigidly	Flexibly	Σ	ΣΣ
n	17	57	74	20	23	43	31	28	6	65	182
%	9	31	41	11	13	24	17	15	3	36	100

Table 9. *Percentage of Children with High–Low Moral Motive Strength Attributing Three or Four Moral Emotions in Stories 1–4*

Moral emotions	Naively amoral (n = 17)	Mainly amoral (n = 57)	Amoral–moral (n = 20)	Moral–amoral (n = 23)	Mainly moral (n = 31)	Rigidly moral (n = 28)	Flexibly moral (n = 6)	Σ (n = 182)
Three or 4 moral emotions	18	47	65	74	77	82	83	62

Table 10. *Number of Cheaters and Noncheaters Among Children Who Attributed Moral Emotions*

Number of moral emotion attributions	Cheaters	Non cheaters
0	24	10
1 or 2	20	12
3 or 4	5	12

Note: $\chi^2(2, N = 83) = 8.2, p < .05$.

tempted to do so by the promise of an attractive reward for success). Three noncheaters were excluded from further analyses because they had detected the camera. Among the remaining 88 participants, 51 (58%) cheated. In the posttask interview, 97% of the children explicitly stated that cheating was not allowed in that situation. For 83 of these children, there were data available on their emotion attributions to hypothetical wrongdoers in Wave 2. Table 10 shows the number of cheaters and noncheaters among children who attributed moral emotions to the protagonist in most, some, or none of the stories in Wave 2.

Although 71% of those children with no moral emotion attributions and 63% of those who gave one or two morally oriented answers cheated, only 29% of those with three or four morally oriented emotion attributions cheated. Thus, consistent moral attributions did predict cheating behavior. There was no significant difference in intelligence among cheaters and noncheaters.

Behavior, of course, will never be fully explained by one motive disposition alone. To explore other influences, we looked at the role of inhibition in further analyses (cf. Asendorpf and Nunner-Winkler 1992). The assumption was that some children might have refrained from cheating because of their subdued temperament, not because of moral scruples. Inhibition toward strangers was assessed in Waves 2 and 4 by the same eight-item parental scale (for details see Asendorpf 1990). For the present analysis children's emotion attributions at age 5–7 (Waves 2 and 4) were aggregated to provide a more robust measure. To explore the relations between moral emotion attributions, inhibition, and cheating behavior, we cross-classified children by median split emotion attribution and inhibition scores. Additionally, children with scores in the lower tercile for both number of moral emotion attributions and inhibition were compared with children with scores in the upper tercile of both distributions, using the remaining children as a control group, in order to test the effects of extremes in the combination of moral emotion attributions and inhibition.

Table 11 presents the means and standard deviations for these analyses. An analysis of variance (ANOVA) showed a main effect for moral attributions, $F(1, 84) = 7.95, p < .01$, and for inhibition, $F(1, 84) = 6.95, p < .01$, and no interaction. These

Table 11. *Cheating Means and Standard Deviations for Children Low or High in Number of Moral Emotion Attributions and Inhibition*

Children		Cheating[a]		
Inhibition	Moral	n	M	SD
Low	Low...	23	.83	.39
Low	High...	28	.58	.50
High	Low...	18	.57	.51
High	High...	23	.28	.46
Very low in both...		11	1.00	.00
Controls...		66	.58	.50
Very high in both...		11	.18	.40

[a] 1 = cheating, 0 = noncheating.

effects, tested by a linear contrast within an ANOVA, were additive: Low-moral unin-hibited children cheated the most, high-moral inhibited children cheated the least, and controls were in between. The contrast was both significant, $F(1, 85) = 17.62$, $p <$ .0001, and of a substantial effect size (nearly 1 SD). An inspection of the group means for the two extreme groups indicated that the cheating behavior of the 22 consistent children could be predicted in 91% of the cases. All of the low-moral uninhibited children cheated, and with only two exceptions, none of the high-moral inhibited children cheated (see Table 11).

In *Episode 2* (Wave 4; Asendorpf and Nunner-Winkler 1992), 126 children were randomly assigned to triads of three unfamiliar same-sex peers. Each group was asked to come to an agreement as to how to distribute scarce resources (one child could watch a funny movie, one child could look through a kaleidoscope, and one child could just watch the others). Triads were cross-classified by a median split on the triadic moral motivation and inhibition scores. An ANOVA explored the relationship between the number of moral emotion attributions, inhibition, and the number of egotistic reactions (e.g., grabbing the kaleidoscope, pushing other chil-dren away, and so forth). There were significant effects for moral emotion attribu-tion, $F(1, 38) = 7.47$, $p < .01$, and inhibition, $F(1, 38) = 6.38$, $p < .02$, that were qualified by an interaction between moral emotion attribution and inhibition, $F(1, 38) = 5.97$, $p < .02$. Further analyses revealed that the number of egotistic reactions is a function of group composition: Three children classified as moral, inhibited, or both, easily came to an agreement; the presence of one low-moral unin-hibited child hardly increased the number of egotistic acts, but the presence of two did so clearly, and of three such children did so dramatically. This suggests that effects of personality variables such as moral motive strength or inhibition on behavior may depend on context variables, in this case, the composition of the group to become visible.

In *Episode 3* (Wave 8; Nunner-Winkler and Asendorpf 1994), 149 children were given a chance to profit unjustifiably from an experimenter's error. One hundred and twenty (80%) of the children corrected the error, and there was no correlation between this behavior and moral motive strength as (assessed by the global rating procedure) or inhibition.

In *Episode 4* (Wave 8; Nunner-Winkler and Asendorpf 1994), 32 dyads of same-sex unfamiliar peers were told that they could see a series of 10 short slapstick films; but for technical reasons, only one person could view the film at a time. They were also told that a chance device had been installed in order to ensure about equal viewing time for both participants. However, unknown to the participants, this device was biased. The two participants alternated only for the first 2 films, and one participant was then consistently favored for the following 8 films. Posttask interviews showed that an overwhelming majority, winners as well as losers, judged that winners had a right to enjoy good luck in this situation, which, by implication, losers had a moral duty to respect. Two scales were constructed for rating participants' behavior after the winners' consistent luck had become obvious: winners' sharing behavior (stepping back from the film box, passing the earphones to the loser, and offering to share) and losers' distance (keeping at a reasonable distance from the winner or from the film box rather than trying to push in on or shove the winner away).

To explore the relationship between moral motivation, inhibition, and behavioral responses (winners' sharing behavior and losers' distance behavior) children were cross-classified by median split for their moral motive and inhibition scores. There was a highly significant main effect of losers' distance on winners' behavior, $F(1, 56) = 27.78$, $p < .0001$; that is, winners shared more with pushy losers. There was a significant main effect of losers' moral motivation on losers' distance, $F(1, 48) = 6.10$, $p > .01$, that is, losers with higher moral motivation kept more at a distance. There were no significant main effects of winners' moral motivation or inhibition on winners' behavior, nor of losers' inhibition on losers' distance, nor any significant interactions between winners' or losers' moral motivation, inhibition, and their respective behaviors.

Discussion. There was a significant correlation between moral motive strength (assessed by number of moral emotion attributions in Episodes 1 and 2 and the global coding procedure in Episodes 3 and 4) and moral behavior in three of the four episodes: Children who consistently expected a moral wrongdoer to feel bad after transgressing at age 4–6 were less likely to cheat (i.e., to transgress a norm they held to be valid for the given situation). They were also less likely to insist egotistically on realizing their own interests at the cost of their peers in the triadic conflict situations; instead, they were more likely to try to find a fair solution. Children who were rated as high in moral motivation at age 10–11 on the basis of interview data were less likely to try ruthlessly to fulfill their own needs at the cost of a peer who, from their perspective, legitimately enjoyed better luck. There was no correlation between moral motive strength and correcting the experimenter's error in Episode 3: Eighty percent of the children corrected the experimenter; the lack of a relation may have been due to ceiling effects or because children may have had nonmoral concerns (e.g., they may have suspected detection or wished to display publicly their own honesty or alterness).

These experimental results provide validation for the two types of measures used for assessing moral motivation: emotion attribution and the global coding procedure. As Episodes 1 and 2 show for children between the ages of 4 and 6, moral emotion attributions to hypothetical wrongdoers indicate moral motivation. The theoretical rationale underlying the operationalization of moral motivation by emotion attributions is thus confirmed for younger children: Young children project what they themselves expect to feel in a similar situation to a hypothetical protagonist. And children expect to feel good when they successfully realize their intentions and bad when they fail to do so. The valence of the emotion attributed (good–bad) thus provides information about the intentions the child assumes to be dominant: Expecting the wrongdoer to feel bad implies that the child assumed the wrongdoer wanted to follow the norm more than he or she wanted to fulfill the conflicting personal desires. The predictive power of this expectation for children's behavior may be accounted for by two different – though concordant – bases: From one, emotions indicate subjective importance: Expecting the wrongdoer to feel bad shows that the child attributes high subjective importance to norm following (and will wish to follow the norms because this is deemed important). From a more functionalist perspective, anticipating negative emotions after wrongdoing might motivate norm conformity in order to avoid feeling bad after transgression.[5]

For older children, moral emotion attributions were no longer a valid measure for moral motivation, probably because of a desire to present themselves favorably by stating what they know to be a more moral answer (e.g., that they expect a person to feel bad after wrongdoing). The *global rating procedure*, in contrast, did measure moral motivation as is shown by the correlation between the global rating and moral behavior: Losers high on moral motivation respected the winners' right to enjoy good luck; losers with low moral motive strength put pressure on the winners – which proved quite successful because winners were more likely to share when pressured. Winners' sharing behavior, however, was independent of their moral motivation. This is not surprising as posttask interviews showed that neither winners nor losers held a sharing rule to be valid in this situation.

Episode 3 failed to show an influence of moral motivation on behavior: There was little variance in behavior and there was (as only became obvious with hindsight) no way of classifying behavior as moral because correcting the interviewer was displayed for a variety of different moral and nonmoral motives.

---

[5] An analogous distinction can be found in the literature on achievement motivation. According to Heckhausen (1989), the motivating force for achievement behavior lies in the anticipation of positive emotions following success. In theoretical conceptualizations emphasizing intrinsic components (e.g., competence motive and flow effect), behavior is taken to be motivated by the desire to master a challenging task, and the positive emotions are seen merely as a by-product of accomplishment.

Table 12. *Q-Sort Correlates of Children High or Low in Moral Motivation (Age 11)*

		Moral motivation		
	Teacher sort (age 6)	High ($n = 53$)	Low ($n = 67$)	p
2	Is considerate and thoughtful of other children	6.62	5.67	.015
6	Is helpful and cooperative	6.92	6.15	.042
11	Attempts to transfer blame to others	3.62	4.68	.026
13	Characteristically pushes and tries to stretch limits; sees what she or he can get away with	3.70	4.94	.019
24	Tends to brood and ruminate or worry	3.77	3.03	.043
28	Is vital, energetic, lively	5.62	6.96	.002
34	Is restless and fidgety	3.13	4.56	.004
66	Is attentive and able to concentrate	6.87	5.89	.031
80	Teases other children (including siblings)	2.91	3.76	.050
	Parent sort (age 10)	High ($n = 58$)	Low ($n = 68$)	
9	Develops genuine and close relationships	6.33	5.68	.050
13	Characteristically pushes and tries to stretch limits; sees what she or he can get away with	4.81	5.87	.017
34	Is restless and fidgety	3.09	4.44	.007
46	Tends to go to pieces under stress, becomes rattled and disorganized	3.41	4.44	.012
37	Tends to dramatize or exaggerate mishaps	4.14	3.30	.036
67	Is planful, thinks ahead	6.33	5.41	.022
74	Becomes strongly involved in what she or he does	5.72	4.91	.036
76	Can be trusted, is dependable	7.57	6.91	.046

Note: Only items are reported that are significant, at least at the level of .05. Item numbers correspond to the original number of the CCQ.

Teacher–Parent Q-Sort Assessments

A further assessment of the validity of moral motivation measurement was provided by Q-sort ratings. The descriptions provided by Q-sort ratings from kindergarten teachers (Wave 3, when children were 5–6 years old) and parents (Wave 7, when children were 9–10 years old) were compared for the groups rated as high or low in moral motivation (Wave 8, global rating at age 10–11).

Results. Table 12 lists all items in which significant differences were found; Table 13 lists those two items that kindergarten teachers and parents rated as most and least characteristic of children who had been classified as high or low in moral motivation in Wave 8. As can be seen from Table 12, teachers had judged children who several years later were rated as high on moral motivation to be more likely to behave in ways that seem morally adequate than children rated low in moral motivation (i.e.,

Table 13. *Most–Least Characteristic Q-Sort Correlates of Children High–Low in Moral Motivation*

Most characteristic		Least characteristic	
Teacher sort			
Moral motivation high			
Gets along well with other children	7.25	Is aggressive	2.69
Uses and responds to reason	7.19	Teases other children	2.91
Moral motivation low			
Is curious, exploring, and eager to learn	7.00	Resorts to more immature behavior	2.94
Is vital, energetic, and lively	6.96	Tends to brood, ruminate, and worry	3.03
Parent sort			
Moral motivation high			
Can be trusted, is dependable	7.57	Is inhibited and constricted	2.14
Gets along well with other children	7.51	Resorts to more immature behavior	2.21
Moral motivation low			
Gets along well with other children	7.47	Resorts to more immature behavior	2.37
Is helpful and cooperative	7.39	Is inhibited and constricted	2.54

to be more considerate, more helpful and cooperative, less likely to transfer blame to others, less likely to push and stretch the limits, and less likely to tease others). They also judged them to be more reflective and self-controlled (i.e., more likely to brood and ruminate, to be attentive and able to concentrate and less likely to be restless and fidgety, vital, energetic, and lively). The two attributes chosen as most–least characteristic fit this picture (cf. Table 13): Children high on moral motivation were judged to be most likely to get along well with other children and to use and respond to reason and least likely to be aggressive and tease other children. Children low in moral motivation, in contrast, were judged to be more vital and less contemplative.

The differences between children high or low in moral motivation that resulted from parents' ratings less often involved morally significant items. Children high in moral motivation were rated as more likely to be dependable and less likely to stretch the limits. Most differences, however, referred to self-control variables: Children high in moral motivation we judged to be less restless and fidgety, less likely to go to pieces under stress, more likely to be planful, and more likely to get involved in what they do. In addition, they were said to be more likely to dramatize mishaps and to develop genuine relations. The items chosen as most and least characteristic for children high or low in moral motivation were almost identical: Both groups were described to be most likely to behave in a positive way (i.e., to get along well with other children and be either dependable or cooperative) and least likely to display undesirable characteristics (e.g., be inhibited or resort to immature behavior).

Discussion. Teacher ratings differentiated the high and low moral motivation groups in a meaningful manner: The high moral motivation group was judged as more moral and more self-controlled. Aspects of self-control may be morally relevant personality assets inasmuch as moral motivation requires taking a stance toward and controlling one's own spontaneous impulses when these conflict with moral concerns. Teachers' ratings thus provide some additional support for the validity of the global rating procedure. In view of the considerable time lag between the two measurements (teachers had rated the children at age 5–6; the global rating for moral motivation was based on children's responses at age 10–11), the finding of relevant differences between the two groups is quite remarkable. It also supports an interpretation given to the longitudinal analyses of developmental paths in the growth of moral motivation (cf. the following section on strength of moral motivation) that pointed to the age of 6–7 as a decisive period for the emergence of moral motivation.

Parents' ratings did not differentiate the criterion variable as well. This may be due to several reasons. It may be more difficult for parents to rate their children on normative behaviors. Teachers have experience with many different children that may allow them to develop implicit standards of "normal" behavior, and they may be in a better position to judge each child. Furthermore, parents may be more likely to express social desirability and choose positive moral attributes as most characteristics for their child.

To conclude, teachers' Q-sort ratings of children at age 5–6 who were rated as high or low in moral motivation at age 10–11 provided additional validity for the measurement of moral motivation by the global rating procedure; they also supported the interpretation that there were behavioral precursors for later development of high moral motivation by age 6.

Longitudinal Analyses: Development of Moral Motivation

Two issues were raised by the cross-sectional results: one about the *strength of moral motivation* and the other about the *type of moral motivation*. For both issues the question arises whether aggregate cross-sectional results reflect individual development. Before presentation of results, some hypotheses are briefly discussed as follows:

> 1. *Continuous Versus Discontinuous Growth in Moral Motivation Strength*
>   The cross-sectional analyses documented a steady increase in the number of moral emotion attributions with age. Does this finding correspond to continuous developmental paths on the individual level ? Is it possible to predict to the strength of moral

motivation in Wave 8 (age: 10–11) as assessed by the global coding procedure from moral emotion attribution in Waves 2, 4, and 6 (age: 4–5, 6–7, and 8–9 years)?

2. *Stability Versus Change in Type of Moral Motivation*
Cross-sectional analyses showed that there are different types of justifications of moral rules and moral emotion attributions: deontic concerns, emphatic concerns (reference to the consequences of wrongdoing to the victim), and concerns over sanctions. Two questions arise from this finding: (a) Are there stable individual preferences for one specific type of justification? Such a hypothesis is, for example, suggested by Gilligan's (Gilligan and Wiggins 1987) distinction between different types of selves evolving from early childhood experiences: an autonomous self that mainly focuses on rights and duties (i.e., deontic concerns) and a relational self that focuses on care and responsibility (i.e., emphatic concerns; cf. Gilligan and Wiggins 1987). On the other hand, preferences for specific justification types may be context dependent (i.e., related to the type of dilemma presented) or may change over development. (b) Do the different types of justifications indicate different predictions for moral development; that is, is it possible to predict moral motivation at age 10–11 (Wave 8) from the types of moral justifications used at ages 4, 6, and 8 (Waves 2, 4, and 6)?

Strength of Moral Motivation: Continuous Versus Discontinuous Growth in Waves 2, 4, and 6

Results. The number of negative emotion attributions justified by truly moral concerns (e.g., the rule is valid, transgression or the transgressor is mean, and victims' needs are thwarted or not met – references to sanctions are excluded) was grouped into three levels: low (0), middle (1 or 2), or high level (3 or 4). Individual developmental trajectories were then calculated for all children for whom data in Waves 2, 4, and 6 were available ($n = 179$). Three patterns emerged: One hundred and seven children

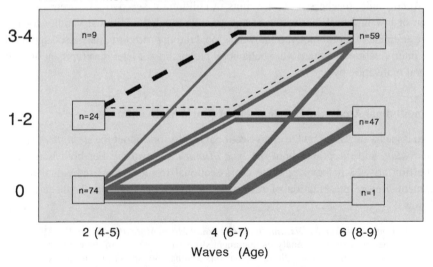

Figure 6. Number of children who at age 8–9 attributed as many or more moral emotions as they had at ages 4–5 and 6–7.

Number of moral emotion attributions

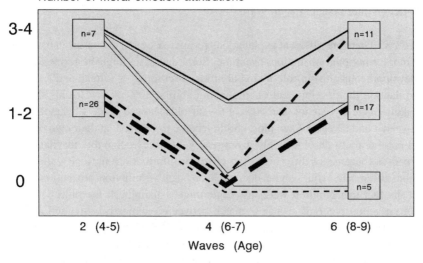

Figure 7. Number of children who at age 6–7 attributed fewer moral emotions than they had at age 4–5, and at age 8–9 as many or more than at 6–7.

Number of moral emotion attributions

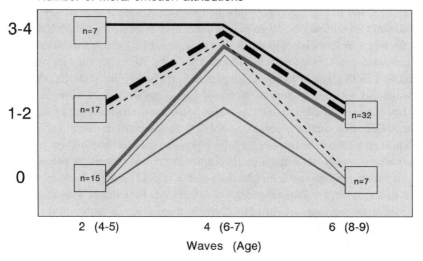

Figure 8. Number of children who at age 6–7 attributed more moral emotions than at ages 4–5 and 6–7.

(61%) showed constant or rising paths. Figure 6 shows the trajectories within this pattern: Eighty-seven children moved up either one (51 children) or two steps (36 children), and 20 remained at a constant level. The second pattern was shown by 33 children (19%) who demonstrated a fall and rise movement, as shown in Figure 7; this pattern resulted in a net growth of one step for 7 participants. The third pattern, shown in Figure 8, was shown by 39 children (22%) who showed a rise and fall movement; of these, 7 moved down a level, and the rest ended up at their starting level after an intermediate rise in Wave 4.

Discussion. There are different explanations for increases and decreases in the number of moral emotional attributions over time: Some decreases might be a consequence of a developmental shift in role-taking abilities. According to Selman and Byrnes's (1974) data on the development of role-taking ability, 80% of 4-year-olds showed role-taking Stage 0 behavior, and 90% of 6-year-olds showed Stage 1 behavior; that is, between 4 and 6 years of age most children come to realize that their own perception is not a copy of an objectively given reality, and they come to understand that other people (because of differing perspectives or information) may view the same situation differently. Thus, some decreases in negative emotion attributions may reflect the fact that children were just beginning to distinguish the objective badness of an action outcome from the match between a subjective intention and an outcome. This interpretation accords with Yuill's (1984) findings that 3-year-olds attribute negative emotions to a protagonist who hurts others because this is an objectively bad action. Older children, in contrast, understand that the protagonist intended to commit a bad act and expected him or her to feel good because the protagonist succeeded in doing what he or she wanted to do. Most decreases, however, reflected the fact that some children became aware of sanctions with increasing age, and negative emotions justified by fear of sanctions were not coded as moral emotion attributions. Rises may reflect either growing moral motivation or they may result from social desirability concerns. It is likely that social desirability concerns did not influence younger children's answers. Although younger children realized that feeling bad after wrongdoing is morally better than feeling good, this knowledge did not induce them to ascribe negative emotions to a wrongdoer. Instead they "naively" attributed to the protagonist the same emotion they expected to feel themselves in a similar situation. Social desirability concerns are possible only when children possess the relevant cognitive prerequisites. When children become aware that others may judge them by their answers (in one theoretical perspective, when they have reached the self-reflexive Stage 3 of role taking, which according to Selman and Byrnes's data, about 50% of 8-year-olds have done), then they have the cognitive prerequisites to attempt to present themselves favorably to the interviewer. Correlations between types of developmental paths through Waves 2, 4, and 6 and the strength of moral motivation at Wave 8 may shed some light on these questions.

Strength of Moral Motivation: Developmental Paths Through Waves 2, 4, and 6 and Moral Motivation at Wave 8

Results. We analyzed whether different developmental paths in the growth of moral motivation (assessed by the number of moral emotion attributions across Waves 2, 4,

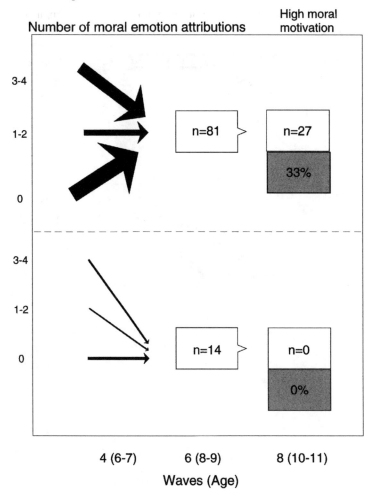

Figure 9. Number and percentage of children with high moral motivation at age 10–11 who at age 6–7 had attributed some versus no moral emotions.

and 6) could predict high moral motivation in Wave 8 (assessed by the global coding procedure).

Prior moral judgments were irrelevant to the developmental path (constant, rising, and falling) leading to Wave 6 responses for children whose Wave 6 performance was at a low (0) or middle (1–2) level. However, regardless of earlier responses, Wave 6 responses did predict Wave 8 performance: One third of those with middle-level performance in Wave 6 were rated as high in moral motivation in Wave 8, whereas none of the children low in moral motivation in Wave 6 were high in moral motivation in Wave 8 (see Figure 9).

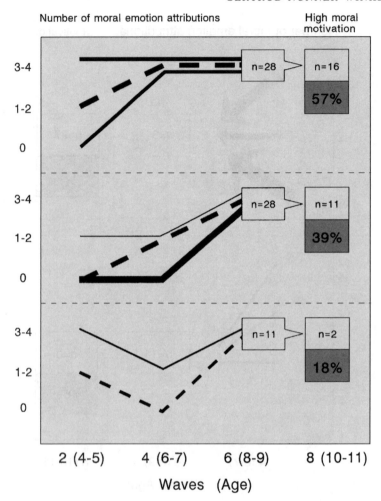

Figure 10. Number and percentage of children with high moral motivation at age 10–11 who at age 6–7 attributed 3–4 versus 1–2 versus 0 moral emotions.

The developmental pattern from Wave 2 on did matter for children who were high in moral emotion attributions in Wave 6 (see Figure 10): Of those who were already high in Wave 4, 57% were still high in moral motivation in Wave 8; among those who were not consistent before Wave 6 but who had a steadily rising path ($n = 28$), 39% were high in moral motivation in Wave 8; and among those who had a falling and rising path ($n = 11$), only 18% were high in moral motivation in Wave 8.

Discussion. It was not possible to predict later moral motivation from the number of moral emotion attributions at age 4–5 (Wave 2). At age 6–7 (Wave 4), however, differential predictions were possible: Of those who consistently attributed moral emotions at age 6–7, a majority (57%) were high on moral motivation at age 10–11 (Wave 8); of those who inconsistently attributed moral emotions at age 6–7, 33% reached the highest level of moral motivation at age 10–11; and of those who never attributed moral emotions at age 6–7, none was high in moral motivation at age 10–11. The prediction from age 8–9 (Wave 6) to moral motivation at age 10–11 (Wave 8) was less powerful. We interpret this as due to the fact that by age 8–9, most children have self-reflexive role-taking abilities and thus may modify their answers because of social desirability concerns. That is, emotion attributions no longer reflect the personal importance of the moral domain alone but also (sometimes exclusively) reflect the child's desire to present him- or herself as moral.

The suggestion that the age of 6–7 marks a crucial period in the development of moral motivation is supported by results of a Q-sort of morally relevant items provided by kindergarten teachers for the children around age 6 (see earlier section on teacher–parent Q-sort assessments). At this age, Q-sort results differed significantly for children high and low in moral motivation at age 10–11. It is noteworthy that this age period has also been marked as decisive for moral development by theorists from quite different perspectives (e.g., Freud and Erikson).

Types of Moral Understanding

Children's justifications for rule validity and negative emotion attributions in Waves 2, 4, and 6 were classified into three categories: deontic concerns (reference to rule validity and moral evaluation of either the act of transgression or the wrongdoer), empathic concerns (reference to consequences ensuing to the victim), or sanction orientation (reference to the consequences ensuing to the wrongdoer). The number of times each of these concerns was mentioned was added across all stories for each child at each wave, yielding scores for the number of deontic, empathic, sanction-oriented and unclassifiable responses (2 justifications per story × 4 stories = score from 0–8). To assess patterns for the type of justification given and developmental changes in mentioning different moral concerns, means and cross-correlations between these scores were calculated for Waves 2, 4, and 6. In addition, we calculated the number of participants who were consistently below or above the mean for each wave across all the waves.

Results. Figure 11 shows the means for each variable across all waves. As can be seen, there was a steady decrease in the frequency of the no-response category and an increase in deontic concerns. There were rather low average values in empathic concerns and very low means in sanction orientation. Table 14 shows the distribution of mentioning each concern across waves. In all, all children mentioned deontic concerns at least once, 32% of the children never referred to sanctions, and 7% never referred to empathic concerns. There was considerable variety within children in

Table 14. *Number and Percent of Children giving Type of Moral Justification across Waves 2, 4, and 6*

	Sanctions		Empathic concerns		Deontic concerns	
Type	n	%	n	%	n	%
Never	58	32	12	7	0	0
Above the mean for that wave	6	3	19	11	14	8
Below the mean for that wave	0	0	11	6	39	22

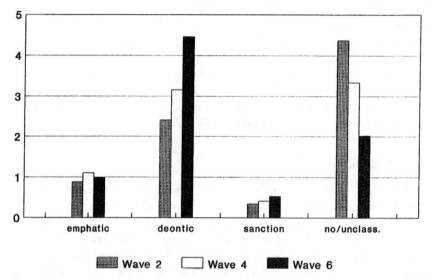

Figure 11. Average number of times children mentioned empathic, deontic, or sanction-oriented concerns in justifying rule-validity and negative emotion attributions in Waves 2, 4, and 6.

the concerns mentioned: Only a few children (sanction 3%, deontic 8%; and empathic concerns 11%) consistently mentioned one specific concern across all three waves with more than average frequency. Fewer than one fourth (sanctions 0%, empathic 6%, and deontic 22%) was consistently lower than average over all three waves.

To look at the effects of justification type on Wave 8 moral motivation, we entered all variables with a correlation coefficient higher than .15 into a multiple regression analysis. Only deontic concerns were related to the strength of moral motivation at Wave 8. The contribution of deontic concerns at Wave 4 was marginal, but at Wave 6 it was clearly significant ($p < .001$). Table 15 presents the pattern of deontic concerns in Wave 4 and 6 and percentages of children high in moral motivation at Wave 8. As can be seen, the percentage of children high in moral motivation at Wave 8 is related

Table 15. *Deontic Justifications in Waves 4 and 6 and Moral Motivation in Wave 8*

Deontic concerns (Wave 4)	Deontic concerns (Wave 6)	n	High in moral motivation (Wave 8)	
			n	%
Low[a]	Low	36	9	25
High[a]	Low	53	17	32
Low	High	35	14	40
High	High	46	21	46

Note: Indicates below and above wave-specific means.

to deontic concerns in Wave 4 and Wave 6 and is highest for those children who were consistently high in deontic concerns over time.

Discussion These findings suggest the following interpretation: Practically all children between 4 and 8 years of age came to understand that empathic and deontic reflections are important concerns in the moral domain, and most also expressed concern with sanctions, although here one third of the sample did not. There were no signs of either a stable person-specific preference for one type of concern or a fixed developmental sequence in acquiring an understanding of these concerns. Emphasizing the deontic nature of morality at age 6–7, and even more so at age 8–9, predicted high moral motivation at age 10–11. Stressing empathic concerns or mentioning sanctions, in contrast, were not related to high moral motivation.

Conclusion

Kohlberg's (1976, 1981, 1984) assumption of a cognitive–affective parallelism in moral development and his description of childhood moral understanding as instrumental have not been corroborated by the present findings. In agreement with Turiel's (1983) findings, the present data suggest that the basics of cognitive moral understanding (i.e., an appreciation of the intrinsic and categorical validity of simple moral rules) seem to be (almost) universally comprehended from very early on. Furthermore (at least by the end of childhood), children understand that exceptions to moral rules are justified when – impartially judged – greater harm can be avoided by transgressing. This suggests that children's moral understanding includes a grasp of abstract principles and is not just rote learning of concrete rules. Their adequate cognitive moral understanding, however, by no means implies that they are competent moral actors. Rather, an overwhelming majority of younger children will "happily" transgress in order to satisfy their own needs when these collide with known and well-understood moral commands. This is compatible with findings from altruism research that children happily commit altruistic acts (i.e., help others, even at their own costs) if they feel like doing so. What younger children lack is moral motivation as a (second-order) disposition to fulfill moral obligations, even when moral conformity does not coincide with their spontaneous desires. Growth of moral motivation is a slow second step in the moral learning process, and it is one that shows large individual differences. The moral domain was an important concern for only one third of the children at age 10–11, and 40% were still willing to transgress if this was in their own interest, provided there was no social control. This finding may explain why Kohlberg interpreted early moral understanding as instrumental: He inquired about action recommendations that children low in moral motivation would guide along strategic cost-benefit calculations, irrespective of their quite adequate cognitive moral understanding. Of those children, however, who had an early start in making morality an important personal concern, almost all did so for intrinsic reasons, mostly for deontic (and not empathic) concerns: They want to do what is right simply because it is right.

This description of early moral development raises several questions concerning: (a) the explanation of the two different types of moral learning processes, (b) the implications for Kohlberg's theory of moral development, and (c) the sociopolitical consequences of the type of moral motivation described in the present study.

(a) How do children acquire an understanding of the intrinsic validity of moral rules? Two mechanisms are plausible. First, acquiring the moral "language game" (to borrow from Wittgenstein) may play an important role in this learning process. In everyday language, all terms denoting transgressions (e.g., theft or murder) are impregnated with negative evaluations, and the fact that these acts are to be condemned is part of the very meaning of the words. Additionally, the intrinsic badness of these acts is quite often emphasized by indignation in the tone of the speaker's voice; sanctions need not be and usually are not mentioned. Second, rule understanding is acquired by social interactions. Nucci and Lee (1993) showed that parents convey the strict validity of moral rules by remaining firm in cases of disciplinary conflicts involving moral rules while being willing to enter into a bargaining process when conventional rules are involved. From these experiences, children may construct an understanding of the categorical obligatoriness of moral commands that contrasts with the merely conventional basis of social rules.

How do children acquire moral motivation? This was not directly assessed in the LOGIC study. Different theoretical traditions imply different facilitative contexts and learning mechanisms: use of sanctions and rewards, effecting conditioning (Skinner); display of command over source recources or competences giving rise to imitation and modeling (social learning theory) and parental use of power or of love withdrawal resulting in identification with the aggressor or in anaclitic identification (Freud, Parsons). I should like to suggest another more intrinsic learning process: Children may attach importance to the moral domain by way of coming to appreciate their parents' high valuation of morality. Research on exceptional achievements in other value domains (e.g., in sports, music, chess, and so forth) of "highly gifted" children may illustrate this type of learning process: It has been shown (cf. Freeman 1993; Sloane 1985) that these children perform well not so much as a result of their unique natural endowments but rather because of their special commitment. This commitment grew in the context of warm relationships with parents who themselves valued the respective domains and supported their children's efforts at becoming competent participators. Parents did not reward their children for their achievements – they took good performances for granted; they did, however, show genuine interest in their children and joy at their growing mastery. Children thus came to estimate the specific value domains for their own worth. These findings agree well with research on the growth of intrinsic motivation (cf. Deci 1975). In a similar way, children may personally come to value morality when their parents' behaviors and ways of resolving conflicts between themselves and with their children show genuine respect for fairness concerns and the dignity of the person (cf. Nunner-Winkler in press).

(b) What are the implications for Kohlberg's theory of moral development? If it is indeed true that the basics of moral understanding are acquired early in development, what then is left to develop in the moral domain? Moral development reduces to two aspects: the development of sociocognitive understanding and the growth of moral motivation. Sociocognitive development includes several dimensions: an increase in formal role-taking abilities, a deepening of the understanding of complex motives acquired through experience (cf. Döbert and Nunner-Winkler 1985a, 1985b, for the distinction between formal and content-bound role taking), the development of an extended time perspective, growth in the understanding of long causal sequences and feedback loops, growth in the understanding that higher order systems cannot be reduced to member characteristics, and so forth (cf. Adelson 1971; Merelman 1969). Moral motivation, in contrast, requires a commitment to the moral domain, making morality an important personal concern, a "personal project," a core element of the identity. Both moral motivation and sociocognitive understanding are necessary prerequisites for an adequate application of moral principles to increasingly complex situations.

(c) The conceptualization of moral motivation as an intrinsic formal second-order desire contrasts with other theoretical conceptualizations of moral motivation, such as fear of external sanctions or desire for social acceptance (focused on in social learning theories), a rigid internalization of concrete rules (implied in the psychoanalytic construct of the superego), a cultural transformation of needs during early socialization processes (as contained in Parsons's (1964) concept of need dispositions), or empathic motives (as assumed in research on altruism). It may also be that the bases of moral motivation have changed with societal change. In modern society, conventional or religious rules are no longer enforced by reference to unquestionable authority: rather, when instilling moral obligations, parents and educators now attempt to appeal to children's understanding, which may mean that moral motivation has acquired a more abstract, content-free nature. Such a formal type of motive structure is functional, given the complexities of modern life: It allows the flexibility that is a prerequisite for following an ethic of responsibility (in which one must impartially calculate all costs ensuing to all involved rather than strictly following clearly specified rules). Also, in contrast to empathy, such a structure may motivate abiding by norms, even when individual transgressions would not cause concrete harm to concrete individuals (e.g., tax evasion, cheating insurance companies, and so forth).

On the other hand, this type of more formal motive structure puts a heavy burden on moral judgment: There is no internally anchored blocking device (as might have been provided by religious authority, the superego, or empathy) to stop cruelty or irrational destruction when a person, no matter how mistakenly, believes that his or her actions are morally justified. Thus, in his central concern – namely, in emphasizing the importance of moral judgment – Kohlberg was right after all.

References

Adelson, J. (1971). The political imagination of the young adolescent. *Daedalus, Journal of the American Academy of Arts and Sciences, 12–16: Early Adolescence*, 1013–1051.
Asendorpf, J. B. (1990). Development of inhibition during childhood: Evidence for situational specificity and a two-factor model. *Developmental Psychology, 26*, 721–730.
Asendorpf, J. B., & Nunner-Winkler, G. (1992). Children's moral motive strength and temperamental inhibition reduce their egotistic tendencies in real moral conflicts. *Child Development, 63*, 1223–1235.
Barden, R. C., Zelko, F. A., Duncan, S. W., & Masters, J. C. (1980). Children's consensual knowledge about the experimental determinants of emotion. *Journal of Personality and Social Psychology, 39*, 968–976.
Blasi, A. (1993). The development of identity: Some implications for moral functioning. In G. G. Noam & T. E. Wren (Eds.), *The moral self* (pp. 99–122). Cambridge, MA: MIT Press.
Block, J. H., & Block, J. (1980). The role of ego-control and ego-resiliency in the organization of behavior. In W. A. Collins (Ed.), *Minnesota Symposium on Child Psychology* (Vol. 13, pp. 39–101). Hillsdale, NJ: Erlbaum.
Colby, A., Kohlberg, L., Speicher, B., Hewer, A., Candee, D., Gibbs, J., & Power, C. (1987). *The measurement of moral judgment: Vol. 1: Theoretical foundations and research validation: Vol. II. Standard issue scoring manual*. Cambridge, England: Cambridge University Press.
Damon, W. (1977). *The social world of the child*. San Francisco: Jossey-Bass.
Deci, E. L. (1975). *Intrinsic motivation*. New York: Plenum.
Döbert, R. (1987). Horizonte der an Kohlberg orientierten Moralforschung [Horizons of research on morality in the Kohlberg tradition]. *Zeitschrift für Pädagogik, 33*, 491–511.
Döbert, R., & Nunner-Winkler, G. (1985a). Interplay of formal and material role-taking in the understanding of suicide among adolescents and young adults: I. Formal and material role-taking. *Human Development, 28*, 225–239.
Döbert, R., & Nunner-Winkler, G. (1985b). Interplay of formal and material role-taking in the understanding of suicide among adolescents and young adults: II. Naive suicide theories and the structural approach. *Human Development, 28*, 313–330.
Frankfurt, H. G. (1988). *The importance of what we care about. Philosophical essays*. Cambridge, England: Cambridge University Press.
Freeman, J. (1993). Parents and families in nurturing giftedness and talent. In K. A. Heller, F. J. Mönks, & A. H. Passow (Eds.), *International handbook of research and development of giftedness and talent* (pp. 669–683). Oxford, England: Pergamon.

Gilligan, C., & Wiggins, G. (1987). The origins of morality in early childhood relationships. In J. Kagan & S. Lamb (Eds.), *The emergence of morality in young children* (pp. 277–305). Chicago: University of Chicago Press.

Göttert, R., & Asendorpf, J. (1989). Eine deutsche Version des California-Child-Q-Sort, Kurzform [A German short version of the California Child Q-set]. *Zeitschrift für Entwicklungspsychologie und Pädagogische Psychologie, 21,* 70–82.

Heckhausen, H. (1989). *Motivation und Handeln* [Motivation and action]. Berlin: Springer.

Kant, I. (1979). Über ein vermeintliches Recht, aus Menschenliebe zu lügen [On a putative right to lie for philanthropic concerns]. In K. Voigtländer (Ed.), *Immanuel Kant: Kleinere Schriften zur Geschichtsphilosophie, Ethik und Politik.* Hamburg: Felix Meiner.

Keller, M., & Edelstein, W. (1993). The development of the moral self from childhood to adolescence. In G. G. Noam & T. E. Wren (Eds.), *The moral self* (pp. 310–336). Cambridge, MA: MIT Press.

Kohlberg, L. (1976). Moral stages and moralization: The cognitive-developmental approach. In T. Lickona (Ed.), *Moral development and behavior: Theory, research and social issues* (pp. 31–53). New York: Holt, Rinehart & Winston.

Kohlberg, L. (1981). *Essays on moral development: Vol. 1. The philosophy of moral development. Moral stages and the idea of justice.* San Francisco: Harper & Row.

Kohlberg, L. (1984). *Essays on moral development: Vol. 2. The psychology of moral development. The nature and validity of moral stages.* San Francisco: Harper & Row.

Merelman, R. M. (1969). The development of political ideology: A framework for the analysis of political socialization. *American Political Science Review, 63,* 75–93.

Montada, L. (1993). Understanding oughts by assessing moral reasoning or moral emotions. In G. G. Noam & T. E. Wren (Eds.), *The moral self* (pp. 292–309). Cambridge, MA: MIT Press.

Nucci, L., & Lee, J. (1993). Morality and personal autonomy. In G. G. Noam & T. E. Wren (Eds.), *The moral self* (pp. 123–148). Cambridge, MA: MIT Press.

Nunner-Winkler, G. (in press). Sozialisationsbedingungen moralischer Motivation. [Contexts for the socialization of moral motivation]. In H. R. Leu & L. Krappmann (Eds.), Zwischen Autonomie und Verbundenheit – Bedingungen und Formen der Behauptung von Subjektivität [Between autonomy and connectedness – terms and ways of asserting subjectivity]. Frankfurt a.M.: Suhrkamp.

Nunner-Winkler, G., & Asendorpf, J. B. (1994). Cross-domain: Inhibition and moral motivation. In F. E. Weinert & W. Schneider (Ed.), *The Munich Longitudinal Study on the Genesis of Individual Competencies (LOGIC): Assessment and results of wave eight* (pp. 108–118). Munich: Max Planck Institute for Psychological Research.

Nunner-Winkler, G., & Sodian, B. (1987). Moral development. In F. E. Weinert & W. Schneider (Eds.), *The Munich Longitudinal Study on the Genesis of Individual Competencies (LOGIC): Documentation of assessment procedures used in waves one to three* (pp. 126–130). Munich: Max Planck Institute for Psychological Research.

Nunner-Winkler, G., & Sodian, B. (1988). Children's understanding of moral emotions. *Child Development, 59,* 1323–1338.

Nunner-Winkler, G., & Sodian, B. (1989). Moral development: Emotion attribution and moral behavior. In F. E. Weinert & W. Schneider (Eds.), *The Munich Longitudinal Study on the Genesis of Individual Competencies (LOGIC): Psychological development in the preschool years: Longitudinal results of wave one to three* (pp. 174–182). Munich: Max Planck Institute for Psychological Research.

Parsons, T. (1964). *The social system.* London: The Free Press of Glencoe.

Perner, J., & Wimmer, H. (1985). "John thinks that Mary thinks that . . ." Attribution of second-order beliefs by 5- to 10-year-old children. *Journal of Experimental Child Psychology, 39,* 437–447.

Selman, R. (1980). *The growth of interpersonal understanding.* New York: Academic Press.

Selman, R. L., & Byrne, F. (1974). A structural–developmental analysis of levels of role taking in middle childhood. *Child Development, 45,* 803–806.

Sloane, K. (1985). Home influence on talent development. In B. S. Bloom (Ed.), *Developing talent in young people* (pp. 439–476). New York: Ballantine Books.

Snarey, J. (1985). Cross-cultural universality of socio-moral development: A critical review of Kohlbergian research. *Psychological Bulletin, 97,* 202–232.

Solomon, R. C. (1976). *The passions*. Garden City, NJ: Anchor Press.

Turiel, E. (1983). *The development of social knowledge: Morality and convention*. Cambridge, England: Cambridge University Press.

Walker, L. J. (1986). Cognitive processes in moral development. In G. L. Sapp (Ed.), *Handbook of moral development* (pp. 109–145). Birmingham, AL: Religious Education Press.

Weber, M. (1956). Der Beruf zur Politik. In M. Weber (Ed.), *Soziologie, Weltgeschichtliche Analysen, Politik* (pp. 67–185). Stuttgart: Kröner.

Yuill, N. (1984). Young Children's coordination of motive and outcome in judgements of satisfaction and morality. *British Journal of Developmental Psychology*, 2, 73–81.

Zelko, F. A., Duncan, S. W., Barden, R. C., Garber, J., & Masters, J. C. (1986). Adults' expectancies about children's emotional responsiveness: Implications for the development of implicit theories of affect. *Developmental Psychology*, 22, 109–114.

Comment: Caring About Morality:
The Development of Moral Motivation
in Nunner-Winkler's Work

Augusto Blasi

The central question that Nunner-Winkler has been pursuing in an interesting series of studies concerns moral motivation, specifically in its relation to moral understanding (Asendorpf and Nunner-Winkler 1992; Nunner-Winkler 1993; Nunner-Winkler and Sodian 1988). To appreciate fully the importance of her question and her approach to it, the significance of her findings, and also some possible problems with her studies, one needs to draw a context, both historical and conceptual. I take this as my first task. Later I address some of the issues that are raised by her research.

The Prescientific Concept of Moral Motivation

Before we put our professional hats on, when we think and interact as normal people with other normal people, what do we mean by "moral motivation"? In a very general sense, we probably refer to the desire to engage in activities that the agent him- or herself considers to be moral because of their moral aspects or qualities. This formula is rather unproblematic as far as it goes, but it has interesting discriminative consequences. Thus, we would not speak of moral motivation if a person tended to perform an action while not grasping its moral meaning, for instance, simply because he or she is told to do it. Similarly, we would not speak of moral motivation if the person understands the moral meaning of an action but is moved by concerns that are quite irrelevant to morality. John, a graduate student, volunteers to work for his professor without asking to be paid. Even though John understands quite well the altruistic aspects of his decision, in fact, he is not motivated by altruism or gratitude but exclusively (if motives are ever so exclusive) by his wish to eventually get a good letter of recommendation. He is aware that his motive is rather selfish and even blushes for it, but "this is what I now need and this is what I want," he tells himself. If we had access to John's well-concealed thoughts and desires, we would not interpret them as relevant to moral motivation. The professor herself may be mistaken about John's motives and may interpret his desire as altruistic, and so may many other people. However, the fact that John's action would be typically interpreted as moral by most people, or the fact that most people in the same situation would be making a similar decision on moral grounds, is irrelevant to whether John's action can be said to be morally motivated.

In summary, when we speak of moral motivation from the perspective of everyday prescientific understanding, we tend to make a number of assumptions: (a) that a person has certain kinds of desires of interests, general or specific that they may be; (b) that these desires are specified by the person's own understanding of the nature of certain actions and motives; (c) that this understanding concerns the specifically moral characteristics of the action; and finally (d) that the desires so specified guide, in principle, the person's intentions and actions, even when, in fact, incompatible desires and interests may be too powerful for moral motives to affect the action. We do not make the same kind of assumptions for other types of motivation. Aggression, for instance, sexuality, or even achievement, may also be recognized in cases in which the agent lacks the understanding of the nature of his or her motives and intentions.

This rather elaborate conceptual introduction may be unnecessary for many of us. However, it is useful sometimes to remind ourselves that whenever social scientists aim to study behaviors that, like morality, are the object of social construction, they must use as their starting point the relevant socially constructed concepts. The main features of what can be called the *everyday understanding of moral motivation* are summarized in Table 1. This view does not carry specific hypotheses concerning which factors would produce moral motivation considered either as a personality characteristic or as a situational process. However, it implies that moral concerns have a necessary relation to moral understanding and interact with the other competing motives of the moment to originate an action, which can be moral, nonmoral, or immoral, depending on which motives ultimately prevail.

Psychological Approaches to the Study of Morality

Interest in moral psychology was present quite early in the history of the discipline on both sides of the Atlantic. As one might expect, psychologists' understandings of what morality is all about and of which questions are worth exploring varied from time to time and were shaped by the cultural preoccupations of each period. In spite of these variations, morality was typically approached, theoretically and methodologically, according to the scientific assumptions of natural sciences, by which psychology wished to be guided. Particularly relevant for us is the idea that moral phenomena can be described objectively; that is, from the perspective of external observers, regardless of, and sometimes against, the personal understanding and intentions of moral agents. Of course, this attitude was not an exclusive property of American behaviorism but was also present in European psychoanalysis and most other theories.

In the area of moral research and theorizing, this view is concretized in the concept of internalization, which, with important differences, is common to both psychoanalysis and learning theories. The learning theory tradition is well represented in the following definition provided by Grusec and Goodnow (1994): "Taking over the values and attitudes of society as one's own so that socially acceptable behavior is

Table 1. *Theoretical Approaches to Moral Motivation*

Antecedent factors	Intraorganismic variables	External manifestations
Everyday understanding	Moral understanding ↓ Moral concerns	⟶ Action
Internalization approach (Learning theories) Social causes: Instruction Models ⟶ Reinforcement Parental discipline	⎡ Processing accurate information Accepting social values ⎦	* ⟶ Action
Kohlberg's theory Disequilibrating social factors: Social participation ⟶ Role taking Cognitive conflict	Constructed moral understanding [Moral motivation]	⟶ Action
Nunner-Winkler's approach ?	Constructed moral understanding ↓ ** Moral motivation	⟋ Emotions ⟋ Action

★ [ ] process only inferred
★★⟿ possible, not necessary relation

motivated not by anticipation of external consequences but by intrinsic internal factors" (p. 4). This definition is clear about three aspects of moral behavior, all three objectively and externally definable, at least in principle: The ultimate sources of morality are (a) society's values and attitudes, those that are "taken over" through internalization; (b) morality is "socially acceptable behavior"; and (c) finally, internalization can be inferred by the absence of behavior-contingent punishments and rewards. However, this definition is hopelessly ambiguous concerning the positive determinants of the behaviors; namely, the intrinsic internal factors from which behavior depends and which ought to define internalization (see Table 1, 2; the brackets in which internal variables are placed represent their theoretical and empirical neglect by these approaches). Grusec and Goodnow (1994) explained that social values are taken over as a result of learning through information processes and acceptance. Because learning alone does not explain the motivation to act and because learning is also needed when one is guided by the expectation of external consequences, it is clear that for internalization, the theoretical burden is placed on acceptance, a notion that unfortunately is left unspecified. What does acceptance mean and, most important, what motivates it? Briefly, in its clarity concerning antecedent environmental factors and responses and in its ambiguity concerning mediating processes, Grusec and Goodnow's definition remains tied to its behavioristic influences; it also remains anchored to the research tradition that has attempted to explain socialization by relating socially acceptable behavior to various forms of parental discipline (see, for example, Hoffman 1970, 1984).

From the perspective of the everyday concept of moral motivation, the internalization approach presents two main problems. Cognitively, in the absence of genuine assimilatory understanding, values seem to remain external (i.e., a more or less accurate copy of external beliefs). The accuracy of the copy, as Grusec and Goodnow (1994) emphasized, would depend on the clarity by which the information is presented and on the sophistication of the processes that transform external information into an internal copy. In addition, the nature of moral motivation and behavior remains ambiguous. Acceptance of external values may be determined by a variety of motives, many having little to do with the intrinsic nature of the values themselves.

The dominance of the objectivistic approach to morality in psychology waned with the advent in psychology of the cognitive and interpretive turn. Kohlberg's (Kohlberg 1984) work, in its singlemindedness, was particularly influential in the shift in perspective. However, it should be clear that its influence was one aspect of a widespread understanding, both in philosophy and in the social sciences, that certain objects of human inquiry, primary among them morality, depend on the social construction of meanings. From this perspective, the ideas of structure, logical consistency, and consequently assimilation acquire a central role, freeing the agent from the externality and the literalness of information. Moral meanings, being constructed by the individual in social interaction, would then become personal in a way that could not be accounted for by the theoretical tools of internalization approaches.[1]

However, it is not sufficiently appreciated that several approaches are possible within the basic parameters derived from the common understanding of morality, depending, for instance, on how moral cognition and the relations between moral cognition and motivation are understood. The Kohlbergian approach (see Table 1) has two central characteristics. First, cognition is understood in strictly structural terms: the contents of moral judgment and specific moral values are deemphasized, whereas the logical relations among basic criteria are stressed. Second, following Platonic assumptions, moral cognition and moral motivation are so intrinsically connected that the former ought to lead inevitably to the latter (see, Kohlberg and Candee 1984). In this context, Nunner-Winkler refers to this aspect of Kohlberg's theory as the cognitive–affective parallelism. She and I may disagree on how Kohlberg's views on moral motivation should be interpreted; however, we would agree that

---

[1] It should be pointed out that cognitive sciences can be as objectivistic and scientistic as any of the approaches and theories that preceded them (see, for example, Searle 1992). What here, too, is frequently neglected or even rejected is the role of human intentionality and agency. One can only conclude that many branches of cognitive psychology are as unsuited to studying morality as any of the noncognitive predecessors.

Kohlberg expected that increasing moral understanding (in terms of his stages) would be accompanied by, and would indeed produce, increasing moral motivation. It is in this sense that his theory of moral motivation could be called *rationalistic* and not simply cognitive.

Nunner-Winkler's Approach to Moral Motivation

It is the motivational component of Kohlberg's theory that Nunner-Winkler attempts to question in her work. However, she does so within the basic parameters of the common everyday understanding of morality and also within the basic cognitive assumptions of Kohlberg's theory. Therefore, it may be misleading on her part to speak of the independence of moral motivation and moral cognition. If the two variables were fully independent, it should be possible to find genuine moral motivation in the absence of moral understanding or with a thoroughly pragmatic view of morality, consequences that, as I believe, Nunner-Winkler would not be ready to accept. I should like to stress this point. It has become almost fashionable to criticize and reject Kohlberg's theory. We should not forget, however, that the assumption that morality, by its very nature, requires subjective understanding and intentional agency – and, at least in this sense, is cognitive in nature – is not an invention of Kohlberg. It is not even a hypothesis that can be proven or disproven by facts. We simply cannot speak of moral phenomena when behavior lacks intention and understanding.

Empirically, however, Nunner-Winkler's work did not focus on moral understanding. She needed, and used, a measure of minimal moral understanding, without which she could not test the hypothesis that moral motivation is not a result of moral cognition. However, she did not pursue this line of inquiry in any depth, for instance, by looking at developmental differences in her participants' moral reasoning. Therefore, she cannot answer the question of whether stage differences in moral understanding have an effect on moral motivation. Theoretically, one could hypothesize that a person's level of understanding limits the types of moral issues that he or she can grasp and, therefore, the breadth of his or her moral motivation. To my knowledge, this question has not been addressed yet by anyone.

Nunner-Winkler resorted to some kind of triangulation to infer the presence or absence of moral motivation, relying on both moral emotions and moral action. I believe that this procedure is conceptually very sound: On the one hand, it maintains the definitional relations between motivation and action; on the other hand, recognizing that the motivation–action relation is only probabilistic, it follows the very sensible view that emotions are principally expressions of concerns and seeks in emotions a more direct index. Practically, emotions were assessed both through projective tasks, in which children were asked to guess how wrongdoers in hypothetical stories would feel, and through self-attribution tasks, in which children were asked to describe the feelings they would experience in the wrongdoer's shoes. In both tasks children were asked to explain the reasons for the attributed emotions. Not only is this information necessary to eliminate the ambiguity of emotion words and to guarantee that children's emotions were indeed moral in nature, but it was also used to begin an analysis of the cognitive structure underlying moral motivation. Moral behavior was assessed through a number of experimental tasks, covering cheating, sharing, and fairness situations.

The empirical procedures adopted by Nunner-Winkler are rich, careful, and sensitive to sound theoretical conceptions – more so than what can be found in similar studies. Even so, the reader should be aware of potential problems. For instance, both projective attribution and self-attribution of emotions may be biased by the distorting effects of social expectations, self-concept, and self-presentation. Most likely these factors are less effective with younger children, still naive and not yet concerned with social appearance. However, these processes may already be operative before the age of 11. More important, the capacity for self-presentational concerns to bias emotion attribution is probably not independent of people's awareness of the moral meaning of emotions. For this reason, in her last testing, Nunner-Winkler supplemented the emotion attribution task with global ratings of moral motivation, on the basis of a variety of considerations (including the reasons given for one's projected emotions, spontaneous references to reparation, and the child's sensitivity to the possible detection of misbehavior).

The assessment of moral action still is one of the most vexing and uncertain aspects in moral development research. Some of the problems with experimental procedures are also present in this study. Each concrete situation may not correspond to the specific areas in which a child's moral motivation is strong. Moreover, it is difficult to generalize from a few behavioral situations to an assessment of the overall motivational status of a child. There probably are more reliable ways of assessing moral behavior, based, for instance, on children's everyday interactions, as seen by parents, teachers, and peers. Nunner-Winkler did look at the relations between a shortened version of the California Child Q-Set – an instrument based on teachers' and parent's evaluations of typical behavior – and global ratings on moral motivation. Several of the items statistically differentiated high and low moral motivation children. Unfortunately, these items had been designed to assess ego resilience and ego control rather than moral motivation or moral behavior. It is therefore difficult to interpret the meaning of these findings.

The Findings

In view of Nunner-Winkler's questions, the most important finding is that there seems to be a gap between moral understanding and moral motivation among the large majority of children between the ages of 4 and 6 or 7. In adults, we would expect that those who understand that a specific behavior is morally wrong would experience a residual negative emotion when, for other motives, they decided to engage in it. This was not the case with Nunner-Winkler's participants. They recognized that an action is wrong but said that they would feel good if, by doing it, they achieved what they wanted. In fact, these children do not even seem to understand that, in these circumstances, negative emotions would be appropriate and socially desirable.

These results appear to be quite solid: They were consistently found with several groups of children and with different situations; moreover, they resisted a careful check of possible confounding factors. Similar findings were recently reported in independent studies by investigators who are unrelated to Nunner-Winkler's laboratory (Yuill, Perner, Pearson, Peerbhoy, and van den Ende 1996). One reason why this finding is interesting is that it brings out a real limitation in young children's moral capacities, at a time when many other investigators stress the early development of moral competence.

How should we interpret Nunner-Winkler's results? We cannot say that younger children have no moral motivation or that genuine moral understanding does not give origin to any degree of concern for moral issues. If this were the case, we should entirely discard a cognitive approach to moral development. Nunner-Winkler's careful studies only show that, in cases of conflict between opposite motives, the moral motivation of young children is too weak to influence action or even to produce emotions. Unfortunately, we do not have the evidence to decide which of several explanations ought to be preferred. It is possible that 4- to 7-year-old children do experience shame or guilt in these situations together with happiness for satisfying their nonmoral desires, but they are not quite capable of articulating simultaneous conflicting emotions. It is also possible that they actually do not care enough about morality to experience negative emotions in case of misbehavior.

In my view, at present, we cannot even completely exclude a cognitive explanation, suggesting that children would care more about morality and would experience the appropriate moral emotions if they understood morality better. Answering this questions would require specifying the meaning of "better understanding" and its parameters, as well as a more differentiated assessment of moral understanding than Nunner-Winkler's method – and her children's verbal capacities – allowed us to achieve. On the basis of other studies (e.g., Arnold 1993; Colby and Damon 1992) it seems clear that Kohlberg's stages, at least beyond the preconventional level, do not account for differences in the presence or the intensity of moral motivation.

Nunner-Winkler reported another finding that, if replicated, would carry interesting developmental implications. She classified her participants as having high, medium, and low moral motivation on the basis of the number of stories in which the attributed emotions were congruent with moral judgment (for the first three assessment waves) or on the basis of global ratings (for the last wave). She found then that the probability of an 11- or 12- year-old child (the age corresponding to the last testing wave) being classified as high was partially related to his or her degree of moral motivation in previous testing waves. No child who was "low" at age 8 or 9 was classified as "high" at age 11 or 12. A "medium" child at age 8–9 had a 33% probability to be high at 11–12; the probability rose to 43% if a child was classified as high at 8 or 9 and rose to 57% if a child was classified as high in moral motivation both at ages 8–9 and 6–7. In Nunner-Winkler's understanding, there seems to be something special, particularly about the age period, 6 to 7, that influences later vicissitudes in moral motivation. This is an intriguing hypothesis. It remains to be determined what the "something special" consists of and what is the psychological meaning of attributing moral emotions in two or three or five different stories.

The Development of Moral Motivation

In reading Nunner-Winkler's chapter, one may observe in the author a note of disappointment with her participants' progress in moral motivation from age to age. Although the overall number of moral emotion attributions increased dramatically from age 4 to age 11–12, the number of children that are classified as high (by the global coding procedure) in the last testing wave still is relatively small (35%), and the number of those who were classified as mainly oriented to strategic and instrumental considerations is relatively high (33%).

Perhaps Nunner-Winkler is justified in her pessimism. Perhaps not much change occurs in the development of moral motivation after the age of 10. Perhaps most people do care about morality, but only up to a certain point. The questions I would like to raise, however, are different ones: If there is development of moral motivation after the end of childhood, where should we find it? What does it consist of?

Probably, as Nunner-Winkler recognizes, the extension of moral emotional attributions to an increasing number of situations is only one index, and perhaps not the best, of development in moral motivation. This index may work best if the situations reflect a general sense of morality and the type of moral understanding that corresponds to each child's moral development.

Whether this type of quantitative extension across moral situations occurs, qualitative changes may take place along different dimensions. One dimension is mainly cognitive, namely, on the basis of the understanding of the nature of morality and of what justifies moral emotions. For instance, even though, as it seems, people that are classified at any one of Kohlberg's stages between 3 and 5 can have equally intense moral commitments (cf. Colby and Damon 1992), it is quite possible that different kinds of moral understanding determine the issues to which a person is likely to become committed. A conventional person would not be expected to invest his or her life, on moral grounds, in activities that question legitimate authorities and laws.

Other dimensions, instead, are not specifically moral, but have to do with the way morality is integrated within the person's overall motivational system and the way moral concerns are taken over by the person's agentic structure. Three interrelated personality aspects are particularly important in this respect: the development of a sense of responsibility, both as obligation and as accountability; the increasing sense of the personal importance of self-consistency; and finally, the development of identity, bringing moral concerns within the domain of what is experienced as the core self. I commented elsewhere on the moral importance of these developmental milestones between adolescence and adulthood (Blasi 1984, 1993, 1995).

Their overall effect should be to make one's moral concerns more reliable in determining action and commitment. In this respect, one last dimension should be added; namely, the increasing awareness of defensive and self-deceptive processes and the increasing resistance to their devious effects. According to Loevinger's data (Loevinger, Wessler, and Redmore 1970), one finds evidence of these characteristics only at the most advanced of the ego development stages.

Conclusion

It seems to me that serious study of moral motivation has barely begun. Nunner-Winkler contributes to our understanding in two major ways. First, she framed the question in a most sensible way, one, that is, that respects the role attributed by common sense to moral understanding while rejecting, at the same time, the rationalistic excesses of cognitive developmentalism. Second, she approached the problem empirically through a methodology that is both careful and theoretically driven.

There is a long way to go. One hopes that Nunner-Winkler herself and others influenced by her work will continue in this line of inquiry. However, it seems to me that the emotion attribution paradigm, so effective so far in bringing clarity to the issues, exhausted its potential. If we wish to make progress in understanding moral motivation, we need different approaches that are better suited to the enormous complexity of this aspect of human life and that are more sensitive to the different variables influencing moral motivation at different ages.

References

Arnold, M. L. (1993). *The place of morality in the adolescent self.* Unpublished doctoral dissertation. Cambridge, MA: Harvard University.

Asendorpf, J. B., & Nunner-Winkler, G. (1992). Children's moral motive strength and temperamental inhibition reduce their immoral behavior in real moral conflict. *Child Development, 63*, 1223–1235.

Blasi, A. (1984). Autonomie im Gehorsam: Die Entwicklung des Distanzierungsvermögens im sozialisierten Handeln [Autonomy in obedience: The development of distancing in socialized action]. In W. Edelstein & J. Habermas (Eds.), *Soziale Interaktion und Soziales Verstehen* (pp. 300–347). Frankfurt am Main: Suhrkamp Verlag.

Blasi, A. (1993). The development of identity: Some implications for moral functioning. In G. G. Noam & T. Wren (Eds.), *The moral self: Building a better paradigm* (pp. 99–122). Cambridge, MA: MIT Press.

Blasi, A. (1995). Moral understanding and the moral personality: The process of moral integration. In W. M. Kurtines & J. L. Gewirtz (Eds.), *Moral development. An introduction* (pp. 128–139). Needham, MA: Allyn & Bacon.

Colby, A., & Damon, W. (1992). *Some do care. Contemporary lives of moral commitment.* New York: Free Press.

Grusec, J. E., & Goodnow, J. (1994). Impact of parental discipline methods on the child's internalization of values: A reconceptualization of current points of view. *Developmental Psychology, 30*, 4–19.

Hoffman, M. L. (1970). Conscience, pesonality, and socialization techniques. *Human Development, 13*, 90–126.

Hoffman, M. L. (1984). Parent discipline, moral internalization, and development of prosocial motivation. In E. Staub, D. Bar-Tal, J. Karylowski, & J. Reykowsky (Eds.), *Development and maintenance of prosocial behavior* (pp. 117–137). New York: Plenum Press.

Kohlberg, L. (1984). *Essays on moral development: Vol. 2. The psychology of moral development. The nature and validity of moral stages.* San Francisco: Harper & Row.

Kohlberg, L., & Candee, D. (1984). The relationship of moral judgment to moral action. In L. Kohlberg (Ed.), *Essays in moral development: Vol. 2. The psychology of moral development* (pp. 498–581). New York: Harper & Row.

Loevinger, J., Wessler, R., & Redmore, C. (1970). *Measuring ego development: II. Scoring manual for women and girls.* San Francisco: Jossey-Bass.

Nunner-Winkler, G. (1993). The growth of moral motivation. In G. G. Noam & T. Wren (Eds.), *The moral self: Building a better paradigm* (pp. 269–291). Cambridge, MA: MIT Press.

Nunner-Winkler, G., & Sodian, B. (1988). Children's understanding of moral emotions. *Child Development, 59,* 1323–1338.

Searle, J. R. (1992). *The rediscovery of the mind.* Cambridge, MA: MIT Press.

Yuill, N., Perner, J., Pearson, A., Peerbhoy, D., & van den Ende, J. (1996). Children's changing understanding of wicked desires: From objective to subjective and moral. *British Journal of Developmental Psychology, 14,* 457–475.

13 A Person-Centered Approach to Development: The Temporal Consistency of Personality and Self-Concept

Marcel A. G. van Aken and Jens B. Asendorpf

After Allport (1937) introduced the debate between an idiographic and a nomothetic approach to the study of personality, numerous researchers have joined in to provide extended reviews of this debate to attempt to clarify idiographic methods and to integrate data analytic techniques from both points of view (see, for example, Hermans 1988; Pelham 1993; Runyan 1983). The nomothetic approach is characterized as concerned with a search for general laws and uses between-subjects analyses of personality, whereas the idiographic approach is characterized as concerned with what is specific to the individual and uses analyses of the patterned uniqueness that exists within a person (Hermans 1988; Pelham 1993). As Ozer (1994) noted, the debate between the approaches has often been discussed on a metatheoretical level, addressing issues such as the uniqueness of a person, the universality of psychological principles, and the scientific status of the idiographic approach. According to Ozer, such issues might be reconciled if the approaches are reformulated in terms of the distinction (first proposed by Stern 1911) between variable-centered methods, in which different people are evaluated on single personality traits, and person-centered methods, in which different traits are evaluated within individual persons.

One of the methods widely suggested for a person-centered approach to the study of personality is the Q methodology. Originally described by Stephenson (1953), this methodology has gained attention in personality research through the work of Jack Block, who developed the California Q-Set, a Q-sort method of personality description (Block 1961), and who demonstrated the use of Q methodology in a longitudinal study (Block 1971). Recently, the advantages of the use of the Q-sort method in the study of personality have been summarized by Ozer (1994).

In a Q-sort method, items have to be sorted into ordered categories, according to a specified criterion (e.g., how salient an item is for the description of a person). Items have to be sorted in a forced distribution (i.e., a specified number of items must be placed in each category). This procedure yields a person-centered personality description because the rater has to compare one attribute with others within the same individual: A high rating for an attribute indicates that this attribute is very salient for a person compared with other attributes in the set of items.

Although most person-centered descriptions use a Q-sort format with a forced distribution, another technique is demonstrated by Pelham (1993), who used a participant's scores on five dimensions of a self-concept measure to yield a person-centered description. Pelham showed that person-centered approaches to personality offer insights that cannot be readily gained by variable-centered approaches, even with a free-choice format and only five attributes.

The person-centered approach has been applied very successfully to assess the consistency of personality over time (also referred to as *ipsative stability*, Caspi and Bem 1990). To compute ipsative stability, Q correlations between two Q-sort profiles of the same person on different measurement occasions are performed. In a Q correlation, the set of attributes of a person at Time 1 is correlated with the set of attributes of that person at Time 2. The higher the correlation, the more the configuration of the attributes has remained stable over time.

Block (1971) used this procedure in his Lives through Time study, which looked at personality consistency and change over time. He focused on two time intervals: from early to late adolescence and from late adolescence to adulthood. He found both high mean Q correlations for each interval and also a wide dispersion, which indicates that there is considerable consistency in personality over time, as well as large individual variation in the extent of this consistency. Block analyzed individuals whose personality changed and did not change and found differences in personality characteristics of the two groups and interactions with the time of measurement and the sex of the participant. Block used Q-factor analyses on his data and found a five-factor solution for the male sample and a six-factor solution for the female sample, suggesting five types of personality development patterns for males and six types for females, each with its own correlates in other data sources. Ozer and Gjerde (1989) replicated Block's study with four time intervals (age 3.5 to 7, 7 to 11, 11 to 14, and 14 to 18). They subjected the four Q correlations to cluster analyses and found four male consistency pattern clusters and five female clusters, again with their own personality correlates, this time provided by the content of the Q items that discriminated among clusters.

Using combined data from the LOGIC study and a longitudinal project conducted in The Netherlands (van Aken 1991), we replicated Ozer and Gjerde's (1989) study and extended it with extreme group comparisons of highly consistent, average, and highly inconsistent children (Asendorpf and van Aken 1991). We found Q correlations in both samples that indicated a temporal consistency in personality patterns that was similar to those reported by Block (1971) and by Ozer and Gjerde, both in mean level and in individual variability. Comparing very consistent children and very inconsistent children to a middle group, we found that consistent children were characterized by culturally desirable traits and inconsistent children by undesirable traits. The items typical for consistent children changed with age in agreement with the change in major developmental tasks, from emotional stability and good peer relations in preschool and kindergarten to intellectual capacities and skills in late childhood.

In this chapter, we extend this earlier work in three ways. First, we extend our questions about the consistency of personality in preschool to the consistency of personality from preschool through elementary school. Second, we extend the generality of our approach. Thus far, person-centered studies on temporal consistency have focused on the consistency of personality descriptions, provided by raters. We, too, address this type of consistency but also study consistency in a person-centered way for another domain: children's self-concept. Third, we extend our scope to address the co-occurrence of consistency in both personality and the self-concept. Are these two related to each other; that is, do children whose personalities are described consistently at two time points also describe themselves consistently at two time points? Are the correlates of personality consistency similar to those of self-concept consistency? What are the correlates of "double" consistency or inconsistency or of children who show consistency in personality but not in self-concept, and vice versa?

Method

Participants

We restricted our analyses to the 138 participants (75 boys and 63 girls) in the LOGIC study with nonmissing data on the two main variables of this chapter: personality consistency and self-concept consistency. Independent t tests comparing the 138 participants to the participants that were excluded from the analyses (ns ranging from 10 to 58) showed no significant differences for any of the variables reported in this chapter.

Instrument: California Child Q-Set

To assess standardized personality descriptions of children, we used a German 54-item version (Göttert and Asendorpf 1989) of the California Child Q-Set (CCQ; Block and Block 1980). The procedure was described in more detail in Section 1.4.3 of LOGIC Report No. 2 (Weinert and Schneider 1987). The set of 54 statements about the behavior and personality of the child had to be sorted in a forced distribution into nine categories, ranging from most characteristic for the child to least characteristic for the child, with each category containing six statements. In this chapter, we use the CCQ descriptions of the children given by kindergarten teachers in Wave 3 (age 6) and by the parents in Wave 7 (age 10; procedure described in Section 2.3 of LOGIC Report No. 10, Weinert and Schneider 1993a). These descriptions were used to construct two variables that we discuss here: personality consistency and an ego-resiliency score.

Personality Consistency. For each child, the two Q-sort profiles (in Waves 3 and 7) were correlated. The resulting Q-correlation coefficient was used as an index for the temporal consistency of the child's personality.

Ego-Resiliency. The Q sort of each child was correlated with the Q-sort prototype for an ego-resilient child (Block and Block 1980) in each wave. The resulting correlation coefficients were used as an index for the ego-resiliency of the child.

Instrument: Harter's Self-Perception Profile

Children in Wave 7 (age 10) and Wave 9 (age 12) completed the 30 items of a German version (Asendorpf and van Aken 1993) of the Self-Perception Profile for Children (Harter 1985). This test contains five 6-item subscales that are answered in a two-step 4-point agreement format. The procedure is described in more detail in Section 7.2 of LOGIC Report No. 9 (Weinert and Schneider 1993b). The five subscales refer to children's perceived cognitive competence, athletic competence, peer acceptance, physical appearance, and global self-worth.

Subscale Scores. Scores on the five subscales were formed by averaging the scores on the 6 items for a specific subscale, after recoding items so that high scores indicated positive self-esteem.

Consistency of Self-Concept. For each child, profiles were formed by 24 items in the domain-specific subscales (the subscales listed earlier except for the subscale for global self-worth). These profiles for Wave 7 and Wave 9 were correlated. The resulting Q-correlation coefficient was used as an index for the temporal consistency of the child's self-concept.

Instrument: Intelligence Tests

Because tests for verbal and nonverbal intelligence were distributed across various time points in the LOGIC study, we constructed intelligence scores for Waves 3 and 7.

Wave 3 (age 6). First, an aggregate score for verbal intelligence was constructed by averaging the score on three verbal subtests of the Hannover–Wechsler–Intelligence Scale for Preschool Children (described in Section 1.2.2. of LOGIC Report No. 2, Weinert and Schneider 1987) in Wave 2 and in Wave 4. An overall aggregate score for intelligence was then constructed by averaging this verbal intelligence score with the score in Wave 3 from the Columbia Mental Maturity Scale, a test that assesses children's nonverbal intellectual skills (described in Section 1.2.1 of LOGIC Report No. 2, Weinert and Schneider 1987).

Wave 7 (age 10). An aggregate score for intelligence was constructed by averaging a composite score from Wave 6 on the verbal subtests of the Hamburg–Wechsler– Intelligence Test for Children (described in Section 2.1 of LOGIC Report No. 9,

Weinert and Schneider 1993b) and the score from the Culture Fair Intelligence Test in Wave 7 (described in Section 2.1 of LOGIC Report No. 10, Weinert and Schneider 1993a).

Results

Personality Consistency

In our previous study (Asendorpf and van Aken 1991), we examined the correlates of the temporal consistency of personality patterns in the LOGIC study from Wave 1 to Wave 3 (age 4 to age 6). The consistency of the personality profile was computed by correlating two Q-sort descriptions, provided by a preschool teacher in Wave 1 and in Wave 3. The median Q-correlation ($n = 151$) was .42, with a minimum of $-.44$ and a maximum of .88. We noted that there was large individual variation in consistency, and we conducted correlational and extreme group analyses to detect the correlates of consistency in the child's behavior and personality. We found that children's ego-resiliency predicted the consistency of their personality patterns. Itemwise extreme group comparisons showed that consistent children were characterized by culturally desirable traits and inconsistent children by undesirable traits. In addition, we found that the items typical for consistent children changed with age, in agreement with an assumed change in major developmental tasks. We interpreted this as suggesting the importance of the age appropriateness of personality.

The consistency of the personality profile from Wave 3 to Wave 7 was computed by correlating the two Q-sort descriptions, provided by a preschool teacher in Wave 3 and by a parent in Wave 7. The median correlation across the 138 children was .40, with a minimum of $-.39$ and a maximum of .85. We consider this median correlation from Wave 3 to Wave 7 to be fairly high (and equal to that during preschool), especially given the long period (4 years compared with 2 years in preschool), the use of more judges providing the personality profile (preschool teacher and parent compared with two preschool teachers), and the change in the school context from preschool to elementary school.[1] A small sex difference in the level of the consistency of personality was found, $t(135) = 2.47, p < .05$, whereby boys ($M = .33$) had a lower mean consistency than girls ($M = .43$).

Similar to our findings on personality consistency in preschool, we expected the personality consistency in this later period to be related to a child's ego-resiliency and intelligence, both prospectively and retrospectively. To test this we computed the correlations for ego-resiliency and intelligence in Wave 3 and in Wave 7 with

---

[1] The consistency of personality from age 6 to age 10 can also be compared with Dutch data, with a similar age gap and a change of judge (but no change of school context). There we computed the consistency of personality between a teacher's sort at age 7 and a parent's sort at age 10: The median consistency ($n = 92$) was .36, range $-.20-.69$.

Table 1. *Mean Ego-Resiliency and Intelligence Scores in Wave 3 and Wave 7 for Groups With Low, Medium, and High Personality Consistency*

	Personality consistency			
Wave	Low	Medium	High	F (2,136)
Wave 3				
Intelligence	-0.15_a	-0.03_a	0.22_a	2.09
Ego-resiliency	0.18_a	0.38_b	0.65_c	22.07***
Wave 7				
Intelligence	-0.17_a	-0.09_a	0.26_a	3.44*
Ego-resiliency	0.28_a	0.39_a	0.64_b	21.86***

Note: Means with different subscripts were significantly different (Tukey, $p < .05$).
*$p < .05$.   ***$p < .001$.

the personality consistency between these waves. Our expectations were confirmed: ego-resiliency in Wave 3 correlated .64 ($p < .001$; boys $r = .62$, girls $r = .65$) with consistency, and ego-resiliency in Wave 7 correlated .49 ($p < .001$; boys $r = .38$, girls $r = .58$) with consistency; intelligence in Wave 3 correlated .20 ($p < .05$; boys $r = .26$, girls $r = .12$) with consistency, and intelligence in Wave 7 correlated .17 ($p = .052$; boys $r = .23$, girls $r = .13$) with consistency.

To find out whether these correlational findings should be attributed to higher than average ego-resiliency and intelligence in the group of consistent children or to lower ego-resiliency and intelligence in the group of inconsistent children, we conducted an extreme group comparison. Groups of high, medium, and low consistent children were formed by selecting the upper, middle, and lower thirds of the distribution of the consistency coefficient.

Separate analyses of variance (ANOVAs) were performed on intelligence and ego resiliency, in Wave 3 and Wave 7, with the extreme groups as an independent variable (three levels: low, medium, and high). The results of these analyses are presented in Table 1.

Table 1 shows a confirmation of the correlational results. For intelligence, the differences between the groups were not significant in Wave 3, and, although significant, no clear group differences emerged in Wave 7. For ego-resiliency, both the high-consistent and the low-consistent group differed from the medium-consistent group in Wave 3. No significant differences were found between the low- and medium-consistent groups in Wave 7, but the high-consistent group was clearly more ego-resilient than the medium- and low-consistent groups. No sex effects were found in these analyses.

Similar group comparisons were made by independent t tests on the 54 single Q-sort items in the Q-sort description by the teacher in Wave 3 and by the parent

Table 2. *California Child Q-Set Items in Wave 3 Discriminating Groups With High or Low Versus Medium Personality Consistency*

Item no.[a]	Content
	Characteristics of consistent children
19/34	Is restless and fidgety ($-$)
07/11	Attempts to transfer blame to others ($-$)
43/76	Can be trusted, is dependable
39/66	Is attentive and able to concentrate
01/02	Is considerate and thoughtful of other children
42/74	Becomes strongly involved in what she or he does
03/05	Is admired and sought out by other children
18/33	Cries easily ($-$)
53/95	Overreacts to minor frustrations ($-$)
31/54	Has rapid shifts in mood, is emotionally labile ($-$)
05/07	Seeks physical contact with others ($-$)
40/67	Is planful, thinks ahead
24/41	Is persistent in activities
	Characteristics of inconsistent children
29/48	Seeks reassurance from others about his or her worth
50/89	Is competent, skillful ($-$)

Notes: [a]German/U.S. version. $p < .01$.

in Wave 7. Because of the many tests performed, we considered an item to differ between groups only when the difference was significant at the .01 level. Table 2 presents the items in Wave 3 that characterized the consistent and the inconsistent groups, as compared with the medium group. A factor analysis was performed on the 13 items that discriminated between groups with high and medium consistency. Three factors emerged, explaining 63% of the variance (44%, 11%, and 9%, respectively). The items in Table 2 are grouped in accordance with the factor structure.

In Table 2, we see a confirmation of the pattern found in the extreme group analyses for the ego-resiliency construct: The correlates for the consistent group are far more salient than the correlates for the inconsistent group. We also see that consistent children are characterized by items that fall on three dimensions: (social) competence, such as positive peer relationships, attention, and involvement; emotional stability; and planfulness and independence.

Table 3 presents the items in Wave 7 that characterized the consistent and the inconsistent groups, compared with the medium group. A factor analysis performed on the 14 items discriminating between groups with high and medium consistency produced four factors, which explained 62% of the variance (35%, 10%, 9%, and 8%, respectively). The items in Table 3 are grouped in accordance with this factor structure.

Table 3. *California Child Q-Set Items in Wave 7*
Discriminating Groups With High or Low Versus Medium
Personality Consistency

Item no.[a]	Content
	Characteristics of consistent children
42/74	Becomes strongly involved in what she or he does
19/34	Is restless and fidgety (−)
39/66	Is attentive and able to concentrate
40/67	Is planful, thinks ahead
14/25	Uses and responds to reason
52/94	Tends to be sulky or whiny (−)
31/54	Has rapid shifts in mood, is emotionally labile (−)
53/95	Overreacts to minor frustrations (−)
08/12	Reverts to more immature behavior under stress (−)
33/56	Is jealous and envious of others (−)
32/55	Is afraid of being deprived (−)
48/85	Is aggressive (physically or verbally) (−)
50/89	Is competent, skillful
24/41	Is persistent in activities; does not give up easily
	Characteristics of inconsistent children
51/90	Is stubborn

Notes: [a] German/U.S. version. $p < .01$.

Again, the characteristics of the consistent group were more pronounced than the characteristics of the inconsistent group. The inconsistent group differed from the medium group only in the fact that they were described as "stubborn."[2] Consistent children were characterized by items that fell on four dimensions: the first and largest dimension representing items related to intelligent behavior, a second dimension of emotional stability, a third dimension of jealousy, and a fourth dimension of (social) competence.

A comparison of Tables 2 and 3 shows both similarities and differences. The similarities are that 7 of the 13 items characteristic of a consistent child in Wave 3 are still characteristic of a consistent child in Wave 7. In addition, two factors (emotional stability and competence–independence) seem to be present in both sets of correlations.

These similarities were also suggested by a comparison of the correlates of consistency in Wave 3 and in Wave 7. We correlated all 54 Q items in Wave 3 and all 54 Q items in Wave 7 with the index of personality consistency and then correlated these

[2] Although this concerns only a single item, it might be an important one: In the study by Caspi et al. (1994), this particular item was strongly ($p < .001$) related to self-reported delinquency, to caregiver-reported disruptive disorders, and to teacher-reported externalizing problems.

two vectors of 54 correlations with each other. The correlation between the two vectors was .90 ($p < .001$), which is remarkably high and which indicates large similarity in the salience of the correlates of personality consistency in Wave 3 and in Wave 7.

However, the differences show a similar pattern to that found in our earlier work, in which we compared the LOGIC sample with a Dutch sample (Asendorpf and van Aken 1991). We again found a shift in the characteristics of consistent children. Those items on the (social) competence factor in Wave 3 that explicitly referred to peer relationships disappeared by Wave 7 and were replaced by items referring to intelligent behavior. In our previous article we interpreted such a shift (then demonstrated by a comparison of separate samples) as a reflection of the developmental tasks that are important in a given period of childhood.

In summary, we again see that ego-resiliency predicts and retroactively explains personality consistency, and we again see that items reflecting the age appropriateness of personality are important correlates of personality consistency.

Self-Concept Consistency

The consistency of the self-concept was computed in the same way as the personality consistency. The profiles created by the 24 items of the four domain-specific scales (cognitive competence, social competence, athletic competence, and physical appearance) from Harter's Self-Perception Scale were correlated across Wave 7 and Wave 9. We regarded this correlation as an index of the profile consistency and used it in further analyses. The median correlation over the 138 children was .22, with a minimum of $-.47$ and a maximum of .78. No sex differences in level of self-concept consistency were found.

First, we looked at the relation between self-concept level and self-concept consistency. We correlated each of the four domain-specific scales and the scale for global self-worth with the consistency score. For data from Wave 7, only the scale for physical appearance correlated significantly with self-concept consistency ($r = .23$, $p < .01$; boys $r = .22$, girls $r = .26$). In Wave 9, physical appearance again correlated with consistency ($r = .42$, $p < .001$; boys $r = .42$, girls $r = .48$), as did global self-worth ($r = .25$, $p < .01$; boys $r = .32$, girls $r = .17$).

We expected self-concept consistency to be related to the child's ego resiliency and intelligence. Because data on these two constructs were not available in Wave 9, we were restricted to the predictive correlations in Wave 7 and the long-term predictive correlations with intelligence and ego-resiliency in Wave 3. Our expectations were confirmed: ego-resiliency measured in Wave 7 correlated .24 ($p < .01$; boys $r = .25$, girls $r = .20$) with self-concept consistency and intelligence correlated .31 ($p < .001$; boys $r = .35$, girls $r = .28$). The long-term prospective correlations were of the same order: ego-resiliency measured in Wave 3 correlated .19 ($p < .05$; boys $r = .10$, girls $r = .26$) with self-concept consistency and intelligence measured in Wave 3 again correlated .31 ($p < .001$; boys $r = .45$, girls $r = .13$).

Extreme group analyses were performed to ask whether these correlations should be attributed to characteristics of the consistent group or the inconsistent group. Again,

Table 4. *Mean Ego-Resiliency and Intelligence Scores in Wave 3 and Wave 7 and Self-Concept Subscale Scores in Wave 7 and Wave 9 for Groups With Low, Medium, and High Self-Concept Consistency*

Wave	Self-concept consistency			$F(2,136)$
	Low	Medium	High	
Wave 3				
Intelligence	$-.39_a$	0.12_b	0.29_b	8.11***
Ego-resiliency	$.33_a$	$0.35_{a,b}$	0.52_b	3.21*
Wave 7				
Intelligence	$-.41_a$	0.12_b	0.30_b	9.51***
Ego-resiliency	$.32_a$	0.48_b	0.50_b	5.17**
Cognitive	2.92	2.91	2.88	0.024
Social	3.04	3.03	3.09	0.167
Athletic	3.08	3.06	2.96	0.494
Appearance	3.19_a	$3.34_{a,b}$	3.48_b	3.96*
Global self-worth	3.09	3.20	3.30	1.88
Wave 9				
Cognitive	2.76	2.77	2.74	0.032
Social	3.02	2.94	2.97	0.272
Athletic	2.91	2.97	2.83	0.739
Appearance	2.74^a	3.04_b	3.30_b	12.33***
Global self-worth	2.88_a	$3.02_{a,b}$	3.19_b	4.67*

Notes: Means with different subscripts were significantly different (Tukey, $p < .05$).
*$p < .05$.　**$p < .01$.　***$p < .001$.

the sample was split into three groups, on the basis of the consistency score tertiles. Separate ANOVAs were performed on intelligence and ego-resiliency for Wave 3 and Wave 7 and on the self-concept subscales for Wave 7 and Wave 9, with the consistency groups as an independent variable (three levels: low, medium, and high).

The results of these analyses, presented in Table 4, show a confirmation of the correlational results. In addition, with the exception of ego-resiliency in Wave 3, all of the significant group effects of ego-resiliency and intelligence could be attributed to a difference between the low-consistent group on the one hand and the medium- and high-consistent groups on the other. Children with low self-concept consistency from Wave 7 to Wave 9 were less intelligent in Wave 3 and Wave 7 and less ego-resilient in Wave 7 than children with medium or high self-concept consistency. The group effects for the self-concept subscales did not show a clear pattern. No sex effects were found in these analyses.

A clearer description of the consistent and the inconsistent children was provided by comparing these groups with the medium-consistency group on the 54 Q-sort

Table 5. *California Child Q-Set Items in Wave 7*
Discriminating Groups With High or Low Versus Medium
Self-Concept Consistency

Item no.[a]	Content
	Characteristics of consistent children
20/35	Is inhibited and constricted
41/69	Is verbally fluent, can express ideas well in language
	Characteristics of inconsistent children
20/35	Is inhibited and constricted
46/82	Is self-assertive (−)
47/83	Seeks to be independent and autonomous (−)

Notes: [a]German/U.S. version. $p < .01$.

items from the CCQ description by a parent in Wave 7. Comparisons were made with independent *t* tests, and an item was only considered to differ between groups if the difference was significant at the .01 level.

The results of these tests, presented in Table 5, show that, for self-concept consistency, the number of items discriminating between the consistent and medium and the inconsistent and medium groups is less than for personality consistency. Consistent children were described as being more verbally fluent, inconsistent children as less self-assertive and less independent. A curvilinear relation with the item "Is inhibited and constricted" was found: Both the consistent group and the inconsistent group were described as being more inhibited than the medium group.

In summary, children with high self-concept consistency are characterized by satisfaction with their physical appearance and tend to have higher self-esteem. They are also more intelligent and ego-resilient.

Co-Occurrence of Consistency in Personality and Self-Concept

Our third question concerned the co-occurrence of personality consistency and self-concept consistency. The correlation between the two indices of consistency was .17 ($p < .05$), indicating a small, but significant relation. To compare the correlates of personality consistency with the correlates of self-concept consistency, we correlated all 54 items of the parental Q sort in Wave 7 with personality consistency and with self-concept consistency. We then correlated these two vectors of 54 correlations with each other. The correlation between the two vectors was .66 ($p < .001$), which indicates that the salient correlates of personality consistency and self-concept consistency are fairly similar. Table 6 shows the 10 items with the highest and the 10 items with the lowest correlations (correlations were standardized and then averaged).

Table 6. *California Child Q-Set Items in Wave 7 Correlating Highest and Lowest With Personality Consistency and Self-Concept Consistency*

Item no.[a]	Content
	Items correlating positively with consistency
40/67	Is planful, thinks ahead
39/66	Is attentive and able to concentrate
50/89	Is competent, skillful
42/74	Becomes strongly involved in what she or he does
41/69	Is verbally fluent, can express ideas well in language
14/25	Uses and responds to reason
49/88	Is self-reliant, confident
28/47	Has high standards of performance for self
24/41	Is persistent in activities
43/76	Can be trusted, is dependable
	Items correlating negatively with consistency
44/78	Is easily offended, sensitive to ridicule or criticism
27/46	Tends to go to pieces under stress
09/13	Pushes and tries to stretch limits
19/34	Is restless and fidgety
51/90	Is stubborn
07/11	Attempts to transfer blame to others
52/94	Tends to be sulky or whiny
18/33	Cries easily
31/54	Has rapid shifts in mood, is emotionally labile
53/95	Overreacts to minor frustrations

Note: [a] German/U.S. version.

Table 6 shows that consistent children were described as being more flexible and intelligent, whereas inconsistent children were described as emotionally labile. In a study of the reliability and validity of a Common-Language version of the CCQ, Caspi et al. (1994) determined the personality correlates of self-reported delinquency, caregiver-reported *DSM–III–R* disruptive disorders, and teacher-reported externalizing behavior problems in a sample of 425 boys. A comparison of the items in Table 6 with the items found by Caspi and colleagues to be indicative of problems in adaptive functioning, especially disruptive disorders, showed a large overlap of items: Of the 10 items correlating highest with consistency, 8 were highly discriminative (beyond the .01 level) between boys with and without disruptive disorders. The same was true for 8 of the 10 items correlating highest with inconsistency. Somewhat less strong results were found for externalizing disorders (5 of the 10 items correlating with consistency and 6 of the 10 items correlating with inconsistency) and self-reported delinquency (5 of the 10 items correlating with consistency and 4 of the 10 items correlating with inconsistency).

Table 7. *Cross-Tabulation of High and Low
Personality and Self-Concept Consistency*

	Personality consistency	
Self-concept consistency	High	Low
High	18 (30%)	10 (16.7%)
Low	12 (20%)	20 (33.3%)

Note: $\chi^2(1, N = 60) = 4.29, p < .05.$

We used an extreme group analysis to provide a more complete description of the co-occurrence of personality consistency and self-concept consistency. The same extreme groups of high, medium, and low consistency as described earlier were formed for both consistency variables. Table 7 shows the cross-tabulation of those children who fell into extreme groups on both consistency indices.

A significant chi-square for this cross-tabulation was found, $\chi^2(1, N = 60) = 4.29, p < .05$, confirming the results found for the analysis of the continuous variables. ANOVAs with ego-resiliency and intelligence as dependent variables and the four subgroups (low–low, high–low, low–high, and high–high) as independent variables showed highly significant effects: for ego-resiliency, $F(3, 59) = 15.51, p < .001$, and for intelligence, $F(3, 58) = 4.43, p < .01$. Post hoc contrast tests showed that the main effect of personality consistency was reflected for ego-resiliency: The groups with high personality consistency (high–high and high–low) differed significantly from the groups with low personality consistency (low–high and low–low). A combined effect was found in intelligence: Only the group with high personality consistency and high self-concept consistency (high–high) differed significantly from the group with low personality consistency and low self-concept consistency (low–low). No sex effects were found in these analyses.

In another person-centered data analytic approach to the question of the co-occurrence of personality consistency and self-concept consistency, and of the relation between this co-occurrence and high or low ego-resiliency and intelligence, we classified groups of individuals according to their characteristic pattern of co-occurrence of personality consistency and self-concept consistency and high or low ego-resiliency and intelligence. The patterns were studied by using configural frequency analyses (CFA; von Eye 1990). In this procedure, observed frequencies of all possible variable combinations are compared with expected frequencies. Groups of variables that contain more individuals than expected by chance are labeled *types*, groups of variables that contain fewer individuals than expected by chance are labeled *antitypes*. To test the significance of types and antitypes, standardized residuals for the difference between observed and expected frequencies can be computed ($z = (o - e)/e^{1/2}$) that are

Table 8. *Configural Frequency Analysis of the Two Consistency Indices: Ego-Resiliency and Intelligence*

PC	SC	IQ	ER	Observed %	Expected %	z score	Type/Antitype[a]
−	−	−	−	9.00 (28.13)	1.97 (6.15)	5.0111	Type
−	−	−	+	0.00 (0.00)	1.97 (6.15)	−1.4031	
−	−	+	−	0.00 (0.00)	1.97 (6.15)	−1.4031	
−	−	+	+	1.00 (3.13)	1.97 (6.15)	−0.6904	
−	+	−	−	2.00 (6.25)	1.53 (4.79)	0.3788	
−	+	−	+	0.00 (0.00)	1.53 (4.79)	−1.2374	
−	+	+	−	2.00 (6.25)	1.53 (4.79)	0.3788	
−	+	+	+	0.00 (0.00)	1.53 (4.79)	−1.2374	
+	−	−	−	1.00 (3.13)	2.53 (7.91)	−0.9625	
+	−	−	+	2.00 (6.25)	2.53 (7.91)	−0.3339	
+	−	+	−	1.00 (3.13)	2.53 (7.91)	−0.9625	
+	−	+	+	4.00 (12.50)	2.53 (7.91)	0.9232	
+	+	−	−	0.00 (0.00)	1.97 (6.15)	−1.4031	
+	+	−	+	2.00 (6.25)	1.97 (6.15)	0.0223	
+	+	+	−	1.00 (3.13)	1.97 (6.15)	−0.6904	
+	+	+	+	7.00 (21.88)	1.97 (6.15)	3.5858	Type

Notes: N = 32. Minus signs represent the lower third, plus signs represent the upper third. PC = personality consistency; SC = self-concept consistency; IQ = intelligence; ER = ego-resiliency.
[a] Alpha level adjusted for number of tests: adjusted level $p < .003$ ($|z| > 2.95$).

approximately standard normally distributed. Because of the simultaneous testing of multiple configurations, adjustment of the alpha level is advised (von Eye 1990); for example, by dividing the usual alpha level (.05) by the number of tests.

The CFA results for the patterns of consistency scores, ego-resiliency, and intelligence are presented in Table 8.

Table 8 shows that two significant types were found. The first type consists of children who are in the lower third of personality consistency and self-concept consistency distributions and in the lower third of the ego-resiliency and intelligence distribution. The observed frequency for this type (9 participants) is 4.57 times larger than the expected frequency (1.97 participants). The second type is the opposite in all respects: These children are in the upper third of personality consistency and self-concept consistency distributions and in the upper third of the ego-resiliency and intelligence distributions. The observed frequency for this type (7 participants) is 3.55 times larger than the expected frequency.[3]

[3] Because of the fact that we combined selected groups from the upper or the lower thirds of the distribution of a total of four variables, the number of participants in a cell sometimes becomes very small. To check whether the small cell size did not lead to unreliable findings, we repeated the CFA by using a median split on the four variables concerned, thus keeping all participants in the analysis. The same two types of pattern of the four variables were found, and there were no other types or antitypes.

Table 8 also provides information on other combinations of low and high scores on the four variables. For example, of the 12 children with low ego resiliency and low intelligence, 9 children also have low personality consistency and self-concept consistency, 1 child only has low personality consistency, and 2 children only have only low self-concept consistency. Results are less clear at the high part: Of the 12 children with high ego-resiliency and high intelligence, 7 children also have high personality consistency and self-concept consistency, whereas 4 children have only high personality consistency, no child has only high self-concept consistency, and 1 child has neither.

Looking at it from another perspective, we see that the combination of low consistencies almost always occurs together with low intelligence and low ego-resiliency, never with low scores on only one of these constructs and only once with high scores on both constructs, a pattern that is less clear with high-consistency combinations: Three participants had dual high consistency but only one high score on intelligence or ego-resiliency.

Discussion

Summarizing the results presented here, we see that, for personality consistency, the results found by Block (1971), Ozer and Gjerde (1989), and in our previous work (Asendorpf and van Aken 1991) are replicated. A fairly high median consistency was found, suggesting that there is considerable temporal consistency for most children in the way they are described by others, even when this includes different others over time. However, we also found large individual differences in the temporal consistency of personality, with values ranging from $-.39$ to $.85$.[4]

As in our previous work, we found that personality consistency was related to a child's ego-resiliency. Consistent children were characterized by a higher level of ego-resiliency and inconsistent children by a lower level, across the temporal spectrum. In addition, high-consistent children tended to show more age appropriate functioning. Earlier, we mentioned three explanations for this finding. First, we suggested that the temporal consistency of personality is related to the fit between specific behaviors and the developmental tasks for a given age. Second, we suggested that high consistency in important others' views of a child promotes ego-resiliency because the social environment is more predictable for these children. Third, we suggested that the stability of the overall environment is an important hidden variable that may simultaneously increase temporal consistency and ego-resiliency.

---

[4] This high consistency does not imply rigidity in the development of those children. First, even a correlation of .85 still only explains around 72% of the variance, leaving ample room for personality changes in that child. Second, consistency is based on the CCQ items, some of which refer to very narrowly defined behaviors (e.g., "teases other children"), but others of which refer to more broad personality attributes (e.g., "is resourceful in initiating activities"). This allows for a certain amount of heterotypic continuity (Kagan 1969) and thus for change combined with consistency.

The median self-concept consistency is lower, indicating that self-concept consistency is lower than personality consistency for most children. One reason for this is that the self-report measures used in our study are less reliable, another is that the self-concept is indeed less consistent over time (cf. Marsh, Craven, and Debus 1991), perhaps especially for young children. The children in our sample left elementary school and entered a new school between Waves 7 and 9; this change in peer groups and in the reference group for scholastic achievement may have destabilized their individual self-concept profile. Despite differences in the level of personality consistency and self-concept consistency, the size of the individual differences in self-concept consistency was fully comparable to the size of the individual differences in personality consistency. Although self-concept consistency was lower than personality consistency for most children, a similar range of (but not necessarily the same) extremely consistent and inconsistent children was observed.

Self-concept consistency was correlated only with the self-concept subscale for physical appearance and, to a somewhat lesser extent, for global self-worth. The importance of these two subscales has been stressed by Harter (1985) and Boivin, Vitaro, and Cagnon (1992). Harter (1990) even coined the terms *outer self* and *inner self* for these two aspects of the self-concept. Apparently, the consistency of the self-concept is related to a child's satisfaction with him- or herself, both in terms of the outer self and in terms of the inner self. Self-concept consistency was also related to ego-resiliency and to intelligence, with a tendency for inconsistent children to deviate from the rest of the sample. It is noteworthy the self-concept consistency was predicted by intelligence measured 4 years earlier.

Although the correlation between personality consistency and self-concept consistency was small, the CCQ item correlates showed large overlap. Thus, although children high or low in personality consistency are not necessarily the same children as those high or low in self-concept consistency, they are nonetheless described in a similar way by their teachers or parents. In addition, for children with low consistencies, these descriptions are similar to how children with disruptive disorders were described in a U.S. sample (Caspi et al. 1994).

It is important to note that, despite some similarities, the two consistency indices differ in one point. To calculate personality consistency, we correlated two profiles that were constructed by an ipsative technique (i.e., a forced number of statements were put into each category, and the number of ties was constant). In contrast, the construction of self-concept profiles did not make use of a forced-choice format. It is not entirely clear how this difference affected our results, nor whether this contributed to the lower median self-concept consistency. We suspect it might have because the correlations between personality consistency and measures based on the same instrument (scores on ego-resiliency and CCQ items) were considerably higher than the correlations between self-concept consistency and subscale scores based on the same instrument, whereas correlations of the consistency indices with measures that were not from the same instrument (intelligence for personality consistency and intelligence and ego-resiliency for self-concept consistency) were of comparable magnitude. Future studies might contrast a forced-choice format with a free-choice format for the same instrument to study this difference in more detail.

Both Block (1971) and Ozer and Gjerde (1989) found sex differences in the correlates of temporal consistency of personality. Although our results show a slightly higher consistency for girls than for boys, no interaction effects were found that could indicate that the pattern of correlations between personality consistency, self-concept consistency, ego-resiliency, and intelligence differed between boys and girls. Although one can only speculate about the lack of sex differences in our study, two arguments should be considered. First, the participants in our sample were considerably younger than those in Block's sample (adolescents and adults) or even Ozer and Gjerde's sample (children from age 3 to 18). Although sex differences in personality have been reported at very young age (for a review see Cohn 1991), most of these findings come from studies that concern the level of personality attributes (and are thus in agreement with our finding that girls show higher consistency of personality) and do not address the external correlates or consistency of personality. Second, Block's results were based on archival data, gathered in studies that started in 1929 and 1932, Ozer and Gjerde's data were gathered in the period 1968–1983, whereas the LOGIC data were gathered in the period 1984–1993. A number of recent meta-analyses by Hyde and colleagues of sex differences in diverse social and cognitive traits such as aggressiveness, sexuality, verbal IQ and mathematical achievement have found that the magnitude of sex differences was decreased during the last 25 years or so (Hyde 1984; Hyde, Fennema, and Lamon 1990; Hyde and Linn 1988; Oliver and Hyde 1993). A similar historic trend may explain the smaller sex effects in the LOGIC study.

One of the major problems in the present study is, of course, that the temporal relation among variables is rather fuzzy. To combine personality consistency and self-concept consistency, we had to drop the distinction between prediction and retrodiction we made in our earlier work. This also meant that it is difficult, if not impossible, to make inferences about the causal relations between consistency and psychological functioning. Future longitudinal studies might address this issue.

Although the purpose of this chapter was to illustrate a person-centered approach to the temporal consistency of personality and the self-concept, our results directly demonstrate the merits of a combination of person- and variable-centered approaches. By entering person-centered indices into variable-centered analyses, as we did when we correlated the consistency indices with ego-resiliency, intelligence, and with the CCQ items, we could combine the advantages of both approaches. The advantages of the person-centered approach were that we could regard temporal consistency as an attribute of a person, not of a variable. However, advantages of the variable-centered approach were that we could use a child's consistency score as an individual-difference variable and could ask about the psychological correlates of interindividual differences in consistency.

By analyzing part of our data with CFA, we introduced another person-centered approach. In CFA (von Eye 1990), the focus is on a group of participants that displays a unique pattern of characteristics. As Magnusson (1996) has noted, the description and the interpretation of these patterns is a first step toward understanding and explaining individual functioning. In this chapter, we found that the pattern combining inconsistency in personality and in the self-concept with low intelligence and low ego-resiliency could be labeled as a type; that is, was more frequently found than was to be expected. Similarly, another type was characterized by the pattern of high consistency in personality and the self-concept, combined with high intelligence and high ego-resiliency. Apparently, low consistencies and inadequate psychological functioning tend to cluster together in the same children, as do high consistencies and adaptive psychological functioning. In addition to the advantages of a person-centered approach that are discussed within the nomothetic–idiographic debate (and that concern the focus on the individual as a whole, and the understanding of the individual person), the identification and further study of these types of children might be one of the important contributions of a person-centered approach to developmental psychology.

References

Allport, G. W. (1937). *Personality: A psychological interpretation*. New York: Holt.

Asendorpf, J. B., & van Aken, M. A. G. (1991). Correlates of the temporal consistency of personality patterns in childhood. *Journal of Personality, 59*, 687–703.

Asendorpf, J. B., & van Aken, M. A. G. (1993). Deutsche Versionen der Selbstkonzeptskalen von Harter [German versions of the Harter self-concept scales]. *Zeitschrift für Entwicklungspsychologie und Pädagogische Psychologie, 25*, 64–86.

Block, J. (1961). *The Q-sort method in personality assessment and psychiatric research*. Palo Alto, CA: Consulting Psychologists Press.

Block, J. (1971). *Lives through time*. Berkeley, CA: Bancroft Books.

Block, J., & Block, J. H. (1980). *The California Child Q-Set*. Palo Alto, CA: Consulting Psychologists Press.

Boivin, M., Vitaro, F., & Cagnon, C. (1992). A reassessment of the Self-Perception Profile for Children: Factor structure, reliability, and convergent validity of a French version among second through sixth grade children. *International Journal of Behavioral Development, 15*, 275–290.

Caspi, A., & Bem, D. J. (1990). Personality continuity and change across the life course. In L. A. Pervin (Ed.), *Handbook of personality: Theory and research* (pp. 549–575). New York: Guilford Press.

Caspi, A., Block, J., Block, J. H., Klopp, B., Lynam, D., Moffitt, T. E., & Stouthamer-Loeber, M. (1994). A "common-language" version of the California Child Q-Set for personality assessment. *Psychological Assessment, 4*, 512–523.

Cohn, L. D. (1991). Sex differences in the course of personality development: A meta-analysis. *Psychological Bulletin, 109*, 252–266.

Göttert, R., & Asendorpf, J. B. (1989). Eine deutsche Version des California-Child-Q-Sort, Kurzform [A German short version of the California Child Q-Set]. *Zeitschrift für Entwicklungspsychologie und Pädagogische Psychologie, 21*, 70–82.

Harter, S. (1985). *Manual for the Self-Perception Profile for Children* (Tech. Rep.). Denver, CO: University of Denver.

Harter, S. (1990). Causes, correlates, and the functional role of global self-worth: A life-span perspective. In R. J. Sternberg, & J. Kollogian, Jr. (Eds.), *Competence considered* (pp. 67–97). New Haven, CT: Yale University Press.

Hermans, H. J. M. (1988). On the integration of nomothetic and idiographic research methods in the study of personal meaning. *Journal of Personality, 56*, 785–812.

Hyde, J. S. (1984). How large are gender differences in aggression? A developmental meta-analysis. *Developmental Psychology, 20*, 722–736.

Hyde, J. S., Fennema, E., & Lamon, S. J. (1990). Gender differences in mathematic performance: A meta-analysis. *Psychological Bulletin, 107*, 139–155.

Hyde, J. S., & Linn, M. C. (1988). Gender differences in verbal ability: A meta-analysis. *Psychological Bulletin, 104*, 53–69.

Kagan, J. (1969). The three faces of continuity in human development. In D. A. Goslin (Ed.), *Handbook of socialization theory and research* (pp. 983–1002). Chicago: Rand McNally.

Magnusson, D. (1996). The patterning of antisocial behavior and autonomic reactivity. In David M. Stoff (Ed.); Robert B. Cairns (Ed.); et-al. *Aggression and violence: Genetic, neurobiological, and biosocial perspectives.* (pp. 291–308). Mahwah, NJ, USA: Lawrence Erlbaum Associates, Inc.

Marsh, H. W., Craven, R. G., & Debus, R. (1991). Self-concept of young children 5 to 8 years of age: Measurement and multidimensional structure. *Journal of Educational Psychology, 83*, 377–392.

Oliver, M. B., & Hyde, J. S. (1993). Gender differences in sexuality: A meta-analysis. *Psychological Bulletin, 114*, 29–51.

Ozer, D. (1994). The Q-sort method and the study of personality development. In D. Funder, R. Parke, C. Tomlinson-Keasy, & K. Widamon (Eds.), *Studying lives through time: Approaches to personality development* (pp. 147–168). Washington, DC: American Psychological Association.

Ozer, D. J., & Gjerde, P. F. (1989). Patterns of personality consistency and change from childhood through adolescence. *Journal of Personality, 57*, 483–507.

Pelham, B. W. (1993). The idiographic nature of human personality: Examples of the idiographic self-concept. *Journal of Personality and Social Psychology, 64*, 665–677.

Runyan, W. M. (1983). Idiographic goals and methods in the study of lives. *Journal of Personality, 51*, 413–437.

Stephenson, W. (1953). *The study of behavior: Q-technique and its methodology.* Chicago: University of Chicago Press.

Stern, W. (1911). *Die differentielle Psychologie in ihren methodischen Grundlagen.* Leipzig: Barth.

van Aken, M. A. G. (1991). *Competence development in a transactional perspective: A longitudinal study.* Kampen, The Netherlands: Mondiss.

von Eye, A. (1990). *Introduction to configural frequency analysis.* Cambridge, England: Cambridge University Press.

Weinert, F. E., & Schneider, W. (1987). *The Munich Longitudinal Study on the Genesis of Individual Competencies (LOGIC), Report No. 2.* München: Max-Planck-Institut für psychologische Forschung.

Weinert, F. E., & Schneider, W. (1993a). *The Munich Longitudinal Study on the Genesis of Individual Competencies (LOGIC), Report No. 9.* München: Max-Planck-Institut für psychologische forschung.

Weinert, F. E., & Schneider, W. (1993b). *The Munich Longitudinal Study on the Genesis of Individual Competencies (LOGIC), Report No. 10.* München: Max-Planck-Institut für psychologische Forschung.

13a   Comment: Regarding a "Person-Centered Approach to Development"

Jack Block

The chapter by van Aken and Asendorpf brings together unusual data of high relevance for important issues. Like all useful research contributions, together with its satisfying findings it raises for subsequent inquiry a host of further questions.

Over the last quarter century, doubts about the across-time consistency of personality have been expressed by various psychologists (e.g., Kagan 1980; Mischel 1968). In response, various longitudinal studies have come forward demonstrating appreciable consistency of personality over extended periods of time (e.g., Asendorpf and van Aken 1991; Block 1971; Block 1993; Ozer and Gjerde 1989; see Moss and Susman [1980] for an extended review of the literature on longitudinally studied consistency). The pertinent questions have changed. Where before the issue was whether there was or was not coherence of development, now we are concerned with the deeper issues of understanding. Why is there more consistency over time for certain individuals than for others? Or during certain periods more than other periods? Conceptually, what appears to underlie the observed consistencies and the observed changes?

The van Aken and Asendorpf chapter brings us closer to these understandings. Their several penetrating analyses converge in their implications. At the risk of some oversimplification, let me summarize their essential findings, adding some personal annotations:

1. There is consistency over time in the personalities of children, as assessed by psychologists. We can accept the data on which this finding is based because such assessments have been demonstrated in a wide variety of contexts to have appreciable validity.
2. There is consistency over time in the self-concepts held by children. We can accept the data on which this finding is based because assessments of self-concepts have been demonstrated in a wide variety of contexts to have appreciable validity.
3. Personality consistency over time is higher than self-concept consistency over time.
4. Individuals who manifest personality consistency also tend to manifest self-concept consistency.
5. Logically, consistency over time, per se, carries no implication whatsoever regarding what substantively underlie such longitudinal consistency. However, both the degree

Preparation of this article was supported in part by National Institute of Mental Health Grant MH16080.

of personality consistency over time and self-concept consistency over time are shown to relate to independent measures of ego-resiliency and of IQ. For personality consistency, the concurrent relations are appreciably higher for ego-resiliency than for intelligence. For self-concept consistency, the predictive relations to assessments at Wave 9 are somewhat higher for intelligence than for ego-resiliency. These relations are important empirical findings; they are not entailed by confound or artifact. Moreover, equivalent findings relating degree of personality consistency to ego-resiliency and IQ have emerged from other longitudinal studies (e.g., Block and Robins 1993).

6. If evaluated from a societal perspective, the personality characteristics associated with personality consistency are "desirable." This observation is conceptually expectable rather than evidence of the intrusion of a "response set." It is not surprising that adaptationally effective characteristics such as ego-resiliency and IQ are evaluated societally as desirable.

7. Within the consistency observed over time, there are appropriate age-related changes "in agreement with the change in major developmental tasks, from emotional stability and good peer relations in preschool . . . to intellectual capacities and skill in late childhood" Personality consistency does not require personality "sameness"; there is developmental maturation. The old maxim applies, "Change within continuity, continuity within change."

Overall, this is an important set of findings that will influence subsequent thinking and research. I now add some personal conjectures and observations evoked in me by their chapter that may have some wider interest.

Why is there a connection between consistency on the one hand and ego-resiliency and IQ on the other? I suggest that if one has evolved a personality system that already is dynamically and resourcefully adaptive, one is not pushed or pulled toward fundamental personality change. In contrast, individuals who have not yet achieved an agreeable modus vivendi will, if they have not yet given up on life, seek change or be more influenceable by environmental shapings.

The relations between ego-resiliency and intelligence are intriguing and warrant particular consideration. The concept of intelligence has generated much controversy over the years and continues to do so. It has been recognized that intelligence is not simply what intelligence tests measure, and, yet, in research operationalizations traditional, narrowly focused intelligence (i.e., IQ) tests continue to be used. However, IQ tests provide only an index of the functioning efficiency of basic information-processing components, such as short-term memory, vocabulary, spatial recognitions, and the like. IQ tests do not provide a sufficient index of the dynamic resourceful adaptability that I have called ego-resiliency, of competence, of what has been called *executive functions*, of the "binding" of cognitive processing units to achieve integration and adaptation. A recent paper (Block and Kremen 1996), in a discussion of the broad implications of ego resiliency, has sought to identify the differences as well as the similarities between the behavioral implications of ego-resiliency and conventional IQ tests. Space here precludes a presentation of these findings and arguments. I suggest, however, that our findings indicate ego-resiliency is more important, adaptively, than is pure IQ. We all know individuals with high IQs who are impressively unresilient. I further suggest that the van Aken and Asendorpf chapter presents results that can similarly be assimilated.

Van Aken and Asendorpf aptly recognize that one reason for the lower average consistency of self-perceptions, as compared with the consistency of personality, may be because the forced choice format was not used in generating the self-concept data. More empiricism is required to evaluate seriously this possibility because a number of factors may be contributing to their finding. However, there is a generally unrecognized difference in the results afforded by unforced-choice as compared with forced-choice methods that warrants mention here. When unforced-choice methods are used and the derived scores are then correlated, these correlations are inevitably lowered – sometimes by a good deal – to the extent that the two distributions being correlated differ in their shape (Carroll 1961). Empirically, the free-choice score distributions offered by participants differ appreciably both within individuals across time and between individuals. When forced-choice methodology is used, however, this logical lowering of subsequent correspondences does not occur – one of the important reasons for using the Q-sort method. To some extent, not now specifiable, the difference between the consistency levels noted by van Aken and Asendorpf is attributable to this psychometric effect.

Van Aken and Asendorpf note that the personality inconsistent group is characterized by "stubbornness." It has been my perception over the years that the term *stubborn* can have at least two meanings, depending on the overall context of observation. Certainly, individuals with strong autonomy needs may indeed express stubbornness. I suggest, however, that what often is labeled *stubbornness* is more simply an indication that the individual does not know what to do, of what else to do, of a limited behavioral repertoire, of adaptational ineffectuality. Such stubbornness is not an expression of personal identity, rather, it is a manifestation of behavioral impotence.

Van Aken and Asendorpf report that over time the self-percept importance of physical appearance increases. This kind of developmental finding has emerged elsewhere as well. It appears to signify the increasing relevance for children of their surrounding culture, which so overvalues physical externalities. Children and preadolescents become increasingly vulnerable to evaluation by their peers, and, consequently, physical attractiveness takes on a central concern in the struggle for a sense of identity. Van Aken and Asendorpf also found that, with increasing age, intelligence becomes a more central basis for an awareness of self-worth, especially for boys. If a boy is smart, he tends to receive evidence from the outside world that he is smart, and self-esteem is thereby enhanced. For a girl, however, in her usual social surrounds, external reinforcements of her intelligence may not become so central as external reinforcements of her attractiveness.

Regarding the van Aken and Asendorpf Table 6, there certainly is strong evidence for the association of maladaptiveness with being, jointly, inconsistent in personality and inconsistent in self-concept. I would emphasize, however, that this maladaptiveness does not seem to have any connection with externalizing disorders or for that matter with internalizing disorders. The notions of externalizing–internalizing are conceptually separate from the issues of adaptation and, in this instance, appear to be empirically unassociated as well. In my view, the concepts of externalizing and internalizing have uncertain meaning and have resulted in a contrary literature. For example, in some studies, externalizing and internalizing are reciprocally (i.e., strongly negatively) related; in other studies, externalizing and internalizing are strongly positively related.

Finally, I wish to remark, if only briefly, on the brief mention by van Aken and Asendorpf of the "important hidden variable that may simultaneously increase temporal consistency and ego-resiliency" (p. 315), namely, the stability of the overall environment. Almost conventionally and to achieve inclusiveness, this kind of interpretation for findings of personality consistency has been frequently and freely invoked over the years by various psychologists, usually as a possible explanation of findings that they would rather attribute to other influences. Of course, environments have influence on behavior. However, it has seemed to me that this proposed explanation, expressed so vaguely, has never been seriously tested. What is meant by terms such as *overall environment?* How is environment to be measured in conceptually valid and psychometrically reliable ways? Has anyone actually ventured empirically to evaluate this conjecture? I know of no such attempts. This supposition implies that, for example, the presence or absence of creativity in individuals would radically come or radically go were the creativity-relevant aspects of the overall environment to change. I do not believe so. Environmental affordances may well influence behavioral manifestations of creativity. However, I suggest that creative accomplishment more importantly requires the existence, however derived, of certain personality configurations.

References

Asendorpf, J. B., & van Aken, M. A. G. (1991). Correlates of the temporal consistency of personality patterns in childhood. *Journal of Personality 59*, 687–703.

Block, J. (1971). *Lives through time*. Berkeley, CA: Bancroft Books.

Block, J. (1993). Studying personality the long way. In D. C. Funder, R. Parke, R. C. Tomlinson-Keasy, & K. Widaman (Eds.), *Studying lives through time: Approaches to personality and development* (pp. 9–41). Washington, DC: American Psychological Association.

Block, J., & Kremen, A. (1996). IQ and ego-resiliency: Clarifying their conceptual and empirical linkage and separateness. *Journal of Personality and Social Psychology, 70*, 349–361.

Block, J., & Robins, R. W. (1993). A longitudinal study of consistency and change in self-esteem from early adolescence to early adulthood. *Child Development, 94*, 909–923.

Carroll, J. B. (1961). The nature of the data, or how to choose a correlation coefficient. *Psychometrika, 26*, 347–372.

Kagan, J. (1980). Perspectives on continuity. In O. G. Brim, Jr. & J. Kagan (Eds.), *Constancy and change in human development* (pp. 26–74). Cambridge, MA: Harvard University Press.

Mischel, W. (1968). *Personality and assessment*. New York: Wiley.

Moss, H. A., & Susman, E. J. (1980). Longitudinal study of personality development. In O. G. Brim, Jr. & J. Kagan (Eds.), *Constancy and change in human development* (pp. 530–595). Cambridge, MA: Harvard University Press.

Ozer, D. J., & Gjerde, P. F. (1989). Patterns of personality consistency and change from childhood through adolescence. *Journal of Personality, 57*, 483–507.

14   Universal, Differential, and Individual Aspects of Child Development From 3 to 12: What Can We Learn From a Comprehensive Longitudinal Study?

Franz E. Weinert, Merry Bullock, and Wolfgang Schneider

As the topics in this volume illustrate, a central and important feature of the LOGIC design was that it measured different domains of development simultaneously. The empirical findings and interpretations from each domain are covered in the individual chapters and commentaries. The aim of this concluding chapter is to complement these chapters and commentaries by considering the more general scientific contribution of the LOGIC findings overall.

There are several ways one could do this. One could adopt a data-driven, bottom-up strategy and use the various findings from each domain to generate a set of empirical and theoretical generalizations. Alternatively, one could follow a more conceptually driven, top-down strategy and ask how compatible the LOGIC data are with different theories and models of development and what changes in these models would be necessary to accommodate the data. In what follows, we generally follow the first of these two strategies because we consider it especially productive to compare the similarities and differences in developmental patterns across such different areas as cognitive abilities, skills and competencies, motivational processes, personality characteristics, and social behavior.

Of course, the developmental phenomena observed across such a range of areas are so variable that it is necessary to cluster them in terms of a smaller number of theoretical perspectives before trying to draw generalizations about developmental processes. By theoretical perspectives, we mean those central tenets that "have the important function of alerting us to particular relations and connections between the building blocks of reality" (Acham 1983, p. 156).

Given that the phenomenon of development cannot be studied as an undifferentiated whole, and that development per se cannot be observed directly, it is necessary to carve developmental phenomena into blocks that can be studied. How this is done depends on which of a number of basic theoretical perspectives in developmental psychology one adopts. That is, how the domains appropriate for scientific scrutiny are chosen, how the research is designed, and how the data are framed, implicitly or explicitly, by an underlying theoretical perspective. There are three areas in which different perspectives can guide a longitudinal research design: (a) in the description of developmental changes, (b) in the description of interindividual differences in developmental changes, and (c) in inferences about the mechanisms of human development and attempts to explain and predict developmental phenomena.

The Description of Developmental Changes

Description of development is not simply an act of recording. First, one must choose a level of analysis for what develops (i.e., on a continuum from elementary units of behavior such as those considered by traditional learning theories, to inferred structures such as those considered by many cognitive models, to inferred systems of interactions such as those considered by contextual theories).

Second, developmental change is, by definition, a process that occurs over time. This can be described with very different degrees of aggregation. In some respects, each person develops like all other people (a universal aspect); in other respects, like only some other people (a differential aspect) and in yet other respects, like no one else (an individual aspect). Thus, the scientific description of change can focus on different aspects of development: the universal (e.g., species-specific patterns of motor development such as reaching in infancy), the differential (e.g., the development of motor skill competencies in subpopulations of children), or the individual (e.g., the development of gymnastics expertise in person X). Which aspect one chooses will determine how one's descriptive developmental psychology addresses a central question: the extent to which developmental change is continuous or discontinuous.

The LOGIC data in the cognitive area offer a good example of the different descriptions provided by different levels of aggregation. Specifically, in agreement with the results from many other studies, the LOGIC data show that

- comparisons across different age groups (either cross-sectionally or longitudinally) yield qualitative differences in behavior and performance that suggest developmental discontinuity and stagelike changes;
- developmental curves (general developmental functions; see Wohlwill 1973) are smoother (e.g., suggest greater continuity) the greater the sample size and the shorter the time span between adjacent measurements; and
- for almost all variables, considerable variability within individuals in developmental patterns of behavior and performance suggest developmental discontinuity.

Observations from carefully conducted microgenetic studies (e.g., Siegler 1994) show that children of all ages simultaneously show behavior, strategies, and performances that are typical (average), accelerated, and retarded for their developmental level. Thus, the accessibility and availability of a developmentally advanced strategy is not a sudden event but represents a process of changing strategy selection and preference. This means that both situational variability and individual continuity must be considered. Whether or not empirical results suggest continuous or discontinuous developmental functions may vary with the variables, measures, and time intervals that one chooses.

In principle, development always implies change. However, regardless of the content studied, be it temperament, individual hierarchies of motive classes, or cognitive abilities, it is important to ask not only what it is that changes during ontogenesis but also what it is that remains constant. Certainly, most people (and also most psychologists, at least in Europe and North America) assume that the individual person is in some sense invariant when ontogenetic changes occur and that subsequent developmental phases are connected to one another. This "constancy assumption" is necessary for our subjectively perceived individual self-identity over the life course (Erikson 1959; Thomae 1957).

Continuity can be expressed in different ways, as illustrated by Kagan (1971), who provided a way to integrate the lay perspective of constancy with the scientific study of developmental change and continuity. He differentiated between what he called *homotypic* and *heterotypic* continuity. While homotypic continuity refers to overt stability in the same or similar behaviors, heterotypic continuity refers to a causal and/ or predictive stability between different behavioral dispositions over time. For example, one can focus on direct (homotypic) continuity in specific overt behaviors over longer periods of time (e.g., physical aggression) or on indirect (heterotypic) continuity between psychological constructs that underlie different behaviors at different points in time (e.g., a need for independence in early childhood and achievement motives in adolescence).

The LOGIC data do not provide ideal conditions for systematically describing developmental change or for answering questions of continuity and discontinuity in development. There is a simple reason: the LOGIC design focused on breadth across developmental domains. This focus did not allow analysis of a constrained set of psychological domains within a consistent network of theoretical constructs and operationalizations (which would also require measurement across rather short time intervals). Rather, the "logic" behind the LOGIC design was to cover a broad spectrum of quite different psychological domains with a small number of indicators that would be tested regularly across 1- to 2-year intervals. These conditions allow us to generate only rather global models of construct- and variable-specific developmental functions within domains and to compare just a few such developmental functions across domains. In contrast to many cross-sectional studies, however, the LOGIC design does allow the analysis of causal connections between different developmental processes over time. An especially good example of this is the analysis of the changing influences of development in specific skill areas on changes in the self-concept of general and specific competencies.

Interindividual Stability in Intraindividual Change Over Time

The question of continuity or discontinuity in intraindividual development is often confounded with the question of the stability of interindividual differences in developmental change. These two issues can be treated as the same only when group performance over time is perfectly correlated; that is, when the rank ordering of individuals within the group does not change. When this is the case, all individuals change at the same rate or in the same way. When there is no differential change, both group and individual changes may be described in the same way.

Adopting a differential perspective becomes more important as group stabilities decrease. In concert with reports from other longitudinal studies, the interindividual stabilities in the LOGIC study ranged from .20 to .80. How should these stabilities be interpreted? There are two very different phenomena that could be responsible for group stabilities of less than 1.0. Take an example of a moderate stability across two measurement points, say, a correlation of .40. This value can arise in two ways: when almost all individuals change their relative rank ordering to a similar, moderate degree over time, or when most individuals retain their relative rank ordering and only a small number changes, but changes substantially. In other words, it is possible that there are individual differences in the stability of change such that stability itself is a differential variable.

To avoid a frequent misunderstanding, we must, in deference to Wohlwill (1973, 1980) note that we have discussed temporal stability or variability only with respect to a group norm (normative stability). In addition, one can analyze temporal stability or variability with respect to different traits or behavioral variables within a single individual (ipsative stability).

The LOGIC data provide estimates of both normative (in cognitive, motivational, and personality areas) and ipsative (in personality variables) stabilities. The differential research perspective (see also Asendorpf and Weinert 1990; Weinert and Schneider 1993) was and is central to the LOGIC project design and analyses. In this regard, the LOGIC data serve a dual role. They both illustrate and provide a counterexample to a criticism made by Wohlwill:

> With only very few exceptions work on stability ... has consisted in the endless proliferation of correlation coefficients to indicate the degree of relationship between measures of behavior over some given time interval.... The result has been that we have learned a little about the "behavior" of *variables* over age, but nothing concerning the behavior of individuals (1973, p. 359).

Mechanisms of Development

One requirement for explaining or predicting empirically observed developmental phenomena is a deeper theoretical understanding of developmental mechanisms (see, for example, Sternberg 1984) and how they are affected by internal and external factors. It is crucial to distinguish explaining and predicting developmental phenomena. Because the necessary conditions for human development are never sufficient for change to occur, it is clearly impossible to predict differential patterns of development, even when there are valid differential explanatory models and when general patterns of development are possible to predict. Important as this methodological truism is, however, it has little pragmatic value because the field lacks generally satisfactory research on explanations of developmental phenomena.

There is pessimism about finding simple explanatory models even for a relatively homogenous class of phenomena, such as the differential development of school achievement. For example, Haertel, Walberg, and Weinstein (1983) noted that

> classroom learning is a multiplicative, diminishing-returns function of four essential factors – student ability and motivation, and quality and quantity of instruction. . . . Each of these essential factors appear to be necessary but insufficient by itself to classroom learning; that is, all four of these factors appear required at least at minimum levels for classroom learning to take place. It also appears that the essential factors may substitute, compensate, or trade-off for one another in diminishing rates of return. (p. 75)

The LOGIC study offers only a limited direct empirical contribution to the analysis of developmental mechanisms. To analyze developmental mechanisms, both controlled experimental studies and fine-grained, small-scale, and short time-span microgenetic studies are necessary. The contribution of the LOGIC data is to provide a rich source of hypotheses necessary for these efforts.

At present, what hampers the measurement and analysis of conditions relevant to development is our lack of methodologies to unpack satisfactorily the multilevel and multisegmental embedding of psychological (explanatory) variables. That is, we cannot satisfactorily disentangle the multilevel effects of the individual child and his or her personal history within a school class, within an individual school, within the school system, and within the larger society. Similarly, there are no methodologically satisfactory ways to separate the multisegmental effects of the child and his or her personal history from effects of the family, the school class, the cohort, and so on. Rather, the best we can deliver are chains and networks of causal relations among variables.

To complicate the matter more, the important conditions of human development are themselves interdependent. A clear example of this is the determination of individual development by genetic and environmental factors. In addition to the fact that these factors are usually confounded (e.g., the biological parents are also the creators of the familial environment), they themselves also covary (i.e., the social environment reacts differentially to different genetically determined phenotypes; in addition, over development children come to select actively those aspects of the environment that most closely match their genotype). The confounding of developmental conditions leads to a permanent overestimation of socialization influences on child development and to an unresolvable conflict between genetic and socialization interpretations of the empirical data.

Because neither a twin nor an adoption study was possible within the LOGIC framework, we explicitly avoided the comprehensive measurement of familial or social class variables. It was, however, possible to include at least one important institutional condition for development within the LOGIC study (see Weinert and Helmke 1997). We regularly observed all children in their kindergarten classes and more than half of the children (along with their schoolmates) in their school classes. Because the German Bavarian State requires that all children attend the nearest school, and because neighborhoods are relatively heterogeneous, this meant that we could assume general independence of genetic and schooling factors. Thus, in combination with the SCHOLASTIC study, the LOGIC data enable analyses of the effects of school learning, teacher instruction, and experiences across different classrooms on cognitive and motivational development.

If one looks across the different chapters, it is clear that there are large differences in what was studied in cognitive areas and what was studied in personality (and motivational) areas. This is because there are substantial differences in the theories, models, and research methodologies typical for these areas. We thus initially consider aspects of cognitive, personality, and motivational development separately. We first discuss the LOGIC findings on cognitive development, then those on personality development, and finally those on the effects of the school on differential development. We end with examples of several hypotheses suggested by the LOGIC findings.

Cognitive Development

The measures used to tap cognitive performance do not represent a unitary set of skills or a uniform level of generality. This makes sense, given that development in a number of different cognitive areas was addressed, including psychometric intelligence, cognitive structure (in a Piagetian sense), memory, mathematics, reading and spelling, scientific reasoning, and school achievement. The researchers in each project area chose or designed measures to explore issues and questions most relevant and germane to their specific areas, as discussions in the individual chapters attest. As separate windows into development, each chapter offers a detailed look at how skills develop and at some of the factors contributing to individual differences in developmental outcomes.

Collectively, however, the data on performance within and across the different areas can be used to address a number of more general questions concerning the description of cognitive development, the utility of early performance information in predicting later behavior, and the importance of general and specific cognitive skills in developmental change. The data can also be used to ask about the importance of interindividual differences in determining the shape and direction of developmental pathways. To frame the discussion, we review the range of cognitive tasks presented to children over the course of the LOGIC Study in Table 1.

Generalizations About Development

Taken together, the LOGIC data provide an overview of changes in a number of developmental functions across a range of cognitive content areas. By developmental function, we mean the pattern of developmental change in a skill, ability, trait, or behavior. Developmental functions can be described according to several dimensions: their trajectory (continuous and discontinuous); their rate (fast and slow), and their specificity in relation to other behaviors in the same individual. Beyond the descriptive

Table 1. *Measurement Points of Several Cognitive Variables*

| | Average at testing | | | | | | | | |
| | Preschool age | | | School age | | | | | |
Variable	4	5	6	7	8	9	10	11	12
General skills									
Psychometric: verbal IQ	X	X		X		X			X
Psychometric: nonverbal IQ	X	X	X		X		X		X
Processing speed: word and number span	X			X	X				
Operational level (Piaget)	X			X			X	X	
Proportional reasoning							X	X	X
Scientific reasoning						X	X	X	X
Specific content areas									
Autobiographical memory	X	X	X	X	X	X	X	X	X
Text memory	X	X	X	X	X	X	X	X	X
List memory, strategy use	X	X		X		X		X	
Spelling	X	X			X	X	X	X	
Reading	X	X			X				
Mathematical word problems					X	X	X		

level, an analysis of similarities and differences in developmental functions across both content areas and individuals provides a heuristic for asking about the extent to which individual development follows general patterns of developmental change and the extent to which developmental patterns should be seen as general or content specific.

The Shape of Developmental Functions

Almost all authors have provided an initial description of their data in terms of mean values across age. When presented in this way, most developmental functions appear to suggest continuous, more or less linear change. Text memory, autobiographical memory, recall performance, raw IQ scores, mathematical problem solving, and the understanding of experimentation each increases fairly continuously with age, at least when corrections for task difficulty level are made. However, an equally consistent finding across the chapters is a considerable variability when data are analyzed in terms of individual differences. There is interindividual variability underlying gradual increases in mean group performance and intraindividual variability in developmental functions across different skill areas. That is, the shape of developmental functions described at the group level may not match the course of developmental change in individuals. This in itself is not surprising, and it is one of the reasons often mentioned in the literature for the importance of longitudinal studies. However, the breadth of the LOGIC data makes it possible to ask further about the meaning of such individual variability.

In the following, we outline some regularities and differences across the different cognitive domains studied. These include changes in the stability of individual performance and interindividual differences across development and changes in the extent to which general or specific skills predict the performance level. We also point out some regularities and differences in developmental function across different content areas: In some areas, the shapes of the developmental functions, even at the individual level, appear to be more or less consistent; in other areas, the shapes of the developmental functions appear more variable. We compare these patterns to suggest ways to understand developmental change across different content areas and to ask about the implications of individual differences in developmental pathways within and across content domains.

What is the importance of similar or different individual patterns of development? The LOGIC data offer several examples. For some basic skills such as those measured by psychometric tests, differences in the rate of development may have long-term facilitating effects. For example, general cognitive skills predict both early performance and subsequent patterns of change in some scientific reasoning and mathematical tasks. In contrast, for other skills, it is the timing and not the rate of component skill acquisition (which is only loosely related to general cognitive ability) that predicts subsequent performance. For example, those children who were most likely to retain memory strategies over time were those who used them first only after such activities were functional in memory performance (see the chapter by Sodian and Schneider). Analogously, the effects of phonological awareness or letter knowledge on subsequent literacy varied with when those component skills were available (see the chapter by Schneider and Näslund).

The adage "past behavior is the best predictor of the future" was illustrated and refined in the analyses reported in many of the chapters. For many cognitive areas, content-specific skills (typically measured as prior performance on the same or similar tasks) were the best predictor of subsequent performance. However, when developmental progress involved the acquisition and integration of initially separate skills, this relation decreased substantially. For example, although interindividual differences in memory performance remained more or less constant across measurement years (the 2-year across-task correlations ranged from .29 to .39 for sort–recall performance and from .35 to .41 for text memory, until the last measurement points when they were higher), there was virtually no cross-measurement correlation in the use of memory strategies. Similarly, although overall scientific reasoning performance was fairly stable (1-year correlations ranged from .43 to .57 and 2-year correlations between .40 and .59), cross-year correlations between the specific tasks contributing to this omnibus score were low. This suggests that the meaning of individual differences in a developmental function depends on what function–competence one is studying. Some functions grow steadily at a homogenous rate. Text memory, with small group variances and relatively stable interindividual differences over time, seems to fit this category, at least as studied here with familiar content. Others grow only when specific conditions are met (e.g., the acquisition of necessary prerequisite skills). Examples in the LOGIC data of important prerequisites for developmental change include the effect of early phonological awareness on later literacy skills or early number competencies on later performance in mathematical problem solving; other examples would be those consistent with Piagetian models. Yet other functions may require a variety of conditions to be met but may be indifferent to the order and sequence of these conditions. There were no pure examples of this in the LOGIC data, but the sort–recall data and the scientific reasoning data come close: For complex tasks in which a number of skills must be assembled for mature performance, the order in which skills are acquired may be irrelevant to individual differences in the final outcome level. Of course, in this case, the quality of component skills may still affect the quality of the final outcome. This is a point to which we return later.

Stability of Developmental Functions

Most of the chapters describing cognitive development in different domains have included analyses regarding the stability of individual differences. As noted before, the stability issue is theoretically independent of the issue of continuity–discontinuity in a developmental function. However, this insight is not always represented in researchers' belief systems. That is, the belief that evidence of a continuous, linear increase in group means for a given variable assessed repeatedly over time also reflects high interindividual stability in changes over time is quite a common myth in the field. The analyses of individual stability described in the various chapters of this volume provide clear evidence to the contrary, showing that in most cases increases in developmental functions are not systematically related to changes in interindividual stability over time.

However, what do we learn about changes in the patterns of interindividual stability in cognitive variables? Is there any typical, domain-general course of development regarding individual differences? For most variables, it was shown that long-term stability (e.g., 1-year stability) was low to moderate when assessed during the preschool and kindergarten years, and that it increased considerably during the elementary school years. For example, the data discussed by Schneider, Perner, Bullock, Stefanek, and Ziegler (Chapter 2) on general mental ability show that stability coefficients obtained for the preschool period were substantial for verbal and nonverbal psychometric intelligence test scores (about .40) and comparably low for Piagetian-type tasks such as number conservation (about .10). Considerable increases in stability were found during the late elementary school years for both the psychometric and Piagetian-type tasks, with test–retest correlations increasing to .80 and .60, respectively. Thus, there was considerable variability in gains during the preschool years, with many children changing their relative status regarding various aspects of mental ability. Later on, interindividual differences in intraindividual changes were much more stable, indicating that children progressed at a more similar rate.

The pattern of individual stabilities found for the memory variables was not so uniform. Although Weber and Strube reported an increase in stabilities of the autobiographical memory recognition measure similar to that observed for the intelligence variables, the patterns in the recall measures of autobiographical memory were less consistent. Depending on the tasks and materials presented, both low (.14) and high (up to .60) stability coefficients were obtained during the preschool years. Similarly, Knopf showed that interindividual differences in intraindividual changes in text recall were already high and stable from the first wave on, with 2-year stabilities of about .60. Interestingly, these stability coefficients were significantly larger than those found for psychometric intelligence tests given at the same measurement points. In contrast, the pattern of long-term stability observed for strategic memory activities (i.e., sort–recall) was clearly different (see the chapter by Sodian and Schneider). From the very beginning, 2-year stabilities of recall and strategic behavior tended to be lower and did not change as a function of age. Given that short-term reliabilities were high for all of these variables, the lack of stability could not be attributed to measurement error. Most likely, large interindividual differences in the stability of children's strategy use at different measurement points decreased the stability of recall performance. Taken together, these findings suggest that the pattern of steady increases in individual stability demonstrated for measures in one area (intelligence) could not be replicated for another area (memory) in which developmental patterns varied considerably as a function of task and contributing skills.

The Timing of Developmental Change

Does the timing of developmental change affect the developmental outcome? At a very general level, there is an indication that developmental speed is an indicator of ability level. That is, those children who showed early general competencies tended to maintain this advantage in later performance. However, there are also indications across the different areas that the effects of the timing of developmental change vary with skill or domain. For example, data in the chapter by Schneider and Näslund suggest that some early skills (e.g., phonological awareness) may have an impact on skill development only if they are present at a particular point in time (i.e., before entering school). Individual differences in preschool phonological awareness were related to spelling success, individual differences later on were not. This makes sense when one considers that competence in some areas such as literacy requires a concatenation of a variety of skills that may be acquired through different routes; in this particular example, it also suggests when and what type of intervention may foster literacy skills. Similarly, in the scientific reasoning chapter, Bullock and Ziegler suggest that individual differences in information-processing skills may be more important than scientific reasoning skills, because they can compensate for less mature logical and inference skills.

Predictability of Outcome From Developmental Functions

For obvious reasons, individual differences in selected cognitive variables such as reading, spelling, and math could not be measured before children entered school. Similarly, scientific reasoning was only assessed during the late elementary school years because of its complexity and intellectual demands. The issue of predictability of individual differences from related preschool measures was raised and tested for variables in all of these content areas by the use of more basic constructs as predictors, such as intelligence or memory capacity. In addition, more specific preschool predictors such as metalinguistic abilities in the case of reading and spelling or number conservation in the case of mathematics were used. The findings by Bullock and Ziegler (scientific reasoning), Schneider and Näslund (reading and spelling), and Stern (mathematics) all demonstrate the predictive power of preschool predictors for the first assessment of school measures, regardless of the domain under study. Although both general cognitive ability and specific preschool measures explained a considerable amount of the variance in the respective dependent variables, their affect on subsequent assessments within in the various domains was negligible. Instead, it was found that earlier assessments of task-specific measures were the best predictors of subsequent task-specific performance, leaving little room for other variables to explain additional variance in the dependent variables (this finding was not explicitly reported in the chapter by Schneider and Näslund but was published in a previous article, see Schneider and Näslund 1993). Thus, the outcome of these analyses illustrates the importance of domain-specific knowledge for skill acquisition in different domains such as reading, spelling, mathematics, and scientific reasoning.

Is Development Domain-Specific?

The current literature on development tends to present a domain-specific view of many developmental functions. Can the LOGIC data provide information about the extent to which the patterns and influences on developmental functions are more domain-specific than not? With the exception of mathematics, the competencies studied in LOGIC are not those more modular and content-rich areas typically construed as distinct domains such as language or intuitive physical or social concepts. However, many authors asked the question in another way, and they analyzed whether performance across different tasks within a content area tends to cohere together and whether it can be predicted better by prior task-specific skills than by general competencies (see chapters by Stern, Knopf, Bullock and Ziegler, and Schneider and Näslund). In general, although there are high correlations between performance and general intellectual skills across many tasks, those correlations are greatly reduced or they disappear when prior task performance is partialled out. For example, text memory is highly correlated with concurrently measured IQ at most measurement points. However, when the analyses control for prior text memory, these relations disappear. The same holds for mathematics and scientific reasoning performance.

An example from the SCHOLASTIC Study data set provides a good quantitative illustration of this point (see Weinert & Helmke 1997). Table 2 shows the pattern of correlations between intelligence test performance, prior domain-specific knowledge, and criterion performance in the mathematics domain. As this table shows, the correlations between mathematics performance and prior knowledge were

Table 2. *Simple and Partial Correlations Between Mathematics Performance (Arithmetic and Word Problems) in Second and Fourth Grades and Between Mathematics Performance (Arithmetic and Word Problems) and Intelligence Test Scores in First Grade*

Comparisons	Arithmetic	Word problems
Simple correlation		
Mathematics performance (2nd grade)[a] and mathematics performance (4th grade)[a]	.57*	.55*
Intelligence test performance (1st grade) and mathematics performance (4th grade)[a]	.26	.47*
Partial correlation		
Mathematics performance (2nd grade)[a] and mathematics performance (4th grade)[a], with intelligence test partialled out	.53*	.42*
Intelligence test performance (1st grade) and mathematics performance (4th grade)[a], with mathematics performance (2nd grade)[a] partialled out	.05	.29

Notes: $n = 852$. $^*p < .01$.
[a] Aggregated score across two measurement points at the beginning and the end of the school year.

consistently higher than those between mathematics performance and intelligence. The correlation between mathematics achievement and prior knowledge was significant when intelligence was partialled out. In contrast, all of the correlations between mathematics performance and intelligence decreased significantly when domain-specific (prior) knowledge was partialled out (from .26 to .05 for arithmetic and from .47 to .29 for mathematical word problems).

These findings support more current componential models of human functioning and suggest that variability in developmental functions across content areas may be the more common pattern.

Effects of Sex and Age on Cognitive Variables

Table 3 lists the range of tasks measuring cognitive variables, ages at which these tasks were given, and the ages at which (at least) a single example of sex differences or of age differences was found. In these analyses, age was determined according to a median split of the sample.

Sex Differences. The presence and meaning of sex differences in cognition is a hotly debated topic. Most authors analyzed sex differences in their measures, with mixed results. Overall, sex differences were neither pervasive nor consistent. Those that did appear (in autobiographical memory recognition tasks, scientific reasoning,

Table 3. *Sex Effects and Age Effects in the Developmental Course of Different Cognitive Variables and Functions*

Content area	Age tested	Sex effect	Age effect
Sort–recall memory	4,6,8,10,12	None	4,6,8,10,12
Autobiographical memory	4,5,6,7,8,9,10,11	8,9,10	8
Text memory	4,5,6,7,8,9,10,12	7,10 (visual)	4,5,6,8,9,10,12
Scientific reasoning	9,10,11,12	10,11	10,12
Mathematical word problems	8,9,10	8,9,	8,9,10
Mathematical proportional problems	9,10	9,10	9,10
Spelling	8,9,10,11	9,10	8,9,10,11
School achievement			
Subjective probability of success	5,6,7,8,9,10,11,12	10,11	
Self-confidence	5,6,7,8,9,10,11,12	8	

mathematics, and spelling) were neither surprising nor unexpected. What was surprising was that most sex differences disappeared by the later measurement points, as skills became more consolidated. In general, the sample is remarkable for the lack of pervasive sex differences (of 120 variables tested for sex differences, only 16 were found).

Age Differences. Far more frequent and far larger in size were age differences. At most measurement points, the younger half of the sample performed consistently lower than the older half across a variety of tasks: math, spelling, text memory, sort–recall memory, and reasoning. This is an important and often overlooked variable, and it underscores the importance of going beyond the group mean in assessing individual competence or readiness.

Personal and Social Development

A legacy from the nineteenth century is that the mind is composed of a number of distinct mental "faculties," agencies, or traits that underlie psychological activities. One result of this legacy is the conceptual separation of psychological phenomena, functions, and traits into distinct constructs. Although modern textbooks agree that there is no theoretical base for this separation, it still exerts an influence on modern psychological concepts. A good example of this is the standard and almost "obvious" distinction between cognitive and personal functioning or between cognitive development (which includes ontogenetic changes in perception, learning, memory, thinking, attention, reading, mathematics, and so on) and social–personality development (which includes temperament, personal traits, motivation, moral development, social attitudes, and so on). Throughout the history of psychology, these areas have been studied with different models, phenomena, and constructs.

Of course, there are some good conceptual reasons for keeping these domains separate. The dominant view is that cognitive (and only cognitive) changes during childhood are, as John Flavell noted, "species-specific, uniform, unavoidable, irreversible and directed toward achieving a mature state" (1970, p. 247). In parallel, it is not supposed to observe such universal, uniform, and systematic changes in personality traits because there are strong socialization effects for many traits and individual preferences, even in early childhood (Zigler and Child 1969), and interindividual personality differences are quite stable from early childhood on. This has led many to assume that there are different sorts of regularities governing cognitive development and personality development. Thus, the theoretical models appropriate for the description and explanation of developmental phenomena must be of different sorts.

The conceptual separation between cognitive and personality domains of development has had some negative effects on research and theory. For example, personality and motivation are scarcely considered in models of the development of cognitive competencies, and cognitive competencies are ascribed an inconsistent role in motivational, social, and moral development: Some believe it is substantial, others that it plays only a little role. A concrete example of this is research on moral development: there is no satisfactory explanation of the large differences between the development of moral judgments (which most agree include a cognitive component) and moral behavior.

Another example is the development of achievement motivation. Achievement motivation (Heckhausen 1982) refers to the personal need to perform as well as possible, to expected success, and to avoid failure (i.e., to try to match one's action outcomes to perceived standards of excellence). Although individual differences in motive strength are quite stable over time even in childhood, the sequence in which components of the achievement motive are acquired is determined by a child's cognitive developmental level, and the structure of the achievement motive itself changes substantially as a function of cognitive development. A mature achievement motive involves applying standards of excellence and attributing success or failure outcomes to the self. This requires a host of cognitively based prerequisites: a child must (a) have a self-concept of his or her own abilities, (b) recognize and center on self-produced outcomes, (c) attribute action outcomes to personal competence, (c) evaluate ability levels, (d) distinguish between ability and effort, (e) judge the subjective probability of success or failure, (f) represent the relation between expected success and calculated incentive values, and (g) anticipate affective self-evaluation after success or failure (Heckhausen 1982). Although each of these components has cognitive prerequisites, and cognitive progress is thus a necessary condition for age-typical changes in achievement motivation, this is not the whole story. Although cognitive inferences about competence are crucial for the development of achievement motivation, it is also clear that "some subgroups with specific personality traits draw these inferences in a way that obscures the image of their own abilities, calls it into doubt, and does not induce self-esteem. Personality characteristics linked with a negative attribution of ability cover a wide range of phenomena: external control; depression; helplessness; fear of failure motive; low self-concept" (Heckhausen 1987, p. 157).

An analysis of empirical findings on cognitive processing and motivation-, or personality-based behavioral preferences suggests three different ways in which they may be related:

> (a) Preferences need no inferences (Zajonc 1980, 1984). Whether one's achievement behavior is governed by hope of success or fear of failure; whether a person is particularly anxious, aggressive, shy, or extroverted; and whether one prefers to work in the garden or read a book cannot be explained as the (psycho-)"logical" consequences of information processing, cognitive inference, insight, or evaluation. Rather, it is a manifestation (or consequence) of personality features, specific social influences, or both. (b) Cognitive competencies provide necessary but not sufficient developmental conditions for change in personal preferences (Heckhausen, 1982). Cognitive competencies that reflect more or less realistic information processing, the use of multiple sources of information, appropriate causal attributions, and critical evaluation of the self play a critical role in changes over elementary school as children set more realistic achievement goals, become able to use variable causal schemes for evaluating their own success or failure, and can anticipate the risks and probabilities of their own actions. This is illustrated by developmental sequences in motivation or personality that are universally observed along with cognitive development. However, stable interindividual differences in the strength of a trait or a motive can remain unchanged despite changes in overt behaviors (e.g., shyness, aggression, and need for affiliation). This stability is not found to the same degree for attitudes, self-judgments, or situational preferences. (c) Individuals "make" use of cognitive inferences to justify or to "explain" trait-dependent behavior. Cognitive processes are set into motion, especially when behavior appears to be deviant, to violate social norms, or to threaten one's own self-worth. Cognitive processes may include excuses, justifications, or subjective explanations that are based on faulty information processing, biased reasoning, and cognitive illusions.

Theoretical constructs such as cognitive structure, cognitive mechanisms, and cognitive processes are evoked when the acquisition and use of knowledge about the world and about the person are considered. Cognitive information-processing regularities are assumed, in principle, to be universal. That is, the outcomes of cognitive information processing are generally assumed to be valid, independent of individual personality. Cognitive inferences and judgments can be evaluated on the basis of quasi-objective, person- and situation-independent measures, and cognitive development can be seen as universal (species-specific) and sequential (from simple to complex, from situationally embedded to general, and from concrete to abstract).

In contrast, there are no universal sequences in personality development. Individual and differential changes are the norm. Thus, one observes not only frequent high stabilities in interindividual differences (which is also true for cognitive skills) but also a strong invariance in the level of behavioral expression of personal dimensions. At the same time, there can be substantial intraindividual differences across situations. Thus, constructs such as anxiety, shyness, or need for achievement are expressed differentially and interindividually and are stable intraindividual psychological dispositions (traits and motives) that first become behaviorally functional as states or motivational tendencies through situationally based stimuli, rewards, and constraints. Individuals differ in the number of situational types that function to release trait-typical behavior, in how strong the situational cues must be, and in the degree to which they actually influence behavior. Developmental studies are primarily concerned with the description and explanation of variability and stability in interindividual differences in personality traits and with the developmental analysis of those situations that elicit trait-specific behaviors. In addition, some studies are concerned with the role of cognitive competencies and their development in changes in personality.

The LOGIC project offers a variety of domain-specific examples in which such issues can empirically be addressed. To frame this discussion, we review the range of personality variables measured over the course of the LOGIC study in Table 4. Overall, the LOGIC data set offers the appropriate conditions for comparative analyses of motivational, social, and moral development between the 3rd and 12th year of life. Specifically important findings are presented in the individual chapters from Helmke, Asendorpf, and Nunner-Winkler. In the following we discuss only a few general regularities in personality development. To do this, we look at data from both the LOGIC and the SCHOLASTIC studies (see Weinert & Helmke 1997).

Schooling and the Development of Learning and Achievement-Related Motives

Over the last few years in the literature on school learning, there has been an inflation in the number of motivational constructs and variables used to explain individual differences in learning performance and school achievement (Weinert 1990). The data used to support these explanations are, however, consistently disappointing. For example, Fraser, Walberg, Welch, and Hattie (1987) reported a meta-analysis with a mean correlation of .12 between motivational variables and school achievement. This correlation shows a typical underestimation of the influence of motivational variables on learning and performance. There are many reasons for this (Helmke & Weinert 1997; Weinert 1990). For example, from a theoretical perspective, it is difficult to justify classifying motivation as an independent variable and school performance as a dependent variable, a practice that is common in the literature. The relations are more dynamic and more complex. The combined results from LOGIC and SCHOLASTIC, in which positive attitudes toward school and learning, domain-specific self-concepts of one's own ability, and test anxiety were regularly assessed over 7 years, provide a good illustration of this. Table 5 provides an overview of the group of those children ($N = 133$) who participated in both the LOGIC and the SCHOLASTIC studies.

The data in Table 5 for the development of three achievement-related motivational variables show a consistent pattern: During the preschool years, there is a relatively high level of positive attitudes toward learning and self-confidence, with low test anxiety during the preschool years. The pattern is even stronger in the first elementary school year. After the second grade, the motivational aspects (attitude toward learning and self-confidence) decrease slightly, and the avoidance tendencies (test anxiety) increase visibly. It is important to note, however, that learning motivation remains consistently in the positive region and that test anxiety is, on average, only weakly expressed. Given the consistent pattern of change in the three motivational

Table 4. *Measurement Points of Several Personality Variables*

| | Average age of testing the child | | | | | | | | |
| | Preschool age | | | School age | | | | | |
Variable	4	5	6	7	8	9	10	11	12
Personality									
Big-Five scale									1,3
Temperament scale								1	
Self-concepts									1
Learning and achievement motivation									
Curiosity and exploration	1,3								
Text anxiety					1	1	1	1	1
Achievement motivation	1	1		1	1	1	1		
School-related expectations			1						
Self-concept of ability		1	1	1,2	1,2	1,2	1,2	1	1
Attitudes toward achievement and learning				1,2	1,2	1,2	1,2	1	1
Social competence and behavior									
Observational measures	1	1	1		1		1		
Questionnaires	2,3	3	3	3	3		3		
Q-sorts	3	3	3						
Ratings				3	3	1	3		
Social self-concept					1	1	1		
Aggression							1		1
Temperamental inhibition							1	1	
Loneliness									1
Social network									1
Moral development									
Moral emotions		1	1	1	1	1	1	1	
Moral judgment (understanding)		1		1		1	1		
Knowledge of moral rules				1	1	1	1	1	
Moral motivation						1	1	1	
Self-ideal								1	
Sociomoral reflections									1

Note: 1 = Child measures (LOGIC); 2 = Child measures (SCHOLASTIC); 3 = Parental, teachers, or both measures.

variables, it would be difficult to interpret them as indicating a dissociation between school learning and achievement motivation as a result of elementary school experiences. Rather, these data show a development from more optimistic to more realistic expectations and attitudes concerning one's own school performance.

Additional findings support such an interpretation of the data. These are data showing the development of the domain-specific self-concept of ability, which is illustrated by the complex relations between self-concept of mathematic ability and mathematics performance. Figure 1 shows a LISREL model with school marks

Table 5. *Changes in Learning Attitudes (Scale: 1–5),*
Self-Concept of Own Abilities (Scale: 1–5), and Test Anxiety
(Scale: 0–4) in Elementary School (N = 126)

Grade	Learning attitude		Self-concept		Test anxiety	
	M	*SD*	*M*	*SD*	*M*	*SD*
Kindergarten	3.00	0.63	2.96	0.59	0.47	0.53
Grade 1	3.47	0.47	3.12	0.48	0.52	0.45
Grade 2	2.99	0.73	2.80	0.44	1.24	0.48
Grade 3	2.94	0.64	2.75	0.44	1.16	0.68
Grade 4	2.92	0.66	2.52	0.42	1.09	0.71

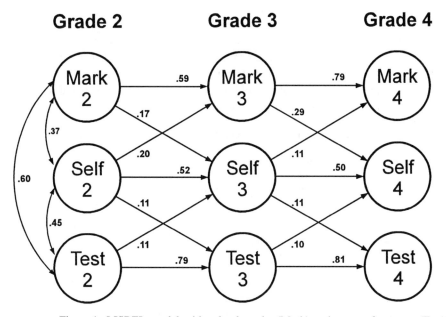

Figure 1. LISREL model with school marks (Mark) and test performance (Test) as separate indicators of mathematics achievement and self-concept of math ability (from Helmke and van Aken 1995, p. 631). Mark = at the end of each school year; Self = Self-concept of ability in mathematics; Test = mathematics test.

(Mark) and test performance (Test) as separate indicators of mathematics achievement and self-concept of mathematics ability (from Helmke and van Aken 1995, p. 631). If one considers teacher assessment of mathematics performance as well as test scores, the self-concept of mathematical ability appears to be more a consequence of prior success and failure than an independent, motivational condition that directs performance. This asymmetrical relation is seen in stronger form in a more complex

LISREL model that accounts for cross-lagged effects for test performance to school marks, and vice versa (see Helmke & van Aken 1995, p. 635; Model 3c).

This finding provides stronger support for a skill-development model than for a self-enhancement model. "It indicates that during elementary school self-concept is mainly a consequence of cumulative achievement-related success and failure and that it does not have a significant impact on later achievement, neither on marks nor on test-performance" (Helmke and van Aken, 1995, p. 635). However, this finding appears to be valid only for the first 4 years of elementary school. A stronger asymmetrical pattern of the reciprocal influence of self-concept of ability and school performance appears as early as the fifth and sixth grades (Helmke 1992).

In addition to this finding, the data from the SCHOLASTIC study indicate that the pattern of simple and reciprocal relations between motivational variables and school achievement depends on the particular domain of learning (e.g., mathematics vs. grammar and spelling) and on classroom context factors (e.g., the dominance of goal-directed, individualized, and direct instruction).

Even within the (necessarily) limited theoretical generalizability of empirical findings on the development of achievement motives, it is evident that the patterns of change and the relevant causes are quite complex. The present data lead to the conclusion that the development of the self-concept of ability and its relation to actual school performance depends (for more details, see Helmke 1992)

- on the early development of individual differences in the direction of the achievement motive (generalized hope of success vs. fear of failure);
- on related attribution style for personal success and failure;
- on the developmental level of cognitive and cognitive–affective competencies for self-evaluation (a component of procedural metacognition);
- on the personal and social salience of school-related performance situations;
- on moderating context factors in classrooms and in the home; and
- on personally experienced success and failure in specific domains of learning (e.g., mathematics) and in the general school context or the social frame of reference in the classroom.

It is not at all surprising that age-typical changes in motivational variables show nonlinear trends over childhood, given such complex and dynamic developmental conditions. Rather, this is consistent with many theoretical expectations.

Social Relations and the Development of Social Behavior

The influences of specific socialization conditions on personality development and on the ontogenesis of motivation are also observed in the development of social behavior. As Asendorpf illustrated in his chapter, the domain of social behavior provides a good demonstration of how large intraindividual differences across different social settings can appear over the course of development so that behavior can often be better predicted from relationship-specific personal attributes than from relationship-unspecific traits.

A review of Asendorpf's developmental and differential analyses reported in his chapter and in a series of journal articles shows an interesting theoretical development from the consideration of single personality variables to the analysis of more cumulative and dynamic Person × Situation interactions. "In this view, relationships shape personality. Individual traits are considered as being outcomes of significant relationships rather than being antecedents of behavior in such relationships" (Asendorpf, Chapter 11, p. 237).

A step-by-step description of Asendorpf's research program on shyness demonstrates those regularities in personal and social development that can be observed and discovered:

The *first step* for developmental analysis is to classify the theoretical constructs being investigated and to specify their behavioral indicators. For example, if shyness or social inhibition is defined as the behavior resulting from an approach–avoidance conflict (i.e., an inhibited social approach motivation), it must be possible to discriminate this behavioral pattern from others such as unsociability, social avoidance, or introversion. The emotional state indicating social inhibition is primarily manifested as inhibition toward strangers and as inhibition in social-evaluation situations.

The *second step* for a developmental analysis is an empirical test of whether the chosen behavioral indices tap the same construct at different ages. Asendorpf (1992a) showed that there is a relatively perfect continuity across age in how shyness is expressed and perceived.

The *third step* in the research program is to study the general developmental sequence of the trait. In the case of social inhibition, it is possible to discern three very similar stages in the development of inhibition toward strangers as well as in social-evaluation inhibition. This general statement is based on data from the LOGIC study and from some of the author's other, related investigations.

> In the first stage, inhibition toward adult strangers is aroused by rather simple physical characteristics of the situation (nearness and body height of the stranger and fastness of the approach), and social–evaluative inhibition is restricted to conditioned cues for punishment or frustrative nonreward.... In the second stage, beginning around the age of 20 months, the emerging new ability of spontaneous perspective taking arouses inhibition toward peer and adult strangers due to the perceived uncertainty of the stranger's intentions, and social–evaluative inhibition due to the anticipation of negative or insufficiently positive social evaluation. Later on, in the third stage of the development of inhibition, the reflections about one's own self presentation reaches awareness and becomes particularly intense during (later childhood and) adolescence. Thus, inhibition toward strangers and social–evaluative situations are assumed to proceed from cognitively rather simple forms in infancy to cognitively more complex forms later on. Furthermore, it is hypothesized that in the third stage of development, a discrepancy arises between inhibition toward strangers and social–evaluative inhibition (Asendorpf 1993).

The *fourth step* in the research program directed by Asendorpf focused on individual differences in the development of shyness. This showed a somewhat confusing pattern. On the one hand, interindividual differences in inhibition toward strangers were very stable over time. Aggregated stability scores increased with increasing age from early childhood on and decreased only temporarily in adolescence. On the other hand, this trait lost its behavioral effects when situations and persons became more familiar, for example, in the kindergarten or school class (for details see Asendorpf, Chapter 11, Figure 1).

The temporal stability of individual differences should be assessed not only at the aggregate level but at the individual level as well. That is, individual social inhibition scores should be used to assess differential stability (i.e., individual differences in stability). Asendorpf (1992b) showed that the stability of children's peer network was positively related to the 1-year stabilities of their inhibition toward peers for three successive 1-year intervals.

This last result points to the *fifth step* of the development analysis of shyness. What are the causes of observed interindividual differences in social inhibition? The LOGIC study itself does not provide data on the influences of genetic or early family socialization conditions (Kagan 1997) for which twin or adoption studies would be necessary. However, observations were available not only for children's behavior with strangers in experimental situations over the preschool years but also for their behavior in free play and for play partners' reactions to contact attempts. As more thoroughly discussed in Chapter 11, Asendorpf found that "peer nonacceptance predicted shy behavior in the same and the following year of observation, whereas the reverse pattern was not found; that is, shy behavior was not correlated with peer nonacceptance in the following year. This asymmetric correlational pattern supported a causal path running from nonacceptance via social–evaluative fears to shy behavior rather than vice versa" (Asendorpf, Chapter 11).

One should not interpret such findings in terms of a simple causal chain. Social inhibition is, of course, not the only determinant of social behavior in various situations. Social competence, for example, may also play an important role. In Chapter 11, Asendorpf provides a short description of the correlations between general intelligence and social competence (peer group competence, operationalized as observed success in children's contact initiation attempts and as kindergarten teachers' Q-sort scores). From a developmental perspective, the reported results for the 4-, 5- and 6-year-olds are very stimulating (for details see Chapter 11, Figure 2). Although social competence is moderately correlated with general intelligence at age 4 ($r = .51$), the correlation decreases at age 6 to $r = .20$. Consistent with expectations, the temporal stability of intelligence between 4 and 6 years of age is quite high ($r = .61$), the stability of social competence is lower ($r = .31$) but clearly increases between 4 and 5 years and 5 and 6 years ($r = .25$ and $r = .44$, respectively). This illustrates a developmental regularity in social behavior that was also found in the cognitive domain. General abilities influence individual differences in the development of cognitive and social skills only in early stages of development. During the course of skill development, developing specific competencies play an increasingly larger role.

If one uses differences in general intelligence and general stranger inhibition on the one hand and differences in peer group competencies and peer inhibition on the other to predict social self-esteem in middle childhood and early adolescence, there is a very interesting pattern of results.

> Our findings suggest that relationship-unspecific traits such as high stranger inhibition or a generally low intellectual ability do not play a major role. . .whereas the more relationship-specific attributes did. . . . This (provides) more support for the developmental significance of early peer relationships than the demonstration of only a predictive relation between peer group behavior and subsequent developmental outcomes. . . . Individual differences in behavior with highly important interaction partners predicted later social–emotional developmental outcomes. Could this be a general principle of development? (Asendorpf & van Aken 1994, p. 1796).

At the moment no definite answer can be given.

Gaps Between Individual Inferences and Preferences: The Case of Moral Development

Modern developmental psychology is replete with cognitive theories of personality development. There are two assumptions that often underlie these models. The first is that increasing intellectual competencies lead to a better and deeper understanding of other people's behavior and intentions, social norms, social interaction rules, and also to a deeper understanding of one's own mental state, personal needs, and individual actions. Second, it is often assumed that subjective preferences (motivations, wishes and so forth) and personal action tendencies will be more rational, more transparent, and more self-reflective through cognitive insight. These assumptions are especially strong in theories of moral development.

Kohlberg, in particular, argued that the postulated unitary construct of moral insight, moral motivation, and moral action led to the theoretical expectation that individual consistency across judgments, feelings, and behavior should increase with moral development. "The reason for doing right is that, as a rational person, one has seen the validity of principles and has become committed to them" (Kohlberg 1981, p. 412) and again "the cognitive definition of the moral situation directly determines the moral emotions which the situation arouses" (Kohlberg 1969, p. 393).

The empirical findings from the LOGIC study question this fundamental theoretical position. In Chapter 12 of this volume, Nunner-Winkler describes a complex pattern of results. Three findings are especially important for the theoretical issue of the (developmental) consistency between cognitive, motivational, and behavioral aspects of action:

- Even very young children of 4 to 5 years understand surprisingly well that moral laws have universal and intrinsic validity; that is, that they are independent of social authorities, sanctions, and individual needs.
- Nevertheless, young children cannot be considered to be competent moral actors. Rather, the large majority of younger children disobey well-known and cognitively well-understood moral rules without visible feelings of guilt ("happily") when these rules collide with their own needs and when they do not expect social sanctions.

- What younger children lack is a form of moral motivation; that is, a learned, secondary need to act morally. The necessary learning processes occur very slowly and show large interindividual differences.

In his commentary on Nunner-Winkler's chapter, Blasi (this volume) cautioned against a theoretical overinterpretation of the empirical findings:

> We cannot say that younger children have no moral motivation or that genuine moral understanding does not give origin to any degree of concern for moral issues.... Nunner-Winkler's careful studies only show that, in cases of conflict between opposite motives, the moral motivation of young children is too weak to influence action or even to produce emotions (Blasi, this volume, p. 297).

From a Variable-Centered to a Person-Centered Approach in Studying Personality Development

The largest part of the LOGIC study and the majority of the findings reported in this volume are variable centered. With such an approach, one can address the development of cognitive abilities, motivational tendencies, personal traits, and social competencies independent of the person as a structural entity. One can ask, How do intellectual competencies develop in general, and which interindividual differences can be observed? How does a particular motive (e.g., the achievement motive) change during childhood, and what socialization effects are important? Of course, this approach allows not only universal (true for all humans) and differential (for subpopulations of humans) conclusions about development but consideration of individual questions as well: How well can one predict a child's relative position on variable x (e.g., social competence) at a later point in time from that child's position on the same variable at an earlier point in time? However, even in this case, the developmental function of variables is the central focus, not the development of the individual (Wohlwill 1973). The individual is only important in providing measures for the variable.

"Variable-centered analyses are useful for understanding the differences between people and what characteristics go with what characteristics in a group of individuals. But as well, and ultimately, psychology will need to seek understanding of the configuration and systematic connection of personality variables as these dynamically operate within a particular person" (Block 1971, p. 13). Some, but by no means many, developmental psychologists adopted this fundamental idea in the last decades. The idea was sharpened theoretically by Magnusson in his person-centered approach: "Thus, the point of departure for the person approach is the proposition that an individual functions as a totality and that each aspect of the structures and processes that are operating (perceptions, plans, values, goals, motives, biological factors, conduct, etc.) takes on meaning from the role it plays in the total functioning of the individual" (Magnusson 1988, p. 22).

To address the equally important person-centered approach, van Aken and Asendorpf (Chapter 13) used a Q-sort-profile procedure in the LOGIC study. In their Q-sort method, 54 items characterizing personality sorted by kindergarten teachers and parents for individual children were classified into nine categories, ranging from *more characteristic for the child* to *least characteristic for the child*. These data were used to develop a personality consistency score and an ego-resiliency score. The statistical analyses of these sortings also used a profile of the child's self-concept (with cognitive, athletic, social, physical, and domain-general aspects) and an intelligence measure. Because some of the results from these analyses have such important implications for both developmental psychology and personality research, they are reviewed again in this concluding chapter.

In the LOGIC data set the Q-sort profiles show large interindividual differences in temporal stability. The stability coefficients of the organization of traits within one individual varied from −.39 to .85. How can one explain such large individual differences in the stability of the pattern of personality traits over a 4-year time interval? The strong relation between individual stability and the child's ego-resiliency provides a first answer to this question. Children with a stable personality pattern were characterized by a higher level of ego resiliency and children with an inconsistent pattern by a lower level. "The more ego-resilient people are, the more they can adapt to changing environments in an active way by controlling their environment within the limits provided by nature and society. One particular consequence of ego resiliency is that people can better seek out, shape, and create environments that are compatible with their personality. . . . In addition, ego-resilient persons will more likely receive positive feedback on their actions. They thus reach a better personality–environment fit which, in turn, stabilizes their personality pattern. Through this process, ego-resiliency stabilizes personality" (Asendorpf and van Aken 1991, p. 692). A finding from the first years of the LOGIC study supports this interpretation. A prototypical Q-sort profile generated by kindergarten teachers for the socially desirable child correlated .61 with the 2-year stability of children's individual personality profiles. In general, the more a child's profile approached that of an "ideal child," the more stable that child's profile was over time.

Of course, this does not imply perfect stability. It implies rather a fit between stability and change in personality with the invariants and changes in the developmental tasks for a given age. On the basis of analyses of a variety of data sets, Asendorpf and van Aken (1991) reached the general conclusion that "because age-appropriateness of personality implies some change in the structure of personality, it may seem paradoxical that highly consistent children do indeed change according to the developmental tasks prescribed by nature and society" (Asendorpf and van Aken 1991, p. 700).

Concluding Remarks

Every developmental psychologist knows it, many have explicitly said it over the years, but only a few have paid attention to this fact in their own research work: Most of our theories of developmental change are not based on the empirical study of these changes but rather on inferences derived from studies of developmental differences between groups of participants of different ages. It is well documented that most published data in developmental psychology arise from cross-sectional studies; in contrast, the results from longitudinal studies play only a minor role. The reasons for this disjunction are both theoretical (a focus on universal laws of development vs. changes in intra- and interindividual differences over time) and practical.

Conducting a longitudinal study presents a large, difficult task, requiring substantial time and money. Often, its scientific contribution becomes evident only after many years. This is also the case for the LOGIC study. Although over the last 10 years there have been 12 reports of the assessment procedures and cross-sectional results of the nine assessment waves (for an overview, see Weinert and Schneider 1995) and more than 70 articles in leading journals as well as an equal number of book chapters (a list of the publications is also available in Weinert and Schneider 1995), the present volume is the first comprehensive presentation of important findings from this longitudinal study. Further publications are in preparation, including single case studies and developmental analyses for groups with particular characteristics (e.g., divergence between intellectual level and school performance). In addition, at the time of the publication of this volume, more than 80% of the original LOGIC sample is participating in a follow-up assessment that began 4 years after the last LOGIC wave.

The scientific community of developmental psychologists may judge whether the effort invested in the LOGIC study was well spent. In this evaluation, it should be remembered that the LOGIC study was and is an exploratory, data-driven study, covering many different domains of development. The next necessary step to allow better description, prediction, explanation, and understanding of the stability and variability of interindividual differences in intraindividual change must be a series of smaller, theoretically driven, and confirmatory longitudinal studies that are built on the basis of the solid data sets provided by exploratory studies like the LOGIC project (see Weinberger 1994).

References

Acham, U. (1983). *Philosophie der Sozialwissenschaften* [Philosophy of social sciences]. Freiburg: Alber Verlag.

Asendorpf, J. B. (1992a). A Brunswikean approach to trait continuity: Application to shyness. *Journal of Personality, 60*, 53–77.

Asendorpf, J. B. (1992b). Beyond stability: Predicting interindividual differences in intraindividual change. *European Journal of Personality, 6*, 103–117.

Asendorpf, J. B. (1993). Social inhibition: A general-developmental perspective. In H. C. Traue & J. W. Pennebaker (Eds.), *Emotion, inhibition and health* (pp. 80–99). Seattle, WA: Hogrefe & Huber Publ.

Asendorpf, J. B., & van Aken, M. A. G. (1991). Correlates of the temporal consistency of personality patterns in childhood. *Journal of Personality, 59*, 689–703.

Asendorpf, J. B., & van Aken, M. A. G. (1994). Traits and relationship status: Stranger versus peer group inhibition and test intelligence versus peer group competence as early predictors of later self-esteem. *Child Development, 65*, 1786–1798.

Asendorpf, J, & Weinert, F. E. (1990). Stability of patterns and patterns of stability in personality development. In D. Magnusson & L. R. Bergman (Eds.), *Data quality in longitudinal research* (pp. 181–197). Cambridge, England: Cambridge University Press.

Block, J. (1971). *Lives through time.* Berkeley, CA: Bancroft Books.

Erikson, E. H. (1959). Identity and the life cycle. *Psychological Issues, 1,* 18–164.

Flavell, J. (1970). Cognitive change in adulthood. In R. Goulet & P. B. Baltes (Eds.), *Life-span developmental psychology: Research and theory* (pp. 248–253). New York: Academic Press.

Fraser, B. J., Walberg, H. J., Welch, W. W., & Hattie, J. A. (1987). Syntheses of educational productivity research. *International Journal of Educational Research, 11,* 145–252.

Haertel, G. D., Walberg, H. J., & Weinstein, T. (1983). Psychological models of educational performance: A theoretical synthesis of constructs. *Review of Educational Reserach, 53,* 75–91.

Heckhausen, H. (1982). The development of achievement motivation. In W. H. Hartup (Ed.), *Review of child development research* (Vol. 6, pp. 600–668). Chicago: University of Chicago Press.

Heckhausen, H. (1987). Causal attribution patterns for achievement outcomes: Individual differences, possible types and their origins. In F. E. Weinert & R. Kluwe (Eds.), *Metacognition, motivation, and understanding* (pp. 143–184). Hillsdale, NJ: Erlbaum.

Helmke, A. (1992). *Leistungsbezogenes Selbstvertrauen und schulische Leistung* [Performance-related self confidence and school achievement]. Göttingen: Hogrefe.

Helmke, A. & van Aken M. A. G. (1995). The causal ordering of academic achievement and self-concept of ability during elementary school: A longitudinal study. *Journal of Educational Psychology, 84*(4), 624–637.

Helmke, A., & Weinert, F. E. (1997). Bedingungsfaktoren schulischer Leistungen. In F. E. Weinert (Ed.), *Psychologie des Unterrichts und der Schule. Enzyklopädie der Psychologie, Serie Pädagogische Psychologie* [Conditions of school achievement in psychology of classroom teaching and schooling] (Vol. 3, pp. 71–176). Göttingen: Hogrefe.

Kagan, J. (1971). *Change and continuity in infancy.* New York: Wiley.

Kagan, J. (1980). Perspectives on continuity. In O. G. Brim, Jr. & J. Kagan (Eds.), *Constancy and change in human development* (pp. 26–74). Cambridge, MA: Harvard University Press.

Kagan, J. (1997). Temperament and the reactions to unfamiliarity. *Child Development, 68*(1), 139–143.

Kohlberg, L. (1969). Stage and sequence: The cognitive–developmental approach to socialization. In D. A. Goslin (Ed.), *Handbook of socialization theory and research* (pp. 347–480). Chicago: Rand McNally.

Kohlberg, L. (1981). *Essays of moral development. Vol. 1: The philosophy of moral development.* San Francisco: Harper & Row.

Magnusson, D. (1988). *Individual development from an interactional perspective: A longitudinal study.* Hillsdale, NJ: Erlbaum.

Schneider, W., & Näslund, J. C. (1993). The impact of early metalinguistic competencies and memory capacity on reading and spelling in elementary school: Results of the Munich Longitudinal Study on the Genesis of Individual Competencies (LOGIC). *European Journal of Psychology of Education, 8,* 273–287.

Siegler, R. S. (1994). Cognitive variability: A key to understanding cognitive development. *Current Directions of Psychological Science, 3,* 1–5.

Sternberg, R. J. (1984). *Mechanisms of cognitive development.* New York: Freeman.

Thomae, H. (1957). Problems of character change. In H. F. David & H. V. Bracken (Eds.), *Perspectives in personality theory* (pp. 242–254). New York: Basic Books.

Weinberger, J. L. (1994). Can personality change? In T. F. Heatherton & J. L. Weinberger (Eds.), *Can personality change* (pp. 333–350). Washington, DC: American Psychological Association.

Weinert, F. E. (1990). Theory building in the domain of motivation and learning in school. In P. Vedder (Ed.), *Fundamental studies in educational research* (pp. 91–120). Amsterdam: Swets & Zeitlinger.

Weinert, F. E., & Helmke, A. (Eds.). (1997). *Entwicklung im Grundschulalter* [Development in the elementary school years]. Weinheim: Psychologie Verlags Union.

Weinert, F. E., & Schneider, W. (1993). Cognitive, social and emotional development. In D. Magnusson & P. Casaer (Eds.), *Longitudinal research on individual development: Present status and future perspectives* (pp. 75–94). Cambridge, England: Cambridge University Press.

Weinert, F. E., & Schneider, W. (Eds.). (1995). *The Munich Longitudinal Study on the Genesis of Individual Competencies (LOGIC), Report No. 12: Assessment Procedures and Results of Wave Nine.* Munich: Max Planck Institute for Psychological Research.

Wohlwill, J. F. (1973). *The study of behavioral development.* New York: Academic Press.

Wohlwill, J. F. (1980). Cognitive development in childhood. In O. G. Brim, Jr. & J. Kagan (Eds.), *Constancy and change in human development* (pp. 359–444). Cambridge, MA: Harvard University Press.

Zajonc, R. B. (1980). Feeling and thinking: Preferences need no inferences. *American Psychologist, 35,* 151–175.

Zajonc, R. B. (1984). On the primacy of affect. *American Psychologist, 39,* 117–123.

Zigler, E., & Child, I. L. (1969). Socialization. In G. Lindzey & E. Aronson (Eds.), *The handbook of social psychology* (2nd ed.) (Vol. 3, pp. 450–589). Reading, MA: Addison-Wesley.

Author Index

351

Subject Index

fear of social evaluation, 229–231, 245. *See also* shyness
fear of strangers, 229–231. *See also* shyness

G-factor, 155–156
gender difference(s), 7, 22–23, 208–213, 223–224, 250. *See also* sex differences
group stabilities, 65, 327
heterotypic continuity, 326
hierarchical linear modeling (HLR), 22–23, 25–26, 47–50, 52, 74
homotypic continuity, 326
hypothesis testing, 39, 56–57

idiographic approach, 301
individual difference variables, 103
individual differences, 2–3, 10–13, 21–25, 29, 33, 35–36, 46–47, 53, 163–167, 333–334
individual differences, genesis of, 3
individual stabilities, 68, 332. *See also* stability
information processing speed, 126, 133–135, 144
inhibition, 271. *See also* behavioral inhibition
instruction, 176, 183. *See also* schooling
intellectual development, 10, 12–14
intelligence, 9–10, 12, 129, 131, 138–139, 143, 176, 189–190, 194–195, 197, 235–236, 304–306, 310, 314–315, 321. *See also* nonverbal intelligence; psychometric intelligence; verbal intelligence
interindividual differences, 2–4, 11, 14, 23, 26, 48, 110–113, 176, 326–327, 330–332
internal working models of relationships, 248
internalizing problems, 238, 292–293
intraindividual change(s), 11–12, 14, 21–26, 326–327, 330
ipsative stability, 302, 316, 327
IQ, 10–11, 16, 42, 127–129, 133, 135, 144, 148. *See also* intelligence; nonverbal IQ; psychometric intelligence; psychometric tests; verbal IQ

judgment accuracy 211

letter knowledge, 126–127, 133, 135–137, 142, 144–145, 331
LISREL, 128, 138–139, 340–342
logical reasoning, 19
longitudinal design, 2–7, 324–325, 348
longterm stability(ies), 16, 26. *See also* stability; stability over time

marks (grades), 201, 211, 213–214, 223, 340–342
mathematics, 154–169, 171–175, 183–184, 186, 188–190, 205, 207, 210–212, 216–217, 335, 341
memory ability(ies), 115
memory capacity, 72–73, 118–119, 126–127, 129–130, 133, 135–136, 143–145, 152
memory development, 65–68, 94–104, 107–110

memory span, 42, 82–83, 85–86, 89–90, 117–118
memory strategies, 61–76, 98–99, 331
metamemory, 61–63, 68–70, 73–74, 88–89, 119
microgenetic studies, 325
moral behavior, 254, 262, 269–275, 292–295
moral conflict(s), 257
moral development, 253, 258–261, 285, 298–299, 340, 345–346
moral motivation, 255–258, 268–269, 275–277, 291–292, 294–298, 346
moral motivation, developmental paths of, 280–283, 298–299
moral motivation, growth of, 277–278, 283, 286–287
moral motivation, strength of, 255, 258, 260–263, 269–275, 277–283
moral motivation, type(s) of, 254, 265–266, 277–278
moral rules, exceptions to, 263, 265
moral rules, justification for, 263–265, 284–285
moral rules, understanding of, 253–256, 262–263, 283–285, 292, 295–298
moral rules, validity of, 254–255, 262–263, 286

nomothetic approach, 301
nonverbal intelligence, 16–17, 21, 25, 30, 35, 116–117, 161, 164–165, 172, 304
nonverbal IQ, 7, 14, 30–31, 132–134
normative stability, 327
number consistency, 18–21, 31–32, 154, 160, 162–165, 167, 332

operational level, 42
optimistic bias, 211

path analyses, 163
peer acceptance, 230–231, 235–236, 238, 245
performance gains, 74
performance, 325
personal development, 336
personality, 88–91, 301, 303
personality consistency, 232–233, 302–303, 305–309, 311–318, 347
personality development, 3–4, 232, 237, 336–347
personality profile, 305, 340
personality, continuity of, 227
person-centered approach (methods), 301–302, 317–318, 346–347
person-situation interaction, 193
phonological awareness, 126–129, 133–138, 143–145, 150–152, 331
phonological processing skills, 126–127, 138–139, 144, 149, 152
phonological tasks, 148–150
Piagetian(-type) tasks, 14, 21, 26, 30–35, 332
procedural information, 101
process-product approach, 187
proportional reasoning, 159–160, 162, 164–165, 167, 169, 173